Patents and Global Administrative Law

The book applies values and concepts from Global Administrative Law (GAL) to international patent law, demonstrating how limiting technocratic and overly economic language can be. Highlighting the administrative foundations of patent law, the book argues that, in its international form, it can be analysed using the same principles of participation, transparency, and accountability found in national administrative law.

At the heart of the book is a simple question: What does international patent law look like when we approach it through the lens of these values? What is being left out when patent law is described predominantly in terms of its technical legal provisions or economic impact? The book presents three interrelated contexts: EU patent law, bilateral trade agreements, and the multilateral space. Modern patent law is increasingly discussed in terms of national competitiveness or economic potential, which reveals only a narrow understanding of how patent law evolves and functions. The vocabulary of administrative law provides a fresh way of recasting, reframing, and re-describing the dynamics of international patent law in a way that is more accessible to those outside of a traditional patent scholarship audience. A fundamental objective of the book is to challenge the tendency towards technocratic isolation in patent law. The book uses accessible vocabulary and represents a new way of conceptualising and understanding how patent law develops on a global scale.

The book will be of interest to researchers in the field of patent law, international law, and administrative law.

David Tilt is a Postdoctoral Fellow at Tokyo College, University of Tokyo, Japan. His research focuses on interdisciplinary approaches to intellectual property, exploring the metaphysical, cultural, and social dimensions of international patent law. He has published comparative legal analysis on specialised courts, the convergence of language around patent law and innovation in government, and national autonomy under the TRIPS Agreement. Currently he is working on a new project that is focused on the Middle East (the GCC in particular) and the potential for patent harmonisation and cooperation.

Patents and Global Administrative Law

Values, Principles, and Challenges

David Tilt

Routledge
Taylor & Francis Group
LONDON AND NEW YORK

First published 2026
by Routledge
4 Park Square, Milton Park, Abingdon, Oxon OX14 4RN

and by Routledge
605 Third Avenue, New York, NY 10158

Routledge is an imprint of the Taylor & Francis Group, an informa business

British Library Cataloguing-in-Publication Data
A catalogue record for this book is available from the British Library

ISBN: 978-1-041-01063-0 (hbk)
ISBN: 978-1-041-01898-8 (pbk)
ISBN: 978-1-003-61685-6 (ebk)

DOI: 10.4324/9781003616856

Typeset in Times New Roman
by Deanta Global Publishing Services, Chennai, India

Contents

Acknowledgements

One day in the late mid-eighties ...

This book project would not have been possible without the support of everyone at Tokyo College, Tokyo. I am grateful for every tea gathering, every seminar, every conversation that showed me the real value of interdisciplinary work. Thank you to Professor Shimazu, Professor Haneda, and Professor Facius in particular. Thank you to the postdocs – to Alarith, Selim, Tamara, and to everyone who has listened to every patent-adjacent thought I have had since joining the College.

I want to thank both Professor Schmidt-Kessen and Professor Tajti for their feedback that was essential in finishing the text. Their efforts in reading, responding to, and challenging the research have had a profound impact that I take into all of my writing. Thank you to Ágnes Diós-Tóth who is responsible for me now questioning how 'reader responsive' every single piece of writing I produce is and for your helpful comments on my research proposal. Thank you to Professor Möschel who, from the very first day, has shown the importance of reaching beyond your own research area and learning from the incredible expertise of those around you.

To my family, who have always supported me in everything, I am forever grateful. To Jessica, you have been a constant in my life ever since that particularly ill-fated coach trip – and it's been too long now, so you'll just have to put up with me forever. To Kirsty, who has been there from a headset and a dream to my first time in Scotland, thank you for everything. To Agnes, Arnisa, Juan, Kate, and Marie – I am thankful for every week and every Suzanne trip, and your influence has been greater than you will ever know. Thank you to Alex who has always provided positivity and entertainment over the years. Thank you to Aziz for being there and providing a steady supply of memes.

The book is dedicated to Basil and his many, *many* brainwaves.

Don't dream it, be it.

David.

Introduction

0.1 Introduction

This book takes seriously the administrative foundations of patent law and argues that it can, therefore, be analysed using the same principles of democratic participation, transparency, and accountability as conventional administrative law.[1] From this perspective, the key element in realising these values is the dynamic relationship between the legislator, patent office, and dispute resolution body. The validity and legal treatment of a patent are predicated on an administrative decision that has national effect, where patent law is increasingly discussed in terms of national competitiveness that presents an overtly economic understanding of the patent.[2] The emphasis on a patent's economic potential narrows how we approach and discuss patent law, as well as how we understand its international development. In many ways, this is a book about patent law that is not aimed at patent law scholars. The vocabulary of administrative law provides a way of deconstructing dynamics in patent law in a language that is much more accessible to those outside of the traditional patent scholarship audience. In consciously challenging the tendency towards technocratic isolation in patent law, the book has been motivated by experiences with different disciplinary audiences.

Patent law, even within legal studies, seems to prompt somewhat of an immediate disengagement with the subject. There is a sense, when trying to engage non-patent scholars on issues of patent law, that it is somehow too technical, too complex, or too detached from law more generally for them to comment. However, when has a lack of technical expertise ever stopped a generalist audience from reacting to, forming a response, or engaging with a discussion on human rights? Or of criminal law? This book is, therefore, primarily aimed at (perhaps counterintuitively) presenting the complex process of global patent development in a vocabulary that is accessible to those who may have previously been hesitant to engage with patent law. It analyses and deconstructs how patent law develops in a way

1 Values which appear through GAL work: Rajeshwar Tripathi, 'Concept of Global Administrative Law: An Overview' (2011) 67(4) India Law Quarterly 356.

2 Particularly as patent law has become a part of national economic strategies: Brad Sherman, 'Towards a History of Patent Law' in Toshiko Takenaka (ed), *Intellectual Property in Common Law and Civil Law* (Edward Elgar 2013) 3.

DOI: 10.4324/9781003616856-1

that not only reflects the administrative foundation of patent law in a theoretical sense but also deploys that vocabulary to invite the reader to engage with questions of patent law. As patent law increasingly affects every aspect of our society and individual lives, it is essential that it not be exclusively the domain of specialists. This book is a first step towards democratising the way in which we analyse patent law and its trajectory, particularly in the global context, and one which attempts to reach between disciplines in law and beyond. As with many areas, the study of patent law is greatly enriched when exposed to challenging and interdisciplinary perspectives. It is my experience that patent law still has a great deal of progress to be made in interdisciplinary or transdisciplinary work. However, it is also important for those within intellectual property to actively demonstrate to scholars outside of the field that questions of patent policy have a fundamental societal impact and would benefit from their disciplinary expertise.

Yet just as patent law has evolved internationally, so too has administrative law. The emergence of Global Administrative Law (GAL) as a fledgling academic subdiscipline questions how administrative values – as inlike democratic participation, transparency, accountability[3] – function in a globalised legal world that lacks an authoritative legislative actor. What does international patent law look like when we approach it from the perspective of global regulation? What does the administrative framing of patent law tell us about not only the current functioning of patent law, but how we arrived at this point? What does the reframing of contemporary patent tensions through an administrative vocabulary help us further explain that a strict patent law approach cannot?

In analysing patent law from this perspective, there is a sense that patents can only be truly understood through a more contextual approach that reaches beyond patent law and even intellectual property more broadly. Centring accountability in patent law, for example, necessarily involves looking beyond the substantive provisions and into the contextual relationship between patent actors, the law, and other systems of regulation. GAL frequently refers to the 'interface' that exists between different systems of law,[4] a margin in which the borders of a legal system encounter another. The interactions in this space are not just a negotiation of a substantive legal provision but a decision as to the extent or reach of a legal system. One clear example of this can be seen in the EU's approach to World Trade Organisation (WTO) treaties. In that context, the European Court of Justice (ECJ), through the doctrine of direct effect,[5] essentially negotiates the relationship between binding

3 Carol Harlow, 'Global Administrative Law: The Quest for Principles and Values' (2006) 17(1) EJIL 193.

4 Predominantly through the concept of interface norms and the concept of a legal 'interface' itself as developed by Nico Krisch: Nico Krisch, 'Framing Entangled Legalities Beyond the State' in Nico Krisch (ed), *Entangled Legalities Beyond the State* (CUP 2022) 1, 2.

5 Marc Maresceau, 'The Court of Justice and Bilateral Agreements' in Allan Rosas, Egils Levit and Yves Bot (eds), *The Court of Justice and the Construction of Europe: Analyses and Perspectives on Sixty Years of Case-Law / La Cour de Justice et la Construction de l'Europe: Analyses et Perspectives de Soixante Ans de Jurisprudence* (Springer 2012) 716.

international obligations and their impact on the EU legal system. The borders or fringes of each legal system are dynamically adjusted. Dispute resolution proceedings operate in this margin to mediate *how* binding these international provisions are while still maintaining the structural relationship and hierarchy between different systems and actors.

The spaces in which different subjects, values, and objectives come into contact produce a distinctly 'entangled' experience of the legal provisions.[6] Entanglement at the margins of a legal system essentially maintains the separate (i.e. not integrated) quality of the different legal systems but highlights how the interactions are not predetermined by law and are produced through the complex interplay of the actors involved.[7] An entangled view of patent law emphasises the interactive quality between different levels of the patent system – national, international, and global – and how dispute resolution bodies are essentially negotiating the boundaries of these systems with an almost improvisational quality. The analysis of patent law, then, cannot be separated from the geopolitical, social, and cultural context of these interactions because they all contribute to the space in which these patent tensions coexist. An international dispute resolution body cannot be isolated from either the structural elements provided by law or the socio-political dimension that informs how they interact with other dispute resolution bodies and systems of law. Together, this produces a more integrated understanding of patent law through administrative values: One which draws on the contextual relationships with other forms of intellectual property; how patent law in specific dispute resolution contexts takes on explicitly political and cultural dimensions; and the persistent tendency towards the technocratic isolation of patent law in global discussions.

0.2 Patents and the foundational values of administrative law

At the centre of patent law's foundation is the exercise of administrative power. Though there are clear indications of this – in the administrative review of patent validity found in many civil law jurisdictions, for example[8] – the relationship between patents and administration speaks to a more fundamental aspect of state power. Administrative law and the discussion of administrative law as an academic discipline have previously been questioned on the basis that it does not clearly articulate its unique contribution.[9] This is the essence of Weinrib's discussion of

6 Where '[a]ctors – litigants, judges, dispute settlers, observers, addressees – make claims about the relation of norms from different backgrounds, and they thus define and redefine the relative weights and interconnection between the norms at play': Nico Krisch, 'Framing Entangled Legalities Beyond the State' in Nico Krisch (ed), *Entangled Legalities Beyond the State* (CUP 2022) 5.

7 Nico Krisch, 'Framing Entangled Legalities Beyond the State' in Nico Krisch (ed), *Entangled Legalities Beyond the State* (CUP 2022) 1.

8 With a specific German influence in China, and a more generalised European influence in Japan: Weinian Hu, *International Patent Rights Harmonisation: The Case of China* (Routledge 2017) 139, 140.

9 In which the discussion of administrative principles does not actually explain why the modern administrative state is necessary: Jacob Weinrib, 'Maitland's Challenge for Administrative Legal Theory' (2021) 84(2) MLR 207, 209.

'Maitland's challenge' to administrative law and the potential of a unified theory of public administration.[10] What exactly does administrative law do that cannot be achieved by another branch of law? Patent law provides a clear example of this unique contribution. Patent law, as the exercise of administrative power through an agency of the state, produces an *erga omnes* right that prevents unauthorised use by a third party with no prior contractual relationship to the owner. The patent extends nationally, and the effect of preventing use by third parties without prior arrangement can only be achieved by the state. Patent law answers Maitland's challenge by demonstrating the uniqueness of administrative power as delegated to and wielded by an agency in a way that cannot be replicated through mechanisms of private law. It also indicates that patent law, much like other forms of administration, can be analysed in terms of accountability and participation beyond thin or procedural understandings of these values.

Together, this presents an integrated view of patent law and administrative principles that centre the idea that:

> The judicial determination of the validity of patents is not a mere 'check' or 'brake' on the accuracy or good judgment of an administrative tribunal, but is itself a fundamental part of the machinery of the patent system.[11]

The language of administrative law then provides a vocabulary through which patent law can be analysed and critiqued, questioning its technocratic isolation and centring substantive understandings of participation, accountability, and transparency. Questioning patent law's current functioning at the national and international level addresses two issues that have become especially prominent in patent law discourse. The first is the fundamental clash between patent law and human rights, which has remained so far unresolved. While there have been some successes in exploring a hierarchical relationship between property rights and human rights,[12] it produces an antagonistic relationship between them. The focus on administrative principles and their realisation in patent law dissolves, rather than resolves, this tension. A critique of patent law through the lens of transparency or accountability is not the application of an external framework to the substantive outcomes of patent law. Instead, it is an internal look at how patent law functions that recognises the exercise of administrative power at its foundation and should, therefore, be subject to certain standards and expectations. In doing so, this book supports a more contextual critique of patent law that encourages integration over hierarchy. This 'internal' approach to patent law also highlights the powerful perception of neutrality in patent law.[13] The distributive outcomes of patent law are masked as

10 Jacob Weinrib, 'Maitland's Challenge for Administrative Legal Theory' (2021) 84(2) MLR 208.

11 William Redin Woodward, 'A Reconsideration of the Patent System as a Problem of Administrative Law' (1942) 55(6) Harvard Law Review 950, 959.

12 Emmanuel Kolawole Oke, *Patents, Human Rights, and Access to Medicines* (CUP 2022) 69.

13 Though the neutrality of patent law and intellectual property more generally is now being questioned through various critical approaches. See generally: Eden Sarid, 'A Queer Analysis of Intellectual Property' (2022) 1Wisconsin Law Review 91.

simply the result of trade policy or regulatory questions on the nature of technology and are presented as neutral. Similar to the rise of Critical Race Theory (CRT) and other approaches such as queer analysis in intellectual property,[14] the administrative framing of patent law presents patent law as contextual and embedded (biased) but without necessarily placing these values in direct opposition to or in confrontation with others. More than advocating for a specific arrangement, it presents an alternative way of problematising patent law that can disrupt, provoke, and invite the reader to think differently about contemporary patent discourse.

The second consequence of framing patent law from the administrative perspective is that it supports broader participation in practice and academia. Patent law, as intellectual property more broadly,[15] has benefited from a perception of complexity and technical character. There have been rare moments when patent law has entered public consciousness, with COVID-19 and the subsequent vaccine development being perhaps the most recent.[16] Nevertheless, it has remained the subject of specialists in academia and, even in practice, seemingly detached from general legal consciousness. There is a sense of technocratic isolation in patent law that prevents broader audiences from engaging with its subjects in a way that is not present in areas like human rights or tort law. Has a lack of expert knowledge ever prevented someone from critiquing human rights or engaging in debate in that area? By using the language of accountability and transparency, this book produces a critique of patent law that encourages the reader to engage with patent issues with a common vocabulary.

This emphasis on the technocratic quality of patent law is directly linked to the debates in GAL scholarship. The rise of global agencies through the 20th century has transformed questions of national regulation and administrative scope into ones of global importance.[17] The administrative law foundation remains clear, though, as these agencies or institutions rely on power that is essentially delegated to them by state actors. The Food and Agricultural Organization (FAO) and Commission for Environmental Cooperation (CEC) are two such examples of bodies that produce technical regulation at a global scale in a way that parallels the traditional

14 On the development of CRT: Mathias Möschel, 'Critical Race Theory' in Emilios Christodoulidis, Ruth Dukes, and Marco Goldoni (eds), *Research Handbook on Critical Legal Theory* (Edward Elgar 2019) 63, 64.

15 With Guan arguing that prior to the introduction of the TRIPS Agreement, intellectual property 'was still the domain of specialists and intellectual property right producers': Wenwei Guan, 'Diversified FRAND Enforcement and TRIPS Integrity' (2018) 17(1) WTR 111.

16 With the HIV/AIDS epidemic another example of public health and patents becoming more prominent outside of academic circles: Ellen 't Hoen, Jonathan Berger, Alexandra Calmy, and Suerie Moon, 'Driving a Decade of Change: HIV/AIDS, Patents and Access to Medicines for All' (2011) 14(1) Journal of the International AIDS Society 15.

17 Ming-Sung Kuo, 'Between Fragmentation and Unity: The Uneasy Relationship between Global Administrative Law and Global Constitutionalism (2009) 10(2) San Diego International Law Journal 443, 444.

scope or role of national administrative agencies.[18] But what about patent law? Though at first the development of the WTO and the TRIPS Agreement represent the explicit joining of intellectual property and trade,[19] this process masks a more fundamental parallel administrative transformation. The patent office, as an administrative agency, exercises delegated power to grant patents according to specific criteria defined in legislation. These decisions can then be initially challenged within the patent office or in court (depending on the jurisdiction). In this sense, there is a clear relationship between the legislative, executive, and judiciary. However, TRIPS establishes binding principles of patent law that shape the fundamental contours of the patent grant without a corresponding global patent office. Issues such as the term of patent protection, appropriate subject matter, and exceptions are all considered in the TRIPS Agreement.[20] From an administrative perspective, these create limits to the exercise of administrative (state) power and, therefore, represent the kind of distinct global regulation considered in GAL.[21] TRIPS constrains the exercise of a patent grant in an almost diffuse way as the global legal context lacks the familiar legislative, executive, and judicial actors that would otherwise stabilise these provisions and their execution. Even when the TRIPS Agreement provisions are transposed nationally, the adjudication of these provisions' fundamental content does not occur in a national court but through the WTO dispute resolution apparatus. Results from this dispute resolution process compel the state to remedy the trade distortion and, in a patent context, fundamentally restrict a state's ability to freely exercise its power as delegated through the patent office.

Patent law and its administrative character also provide a different way of interpreting the tensions in international patent law, which have become characteristic of this area since the conclusion of the Uruguay Round.[22] The relationship between developed and developing countries,[23] the inclusion of pharmaceuticals within patent law,[24] and the protection of genetic materials are all points of tension that can be reframed through the administrative foundation of patent law.[25] Rather than focusing on the human rights dimension of pharmaceutical protection, the emphasis on

18 Benedict Kingsbury and Lorenzo Casini, 'Global Administrative Law Dimensions of International Organizations Law' (2009) 6 International Organizations Law Review 355.

19 Wenwei Guan, 'Diversified FRAND Enforcement and TRIPS Integrity' (2018) 17(1) WTR 112.

20 Article 33; Article 27(1); Article 27(2) of the TRIPS Agreement.

21 With global regulation cast in the language of administration: Benedict Kingsbury, Nico Krisch, and Patrick B Stewart, 'The Emergence of Global Administrative Law' (2005) 68(3/4) Law and Contemporary Problems 15, 27.

22 Jörg Reinbothe and Anthony Howard, 'The State of Play in the Negotiations on TRIPS (GATT/Uruguay Round)' (1991) 13(5) EIPR 157.

23 John Whalley, 'Developing Countries and System Strengthening in the Uruguay Round' in Will Martin and L Alan Winters (eds), *The Uruguay Round and Developing Countries* (CUP 1996) 429.

24 Alan O Sykes, 'TRIPS, Pharmaceuticals, Developing Countries, and the Doha "Solution"' (2002) 3(1) Chicago Journal of International Law 50, 51.

25 Daniel J Gervais, 'Traditional Knowledge & Intellectual Property: A TRIPS-Compatible Approach' (2005) Michigan State Law Review 151, 152.

participation presents a different question: Who has the power to modify, enforce, or subvert these provisions? In doing so, the analysis focuses more clearly on the functioning of patent law as an integrated whole rather than a neutral technical area being interpreted through an 'external' framework of values.

0.3 But why do we need this administrative interpretation of patent law now? (And is it really that important?)

There is a sense in reading patent law scholarship that little has changed about the fundamental relationship between intellectual property rights and contentious distributive outcomes. COVID-19, like HIV/AIDS before it, has demonstrated that current ways of discussing patent law still reflect a strong opposition between patent and non-patent values. Critical approaches to patent law, as the application of a specific and biased value system, can be disregarded by academics or policymakers as a distortion of the patent bargain.[26] From this perspective, the technical neutrality of patent law as a form of regulation is essentially incompatible with approaches based on the right to health or the right to food.[27] There is still a persistent tension that recognises (implicitly or otherwise) a perceived neutrality to patent law provisions that centres on the economic importance of the patent right.[28] Critical approaches to patent law may work for achieving practical outcomes in specific areas, though they are still predicated on a strict separation of what patent law *is* and *does* with the application of an external tool or perspective to modulate this. The issue is that this structure presents little opportunity for communication with those who view human rights or distribution concerns as distortions to the ordinary functioning of the patent system. The values of a human rights lawyer in medicine and an international investment lawyer are incompatible because they are fundamentally in opposition. The vocabulary with which each would speak about patent law means that communication is difficult and conflict-driven. The separation and opposition of strict binary values in patent discussions (primarily in the sense of what is internal or inherent to patent law and that which is external) encourages viewpoints in which there is little space for compromise and or meaningful communication.

In this, the way patent law is written about – in its ordinary functioning and particularly in more specialist issues of medicine – contributes to its technical perception and a certain 'closed off' quality. Even in other areas of law, it is very rare for academics to enter discussions of patent law.[29] There have been some notable

26 Bryan Mercurio, 'The IP Waiver for COVID-19: Bad Policy, Bad Precedent' (2021) 52 IIC 983.

27 Emmanuel Kolawole Oke, 'Defining the Right to Health Responsibilities of Patent-Owning Pharmaceutical Companies' (2019) 1 IPQ 45.

28 Emphasising that it makes financial sense for IP owners to have an expansive approach to licensing generics and so framing accessibility through the lens of economics: Bryan Mercurio, 'The IP Waiver for COVID-19: Bad Policy, Bad Precedent' (2021) 52 IIC 987.

29 Lorenzo Casini, 'The Expansion of the Material Scope of Global Law' in Sabino Cassese (ed), *Research Handbook on Global Administrative Law* (Edward Elgar 2016) 28.

exceptions in intellectual property more broadly, where topics have entered public consciousness and become more accessible as subjects of debate.[30] The vocabulary of accessibility and participation can be used to interpret patent law in a way that promotes exactly this type of broader engagement, inviting both academics and the public to consider patent law from a more relatable and familiar perspective. This approach also recognises the administrative foundation of patent law in a way that can be used to critically deconstruct contemporary patent issues without reinforcing the conventional sense of an imposed external approach. Participation is a value that can be recognised not only by the human rights advocate and investment professional, but also by a non-law and non-patent audience more generally. In doing so, it also works towards one of the major elements of GAL: The questioning of 'neutrality' in law and regulation.[31] By dissolving the question of whether it is appropriate to apply a human rights lens to patent law and instead centring fundamental administrative values in the exercise of state power, it reveals that the values that make up patent law are malleable social constructs. Just as particular priorities and commitments necessarily shape the right to health advocacy in patent law, the patent framework itself is also made up of a series of particular normative choices.[32] GAL and the administrative focus invite the reader to question the perceived legitimacy or 'natural' quality of patent law. From this perspective, qualities and values such as 'inventiveness' or even 'industrial applicability' are just as biased, just as contextually inflected, as the value frameworks employed by human rights advocates within patent law. Patent law is not a natural phenomenon and its concepts, values, and objectives are not natural either.

0.4 Establishing some guiding research questions

Given the complexity of international patent law and the potential range of administrative values, this book is intended to explore two particular questions. These questions – just as with the choice of transparency, accountability, and participation as the guiding administrative values for the project – represent design choices

30 The visible protests around ACTA are perhaps the clearest example of this in recent times: Peter K Yu, 'Development Bridge Over Troubled Intellectual Property Water' in Xavier Seuba and Carlos Correa (eds), *Intellectual Property and Development: Understanding the Interfaces* (Springer 2019) 112.

31 Particularly as narrow understandings of legitimacy are no guarantee of normatively fair or just outcomes, nor do they actually render the process somehow neutral: Richard B Stewart, Michelle Ratton and Sanchez Badin, 'The World Trade Organisation: Multiple Dimensions of Global Administrative Law' (2011) 9(3–4) ICON 556, 584; on the way in which global regulation does not proceed in a 'value-free manner': BS Chimni, 'Co-Option and Resistance: Two Faces of Global Administrative Law' (2005) 37 NYU Journal of International Law and Politics 799, 804, 805, 827.

32 What is significant about the normative choices in patent law design is that their normative content is rendered almost invisible. See generally: David Tilt, 'International Perspectives on Regulatory Frameworks: AI Through the Lens of Patent Law' in Angelos Kornilakis, Georgios Nouskalis, Vassilis Pergantis, and Themistoklis Tzimas (eds), *Artificial Intelligence and Normative Challenges: International and Comparative Legal* Perspectives (Springer 2023) 171.

and are the result of my own reaction to and interpretation of GAL scholarship. More generally, the objective of these questions and the book is to provide one specific way of interpreting patent law and its functioning rather than providing a definitive account.

i. *Does patent law have tensions, problems, or dynamics that can be expressed through the vocabulary of accountability, transparency, and participation?*
ii. *How do dispute settlement bodies support or undermine these values in the functioning of patent law?*

In terms of the second question, the element of 'positioning' is particularly significant for the book. Dispute resolution bodies, in providing an authoritative interpretation of a legal provision, necessarily operate at the very borders of a legal system. This is specifically the case for areas of law with international sources of law, such as patent law. In this case, the decision of a national court on an issue of patent law is not negotiating the legal boundaries of the principle under consideration (inventive step, for example) but modulating the relationship between the national and international and the degree to which one influences the other. The interpretation of a binding international obligation is not simply a question of applicability to the case at hand, but is a process through which the dispute settlement body contextualises and interprets that obligation to produce something more embedded or grounded. Dispute settlement bodies are not involved in just identifying the substantive elements of a provision but can direct the legal reality of that obligation. This can reinforce the boundaries between national and international law,[33] it can be used to solidify their jurisdictional reach over a particular subject, or to establish new or specific normative standards for dispute resolution in that area more broadly. The role of the dispute settlement body is creative and dynamic, and it is how it operates at the interface of legal spaces that makes it so important for analysing accountability, transparency, and participation in patent law.

0.5 Establishing the conceptual scope of the book

0.5.1 Identifying some core administrative concepts and themes

National administrative law and GAL both incorporate a variety of values and perspectives that make it impossible to definitively establish the scope (or even purpose) of these areas of law.[34] Yet three major values appear repeatedly: transparency, participation, and accountability. These values are the lens through which

33 Such as the muted dialogue between the CJEU and WTO Panel decisions: Michelle Q Zhang, 'Shall We Talk? Judicial Communication between the CJEU and WTO Dispute Settlement' (2017) 28(1) EJIL 273, 292.

34 Disagreements as to the purpose of even national administrative law are found throughout the literature: Richard B Stewart, Michelle Ratton, and Sanchez Badin, 'The World Trade Organisation: Multiple Dimensions of Global Administrative Law' (2011) 9(3–4) ICON 556, 583.

patent law is interpreted in this book. Helpfully, these values also provide important links to other concepts that appear throughout administrative law and GAL literature, connecting with discussions on legitimacy,[35] authority,[36] and control.[37] The complexity of patent law means that deliberately interpreting it through a narrow set of values necessarily incorporates elements of these broader values. The emphasis on dispute resolution bodies also reflects the important role of these bodies within a national administrative law context, but especially recognises the unique creative potential of international dispute resolution bodies and their more unusual relationship to (national) legislative power.

One of the immediate challenges in applying an administrative lens to patent law is a fundamental question of whether a global administrative system even exists. Work from Kingsbury, Krisch, and Stewart touches on the question of whether a global administrative 'space' truly exists,[38] though Xavier has focused on the potentially contentious relationship between the global administrative space and the character of domestic administrative law.[39] This type of discussion is linked to the issue of defining GAL because it substantially overlaps with international regulation and multilevel governance.[40] Even from a more administrative-focused perspective, global administration work generally appears to embrace a more inclusive approach that includes elements from outside of domestic administrative law.[41] Fundamental to these discussions is a particularly spatial way of understanding how legal systems interact. Global administration often involves discussions on the 'interfaces' of law in which multiple, often competing, areas or perspectives of law interact.[42] Though this sense of legal interface appears throughout, there is very little discussion of what it entails beyond its existence – what are the qualities of a legal interface? What characteristics of a legal interface support or hinder the autonomy of different actors in navigating the impact of binding obligations?

35 Sujith Xavier, 'Top Heavy: Beyond the Global North and the Justification for Global Administrative Law' (2018) 57 Indian Journal of International Law 353.

36 Nico Krisch and Benedict Kingsbury, 'Introduction: Global Governance and Global Administrative Law in the International Legal Order' (2006) 17(1) EJIL 4, 5.

37 Carol Harlow, Päivi Leino, and Giacinto Della Cananea, 'Introduction: European Administrative Law – A Thematic Approach' in Carol Harlow, Päivi Leino, and Giacinto Della Cananea (eds), *Research Handbook on EU Administrative Law* (Edward Elgar 2017) 7.

38 Benedict Kingsbury, Nico Krisch, and Richard B Stewart, 'The Emergence of Global Administrative Law' (2005) 68(3–4) Law and Contemporary Problems 18.

39 Deconstructing the sense of an American-inflected global administrative space as a result of 'intellectual influence' rather than a colonisation: Sujith Xavier, 'Top Heavy: Beyond the Global North and the Justification for Global Administrative Law' (2018) 57 Indian Journal of International Law 342, 343.

40 Discussing the mutual shaping of administrative law, global governance, and constitutional law post-Cold War: Santiago Montt, *State Liability in Investment Treaty Arbitration: Global Constitutional and Administrative Law in the BIT Generation* (Hart 2009) 131, 132.

41 Sabino Cassese, 'Global Administrative Law: The State of the Art' (2015) 13(2) ICON 466.

42 Nico Krisch, 'Framing Entangled Legalities Beyond the State' in Nico Krisch (ed), *Entangled Legalities Beyond the State* (CUP 2022) 1, 2.

Yet what underlies much of the global understanding of administration (and works to distinguish it from a simpler sense of international regulation) is that it concerns the exercise of public power or the power of the state.[43] Because global administration as a discrete research area is a relatively recent development, identifying the *purpose* of administrative regulation appears to draw on a mix of domestic administrative law traditions. Harlow considers more European approaches to administrative law (and the judiciary that supports this system) as fundamental parts of 'the legislation and regulations set in place by government and administrators for the implementation of policy'.[44] In doing so, values central to administrative law analysis, like accountability, transparency, and participation, are transposed and become fundamental aspects of global administration. Kingsbury, Krisch, and Stewart have focused on how transparency and accountability function as important points of analysis when looking at the international institutional context from a global administrative perspective.[45]

In terms of dispute resolution actors, a number appear repeatedly. D'Alterio has discussed the role of the International Court of Justice (ICJ) in creating a 'significant effect on public interests and fundamental rights'.[46] Madsen instead considers the role of international courts more generally and how the proliferation of these institutions (as well as their expansion) happened parallel to the emergence of GAL.[47] Despite the emphasis on 'legal orders' in the work of Michaels,[48] the actual process of recognition, of mediation, and creation of the legal order is realised through the actions of courts. The emphasis may be on the lack of hierarchy between legal systems and the sense of coexistence that 'brings about the possibility that conflicts … about the place of the border between legal systems … may exist'[49] – yet, in which venue are these tensions visibly deconstructed? The court, less frequently but more importantly, becomes a central environment in which the entanglement of legal

43 Discussing a paradigm within administrative law, where 'there are two normative remarks, which must be highlighted: first, administrative law is a product of the state, of *each* state; second, it is a product *only* of the state': Giacinto Della Cananea, 'Administrative Law Beyond the State: The Influence of International and Supranational Organizations' in Peter Cane, Herwig CH Hofmann, Eric C Ip and Peter L Lindseth (eds), *Oxford Handbook of Comparative Administrative Law* (OUP 2021) 358.

44 Carol Harlow, 'Global Administrative Law: The Quest for Principles and Values' (2006) 17(1) EJIL 192.

45 Where Kingsbury, Krisch, and Stewart define GAL as principles, practices and mechanisms that support accountability, standards of transparency, participation, legality, and review: Benedict Kingsbury, Nico Krisch, Richard B Stewart, 'The Emergence of Global Administrative Law' (2005) 68(3–4) Law and Contemporary Problems 17.

46 Elisa D'Alterio, 'Judicial Regulation in the Global Space' in Sabino Cassese (ed), *Research Handbook on Global Administrative Law* (Edward Elgar 2016) 304.

47 Mikael Rask Madsen, 'Judicial Globalisation: The Proliferation of International Courts' Sabino Cassese (ed), *Research Handbook on Global Administrative Law* (Edward Elgar 2016) 299, 300.

48 Ralf Michaels, 'Tertiary Rules' in Nico Krisch (ed), *Entangled Legalities Beyond the* State (CUP 2022) 442, 443.

49 Ralf Michaels, 'Tertiary Rules' in Nico Krisch (ed), *Entangled Legalities Beyond the* State (CUP 2022) 440.

regimes is both realised and explored.[50] Duval extensively discusses the role of the Court of Arbitration for Sport (CAS) to explore how it functions as an example of hybrid and transnational legal practice.[51] Duval specifically highlights the tension that comes from lacking a single authoritative actor, which leads to the creation of transnational legal practice through 'strange loops and contextual assemblages'.[52] Together, these present a much more contextual lens through which to view patent law – partly or entirely because it lacks an international specialised dispute resolution body to focus these tensions.

While the WTO Dispute Settlement Body (DSB) and Appellate Body (AB) appear occasionally in the literature as examples of international dispute resolution bodies,[53] there does not appear to be work that specifically explores the relationship of international dispute resolution with the issues (and values) of international patent law and WTO law more generally. Adopting the language of administration, and particularly of GAL, represents an important step towards investigating this relationship of international dispute resolution, patent law, and administrative values. This approach bridges the typical focus on dispute resolution and how the DSB and AB could promote accessibility and transparency in their cases but grounds it in a more intellectual property-specific context.[54] In terms of objectives, the book can also be read as a starting point for understanding how administrative values can be used as a tool of analysis in a less traditional area of law. Though this gap is not surprising given the general lack of attention to patent law within GAL scholarship, TRIPS and the WTO are both fundamental features of global regulation (in trade and beyond). As such, applying this lens to patent law is then not necessarily a radical departure from core administrative areas and can instead be seen as a more measured extension. Exploring the role of dispute settlement bodies in patent law is especially valuable for understanding transparency and accountability from a GAL perspective because of the broadly harmonised quality of patent law. This means that while the institutional setup and identity differ in each national context, the

50 The importance of dispute resolution bodies appears early in *Entangled Legalities*, though specifically explores the impact of the 'situatedness' of the court or dispute resolution body on the ability (or will) to act as 'bridge-builders' between legal orders and norms: Nico Krisch, 'Framing Entangled Legalities Beyond the State' in Nico Krisch (ed), *Entangled Legalities Beyond the State* (CUP 2022) 13, 14.

51 Antoine Duval, 'Seamstress of Transnational Law: How the Court of Arbitration for Sport Weaves the Lex Sportiva' in Nico Krisch (ed), *Entangled Legalities Beyond the State* (CUP 2022) 286.

52 Antoine Duval, 'Seamstress of Transnational Law: How the Court of Arbitration for Sport Weaves the Lex Sportiva' in Nico Krisch (ed), *Entangled Legalities Beyond the State* (CUP 2022) 286, 287.

53 Specifically how the DSB uses interface norms to engage with elements of international environmental law on a 'case-by-case basis … while keeping them formally at bay.': Lucy Lu Reimers, 'International Trade Law: Legal Entanglement on the WTO's Own Terms' in Nico Krisch (ed), *Entangled Legalities Beyond the State* (CUP 2022) 193, 194.

54 Scholarship has explored how the DSB and the AB could impose GAL norms on the standards agencies that they essentially legitimise in their decisions as a form of judicial review: Richard B Stewart, Michelle Ratton, and Sanchez Badin, 'The World Trade Organisation: Multiple Dimensions of Global Administrative Law' (2011) 9(3–4) ICON 577.

general framework of patent obligations that each dispute resolution body, patent office, and legislator are subject to are the same.

0.5.2 Bringing patent law within the framing of global administration

While intellectual property features in GAL scholarship, it has generally been very limited. Patent law rarely appears in GAL scholarship and even the TRIPS Agreement is often mentioned only in passing. Casini is representative of how intellectual property is incorporated in GAL scholarship because the TRIPS Agreement is simply presented as an element of the broad normative reach of the WTO.[55] While the TRIPS Agreement is mentioned in Tamanaha's work,[56] the analysis is focused on TRIPS and the WTO as elements of a 'burgeoning multiplicity of transnational legal and regulatory regimes'.[57] Together, these approaches demonstrate the important entangled nature of patent law in a global setting. An investigation into patent law from an administrative perspective necessarily incorporates elements from other areas of intellectual property because, in practice, they are linked. Intellectual property is sometimes discussed as a contentious area in global administration,[58] though there does not appear to be a meaningful distinction between the administrative elements of intellectual property generally and patent law more specifically. More attention is given to the interaction of the TRIPS Agreement with the more conventionally administrative dimensions of Sanitary and Phytosanitary Measures (SPS Agreement) or Technical Barriers to Trade (TBT Agreement).[59]

This book is aimed at exploring this important gap. In fact, the lack of work considering the TRIPS Agreement, intellectual property, or patent law is particularly stark given that the WTO otherwise appears quite regularly in global administration work.[60] Despite significant analysis exploring the WTO as an important actor in global regulation and administration,[61] TRIPS and patent law have been overlooked as fundamental elements of the global administrative system. Importantly,

55 Lorenzo Casini, 'The Expansion of the Material Scope of Global Law' in Sabino Cassese (ed), *Research Handbook on Global Administrative Law* (Edward Elgar 2016) 28.

56 Brian Z Tamanaha, 'A Reconstruction of Transnational Legal Pluralism and Law's Foundations' in Nico Krisch (ed), *Entangled Legalities Beyond the State* (CUP 2022) 452.

57 Brian Z Tamanaha, 'A Reconstruction of Transnational Legal Pluralism and Law's Foundations' in Nico Krisch (ed), *Entangled Legalities Beyond the State* (CUP 2022) 452.

58 Specifically in the enforcement of intellectual property rights by multinational firms: Benedict Kingsbury, Nico Krisch, and Richard B Stewart, 'The Emergence of Global Administrative Law' (2005) 68(3–4) Law and Contemporary Problems 47.

59 Lorenzo Casini, 'The Expansion of the Material Scope of Global Law' in Sabino Cassese (ed), *Research Handbook on Global Administrative Law* (Edward Elgar 2016) 28.

60 Particularly the dispute resolution system of the WTO: Jan Wouters, 'Government by Regulation' in Sabino Cassese (ed), *Research Handbook on Global Administrative Law* (Edward Elgar 2016) 209.

61 Where the WTO shows 'comparable potential' to the EU, where the EU 'transitioned from clearing away a dense web of national regulations inhibiting cross-border trade, to itself creating a dense web of transnational regulation.': Martin Shapiro, '"Deliberative," "Independent" Technocracy v. Democratic Politics: Will the Globe Echo the E.U.?' (2005) 68(3/4) Law and Contemporary Problems 341.

the broader lens of administrative values develops the idea that patent regulation in this global setting has an impact that extends far beyond the more conventional context of technical standards. International patent law is a fundamental element of the modern trade environment and, because of this importance, should be subject to the same type of scrutiny as more conventional examples of administrative power. It also provides a shift in focus, in keeping with the book's objective of promoting engagement and accessible discussion, centring a technical subject rather than some of the extremely contentious issues facing the international community.[62]

As highlighted earlier, one of my own issues with the way in which patent law is discussed is the significant economic element that has appeared in two distinct ways. The first is from a methodological perspective, with the rise in the early 2000s of law and economics concepts being applied to patent law. Work from Lemley is fairly typical of this type of approach to patent law in this area,[63] emphasising how patent law relates to efficiency,[64] innovation,[65] and incentive.[66] While critical perspectives on patent law have become more mainstream in recent years,[67] this economic focus on patents reflects a broader perception of patent law as a market or economic tool. Though it recognises that there are distributional outcomes, the economics approach renders them almost as abstract, periphery, or somehow secondary elements of patent law. The second issue with the dominant construction of patent law through an economics vocabulary is the *reach* that this approach has had. Framing the purposes of patent law in terms of its economic characteristics has extended beyond academic scholarship and has made its way into the innovation policy of many countries.[68] This presentation of patent law as innovation

62 Understanding patent law from a GAL perspective would seem to be generally less controversial than other studies that have investigated areas like foreign relations law and touched on issues of military force, conflict, and human rights. See generally: Angelo Jr Golia, 'Judicial Review, Foreign Relations and Global Administrative Law: The Administrative Function of Courts in Foreign Relations' in Helmut Philipp Aust and Thomas Kleinlein (eds), *Encounters between Foreign Relations Law and International Law: Bridges and Boundaries* (CUP 2021) 130.

63 Applying an empirical and economic perspective to elements of the patent like patent term: Mark A Lemley, 'An Empirical Study of the Twenty-Year Patent Term' (1994) 22(3–4) AIPLA Quarterly Journal 369, 370.

64 Particularly on the role of licensing in static and dynamic efficiency: Thomas Cotter, 'Antitrust, Intellectual Property, and Dynamic Efficiency: An Essay in Honor of Herbert Hovenkamp' (2020) 3 Concurrences 6.

65 Robert D Cooter and Uri Y Hacohen, 'Progress in the Useful Arts: Foundations of Patent Law in Growth Economics' (2020) 22 Yale Journal of Law & Technology 191, 195.

66 Exploring incentives in a law and economics approach: Richard A Posner, 'The Law & Economics of Intellectual Property' (2002) Dædalus 10.

67 For an overview of how critical perspectives in intellectual property have continued to impact the discipline: Margaret Chon, 'Intellectual Property and Critical Theories' in Irene Calboli and Maria Lillá Montagnani (eds), *Handbook of Intellectual Property Research: Lenses, Methods, and Perspectives* (OUP 2021) 746, 747.

68 One example that appears in many jurisdictions is the relationship between universities, patents, and national economic growth. The chairman of the Japanese Intellectual Property Strategy Committee has previously commented on the importance of creating and exploiting intellectual property in this

policy legitimises the economics approach to regulation while, at the same time, simplifying the complex functioning of patent law in a globalised world. Here, simplification is not a helpful tool of accessibility but is closer to a distortion of how patent law is produced and functions. It centres idealistic ideas of profitable start-ups and economic prosperity but minimises the normative aspects of patent law and the very real impact that they have on global communities.[69]

Applying an administrative law perspective to patent law is an attempt to address this simplification of patent law, though administrative law concepts are not necessarily completely detached from the values in economics-focused work. There is a significant practical overlap between the effect of maximising efficiency in the law and economics scholarship and the impact of increased transparency and accountability. Informational transparency is a frequent concept that often explicitly links transparency with economic efficiency,[70] while accountability has broad parallels with how the rule of law is essential in supporting effective economic activity.[71] While the administrative law perspective would first appear to focus on non-economic concepts, the accessible nature of the GAL vocabulary (and the particularly versatile nature of accountability, transparency, and participation) can promote meaningful and mutual dialogue with economic priorities or objectives. Using these concepts as a more inclusive vocabulary also integrates, as it removes questions of internal and external, economic perspectives within administration rather than isolating them. The result is that the analysis reflects not only an internal critique of patent law, but one that incorporates or reflects the complexity of patent law as an economic, political, and legal area.

Aside from the more abstract relationships between patent law and systems of international regulation, substantive outcomes in patent law are one of the most important elements of contemporary patent discourse. One perennial example would be the role of patents in restricting access to medicine, particularly in developing countries,[72] and is presented as one of the most significant issues in

---

context: Hisamitsu Arai, 'Intellectual Property Strategy in Japan' (2005) 1 International Journal of Intellectual Property Law, Economy and Management 6, 7.

69 In that it renders the normative aspects of patent law, and the normative design choices, invisible. See generally: David Tilt, 'International Perspectives on Regulatory Frameworks: AI Through the Lens of Patent Law' in Angelos Kornilakis, Georgios Nouskalis, Vassilis Pergantis, and Themistoklis Tzimas (eds), *Artificial Intelligence and Normative Challenges: International and Comparative Legal Perspectives* (Springer 2023) 171.

70 Gianna Lotito, Matteo Migheli, and Guido Ortona, 'Transparency, Asymmetric Information and Cooperation' (2020) 50 European Journal of Law and Economics 267, 268.

71 Specifically discussing the role of risk reduction as 'an important channel through which strong, accountable, transparent and efficient institutions support financial markets': Bogdan Dima, Flavia Barna, and Miruna-Lucia Nachescu, 'Does Rule of Law Support the Capital Market?' (2018) 31(1) Economic Research–Ekonomska Istraživanja 475.

72 Olufemi Soyeju and Joshua Wabwire, 'The WTO–TRIPS Flexibilities on Public Health: A Critical Appraisal of the East African Community Regional Framework' (2017) 17(1) WTR 150, 151.

the development of international patent law.[73] Here, the contextual complexity of patent law and its social impact supports engagement from a variety of theoretical backgrounds. Access to medicine has been critiqued from a feminist perspective,[74] work that uses approaches from political science,[75] and more embedded work that draws on indigenous or post-colonial perspectives.[76] From these perspectives, two consistent elements appear in the analysis of patent law. The first is the central role of human rights and their deployment as tools of critique. Across the various critical approaches to patent law, the substantive outcomes of patent law are being understood in terms of rights like the right to health,[77] the right to self-determination,[78] and the right to development.[79] What this does, however, is produce a contentious framing of the issue. The practical impact of framing these areas as being in conflict is a clear way of articulating and challenging injustices,[80] yet it also, in some ways, inhibits communication.

This reflects the second consistent element in the literature, which is a fairly explicit recognition that these tools of critique are *external* to patent law and thereby work to reinforce the economic character of the patent. Significant work has been dedicated to legitimising or otherwise grounding the critique of the substantive outcomes within patent law in a way that justifies the approach at a conceptual level. Owoeye has presented patent law and medicine from the perspective of the right to development and how this should shape the international trajectory of patent law.[81] This represents one of the more common approaches when look-

73 Dhanay M Cadillo Chandler, 'The Never-Ending Story of Access to Medicines' (2016) 8 WIPOJ 55, 56.

74 Though it appears prominently as an epistemological critique of patents and copyright: Debora Halbert 'Feminist Interpretations of Intellectual Property' (2006) 14(3) Journal of Gender, Social Policy & the Law 437, 438.

75 Particularly using social network analysis techniques: Jiaming Jiang and Xingyuan Zhang, 'Essential Patents and Knowledge Position, a Network Analysis on the Basis of Patent Citations' (2021) 1 Standards 90, 91.

76 Laura A Foster, 'Situating Feminism, Patent Law, and the Public Domain' (2011) 20(1) Columbia Journal of Gender and Law 261.

77 Where '[p]atent rights have a direct impact on the right to health, especially in developing countries where pharmaceutical products are priced beyond the reach of poor patients.': Emmanuel Kolawole Oke, 'Defining the Right to Health Responsibilities of Patent-Owning Pharmaceutical Companies' (2019) 1 IPQ 45.

78 Though considered in a Hawaiian context, converting 'the traditional knowledge and cultural heritage of the Native Hawaiian people into definitions of patents, copyrights, trade-marks, personality, and trade secrets … makes a mockery of the Native Hawaiian struggle for freedom and self-determination.': Danielle Conway-Jones, 'Safeguarding Hawaiian Traditional Knowledge and Cultural Heritage: Supporting the Right to Self-Determination and Preventing the Commodification of Culture' (2005) 48(2) Howard Law Journal 752.

79 Ruth L Gana, 'The Myth of Development, the Progress of Rights: Human Rights to Intellectual Property and Development' (1996) 18 Law & Policy 316, 316.

80 A theme reflected more broadly on the productive aspect of conflict, of conflictual consensus: Chantal Mouffe, *Agonistics: Thinking the World Politically* (Verso 2013).

81 Olasupo Owoeye, 'Patents for Drugs and the Right to Development in International Law' (2015) 8(1) Law and Development Review 69, 70.

ing at patent law and distributional outcomes, which is to integrate patent law with an established discipline. This produces a legitimate basis for the work as a piece of human rights scholarship rather than just patent work. The undercurrent of the book is that it seeks to dissolve, rather than resolve,[82] this issue by constructing patent law as a form of administrative power within an emerging system of GAL. Patent law as administration realises this without needing to deal with the legitimacy of assessing patent law outcomes using non-patent disciplines as a lens. This broader and more accessible approach to the framing of patent law also works to destabilise the distinction between systemic and discrete issues in international patent law. The difficulty of dealing with critiquing access to medicine, even when it is presented as a systemic issue,[83] is that each discrete issue requires its own legitimation. Whether it is the negotiating capacity of developing countries,[84] access to medicine,[85] or the treatment of genetic material,[86] work in each of these areas takes on the difficult task of establishing a sufficient link between patent law and the specific issue under consideration as a reason why it needs to be critiqued in that particular way. Understanding the administrative law dimensions of patent law removes this tension by emphasising the systemic nature of transparency, accountability, and responsiveness as inherent elements of patent law rather than working to establish a hierarchical relationship between economic and non-economic objectives, rights, or perspectives.

0.6 Structure of the book

0.6.1 Chapter 1: Connecting patents, administration, and Global Administrative Law concepts

Chapter 1 explores the development of GAL and the prominent themes and values that emerge in the literature. This chapter is essentially the foundation for the book's approach because it frames how the later chapters construct the relationship

82 Referencing Wittgenstein's description of pseudo-problems that 'cannot be solved, but only *dissolved*' and the tension between Wittgenstein's earlier and later work (with a subsequent emphasis on *resolving* problems): Jerry H Gill, 'Wittgenstein and the Function of Philosophy' (1971) 2(2) Metaphilosophy 137.

83 Where the 'continued demands by developing countries for systemic solutions to address systemic solutions to address structural inequities and the dominance of the market over health rights and socio-economic justice remain largely ignored.': Gaëlle Krikorian and Els Torreele, 'We Cannot Win the Access to Medicines Struggle Using the Same Thinking That Causes the Chronic Access Crisis' (2021) 23(1) Health and Human Rights Journal 121, 123.

84 Particularly in the information asymmetry between developed and developing countries during the TRIPS negotiation: Coenraad J Visser, 'Making Intellectual Property Laws Work for Traditional Knowledge' in J Michael Finger and Philip Schuler (eds), *Poor People's Knowledge: Promoting Intellectual Property in Developing Countries* (OUP 2004) 208.

85 Olasupo Owoeye, 'International Patent Laws and Health: Resisting the TRIPS Compulsory Licensing Regime and the Doha Paragraph 6 System' (2015) 37(4) EIPR 794, 795.

86 Prashant Reddy, 'Access to Plant Genetic Resources and Benefit Sharing: Has India Lost the Plot?' (2018) 3 IPQ 181.

between patent law, intellectual property, and the system of global administration itself. The latter half of the chapter considers how these administrative values can be applied to the distinct contexts that appear throughout the rest of the book. Applying this GAL framing to patent law requires an exploration of how values and concepts have developed in GAL scholarship. Work in this area emphasises the role of accountability, transparency, and participation in international administration, although it also discusses the challenges of realising these values in a global space without systems of direct oversight. Patent law highlights exactly these tensions and reflects other administrative-specific concerns in the global space, such as the normative character of procedure in law-making and potential capture by technocrats. The institutional focus throughout the book – on dispute resolution bodies – also reflects the central role of these actors in global administration.

0.6.2 Chapter 2: Current developments in European patent law through the lens of administrative values

Chapter 2 considers the development of the European Patent with Unitary Effect (EPUE) as an example of creating a new interface in international patent law, deconstructing it through the lens of participation and accessibility. The EPUE and Unified Patent Court (UPC) bring together tensions of harmonisation, meaningful participation, and systemic coherence in a way that contextualises the legal content of the patent provisions. The EPUE and UPC provide a very specific environment for understanding the role of a dispute settlement body and participation. This is because the EPUE was introduced with the very specific purpose of improving the efficiency of dispute settlement and the overall competitiveness of European patent law.[87] The current form of the EPUE is dramatic from the perspective of participation and how it functions as a legal interface because its legal configuration fails to realise the objectives that have underpinned the decades-long project of a European patent right.

The EPUE, from an administrative values perspective, is particularly interesting because while it claims to bring harmonisation and simplify patent law in Europe, it actually exacerbates existing tensions in European law. Crucially, the issues of participation in the development of the EPUE connect with concerns beyond patent law and to the broader relationship between large and small Member States within Europe. The impairment in meaningful participation within the EPUE project then provides a way of interpreting how the EPUE emerged with both substantive and procedural flaws. The latter half of the chapter considers how the enhanced cooperation process risks permanently shifting the dynamic involved in the creation of new legal projects in a way that minimises transparency and accountability. This is because the EPUE, unlike the CPC,[88] is the product of enhanced coopera-

87 Klaus Haft, 'The Unitary Patent System from an SME's Perspective' (2017) 52(4) Les Nouvelles 274.

88 Dennis Thompson, 'The Draft Convention for a European Patent' (1973) 22(1) ICLQ 51, 52.

tion that allows a group of EU Member States, as a last resort, to proceed with their own projects when their objectives cannot be agreed upon by the Union as a whole.[89] Using enhanced cooperation to establish a patent interface distinguishes it from other uses of enhanced cooperation and highlights the importance of contextual analysis in international patent law. When considered in light of the previous uses of enhanced cooperation, the EPUE represents a potential turning point in the dynamic of EU law-making specifically for participation and transparency.

0.6.3 Chapter 3: Applying administrative values to bilateral trade agreements in patent law and beyond – Identifying a distinct 'bilateral space'

The development of bilateral trade agreements and their relationship to the broader, global trade environment present an important perspective on the creation of legal interfaces and how the 'bilateral space' constitutes a distinct environment for binding obligations in patent law. A primary question that has followed their development in history has been whether bilateral agreements are a supplement to, or replacement for, multilateral instruments.[90] Chapter 3 explores the degree to which these bilateral frameworks constitute legal interfaces and how they present unique challenges (and a unique space) for realising administrative values. The issue of accountability between these multilateral frameworks and bilateral agreements also takes on a specific dynamic due to the accompanying growth of enforcement mechanisms that shift, in context, how transparency and participation emerge in a bilateral environment. As with early work on global administration that attempted to establish the idea of a global administrative space that differed from national administration,[91] the chapter is aimed at analysing how these values are produced and challenged within a distinct 'bilateral space' that is separate from (and yet connected to) the dynamics of multilateral initiatives and the global space.

Beyond the specific interplay of agreements with developed enforcement models and those without, transparency and responsiveness become a problem between these interfaces with binding enforcement measures. In this, the chapter actively embraces a more inclusive approach to intellectual property and the entangled quality of patent law. The entanglement is particularly dynamic here because bilateral agreements do not separate out patent provisions to a different agreement. Instead, patent law provisions are produced alongside every other legal provision in intellectual property and beyond. An expansive approach to contextualising patent law provisions also helps to integrate administrative values in the broader bilateral

89 Article 20(1) TEU.

90 Knut Brünjes and Milena Weidenfeller, 'Multilateral Trade Policy Is Back' in Christoph Herrmann, Bruno Simma and Rudolf Streinz (eds), *Trade Policy between Law, Diplomacy and Scholarship* (Springer 2015) 52.

91 Drawing on perspectives and themes that were prominent in the early development of GAL, where much of the work deals with establishing that there is a 'global space' at all: Elisa D'Alterio, 'Judicial Regulation in the Global Space' in Sabino Cassese (ed), *Research Handbook on Global Administrative Law* (Edward Elgar 2016) 321.

space, given the (relatively) little space dedicated to patent law in each agreement. As such, analysing patent law alongside other forms of intellectual property in the same agreement helps to understand the dynamic of the agreement and how it contributes overall to a distinct sense of bilateral space. In terms of enforcing these agreements, it is very much a narrow and developing area because the overlap between WTO dispute settlement and enforcement mechanisms contained in specific agreements has been generally small.[92] Yet, it does present a particular challenge in intellectual property due to the fuzzy scope of these rights and how they can be deployed.[93] The difficulty here is the presumption that WTO Panels would be unable to decline these disputes just because the facts may also give rise to an action in a different dispute context.[94] Taken together, it is not only the textual provisions of an agreement that can produce tensions in accountability, transparency, and participation, but the interplay of these agreements within a specific legal space.

0.6.4 Chapter 4: Multilateral tensions and the future of international patent law – Using the language of global administration to interpret modern developments and challenges

The final substantive chapter explores the dynamic of multilateral patent law and its relationship to the broader trade environment. The TRIPS Agreement, as the foundation of an essentially global patent law, represents an important space in which different objectives and tensions are modulated. Central to the administrative perspective here is the application not only to contemporary issues of patent law but also to deconstruct how the global regulatory space has been sustained. Participation, again, is a central value here because the TRIPS Agreement provides for compulsory licensing and *l'ordre public* exceptions, allowing states to modulate how binding international obligations are effective in practice. Understanding these mechanisms as tools that actors can use to interpret patent law to enhance their ability to participate also centres some concerns around autonomy. More conventional patent analysis has focused on the fact that the mere existence of textual flexibilities does not mean that they are used in practice,[95] but the focus on

92 Peter-Tobias Stoll, 'The WTO Dispute Settlement System and Regional Trade Tribunals: The Potential for Conflict and Solutions' in Alberto do Amaral Júnior, Luciana Maria de Oliveira Sá Pires, and Christiane Lucena Carneiro (eds), *The WTO Dispute Settlement Mechanism: A Developing Country Perspective* (Springer 2019) 235.

93 One example would be the challenges to Canada's promise doctrine in patent law: Pratyush Nath Upreti, 'Eli Lilly v Government of Canada: The Tale of Promise v Expectation' (2018) 21(3) IntALR 84.

94 Peter-Tobias Stoll, 'The WTO Dispute Settlement System and Regional Trade Tribunals: The Potential for Conflict and Solutions' in Alberto do Amaral Júnior, Luciana Maria de Oliveira Sá Pires, and Christiane Lucena Carneiro (eds), *The WTO Dispute Settlement Mechanism: A Developing Country Perspective* (Springer 2019) 237.

95 Debora J Halbert, 'The Curious Case of Monopoly Rights as Free Trade: The TPP and Intellectual Property and Why It Still Matters' (2017) 7 Journal of Information Policy 212.

administrative values further contextualises the qualities of this distinct international space in which competing tensions are negotiated.

The states involved have necessarily consented, legally, to the binding obligations of the TRIPS Agreement, and yet in practice the ability for specific states to meaningfully participate is obviously impaired. This goes back to the fundamental elements of GAL and how participation, in particular, can be used to deconstruct tensions in patent law. Participation in the multilateral context especially has to go beyond a formal or thin understanding because these provisions were negotiated and accepted rather than imposed.[96] Similar to the UPC in Chapter 2, a more nuanced understanding of participation recasts the configuration between patent actors, legislative power, and dispute resolution. Which actors have the power to meaningfully alter the content of binding obligations in this context? In which fora are impactful decisions being made on the quality or characteristics of these binding obligations?

Balance in the WTO membership and the potential for strategic coalitions to address contemporary issues like biopiracy or access to medicine also appear in more conventional patent work.[97] This chapter centres the African Union (AU) as a potential counterbalance not only in specific or isolated issues of patent law but also in the impaired ability to participate more broadly. As discussed in Chapter 1, the three administrative values of the book have a mutual effect and, in practice, cannot be easily separated. Patent law in the global context is perhaps the most clearly entangled because it, too, cannot be easily separated out from the broader political and economic forces. From this perspective, the AU is not simply a way of counterbalancing Western hegemonic power within the WTO to achieve more equitable access to patented medicines or benefit sharing. Rather, the AU represents a multilateral trading system in which participation is meaningful for each member, and one way of achieving this is through cooperative coalition building.

The chapter also considers the treatment of COVID-19 vaccines in terms of compulsory licensing and how it reflects the unresolved tensions of the Doha Health Declaration. However, the focus shifts away from just analysing the legal provisions and framework towards a broader understanding of autonomy and participation between countries. Throughout the pandemic and its discussion in the WTO, the role of vaccine donations appeared repeatedly.[98] Questions of patent law were essentially subsumed by the geopolitical relationships between WTO members, which allowed countries like the UK to appear supportive of the

96 There would later be a sense that the TRIPS Agreement was, in fact, imposed on developing countries and an ongoing dissonance between developing and developed countries: Jörg Reinbothe and Anthony Howard, 'The State of Play in the Negotiations on TRIPS (GATT/Uruguay Round)' (1991) 13(5) EIPR 157.

97 Brendan Vickers, 'Africa and the Rising Powers: Bargaining for the "Marginalised Many"' (2013) 89(3) International Affairs 676.

98 Jessica Elgot, 'UK's Covid Vaccine Donations Alongside Move to Block Waiver "Shameful"' (*The Guardian*, 28 July 2021) <https://www.theguardian.com/politics/2021/jul/28/uks-covid-vaccine-donations-alongside-move-to-block-waiver-shameful>.

difficulties in developing countries.[99] This centring of European and US interests with African countries firmly on the margins established a configuration between states that further, perhaps permanently, impairs participation. Rather than supporting a meaningful reform of the Doha Health Declaration and more fundamentally reviewing the functioning of international patent rules,[100] the pandemic further entrenched the sense that *even in times of crisis*, the interests and objectives of all states do not have equal weight.

0.7 Conclusion

Patent law is rarely critiqued in the language of administrative law, though many critical approaches to intellectual property implicitly work to draw out elements of transparency, accountability, and participation. Taking patent law's administrative foundation seriously centres these values as a way of analysing the relationship between the patent office, courts, and the patent itself. The national understanding of patent law is obviously administrative, especially in civil law or civil law-inspired jurisdictions,[101] where the structure of a patent challenge recognises that validity is legally distinct from infringement.[102] Patent law and its administrative foundation are interesting to explore from the perspective of accountability, transparency, and participation precisely because this national context persists even as international patent law has transformed its functioning. GAL questions the expanding reach of administrative agencies and power,[103] the way in which hierarchies become legitimised and embedded,[104] and how the technical character of regulation can work to insulate specific areas of law from critique.[105]

From this perspective, these values can be used to deconstruct how patent law develops in both a national and international setting. In particular, and drawing

99 Sarah Newey, '"Trojan Horse": Bulk of UK Vaccine Donations to Poor Countries Set to Expire in September' (*The Telegraph*, 28 July 2021) <https://www.telegraph.co.uk/global-health/science-and-disease/trojan-horse-bulk-uk-vaccine-donations-poor-countries-set-expire/>.

100 Siva Thambisetty, Aisling McMahon, Luke McDonagh, Hyo Yoon Kang, and Graham Dutfield, 'The TRIPS Intellectual Property Waiver Proposal: Creating the Right Incentives in Patent Law and Politics to End the COVID-19 Pandemic' (*LSE Legal Studies Working Paper*, 2021) 35. Available on SSRN at: <https://papers.ssrn.com/sol3/papers.cfm?abstract_id=3851737>.

101 Weinian Hu, *International Patent Rights Harmonisation: The Case of China* (Routledge 2017) 139, 140.

102 On the bifurcation of validity and infringement, see: David Tilt, 'Exploring Bifurcation in the Unified Patent Court from a Comparative Perspective: Japan and the EU' (2023) 12(4) QMJIP 470.

103 Mikael Rask Madsen, 'Judicial Globalisation: The Proliferation of International Courts' Sabino Cassese (ed), *Research Handbook on Global Administrative Law* (Edward Elgar 2016) 299, 300.

104 Sujith Xavier, 'Top Heavy: Beyond the Global North and the Justification for Global Administrative Law' (2018) 57 Indian Journal of International Law 353.

105 On the complexity of designing an appropriate relationship between experts and the broader decision-makers: Martin Shapiro, '"Deliberative," "Independent" Technocracy v. Democratic Politics: Will the Globe Echo the E.U.?' (2005) 68(3–4) Law and Contemporary Problems 343, 344.

from GAL's focus on courts, the book centres the role of dispute settlement bodies and how contemporary patent issues can be reinterpreted from an administrative perspective. At a fundamental level, can these tensions in patent law actually be understood as deficiencies in transparency, participation, and accountability? Yet the administrative deconstruction of patent law also serves to explore the nature of administrative law and administrative power. It demonstrates that administrative law is a unique power that cannot be replicated through private means. For patents, administrative power means that only within national borders can their existence and effectiveness be guaranteed. The book considers patent law at the borders of national and international systems in a way that necessarily questions the limits of administrative power. Particularly in Chapters 3 and 4, the creative potential of a dispute settlement body is enabled in the international context precisely because the system of global administration lacks an authoritative legislative power. Instead, the dispute settlement bodies that are deployed in patent law and intellectual property more broadly are engaged in a mutual process of confirmation and negotiation. The creation of distinct spaces and complex modes of communication between dispute settlement bodies and legislative instruments means that the underlying values – notably participation – take on a markedly different quality than in a purely national context.

Rather than framing contemporary issues in patent law through the lens of human rights or a specific critical approach, the book incorporates the language of accountability and transparency to promote broader engagement with people from outside patent law. The language and vocabulary of administrative law and administrative values explicitly frame the development of patent law, which moves against technocratic isolation. Again, patent law affects our societies in a variety of profound ways. The administrative law vocabulary encourages a reader to have at least some response to issues of patent law and connect those concerns, priorities, and values with their own knowledge systems. The future of patent law, because of its global societal impact, is a future in which perspectives from other disciplines and other audiences will meaningfully contribute to our understanding of it. This approach also promotes a more integrated understanding of patent law, one in which it is recognised as a normatively complex subject and where technical regulation should always be contextualised alongside its social, cultural, and political dimensions. An approach based on administrative values discards the internal/external debate on the validity of applying a human rights perspective to patent law in favour of a more integrated analysis. Considerations of accountability or transparency are not imposed on the substantive outcomes of patent law, but instead come from within and can be used to reveal the type of value judgments which have become normalised (and thus invisible) to us. Crucially, it is those normalised or invisible assumptions that can be used to integrate interdisciplinary perspectives and demonstrate the value of broad engagement in patent law.

Bibliography

Articles

Arai H, 'Intellectual Property Strategy in Japan' (2005) 1 *International Journal of Intellectual Property Law, Economy and Management* 1.

Cassese S, 'Global Administrative Law: The State of the Art' (2015) 13(2) *International Journal of Constitutional Law* 465.

Chandler DMC, 'The Never-Ending Story of Access to Medicines' (2016) 8 *WIPO Journal* 42.

Chimni BS, 'Co-Option and Resistance: Two Faces of Global Administrative Law' (2005) 37 *NYU Journal of International Law and Politics* 799.

Conway-Jones D, 'Safeguarding Hawaiian Traditional Knowledge and Cultural Heritage: Supporting the Right to Self-Determination and Preventing the Commodification of Culture' (2005) 48(2) *Howard Law Journal* 737.

Cooter RD and UY Hacohen, 'Progress in the Useful Arts: Foundations of Patent Law in Growth Economics' (2020) 22 *Yale Journal of Law & Technology* 191.

Cotter T, 'Antitrust, Intellectual Property, and Dynamic Efficiency: An Essay in Honor of Herbert Hovenkamp' (2020) 3 *Concurrences* 1.

Dima B, F Barna, and ML Nachescu, 'Does Rule of Law Support the Capital Market?' (2018) 31(1) *Economic Research–Ekonomska Istraživanja* 461.

Gana RL, 'The Myth of Development, The Progress of Rights: Human Rights to Intellectual Property and Development' (1996) 18 *Law & Policy* 315.

Gervais DJ, 'Traditional Knowledge & Intellectual Property: A TRIPS-Compatible Approach' (2005) 2005 *Michigan State Law Review* 137.

Gill JG, 'Wittgenstein and the Function of Philosophy' (1971) 2(2) *Metaphilosophy* 137.

Guan W, 'Diversified FRAND Enforcement and TRIPS Integrity' (2018) 17(1) *World Trade Review* 91.

Haft K, 'The Unitary Patent System from an SME's Perspective' (2017) 52(4) *Les Nouvelles* 274.

Halbert D, 'Feminist Interpretations of Intellectual Property' (2006) 14(3) *Journal of Gender, Social Policy & the Law* 431.

Halbert DJ, 'The Curious Case of Monopoly Rights as Free Trade: The TPP and Intellectual Property and Why it Still Matters' (2017) 7 *Journal of Information Policy* 204.

Harlow C, 'Global Administrative Law: The Quest for Principles and Values' (2006) 17(1) *European Journal of International Law* 187.

Hoen E, J Berger, A Calmy, and S Moon, 'Driving a Decade of Change: HIV/AIDS, Patents and Access to Medicines for All' (2011) 14(1) *Journal of the International AIDS Society* 15.

Jiang J and X Zhang, 'Essential Patents and Knowledge Position, a Network Analysis on the Basis of Patent Citations' (2021) 1 *Standards* 90.

Kingsbury B and L Casini, 'Global Administrative Law Dimensions of International Organizations Law' (2009) 6 *International Organizations Law Review* 319.

Kingsbury B, N Krisch, and PB Stewart, 'The Emergence of Global Administrative Law' (2005) 68(3/4) *Law and Contemporary Problems* 15.

Krikorian G and E Torreele, 'We Cannot Win the Access to Medicines Struggle Using the Same Thinking That Causes the Chronic Access Crisis' (2021) 23(1) *Health and Human Rights Journal* 119.

Krisch N and B Kingsbury, 'Introduction: Global Governance and Global Administrative Law in the International Legal Order' (2006) 17(1) *European Journal of International Law* 1.

Kuo MS, 'Between Fragmentation and Unity: The Uneasy Relationship Between Global Administrative Law and Global Constitutionalism (2009) 10(2) *San Diego International Law Journal* 439.

Lemley MA, 'An Empirical Study of the Twenty-Year Patent Term' (1994) 22(3–4) *AIPLA Quarterly Journal* 369.
Lotito G, M Migheli, and G Ortona, 'Transparency, Asymmetric Information and Cooperation' (2020) 50 *European Journal of Law and Economics* 267.
Mercurio B, 'The IP Waiver for COVID-19: Bad Policy, Bad Precedent' (2021) 52 *International Review of Intellectual Property and Competition Law* 983.
Oke EK, 'Defining the Right to Health Responsibilities of Patent-Owning Pharmaceutical Companies' (2019) 1 *Intellectual Property Quarterly* 43.
Owoeye O, 'International Patent Laws and Health: Resisting the TRIPS Compulsory Licensing Regime and the Doha Paragraph 6 System' (2015) 37(4) *European Intellectual Property Review* 782.
Owoeye O, 'Patents for Drugs and the Right to Development in International Law' (2015) 8(1) *Law and Development Review* 69.
Posner RA, 'The Law & Economics of Intellectual Property' (2002) *Dœdalus* 5.
Reddy P, 'Access to Plant Genetic Resources and Benefit Sharing: Has India Lost the Plot?' (2018) 3 *Intellectual Property Quarterly* 181.
Reinbothe J and A Howard, 'The State of Play in the Negotiations on TRIPS (GATT/ Uruguay Round)' (1991) 13(5) *European Intellectual Property Review* 157.
Sarid E, 'A Queer Analysis of Intellectual Property' (2022) 1 *Wisconsin Law Review* 91.
Shapiro M, '"Deliberative," "Independent" Technocracy v. Democratic Politics: Will the Globe Echo the E.U.?' (2005) 68(3/4) *Law and Contemporary Problems* 341.
Soyeju O and J Wabwire, 'The WTO-TRIPS Flexibilities on Public Health: A Critical Appraisal of the East African Community Regional Framework' (2017) 17(1) *World Trade Review* 145.
Stewart RB, M Ratton, and S Badin, 'The World Trade Organisation: Multiple Dimensions of Global Administrative Law' (2011) 9(3-4) *International Journal of Constitutional Law* 556.
Sykes AO, 'TRIPS, Pharmaceuticals, Developing Countries, and the Doha "Solution"' (2002) 3(1) *Chicago Journal of International Law* 47.
Thompson D, 'The Draft Convention for a European Patent' (1973) 22(1) *International & Comparative Law Quarterly* 51.
Tilt D, 'Exploring Bifurcation in the Unified Patent Court from a Comparative Perspective: Japan and the EU' (2023) 12(4) *Queen Mary Journal of Intellectual Property* 470.
Tripathi R, 'Concept of Global Administrative Law: An Overview' (2011) 67(4) *India Law Quarterly* 355.
Upreti PN, 'Eli Lilly v Government of Canada: The Tale of Promise v Expectation' (2018) 21(3) *International Arbitration Law Review* 84.
Vickers B, 'Africa and the Rising Powers: Bargaining for the "Marginalised Many"' (2013) 89(3) *International Affairs* 673.
Weinrib J, 'Maitland's Challenge for Administrative Legal Theory' (2021) 84(2) *Modern Law Review* 207.
Woodward WR, 'A Reconsideration of the Patent System as a Problem of Administrative Law' (1942) 55(6) *Harvard Law Review* 950.
Xavier S, 'Top Heavy: Beyond the Global North and the Justification for Global Administrative Law' (2018) 57 *Indian Journal of International Law* 337.
Zhang MQ, 'Shall We Talk? Judicial Communication Between the CJEU and WTO Dispute Settlement' (2017) 28(1) *European Journal of International Law* 273.

Books

Hu W, *International Patent Rights Harmonisation: The Case of China* (Routledge 2017).

Montt S, *State Liability in Investment Treaty Arbitration: Global Constitutional and Administrative Law in the BIT Generation* (Hart 2009).
Mouffe C, *Agonistics: Thinking the World Politically* (Verso 2013).
Oke EK, *Patents, Human Rights, and Access to Medicines* (CUP 2022).

Chapters

Brünjes K and M Weidenfeller, 'Multilateral Trade Policy is Back' in Christoph Herrmann, Bruno Simma, and Rudolf Streinz (eds), *Trade Policy Between Law, Diplomacy and Scholarship* (Springer 2015) 47.
Cananea GD, 'Administrative Law Beyond the State: The Influence of International and Supranational Organizations' in Peter Cane, Herwig Ch Hofmann, Eric C IP, and Peter L Lindseth (eds), *Oxford Handbook of Comparative Administrative Law* (OUP 2021) 357.
Casini L, 'The Expansion of the Material Scope of Global Law' in Sabino Cassese (ed), *Research Handbook on Global Administrative Law* (Edward Elgar 2016) 25.
Chon M, 'Intellectual Property and Critical Theories' in Irene Calboli and Maria Lillá Montagnani (eds), *Handbook of Intellectual Property Research: Lenses, Methods, and Perspectives* (OUP 2021) 746.
D'Alterio E, 'Judicial Regulation in the Global Space' in Sabino Cassese (ed), *Research Handbook on Global Administrative Law* (Edward Elgar 2016) 303.
Duval A, 'Seamstress of Transnational Law: How the Court of Arbitration for Sport Weaves the Lex Sportiva' in Nico Krisch (ed), *Entangled Legalities Beyond the State* (CUP 2022) 260.
Golia AJ, 'Judicial Review, Foreign Relations and Global Administrative Law: The Administrative Function of Courts in Foreign Relations' in Helmut Philipp Aust and Thomas Kleinlein (eds), *Encounters Between Foreign Relations Law and International Law: Bridges and Boundaries* (CUP 2021) 130.
Harlow C, P Leino, and GD Cananea, 'Introduction: European Administrative Law – A Thematic Approach' in Carol Harlow, Päivi Leino, and Giacinto della Cananea (eds), *Research Handbook on EU Administrative Law* (Edward Elgar 2017) 1.
Krisch N, 'Framing Entangled Legalities Beyond the State' in Nico Krisch (ed), *Entangled Legalities Beyond the State* (CUP 2022) 1.
Madsen MR, 'Judicial Globalisation: The Proliferation of International Courts' Sabino Cassese (ed), *Research Handbook on Global Administrative Law* (Edward Elgar 2016) 282.
Maresceau M, 'The Court of Justice and Bilateral Agreements' in Allan Rosas, Egils Levit and Yves Bot (eds), The Court of Justice and the Construction of Europe: Analyses and Perspectives on Sixty Years of Case-Law / La Cour de Justice et la Construction de l'Europe: Analyses et Perspectives de Soixante Ans de Jurisprudence (Springer 2012) 693.
Michaels R, 'Tertiary Rules' in Nico Krisch (ed), *Entangled Legalities Beyond the* State (CUP 2022) 424.
Möschel M, 'Critical Race Theory' in Emilios Christodoulidis, Ruth Dukes, and Marco Goldoni (eds), *Research Handbook on Critical Legal Theory* (Edward Elgar 2019) 63.
Reimers LL, 'International Trade Law: Legal Entanglement on the WTO's Own Terms' in Nico Krisch (ed), *Entangled Legalities Beyond the State* (CUP 2022) 193.
Sherman B, 'Towards a History of Patent Law' in Toshiko Takenaka (ed), *Intellectual Property in Common Law and Civil Law* (Edward Elgar 2013) 3.
Stoll PT, 'The WTO Dispute Settlement System and Regional Trade Tribunals: The Potential for Conflict and Solutions' in Alberto do Amaral Júnior, Luciana Maria de Oliveira Sá Pires, and Christiane Lucena Carneiro (eds), *The WTO Dispute Settlement Mechanism: A Developing Country Perspective* (Springer 2019) 229.

Tamanaha BZ, 'A Reconstruction of Transnational Legal Pluralism and Law's Foundations' in Nico Krisch (ed), *Entangled Legalities Beyond the State* (CUP 2022) 449.

Tilt D, 'International Perspectives on Regulatory Frameworks: AI Through the Lens of Patent Law' in Angelos Kornilakis, Georgios Nouskalis, Vassilis Pergantis, and Themistoklis Tzimas (eds), *Artificial Intelligence and Normative Challenges: International and Comparative Legal* Perspectives (Springer 2023) 171.

Visser CJ, 'Making Intellectual Property Laws Work for Traditional Knowledge' in J Michael Finger and Philip Schuler (eds), *Poor People's Knowledge: Promoting Intellectual Property in Developing Countries* (OUP 2004) 207.

Whalley J, 'Developing Countries and System Strengthening in the Uruguay Round' in Will Martin and L Alan Winters (eds), *The Uruguay Round and Developing Countries* (CUP 1996) 305.

Wouters J, 'Government by Regulation' in Sabino Cassese (ed), *Research Handbook on Global Administrative Law* (Edward Elgar 2016) 209.

Yu PK, 'Development Bridge Over Troubled Intellectual Property Water' in Xavier Seuba and Carlos Correa (eds), *Intellectual Property and Development: Understanding the Interfaces* (Springer 2019) 97.

Legislation

Article 20, TEU.

Article 27, TRIPS Agreement.

Article 33, TRIPS Agreement.

Other

Elgot J, 'UK's Covid Vaccine Donations Alongside Move to Block Waiver "Shameful"' (*The Guardian*, 28 July 2021) <https://www.theguardian.com/politics/2021/jul/28/uks-covid-vaccine-donations-alongside-move-to-block-waiver-shameful>.

Newey S, '"Trojan Horse": Bulk of UK Vaccine Donations to Poor Countries Set to Expire in September" (*The Telegraph*, 28 July 2021) <https://www.telegraph.co.uk/global-health/science-and-disease/trojan-horse-bulk-uk-vaccine-donations-poor-countries-set-expire/>.

Thambisetty S, A McMahon, L McDonagh, HY Kang, and G Dutfield, 'The TRIPS Intellectual Property Waiver Proposal: Creating the Right Incentives in Patent Law and Politics to End the COVID-19 Pandemic' (LSE Legal Studies Working Paper, 2021) 35 <https://papers.ssrn.com/sol3/papers.cfm?abstract_id=3851737>.

1 Connecting patents, administration, and Global Administrative Law concepts

1.1 Introduction

Patent law is a complex area of law that involves the interaction of national and international systems across a variety of different hierarchies. Patents stand out from other conventional forms of intellectual property because the drive towards harmonisation has yet to produce a truly global system of protection.[1] Instead of a single global patent emerging, there has been cooperation between legal systems on what the fundamental qualities of a patent granted by the relevant administrative agency should be.[2] The actual enforcement and the grant of the patent have, however, remained distinctly national.[3] International patent law is, then, at once produced through interactions between actors in a horizontal sense (national agencies in relation to one another) and a more vertical sense (direct hierarchies of legal primacy that structure international relationships). Crucial to the book's focus on administrative values in the context of patent law is the emphasis on procedural, rather than substantive, features of patent law. As with the isolation of administrative values more fundamentally, the reality is that the procedural aspects of patent law can never truly be separated from the substantive content. Understanding patent law as being produced through a diffuse network of controls over the exercise of administrative power emphasises the importance of the *values* that can be used to shape, interpret, and critique this dynamic process. The central values considered here are drawn from both national administrative law and global administration, exploring how values like transparency, participation, and accountability can be used to reinterpret and reframe the process of patent law development.

1 Randy Campbell, 'Global Patent Law Harmonization: Benefits and Implementation' (2003) 13(2) Indiana International & Comparative Law Review 605. And while Rajec remains unconvinced by the explanatory value of harmonisation within international intellectual property (preferring maximalism instead), it remains that there is no global system that deals with the grant and enforcement of patent rights: Sarah R Wasserman Rajec, 'The Harmonization Myth in International Intellectual Property Law' (2020) 60 Arizona Law Review 735, 740.

2 Such as the length of a patent and the technological scope of patent law: Adam Isaac Hasson, 'Domestic Implementation of International Obligations: The Quest for World Patent Law Harmonization' (2002) 25 Boston College International & Comparative Law Review 379, 380.

3 Randy Campbell, 'Global Patent Law Harmonization: Benefits and Implementation' (2003) 13(2) Indiana International & Comparative Law Review 614.

DOI: 10.4324/9781003616856-2

Europe highlights how tensions can emerge at the borders of legal orders in a more general sense (as with the process of EU enlargement),[4] but the history of patent harmonisation more specifically demonstrates the dynamic negotiation that occurs between the national, international, and global spheres.[5] Non-intellectual property contexts in Europe provide many examples of mechanisms and values used to moderate how legal systems interact, with some drawing specifically on the vocabulary of domestic administrative law.[6] Intellectual property has generally not been analysed from a perspective that emphasises its connection to the exercise of delegated public power and the use of administrative concepts to interpret it. Patents (and more specifically, the *grant* of a patent) are produced through state power exercised through an administrative agency. International agreements and institutions that produce international patent law, in some way, can then be considered restrictions or limitations on the ability of a state to grant patents and freely delegate this power. From this perspective, international patent law – particularly with its important economic and regulatory character – fits closely with global administration's more conventional subject matter. There is certainly a tension in presenting patent law as subject to administrative (conceptual and practical) oversight rather than identifying it as an area of regulation (trade or otherwise). Yet precisely because the patent relies on a delegated exercise of public power, the rules that govern its use function in much the same way as conventional administrative law in providing limits and expectations around state power. So, while Ghosh is correct in presenting patent law as an element of international trade regulation,[7] this is *in addition* to a more fundamental administrative character of the patent that carries with it an inherently value-laden perspective. Patent law presents an interesting opportunity for this type of approach because its economic framing has often been used to push for harmonisation on the basis of efficiency. However, in practice, what is actually being regulated is intensely connected to the autonomy of national legal systems and the way in which power is exercised within those boundaries. The patent system, though it necessarily produces a legal right that has an economic impact,[8] is informed by many considerations from outside this narrow economic framing that reflects its capacity for entanglement. The operation of

4 Günter Burghardt, 'The EU/US Transatlantic Relationship: The Indispensable Partnership' in Christoph Hermann, Bruno Simma, and Rudolf Streinz (eds), *Trade Policy between Law, Diplomacy and Scholarship* (Springer 2015) 197.

5 Victor Rodriguez, 'Constructing a Unitary Title for the European Patent System' (2011) 6(8) JIPLP 576.

6 Giacinto Della Cananea, 'Administrative Law Beyond the State: The Influence of International and Supranational Organizations' in Peter Cane, Herwig CH Hofmann, Eric C Ip, and Peter L Lindseth (eds), *Oxford Handbook of Comparative Administrative Law* (OUP 2021) 359, 373.

7 With patent law proposed as a tool of marketplace regulation, suggesting that the patent bargain theory of patent law is misguided: Shubha Ghosh, 'Patents and the Regulatory State: Rethinking the Patent Bargain Metaphor after Eldred' (2004) 19(4) Berkeley Technology Law Journal 1315, 1318.

8 Discussing the utilitarian perception of patents as 'economic instruments' that should protect only the minimum term required to incentivise innovation: Federica Baldan, *Judicial Coherence in the European Patent System: Lessons from the US and Japan* (Edward Elgar 2022) 91.

patent law brings together a mix of national conditions and societal values that distinguish between what is or is not inventive,[9] which inventions could be contrary to public morals,[10] and the appropriate role of the patent system in national growth.[11]

This chapter first looks into the development of GAL as an academic perspective and some of the prominent features of this area of scholarship. Particular attention is given to the role of dispute settlement bodies across a variety of international contexts. The chapter then explores more concretely how administrative concepts and values will be incorporated throughout the rest of the book, emphasising more recent developments in GAL that explore the dynamic and interactive quality of legal interfaces. Applying this type of administrative lens to dispute resolution institutions helps to direct the analysis in terms of administrative values. The interactional quality central to dispute resolution brings form to administrative values and investigates how, in context, the process can be interpreted as maximising, promoting, or elaborating the traditional administrative values of accountability, participation, and transparency in a patent setting. The focus on dynamic relationships in a dispute setting also helps to more explicitly incorporate administrative values as an analytical lens with the more specific work on managing legal interfaces. Beyond clarifying how these institutions facilitate the interactions between legal systems and through which mechanisms, the chapter also looks at the extent to which this facilitative role of the dispute settlement body is also creative. There is a fundamentally generative element to global administration in that dispute resolution is the process through which meaning and specific legal form are given to values.[12] Here, this centring of the creative, dynamic, somewhat improvisational process helps to produce a more active understanding of dispute resolution bodies, their function, and how the economic dimension of a patent is only a single element of its legal constitution.

9 Such as excluding mathematics from patentability: Hazel VJ Moir, *Patent Policy and Innovation: Do Legal Rules Deliver Effective Economic Outcomes?* (Edward Elgar 2013) 64.

10 The changing approach to 'products manufactured by an atomic transformation' in Japan is one example: Nobuhiro Nakayama, 'The Enforcement of the TRIPS Agreement in Japan' (1995) 38 Japanese Annual of International Law 58.

11 Like the reforms around universities and patent commercialisation that appeared around the world: Hiroyuki Odagiri, Akira Goto, and Atsushi Sunami, 'IPR and the Catch-Up Process in Japan' in Hiroyuki Odagiri, Akira Goto, Atsushi Sunami, and Richard R Nelson (eds), *Intellectual Property Rights, Development, and Catch-Up: An International Comparative Study* (OUP 2010) 120.

12 Discussing the central (and fundamentally creative) role of courts in developing and applying norms: Li-Ann Thio, 'Courts and Judicial Review' in Peter Cane, Herwig CH Hofmann, Eric C Ip, and Peter L Lindseth (eds), *Oxford Handbook of Comparative Administrative Law* (OUP 2021) 721, 722.

1.2 Exploring the fundamentals of Global Administrative Law

1.2.1 Integrating the global administration perspective with patent law

1.2.1.1 Values, patent law, and administrative power

In terms of academic focus, the project draws on the vocabulary and history of GAL for its conceptual framing. GAL emerged perhaps more formally as a field in the early 2000s as a response to increasing globalisation and the impact of international regulation and governance,[13] focusing on the relationship between these international modes of governance and values like accountability and transparency in the exercise of administrative power.[14] GAL has been presented essentially as a response to the

> vast increase in the reach and forms of transgovernmental regulation and administration signed to address the consequences of globalized interdependence in such fields as security … environmental protection … intellectual property ... and cross-border movements of populations, including refugees.[15]

GAL scholarship is important for understanding the trajectory and dynamic of international patent law because of the type of institutional focus and legal values that underpin the analysis in this area. By focusing on sources of law that are outside of legislation or international treaties, dispute settlement bodies become central institutions in studying how values develop in regulatory practice.[16] Dispute settlement bodies are crucial for giving actual meaning or force to these concepts precisely because they work directly with the type of general language that provides the space for interpretation. In looking at global administration, the fact that this type of framing has not been applied directly to patent law is somewhat stark. Recent decades have seen the increasingly regulatory character of patent law take on a particularly global quality, with the WTO itself emerging as an important international actor for global administration. When patent or intellectual property elements appear in GAL work, they are often covered briefly and work has tended to focus on the relationship between the TRIPS Agreement and technical standard-setting.[17] As with the analysis throughout the rest of the book, the approach here

13 Benedict Kingsbury, Nico Krisch, and Patrick B Stewart, 'The Emergence of Global Administrative Law' (2005) 68(3/4) Law and Contemporary Problems 15; though Aman presents the beginning of 'the global era of administrative law' as being in the 1980s: Alfred C Aman, 'Administrative Law in the United States: Present and Future' (1991) 16 Queen's Law Journal 179.

14 Rajeshwar Tripathi, 'Concept of Global Administrative Law: An Overview' (2011) 67(4) India Law Quarterly 356.

15 Benedict Kingsbury, Nico Krisch, and Patrick B Stewart, 'The Emergence of Global Administrative Law' (2005) 68(3/4) Law and Contemporary Problems 16.

16 Mikael Rask Madsen, 'Judicial Globalization: The Proliferation of International Courts' in Sabino Cassese (ed), *Research Handbook on Global Administrative Law* (Edward Elgar 2016) 282.

17 Lorenzo Casini, 'The Expansion of the Material Scope of Global Law' in Sabino Cassese (ed), *Research Handbook on Global Administrative Law* (Edward Elgar 2016) 28.

reflects perhaps an early attempt at integrating patents within the more traditional scope of global administration.

Patent law provides then an interesting way of looking at the complex role of the WTO as an international organisation. The WTO does appear regularly in work on global administration in terms of its capacity to manage international regulation,[18] how it can actually apply administrative law principles,[19] and provide a critical case study in terms of how harmonisation or uniformity can be interpreted.[20] Even returning to the creation of the WTO, the lack of patent or intellectual property focus stands out given that the successful conclusion of the TRIPS Agreement was a key development. The TRIPS Agreement regulates the fundamental aspects of patent law and so reflects very real changes to the ability to grant patents, though its provisions and negotiation process were shaped by a profound dissonance and imbalance between developing and developed countries.[21] The TRIPS Agreement is perhaps most notable in terms of patent law because it bound international intellectual property with a system of dispute resolution.[22] The general contours of patent law have been generally settled since the Paris Convention in 1883, and so the TRIPS Agreement represented very minor modifications in terms of what a patent is. From an approach that centres meaningful participation and transparency, the relationship between the TRIPS Agreement and dispute settlement is especially important. The provisions in the TRIPS Agreement not only further specify the parameters around the state grant of a patent (and so, what a patent *is*) but also attach legal consequences to these obligations and establish an effective system of dispute resolution. The provisions provide legally enforceable understandings of the type of invention that may be patented,[23] the length of the protection to be granted,[24] and the mechanisms through which patent protection can be limited or otherwise minimised.[25] All of these regulate an exercise of state power and yet have not been investigated or presented as such in the literature. The imbalance in negotiating and economic position has been discussed extensively in the development of the TRIPS Agreement and so,[26] despite the official consent of developing

18 Martin Shapiro, '"Deliberative," "Independent" Technocracy v. Democratic Politics: Will the Globe Echo the E.U.?' (2005) 68(3/4) Law and Contemporary Problems 341, 342.

19 Giacinto Della Cananea, 'Administrative Law Beyond the State: The Influence of International and Supranational Organizations' in Peter Cane, Herwig CH Hofmann, Eric C Ip, and Peter L Lindseth (eds), *Oxford Handbook of Comparative Administrative Law* (OUP 2021) 373.

20 René Fernando Urueña Hernandez, 'Global Administrative Law and the Global South' in Sabino Cassese (ed), *Research Handbook on Global Administrative Law* (Edward Elgar 2016) 395, 396, 397.

21 Jörg Reinbothe and Anthony Howard, 'The State of Play in the Negotiations on TRIPS (GATT/Uruguay Round)' (1991) 13(5) EIPR 157.

22 Srividhya Ragavan, *Patent and Trade Disparities in Developing Countries* (OUP 2012) 74.

23 Patentable subject matter: Article 27(1), TRIPS Agreement.

24 Term of protection: Article 33, TRIPS Agreement.

25 *L'ordre public*: Article 27(2), TRIPS Agreement.

26 With particular attention to future trade negotiation and analysis, 'it will be impossible to isolate the influence of the Uruguay Round imbalance from the many other elements that go into negotiating

countries, there is something almost explicitly limiting about how it practically affects their ability to grant patents. Even when the provision appears to be permissive and not a restriction on state power per se, the reality is that these parameters only exist as they are provided for by the TRIPS Agreement. One example would be the provisions on patentable subject matter. This provides that patents must be granted for all areas of technology and, on the surface, does not immediately read as a restriction of state power. In practice, however, this means that the 'freedom' to grant patents still represents a directing of state power that is produced *through* the operation of the TRIPS Agreement – states are *obliged* to grant patents in all areas of technology and the operation of delegated state power is therefore in some way subject to a (binding) restriction. In the broader context, then, the TRIPS Agreement provisions necessarily frame the legitimate scope of autonomy of participants within the global system of trade regulation.

1.2.1.2 Situating dispute resolution, the WTO, and the values of Global Administrative Law

The WTO has, even beyond the specific issues that have emerged in patent law,[27] been discussed critically in terms of accountability and transparency.[28] In this, there is a significant parallel between the way in which the language of democratic deficit has been applied to both the WTO and the EU.[29] And yet despite this, the distinct global administrative language and values have not been directly applied to the patent or intellectual property aspects of the WTO and its dispute settlement apparatus. The role of dispute settlement bodies appears throughout global administration in a variety of different legal contexts[30] – though it is important to recognise that courts are only one element within a broader institutional setting with an important role in administration.[31] The book focuses more closely on dispute settlement bodies because, especially with patent law and the mirrored institutional setups across different hierarchies, an institution's ability to produce a

motivations and tactics': J Michael Finger, 'Implementation and Imbalance: Dealing with Hangover from the Uruguay Round' (2007) 23(3) Oxford Review of Economic Policy 442.

27 Noah Benjamin Novogrodsky, 'Beyond TRIPS: The Role of Non-State Actors and Access to Essential Medicines' in Thomas Pogge, Matthew Rimmer, and Kim Rubenstein (eds), *Incentives for Global Public Health: Patent Law and Access to Essential Medicines* (CUP 2010) 346, 347.

28 Sarah Joseph, 'Democratic Deficit, Participation and the WTO' in Sarah Joseph, David Kinley, and Jeff Waincymer (eds), *The World Trade Organization and Human Rights: Interdisciplinary Perspectives* (Edward Elgar 2009) 313, 314.

29 Kevin Featherstone, 'Jean Monnet and the "Democratic Deficit" in the European Union' (1994) 32(2) JComMarSt 149, 150.

30 Particularly in the European context: Giulio Vesperini, 'Europe and Global Law' in Sabino Cassese (ed), *Research Handbook on Global Administrative Law* (Edward Elgar 2016) 386, 387.

31 Such as the role of private and hybrid institutional arrangements in the creation of regulation, such as the Codex Alimentarius Commission or International Organization for Standardization: Stefano Battini, 'The Proliferation of Global Regulatory Regimes' in Sabino Cassese (ed), *Research Handbook on Global Administrative Law* (Edward Elgar 2016) 52, 59.

binding decision as to the precise state of law provides a common foundation. The interactions, despite their functionally similar elements, can then be deconstructed through the lens of accountability, transparency, and participation.

Rather than exploring how these values can be realised through court structures in intellectual property, it is important to deconstruct their dynamic and interactive quality. In this context, the focus has been on interfaces – the points of contact between different legal regimes and the tools and mechanisms necessary to realise a workable system of law.[32] As with GAL more generally, patent law provides an interesting environment in which to investigate interfaces precisely because of its multilevel nature. Patent law is constructed from national and international instruments, standards of protection required by these international instruments but that still rely on the grant of patents by national bodies and an enforcement environment that involves decisions from both national and international actors. This means that even international patent law alone is made up of a mosaic of legal sources. It draws on the Paris Convention, the TRIPS Agreement, and national patent laws that together establish the foundations of the international patent system. Additional legal instruments with a more specific disciplinary focus can build on this system (such as the Biotechnology Directive) and support future cooperation or harmonisation (for example the European Patent Convention). Rather than just exploring the role of a dispute settlement body in promoting or realising general administrative values, additionally incorporating the language of legal interfaces instead highlights the powerful role of the dispute settlement body in this context. From this perspective, dispute settlement bodies are involved in creating regulation, managing these hierarchical interactions between actors and legal systems, and exploring the extent to which these interactions produce outcomes that can be interpreted through the language of transparency and participation.

1.3 What exactly counts as Global Administrative Law?

1.3.1 Approaching the disciplinary boundaries of global administration

1.3.1.1 The permeable quality of 'global' 'administrative' 'law'

It is clear that, throughout work on administrative law, there is a variety in how administrative law (even without considering the complicating 'global' dimension of this area) can be constructed. There is certainly a diversity in how different audiences understand or construct the precise nature of administrative power and even the boundaries of what exactly should be considered 'administrative' law. The indistinct boundaries between what is administrative and what is not are also reflected internally, where there is often a distinction between general and special

32 Predominantly through the concept of interface norms and the interface itself as developed by Nico Krisch: Nico Krisch, 'Framing Entangled Legalities Beyond the State' in Nico Krisch (ed), *Entangled Legalities Beyond the State* (CUP 2022) 1, 2.

administrative law.[33] Ziller, for example, suggests that this distinction between general and special emerges from the difficulty in cleanly separating the law 'applying to the substance of policies … and the law applying to policy-making'.[34] This is further complicated by the diversity of national perspectives on what is typically considered administrative. The specific examples of French, German, and Italian administrative law can incorporate elements of contract law or more general adjudication.[35] The concept of liability appears in the French context, and a narrower construction with elements of adjudication by public agencies in Italy and Germany emerged in the 20th century.[36] While the US has a particularly distinct history of administrative law, the role of the courts in restraining or otherwise checking the exercise of power by administrative agencies remains a prominent part of the system.[37] The element of restraint, of control, is fundamental to all of these contexts and centre mechanisms intended to manage the creative potential of state power – especially when it is delegated away from the primary institutions of the state.

Along with the variety of approaches to administrative law, there is also a spectrum in terms of the functioning (and expectations) of administrative law itself. The extremes of this spectrum are perhaps most clearly represented, ranging from thin or more procedural understandings of administration to a thicker, more substantive perspective. Harlow suggests that this thin version of administrative law, with its emphasis on procedural guarantees of the rule of law, aligns with the perspective of economic liberals.[38] In this economic framing, the institutions central to entrenching the procedural form of administrative law are the institutions of international trade law, such as the WTO, thc World Bank (WB), and the International Monetary Fund (IMF).[39] In this, there is a persistent undercurrent in global administration of both the security of capital and property. The presence of developed dispute resolution mechanisms within these institutions is also central to the attempts to 'juridify' the values of thin administrative law principles because it establishes a language in

33 Jacques Ziller, 'Comparison within Multi-Level Polities and Governance Regimes' in Peter Cane, Herwig CH Hofmann, Eric C Ip, and Peter L Lindseth (eds), *Oxford Handbook of Comparative Administrative Law* (OUP 2021) 139.

34 Jacques Ziller, 'Comparison within Multi-Level Polities and Governance Regimes' in Peter Cane, Herwig CH Hofmann, Eric C Ip, and Peter L Lindseth (eds), *Oxford Handbook of Comparative Administrative Law* (OUP 2021) 139.

35 Jacques Ziller, 'Comparison within Multi-Level Polities and Governance Regimes' in Peter Cane, Herwig CH Hofmann, Eric C Ip, and Peter L Lindseth (eds), *Oxford Handbook of Comparative Administrative Law* (OUP 2021) 139.

36 Jacques Ziller, 'Comparison within Multi-Level Polities and Governance Regimes' in Peter Cane, Herwig CH Hofmann, Eric C Ip, and Peter L Lindseth (eds), *Oxford Handbook of Comparative Administrative Law* (OUP 2021) 139.

37 Alfred C Aman, 'Administrative Law in the United States: Present and Future' (1991) 16 Queen's Law Journal 184.

38 Carol Harlow, 'Global Administrative Law: The Quest for Principles and Values' (2006) 17(1) EJIL 187, 208.

39 Carol Harlow, 'Global Administrative Law: The Quest for Principles and Values' (2006) 17(1) EJIL 187, 208.

which they can be authoritatively framed.[40] Given the attention to the impact of binding dispute resolution systems in patent law through the TRIPS Agreement,[41] it is clear that the multifaceted nature of the WTO presents an understanding of administration (and also patent law) that is profoundly entangled. Here, there is no simple way of separating the development of the WTO, the role of binding dispute resolution bodies in a patent context, and the degree to which the system itself represents an attempt to juridify or otherwise legitimise a thin understanding of administrative values. The very interconnected nature of global regulation means that all of its constituent elements are brought into contact in varying degrees, presenting a global space in which these discrete spheres of law are configured relationally. Procedural developments in the WTO necessarily shape howinternational dispute resolution functions and, in turn, impact patent law and all other forms of intellectual property.

In this, there is a sense that the role or purpose of administrative law in the global space is fundamentally connected to or dependent on the specifically global character of the institutional context. The focus on the institutional arrangement that emerges when regulation occurs at the global level is important because in the absence of a familiar national system, it challenges the ability to draw a clear connection between domestic, administrative work within a single state and parallel activities of a similar nature at the international or global level.[42] Indeed, it is this institutional arrangement that highlights the issues in constructing a sufficient, in both a descriptive and a functional sense, definition of what administration *is*. One definition that has been used is functionally very broad, essentially incorporating all modes of law and law-making except international treaties, formal international agreements, and episodic dispute resolution bodies.[43] A challenge that is fundamental to the issue of understanding or mapping global regulation is that the vocabulary of domestic administration does not necessarily fit the institutions that have emerged in the international space.[44] Even at the national level, the bureaucratic understanding of administration is being challenged by other approaches to regulatory activity, such as those of 'new governance' regulation.[45] Taken together,

40 In using these dispute mechanisms to gain authority, if not always legitimacy: Carol Harlow, 'Global Administrative Law: The Quest for Principles and Values' (2006) 17(1) EJIL 187, 208.

41 Srividhya Ragavan, *Patent and Trade Disparities in Developing Countries* (OUP 2012) 74.

42 Richard B Stewart, Michelle Ratton, and Sanchez Badin, 'The World Trade Organisation: Multiple Dimensions of Global Administrative Law' (2011) 9(3–4) ICON 556, 583.

43 Richard B Stewart, Michelle Ratton, and Sanchez Badin, 'The World Trade Organisation: Multiple Dimensions of Global Administrative Law' (2011) 9(3–4) ICON 556, 583.

44 Richard B Stewart, Michelle Ratton, and Sanchez Badin, 'The World Trade Organisation: Multiple Dimensions of Global Administrative Law' (2011) 9(3–4) ICON 556, 583.

45 Specifically considered from the perspective of democratic accountability: Adrienne Héritier and Dirk Lehmkuhl, 'New Modes of Governance and Democratic Accountability' (2011) 46(1) Government and Opposition 126, 127; Though see also the discussion on new governance paradigms and 'instances of "new governance" regulation' in political science: Neli Frost, 'Out with the "Old", In with the "New": Challenging Dominant Regulatory Approaches in the Field of Human Rights' (2021) 32(2) EJIL 507, 515.

there is certainly something distinct that changes as administration extends into the global space, but not necessarily in function or content. The sense of positionality of these institutions and their relationships to other actors and fields of law become central as the context in which they operate lacks the definitive framing of the national context. Though their functions are necessarily prescribed by legal instruments, the way in which their activities cross over, interact, or come into conflict is relative to one another in a way that is not the case with a national legislator and apex court. There is a dynamic quality to administration in this context that at once generates significant complexity for accurately mapping these interactions and a great potential for cooperation in particularly interdisciplinary areas of regulation. Even at this early stage, there is a tension in accepting a definition of global administration that excludes treaties – the TRIPS Agreement is a treaty, but as mentioned throughout, its provisions regulate state power in a way that is functionally similar to conventional domestic administrative law. What would be gained, with a view to exploring global administration, by excluding the TRIPS Agreement as a legitimate source of administrative regulation?

Turning to how we can understand the actual purpose of administrative law, this is also subject to discussion. What exactly is the primary function of administrative law? For some, European legal systems generally follow an approach in which administrative law is framed predominantly as a tool for restraining or otherwise controlling the exercise of public power.[46] From this, Harlow suggests that this element of legal mechanisms that control or contain state power is central to defining and understanding administrative law in those systems.[47] The French perspective, and its perhaps more expansive construction of administrative law,[48] reflects a broader understanding of administrative law that is beyond this procedural control exercised through courts and dispute resolution.[49] Yet even these national bodies and courts operate within a legal system and, through the interpretation of administrative law, represent not just a controlling of state power but an elaboration as to the standards, values, and dynamics of that control. One example that is discussed in administrative law is the approach of French judges, where administrative judges work from *inside* the framework to develop the substantive character of administrative norms.[50] Harlow argues that this facilitates an understanding, or perhaps an alternative definition, of administrative law that considers all rules and

46 Carol Harlow, 'Global Administrative Law: The Quest for Principles and Values' (2006) 17(1) EJIL 191.

47 Carol Harlow, 'Global Administrative Law: The Quest for Principles and Values' (2006) 17(1) EJIL 191.

48 Jacques Ziller, 'Comparison within Multi-Level Polities and Governance Regimes' in Peter Cane, Herwig CH Hofmann, Eric C Ip, and Peter L Lindseth (eds), *Oxford Handbook of Comparative Administrative Law* (OUP 2021) 139.

49 Carol Harlow, 'Global Administrative Law: The Quest for Principles and Values' (2006) 17(1) EJIL 192.

50 Carol Harlow, 'Global Administrative Law: The Quest for Principles and Values' (2006) 17(1) EJIL 192.

laws that apply to the administration and not just restrictions on the exercise of state power itself.[51]

Applying these perspectives on the function and role of administrative power to patent law highlights the overlooked administrative foundation of patent law and the patent grant itself. Turning first to the breakdown between a clear (or effective) distinction between national and international administration because of globalisation, patent law highlights the tense relationship between international systems of regulation and state sovereignty. Patents are granted by the state and rely on the power of the state to enforce these property rights. Since the international elements of patent law are produced by states (and consented to by them as well), does this demonstrate a system of global administration that fundamentally enables (or requires, presupposes) effective standards of participation and transparency? In the face of negative distributional outcomes in patent law, why do states not simply use their sovereign power to modify patent law? Are all states' interests (and therefore participation) equally capable of meaningfully shaping the binding obligations of international patent law? The values involved in deconstructing global administration can then be an important tool in understanding how we evaluate or understand these systems and how they interact.

1.3.2 Prominent values and principles of Global Administrative Law

1.3.2.1 The role of law, democracy, and accountability in administration

Two other values of GAL that emerged as it developed as an academic subdiscipline are the rule of law and democracy, which are considered in some parts as the 'legitimating principles' in Western administrative legal systems.[52] Indeed, a strong theme is the importance of a particularly contextualist analysis that considers not just the functioning of administrative law in states, but the specific legal features of these states and the interplay of institutions more broadly. In this, the potential of exploring global administration and its value as distinctly global concepts must be understood in the context of an interconnected environment of regulation in which the 'functions, governance arrangements, and the ability of different players to use GAL tools are all relevant'.[53] Rule of law and democracy are usually complemented with discussions of accountability, though there appears to be some flexibility as to whether it is framed solidly as a general aspect of democratic order or represents values that are essentially derived from administrative law.[54] Taggart's

51 Carol Harlow, 'Global Administrative Law: The Quest for Principles and Values' (2006) 17(1) EJIL 192.

52 Carol Harlow, 'Global Administrative Law: The Quest for Principles and Values' (2006) 17(1) EJIL 190.

53 Richard B Stewart, Michelle Ratton, and Sanchez Badin, 'The World Trade Organisation: Multiple Dimensions of Global Administrative Law' (2011) 9(3–4) ICON 556, 586.

54 'While liberal democratic orders are committed to democratic values such as transparency, accountability, and participation, whether judicial review of executive rule or policy-making is robust or minimal turns on contextual factors': Li-Ann Thio, 'Courts and Judicial Review' in Peter Cane,

work represents perhaps a third approach, where accountability appears alongside other conventional rule of law principles (along with participation and openness) but in a way that characterises them as elements of public law that are derived predominantly from the development of administrative law.[55]

Beyond the classification of accountability as an administrative law value, a more specific construction of legal accountability can be understood as the way in which the less powerful actors are protected within a legal framework.[56] Despite the important function of accountability in directly presenting a path towards decisional review of an agency, there appears to be an important relationship between administrative accountability and administrative legitimacy.[57] The emphasis appears to land on *where* this accountability is directed. If accountability leads to 'powerful states or organized economic interests',[58] then accountability is especially limited in its connection to legitimacy and can be no guarantee of normatively just or fair outcomes.[59] More recent work has focused specifically on how institutions relate to values such as accountability and legitimacy, particularly in how legitimacy is connected with effectiveness.

As with the difficulty in isolating the legal treatment of patent law in a system of global regulation, this entanglement also extends to administrative values in practice. There is a mutual relationship between these values because organisations are interested in promoting inclusiveness (as participation) to increase their legitimacy and demonstrate how representative they are.[60] Yet the shift away from the domestic administrative space and into a new global paradigm also affects the construction of these values as they exist relative to systems of oversight or control. Central to this, and specifically for investigating patent law from this perspective, is how legitimacy and accountability are incorporated through the exercise

---

Herwig CH Hofmann, Eric C Ip, and Peter L Lindseth (eds), *Oxford Handbook of Comparative Administrative Law* (OUP 2021) 727; with Krisch arguing that the purpose of GAL is '... whether and to what extent ideas from domestic administrative law can help us solve accountability problems in global governance.': Nico Krisch, 'The Pluralism of Global Administrative Law' (2006) 17(1) EJIL 247, 248.

55 Michael Taggart, 'The Province of Administrative Law Determined' in Michael Taggart (ed), *The Province of Administrative Law* (Hart 1997) 3; though these principles are further analysed through a public law and governance framing in Megan Donaldson and Benedict Kingsbury, 'The Global Governance of Public Law' in Cormac Mac Amhlaigh, Claudio Michelon, and Neil Walker (eds), *After Public Law* (OUP 2013) 271.

56 Richard B Stewart, Michelle Ratton, and Sanchez Badin, 'The World Trade Organisation: Multiple Dimensions of Global Administrative Law' (2011) 9(3–4) ICON 556, 584.

57 Richard B Stewart, Michelle Ratton, and Sanchez Badin, 'The World Trade Organisation: Multiple Dimensions of Global Administrative Law' (2011) 9(3–4) ICON 556, 584.

58 Richard B Stewart, Michelle Ratton, and Sanchez Badin, 'The World Trade Organisation: Multiple Dimensions of Global Administrative Law' (2011) 9(3–4) ICON 556, 584.

59 Richard B Stewart, Michelle Ratton, and Sanchez Badin, 'The World Trade Organisation: Multiple Dimensions of Global Administrative Law' (2011) 9(3–4) ICON 556, 584.

60 Laurence Boisson de Chazournes, 'Changing Roles of International Organizations: Global Administrative Law and the Interplay of Legitimacies' (2009) 6(2) International Organizations Law Review 655, 657.

of legal mechanisms. Cassese argues that, unlike the domestic space, legitimacy and accountability mechanisms operate horizontally rather than being introduced through vertical hierarchies.[61] For this reason, Cassese suggests it is a mistake to bring the same national paradigm and understanding of the state into a global context and instead move away from efforts to identify a sufficiently legitimate relation between the institutions and the demos.[62] Global regulation, therefore, even in a patent setting, does not necessarily demonstrate its accountability and representative quality by mirroring the national administrative relationships to state power. This emphasises the dynamic relationship (and the relative character of this relationship) between institutions and states rather than reproducing a national understanding of patent law (and its institutions) in an international context. While many institutions are involved in establishing the provisions of international patent law, dispute settlement bodies are important precisely because they more easily transcend this national/international paradigm. Dispute resolution bodies, the binding trade obligations, and their interpretation by national patent offices still operate in a hierarchy of authority but in a filtered or somehow more diffuse way. The obligations remain binding on the national patent office and its ability to grant patents but in a way that provides space for interpretation and negotiation of their impact in practice.

1.3.3 The complexity of 'global' administration

1.3.3.1 The interconnected character of administrative law – global or otherwise

The type of 'internal' difficulty in defining what exactly constitutes administrative law is also mirrored at the international and global levels. This has been attributed to the very nature of global space, where 'economic globalization, liberalization and privatization are so closely linked to be indistinguishable'.[63] In centring the interconnected nature of regulation, administration, and broader political or legal developments, administration emerges as both the subject of regulation *and* a way of developing the norms that apply to global regulation. Law, in this circumstance, is then the tool by which, in this new 'global era', an institutional framework that is essential for democracy can be created.[64] Here, though, Aman argues that the role of law in promoting democracy through institutional frameworks extends far beyond governmental institutions and into the private sector.[65] As with many technical areas of international trade regulation, patent law can certainly be interpreted as a complex subject with a strong economic focus. Nevertheless, it cannot be

61 Sabino Cassese, 'Global Administrative Law: The State of the Art' (2015) 13(2) ICON 465, 467.
62 Sabino Cassese, 'Global Administrative Law: The State of the Art' (2015) 13(2) ICON 465, 467.
63 Carol Harlow, 'Global Administrative Law: The Quest for Principles and Values' (2006) 17(1) EJIL 208.
64 Alfred C Aman, 'Globalization, Democracy, and the Need for a New Administrative Law' (2003) 10(1) Indiana Journal of Global Legal Studies 125, 126.
65 Alfred C Aman, 'Globalization, Democracy, and the Need for a New Administrative Law' (2003) 10(1) Indiana Journal of Global Legal Studies 125, 126.

divorced from either its broader institutional context or the process by which international patent law was (and is) constituted that necessarily impacts private (rather than state) interests and actions. The functioning of the TRIPS Agreement, despite its technical subject matter, is necessarily a part of the contentious relationship between developing and developed countries. It represents a coming together of related issues like the role and function of representation and autonomy in international law,[66] as well as the enforcement of binding provisions in international agreements.[67] All of these reflect aspects of how democratic accountability and transparency function in the context of international or global actors and the difficulty with which they can be meaningfully incorporated in technical legal contexts.

Despite the discussion so far, it is also important to recognise that both the definition and scope of global administration remain contested. Beyond the definitional difficulties in establishing the boundaries of GAL,[68] there is also ongoing work to explore how it is (and becomes) interconnected with other areas of law. The lack of settled status in what exactly GAL is has been described as coming not simply from a missing single definition but a more fundamental uncertainty around its interactions with constitutional law and international law.[69] At this general level, Cassese has highlighted work that shifts away from the explicit vocabulary of global administration and instead develops a sense of an 'exercise of international public authority' or a 'law of global governance'.[70] In these works, the language of administrative law essentially takes on the vocabulary and approach of constitutional law.[71] However, the clearly interconnected nature of what is being articulated by the concepts in global administration challenges a strict focus on maintaining traditional or typical understandings of administration (national or otherwise). Even describing patent law and intellectual property in terms of global regulation highlights a significant overlap with the concerns and priorities of conventional regulation or governance work. Patent law is interesting because, particularly at the global level, it reflects this type of intersectional relative position that at once embodies elements of regulation, administration, and governance. Described as such, these terms also reflect perhaps a spectrum in terms of how value-laden they are – where regulation can be considered as economic, technical, and neutral; while governance is something more amorphous, interventionist, normative. This type of

66 On the flexible quality of autonomy available to developing countries in the WTO (though also specifically discussing this in the context of the TRIPS Agreement): Alvaro Santos, 'Carving Out Policy Autonomy for Developing Countries in the World Trade Organisation: The Experience of Brazil and Mexico' (2012) 52(3) Virginia Journal of International Law 570, 588.

67 Peter K Yu, 'TRIPS Enforcement and Developing Countries' (2011) 26(3) American University International Law Review 728, 729.

68 Sabino Cassese, 'Global Administrative Law: The State of the Art' (2015) 13(2) ICON 465.

69 Sabino Cassese, 'Global Administrative Law: The State of the Art' (2015) 13(2) ICON 465.

70 Armin von Bogdandy, Matthias Goldmann, and Ingo Venzke, 'From Public International to International Public Law: Translating World Public Opinion into International Public Authority' (2017) 28(1) EJIL 116, 117; Eyal Benvenisti, *The Law of Global Governance* (Hague Academy of International Law 2014) 25.

71 Sabino Cassese, 'Global Administrative Law: The State of the Art' (2015) 13(2) ICON 465.

indistinct boundary has been discussed as affecting the 'global' of 'global administrative law' given that what is being explored by GAL is not just global, not just administration, and not just law.[72]

From a more institutional perspective, the unique challenges of regulation in a global space have been met in two distinct ways. These can broadly be divided between approaches that emphasise the creation of new institutions and those which propose amendments to existing international institutions.[73] It is a common theme in writing on global administration that global challenges require the introduction of global institutions to adequately address the unique character of the space.[74] Yet, it is precisely these global challenges that have raised questions about the capacity of these organisations to meet challenging developments and whether their institutional mandate is sufficient.[75] Though the responses to this question of sufficient mandate have varied over time,[76] an alternative to adjusting existing institutions has been to simply create a new organisation (like with the rise of field organisations) more closely aligned with specific issues.[77]

One of the complicating factors of translating governance and administration, specifically from a national level to a global level,[78] is that much of the administrative framework and decision-making is characterised by a less formalised normative

72 'It is now clear that global administrative law is not only global, not only administrative, and not only law. It is not only global because it includes many supranational regional or local agreements and authorities. It is not only administrative, because it includes many private and constitutional elements … Global administrative law is not only law, because it also includes many types of "soft law" and standards': Sabino Cassese, 'Global Administrative Law: The State of the Art' (2015) 13(2) ICON 466.

73 Laurence Boisson de Chazournes, 'Changing Roles of International Organizations: Global Administrative Law and the Interplay of Legitimacies' (2009) International Organizations Law Review 655, 656; on the complex relationship between new institutions in a global governance framework from a critical perspective: Yakub Halabi, 'The Expansion of Global Governance into the Third World: Altruism, Realism, or Constructivism?' (2004) 6(1) International Studies Review 21, 35, 36.

74 Sabino Cassese, 'Global Administrative Law: The State of the Art' (2015) 13(2) ICON 465, 466.

75 Laurence Boisson de Chazournes, 'Changing Roles of International Organizations: Global Administrative Law and the Interplay of Legitimacies' (2009) 6(2) International Organizations Law Review 655, 656.

76 Laurence Boisson de Chazournes, 'Changing Roles of International Organizations: Global Administrative Law and the Interplay of Legitimacies' (2009) 6(2) International Organizations Law Review 655, 656.

77 Laurence Boisson de Chazournes, 'Changing Roles of International Organizations: Global Administrative Law and the Interplay of Legitimacies' (2009) 6(2) International Organizations Law Review 655, 656.

78 Though the relationship between regulation and administration was discussed earlier in the chapter, governance appears throughout GAL scholarship. With the WTO, it has been examined as an 'important example of the many dimensions of global administrative law (GAL) in multilevel global regulatory governance' and how '[m]uch of this global regulatory governance – especially in fields such as trade and investment, financial and economic regulation – can now be understood as administration'. Beyond this, the references to governance appear to emphasise the institutional elements of GAL systems: Richard B Stewart, Michelle Ratton, and Sanchez Badin, 'The World Trade Organisation: Multiple Dimensions of Global Administrative Law' (2011) 9(3–4) ICON 556, 557.

output and a non-hierarchical institutional structure that centres the work of administrative committees.[79] There is a recurring tension in the institutional design of global administration that fundamentally shapes the contours and dynamics of both the space and institutions themselves. In emphasising the 'global' aspect of global administration, an obvious question emerges: What exactly distinguishes GAL and its 'peculiarities' from ordinary administration?[80] Institutionally, the global space is particularly interesting in answering this question because it produces an environment in which law is created without traditional legislatures and regulation implemented without a singularly authoritative executive.[81] All of this is then monitored and enforced through a very limited number of dispute resolution bodies, where the emphasis is shifted towards a complex network of reviewing bodies that perform what is essentially a quasi-judicial function.[82]

International patent law reflects many of these same tensions but has not typically been characterised as an element of GAL. Applying this institutional focus to international patent law highlights the fundamental impact of the dysfunctional relationship between the WTO dispute settlement system and the WTO's mandate as an organisation.[83] Even with a functional AB, it remained a dispute settlement body essentially disconnected from democratic oversight that nevertheless decided on issues of law that restrict or otherwise constrain the state power involved with a patent grant. One illustrative example would be *Eli Lilly* that questioned the clarity and underlying principles of Canada's promise doctrine.[84] While this case is obviously framed in terms of an expropriation claim and the economic features of patent law,[85] it nevertheless is an international dispute settlement body of a trade organisation issuing binding recommendations as to how patents should and should not be granted. It renders these decisions from a trade perspective and, therefore, appears to be completely in accordance with the terms and mandate of the WTO. Yet it is precisely this economic focus and language of trade that work to obscure how state power is being mediated and negotiated in the context of patent law. Framed as a question of participation, what means would a developing country have to

79 'It is more challenging, however, to successfully apply GAL requirements to "horizontal" decision making processes, like those within regulatory committees composed of member representatives … or regulatory networks of diverse actors that are not hierarchically organized and whose normative output is often much less formalized.': Richard B Stewart, Michelle Ratton, and Sanchez Badin, 'The World Trade Organisation: Multiple Dimensions of Global Administrative Law' (2011) 9(3–4) ICON 582, 583.

80 Sabino Cassese, 'Global Administrative Law: The State of the Art' (2015) 13(2) ICON 466.

81 Sabino Cassese, 'Global Administrative Law: The State of the Art' (2015) 13(2) ICON 466.

82 Sabino Cassese, 'Global Administrative Law: The State of the Art' (2015) 13(2) ICON 466.

83 On the paralysis of the Appellate Body: Georgie Juszczyk, 'Legitimacy Crisis in the World Trade Organisation Appellate Body: Other Ways than the MPIA?' in Jelena Bäumler, Christina Binder, Marc Bungenberg, Markus Krajewski, Giesela Rühl, Christian J Tams, Jörg Philipp Terhechte, and Andreas R Ziegler (eds), *European Yearbook of International Economic Law* (Springer 2022) 90.

84 *Eli Lilly and Company v The Government of Canada* UNCT/14/2.

85 See generally Pratyush Nath Upreti, 'Eli Lilly v Government of Canada: The Tale of Promise v Expectation' (2018) 21(3) IntALR 84, 85.

meaningfully shape the content of a binding obligation with which it disagreed? To what extent would that country be able to successfully balance the economic aspect of a binding dispute outcome with its own social considerations?

1.4 Critical perspectives on GAL

1.4.1 Fundamental tensions and the role of the Global North

1.4.1.1 Harlow's 'double colonization'

Despite the significant potential of the values developed in global administration to deconstruct or reframe tensions in administration and regulation, the exact status and content of these values are not necessarily settled. Harlow argues that, in the development and dissemination of GAL, there has been something of a 'double colonization'.[86] This development is presented as a result of the general bias in GAL concepts and principles towards Anglo-American understandings of administrative law more generally.[87] The first of these colonisations is suggested to occur when administrative law (and the administrative law system) 'absorbs' the values that underpin global governance or human rights,[88] but specifically in how democracy, participation, transparency, and accountability are incorporated.[89] In doing so, the form of administrative law itself reflects a set of normative values that are themselves contextually specific and have meaning only in a profoundly relative way. While this framing evocatively uses the language of 'colonisation', from a more abstract perspective, there is no inherent problem with administrative law embodying values like accountability and transparency.

The second 'colonisation' occurs through the legal processes of cross-fertilisation, or more explicitly, through legal transplants.[90] Though Harlow recognises that this type of diffusion of legal norms, institutions, or principles can happen spontaneously,[91] specific emphasis is given to the role of the 'powerful transnational juristocracy' that operates in human rights courts and across European legal systems to eventually form an abstract common European standard.[92] Underlying Harlow's approach to legal transplants, however, is the suggestion that there are

86 Carol Harlow, 'Global Administrative Law: The Quest for Principles and Values' (2006) 17(1) EJIL 209.
87 Carol Harlow, 'Global Administrative Law: The Quest for Principles and Values' (2006) 17(1) EJIL 209.
88 Carol Harlow, 'Global Administrative Law: The Quest for Principles and Values' (2006) 17(1) EJIL 209.
89 Carol Harlow, 'Global Administrative Law: The Quest for Principles and Values' (2006) 17(1) EJIL 209.
90 Carol Harlow, 'Global Administrative Law: The Quest for Principles and Values' (2006) 17(1) EJIL 209.
91 Carol Harlow, 'Global Administrative Law: The Quest for Principles and Values' (2006) 17(1) EJIL 209.
92 Carol Harlow, 'Global Administrative Law: The Quest for Principles and Values' (2006) 17(1) EJIL 209.

no inherent characteristics of either the source of the principle or the principle itself that necessarily mark this process negatively.[93] Yet this highlights a tension in how we understand the relationship between developing and developed countries in both patent law and global administration. In a GAL context, this can be seen perhaps most clearly when developed countries attempt to impose external standards (and thus, normative values embodied in the law) on less-developed countries while either remaining unwilling to give proper effect to these standards (or actually practically unable to).[94] For patent law, there is a persistent theme of exploring precisely that double standard of developed countries encouraging high standards of protection when their own industrialisation benefited from lax intellectual property enforcement.[95]

Even when the focus is on this 'thin' understanding of GAL, emphasising the use of procedural safeguards rather than substantive objectives, there is considerable tension around presenting values such as accountability or participation as being value-neutral in practice. Accepting these values as being neutral standards of administration enables a similar masking of normative direction that occurs in trade regulation and patent law. Accepting participation as a technical quality that is present or not present risks rendering its normative biases invisible and producing the exact kind of naturalisation and legitimisation criticised in GAL. Chimni argues that, by focusing on the procedural elements,[96] GAL principles in the procedural dimension work to legitimise the types of unjust or unfair outcomes that GAL principles are intended to combat.[97] Here, global regulation is presented as proceeding not in a 'value-free manner', but in a way that is necessarily informed

93 'There is, of course, no particular reason why administrative law norms borrowed from Western systems should not be successfully diffused throughout the world': Carol Harlow, 'Global Administrative Law: The Quest for Principles and Values' (2006) 17(1) EJIL 209.

94 Carol Harlow, 'Global Administrative Law: The Quest for Principles and Values' (2006) 17(1) EJIL 211.

95 Where 'the patent law policies of European countries during their early years of industrialization reveal a clear instrumentalist policy of appropriating the ideas and technologies of other states.': Ikechi Mgbeoji, *Biopiracy: Patents, Plants, and Indigenous Knowledge* (UBC Press 2006) 34; though this sense of a double standard in patent law also extends to biological materials and how non-Western contributions to plant development 'systematically relegated to an inferior status for appropriation through the patent system': ibid 14; and also in discussions around how the use of fossil fuels in developing countries is condemned by Western governments (despite their own industrialisation benefiting from fossil fuels): Augustine Sadiq Okoh, *Oil Mortality in Post-Fossil Fuel Era Nigeria: Beyond the Oil Age* (Springer 2021) 66.

96 Though Chimni also argues that the reality of our current international law necessarily requires a broad definition of GAL, that does not try to maintain a distinction between substantive law and administrative law. Where '[a] broader definition of GAL does not, in the face of the democracy deficit that characterizes international institutions and bodies, accept the strict separation between substantive law and administrative law': BS Chimni, 'Co-Option and Resistance: Two Faces of Global Administrative Law' (2005) 37 NYU Journal of International Law and Politics 799, 804, 805, 827

97 BS Chimni, 'Co-Option and Resistance: Two Faces of Global Administrative Law' (2005) 37 NYU Journal of International Law and Politics 805.

by the market dynamics between developed and developing countries that focus on the important role of 'fair competition' through regulation.[98] The entanglement of values, institutions, and actors demonstrates that administration must be approached in a way that is responsive to the contextual features of the space. Patent law can never simply be an element of trade regulation because to approach it as such is to mask the multifaceted way it develops and functions.

This is also an important element of the broader academic treatment of the TRIPS Agreement, where the process – created and agreed upon by WTO Members – works to legitimise or stabilise any negative welfare outcomes and current paradigms within intellectual property.[99] The concerns over stability and legitimacy stand out here given the emphasis on the WTO as being led by its members and the persistent reliance on a strict understanding of sovereignty.[100] As such, the value of procedural transparency and accountability has to be interpreted in light of the fact that the TRIPS Agreement was created by its members and voluntarily accepted. Yet it is clear that there is some tension between this visible consent and a more functional approach that recognises that TRIPS did involve, to a degree, a coercive dimension. This type of contrast between substantive outcomes and procedural legitimacy is also mirrored in patent exceptions and flexibilities. The presence of these flexibilities works to legitimise the international patent system more generally by performing a sense of openness to divergent interests or understandings. These flexibilities facilitate a perception of inclusivity and genuine concession to the varied interests of different states. This procedural legitimation frames the context in which the TRIPS Agreement is approached, disguising the difficulty with which countries have had in actually making use of these mechanisms.[101]

Indeed, legitimacy and its potential to mask tensions appear throughout many discussions on global administration. Specifically in the shift away from purely national contexts, focusing on procedural transparency or narrow accountability can be a way of legitimising or stabilising specific institutions or relationships between

98 Yakub Halabi, 'The Expansion of Global Governance into the Third World: Altruism, Realism, or Constructivism?' (2004) 6(1) International Studies 33, 34.

99 Using a similar vocabulary found in GAL scholarship more broadly, Cloatre suggests that even with progress in medicine accessibility, '… certain patterns of inequality and exclusion seem to persist … TRIPS, by inscribing them into law, has stabilized some of the patterns of dominance that allowed it emerge': Emilie Cloatre, *Pills for the Poorest: An Exploration of TRIPS and Access to Medication in Sub-Saharan Africa* (Palgrave 2013) 175, 176.

100 'The WTO is run by its member governments' and '[i]n this respect, the WTO is different from some other international organizations such as the World Bank and the International Monetary Fund. In the WTO, power is not delegated to a board of directors or the organization's head': WTO, 'Understanding the WTO: The Organization' (*WTO*) <https://www.wto.org/english/thewto_e/whatis_e/tif_e/org1_e.htm>.

101 On the bureaucratic burden involved in the use of TRIPS flexibilities (specifically for medicine and licensing): Roy Love, 'Corporate Wealth or Public Health? WTO/TRIPS Flexibilities and Access to HIV/AIDS Antiretroviral Drugs by Developing Countries' (2007) 17(2) Development in Practice 211, 212.

particular actors.[102] Kingsbury, Krisch, and Stewart argue that this is an issue which is fundamental to global administration and how we define what exactly it entails. From this perspective, accepting that there is a global administrative space – a distinct legal environment in which global regulation is expressed through the language of administration[103] – has the potential to legitimise and stabilise the current configurations of power.[104] Legitimacy then takes on a more nuanced role in our understanding of global administration, precisely because it cannot be uncritically adopted as a standard of evaluation. The normative aspect of legitimacy has been discussed as a way in which Global North and Western understandings of governance become further entrenched.[105] This is not to say that legitimacy, much like transparency or accountability, is useless because it is normatively inflected. Rather, recognising that these values are contextually developed through the interplay of institutions, law, and actors emphasises thoughtful and measured reflection. It speaks perhaps to the broader interconnected quality of global administration, where attempting to isolate or strictly separate concepts and principles instead produces a profoundly distorted understanding of how these systems of regulation interact in practice. Thoughtful reflection on this relative quality of administrative values encourages an approach that goes beyond a 'thin' construction, in which procedural aspects of regulation and administration remain disconnected from the dynamic institutional, legal, and political setting in which they function.

This limitation of values within global administration mirrors many elements of a broader critique of administrative law itself as a 'Western' legal construct.[106] Though there are significant examples that demonstrate the measurable (positive) developmental impact of strong administrative principles – China, for example, appears repeatedly[107] – the fundamental nature of administrative law requires that we examine and work to deconstruct the potential for 'structural biases' within administration.[108] This approach suggests that, to examine administration, the analysis must counterintuitively go beyond the administrative context. The political, cultural, and social forces of a legal setting cannot be detached from mere 'technical' rules of administration as both are responsive to the spatial and temporal environment in which they were produced. It is precisely the type of discussion that

102 Benedict Kingsbury, Nico Krisch, and Patrick B Stewart, 'The Emergence of Global Administrative Law' (2005) 68(3/4) Law and Contemporary Problems 15, 27.

103 Benedict Kingsbury, Nico Krisch, and Patrick B Stewart, 'The Emergence of Global Administrative Law' (2005) 68(3/4) Law and Contemporary Problems 15, 27.

104 Benedict Kingsbury, Nico Krisch, and Patrick B Stewart, 'The Emergence of Global Administrative Law' (2005) 68(3/4) Law and Contemporary Problems 15, 27.

105 Benedict Kingsbury, Nico Krisch, and Patrick B Stewart, 'The Emergence of Global Administrative Law' (2005) 68(3/4) Law and Contemporary Problems 15, 27.

106 Richard B Stewart, Michelle Ratton, and Sanchez Badin, 'The World Trade Organisation: Multiple Dimensions of Global Administrative Law' (2011) 9(3–4) ICON 573.

107 Sarah Biddulph, 'Administrative Power' in Peter Cane, Herwig CH Hofmann, Eric C Ip, and Peter L Lindseth (eds), *Oxford Handbook of Comparative Administrative Law* (OUP 2021) 381.

108 Richard B Stewart, Michelle Ratton, and Sanchez Badin, 'The World Trade Organisation: Multiple Dimensions of Global Administrative Law' (2011) 9(3–4) ICON 573.

focuses on the contextual features of a legal development's *origin* (and of bias even in technical areas) that have formed an important part of deconstructing intellectual property from a critical perspective.

The emphasis is not only on the inherently value-laden nature of administration or regulation (in intellectual property and more generally) but the interconnected and overlapping quality of these areas in practice. The global space is characterised by polycentric systems and the dynamic interactions between actors in the absence of strict vertical hierarchies. Patent law demonstrates exactly these structural tensions because, despite the TRIPS Agreement, the legal provisions and how they modify state power are found in a multitude of overlapping legal frameworks. Just as GAL is necessarily constructed from elements that challenge distinctions between global and national, or administrative and non-administrative, the structural tensions in patent law operate at a variety of different scales that are simultaneously responsive to (and challenge) local, regional, and global legal developments. Rather than simply rejecting administrative law values like democratic accountability or legitimacy on the basis of their 'Western' character, centring them in an analysis of patent law involves recognising their contested status within administration and their inflected quality. The sense of administrative values being 'Western' takes on a distinctive character when considering the functioning of the TRIPS Agreement that is not necessarily found in other contexts (like when analysing the UPC in a European context). There are broad parallels between the colonialist critique of global administration and how patent law has been variously 'imposed' on developing countries,[109] yet the failure to centre the administrative value of participation is an oversight. In doing so, patent work has effectively not taken seriously the idea that these frameworks were truly 'imposed' and the ability for states to participate meaningfully had been impaired. Discussing TRIPS as an imposed legal framework without then firmly incorporating considerations of participation then misses a more nuanced understanding of how state power is exercised under global legal initiatives that were (unequivocally) consented to.

1.4.1.2 The normative and descriptive overlap of Global Administrative Law

A fundamental element of both global administration and its application to patent law is a question as to the extent to which it represents a descriptive or prescriptive account of international regulation. More accurately, perhaps, given the explicit acceptance by many authors that their work is normative,[110] the question that

109 David Lea, *Property Rights, Indigenous People and the Developing World: Issues from Aboriginal Entitlement to Intellectual Ownership Rights* (Martinus Nijhoff 2008) 194, 195.

110 'Participants in either the study or the construction of a global administrative law recognise that these are normative projects, and not simply a taxonomical exercise or the promulgation of practical technical solutions to well-defined and accepted problems posed by global regulatory administration. But the potential normative foundations are as varied as their practical administrative counterparts.': Benedict Kingsbury, Nico Krisch, and Patrick B Stewart, 'The Emergence of Global Administrative Law' (2005) 68(3/4) Law and Contemporary Problems 42.

emerges implicitly is the *degree* to which the global administrative lens and its concepts are normative. Kingsbury, Krisch, and Stewart argue that it is well-accepted amongst those involved in the study of global administration, that many projects go beyond establishing a taxonomy or the technocratic advocacy for technical solutions to regulatory problems.[111] Approaching patent law from the perspective and values of global administration is at once a way of redescribing and remapping the way patent law is produced, but it is also necessarily a normative statement as to how global patent law should function. Patents occupy a unique space normatively because intellectual property rights are intangible.[112] From this, Peukert's work emphasises that the form, function, and values that animate patent law are all co-produced by the participants of a legal system rather than occurring as a natural fact.[113] Patent law is not a natural occurrence, the rights that it produces are not natural or inherent, and the design choices reflect specific priorities and objectives. There is, therefore, no inherent tension or contradiction when critiquing patent law from a normative perspective because the conventional economic approach is equally normatively biased. Emphasising that patent law is produced essentially as a form of community acceptance, or phantasm, mirrors the persistent metaphor in global administration of interfaces as creative and dynamic interactive spaces.[114]

1.4.2 Deconstructing the structural dimension of values in global administration

1.4.2.1 The embedded relationship between accountability, transparency, and participation

There is a distinctly embodied dimension of administrative values in global institutions that moderates their relationships to participation, accountability, and other legal institutions. The development of arbitral remedies in investment treaties has

111 Benedict Kingsbury, Nico Krisch, and Patrick B Stewart, 'The Emergence of Global Administrative Law' (2005) 68(3/4) Law and Contemporary Problems 42.

112 Alexander Peukert, *A Critique of the Ontology of Intellectual Property Law* (CUP 2021) 1.

113 Describing debates on the ontological character of intellectual property, where the 'relationship between "is" and "ought" is particularly unstable'. Patents are presented as paradigmatic of these ontological concerns because they '[generate] its object from itself – namely from highly formalised patent documents.': Alexander Peukert, *A Critique of the Ontology of Intellectual Property Law* (CUP 2021) 7, 8; Yet this analysis of normative value also appears in a GAL context, where 'the GAL approach claims to retain a soft normative value, aiming to bridge a relatively little gap between an "Is" and "Ought" at a global level, by expanding guarantees in administrative action, in fields where they have not been established yet': Angelo Jr Golia, 'Judicial Review, Foreign Relations and Global Administrative Law: The Administrative Function of Courts in Foreign Relations' in Helmut Philipp Aust and Thomas Kleinlein (eds), *Encounters between Foreign Relations Law and International Law: Bridges and Boundaries* (CUP 2021) 139.

114 Where legal systems, and the tertiary rules that Michaels focuses on, are part of the creation of the legal order itself. 'Tertiary rules thus do not only respond to, and organize, a world of separated legal systems, they are themselves involved in the creation of such a system', and from a broader perspective, '[w]hile the law at large is autopoietic, individual legal systems are not; they constitute each other through mutual recognition.': Ralf Michaels, 'Tertiary Rules' in Nico Krisch (ed), *Entangled Legalities Beyond the State* (CUP 2022) 426, 427.

been highlighted as reflective of these complex interactions,[115] with examples of expropriation claims under North American Free Trade Agreement (NAFTA) for environmental legislation and the cancellation of a water service franchise.[116] And yet even if the results of arbitral mechanisms of dispute resolution functioned well in both a substantive and procedural sense, there are still structural issues about how these bodies can be sufficiently connected or subject to considerations of participation, transparency, and accountability.[117] It is here that there is then a tension between effectiveness in international regulation and imposing standards or expectations that could otherwise temper the ability of these bodies to respond in a way that fully reflects their technocratic expertise. This difficulty, and particularly in patent law, has also given rise to issues in both arbitral agreements and the specialised bodies of global administration – that they consider issues of global importance that are complex, interconnected, and overlapping. Effectiveness and the attractive prospect of efficient and effective enforcement of international regulation is perhaps most visible at the global level but not uniquely so. It provides a way of looking at complex issues of international trade, simplifying and narrowing how competing priorities and objectives should (or can) be evaluated. But doing so masks the interconnected nature of regulation and its specific agreements, isolating them in narrow technical vocabularies that are contrary to the very global impact of what they are considering.

Patent law represents one way of deconstructing the concept of administrative accountability precisely because of the tendency towards language that emphasises economic impact and efficiency. As a discipline, patent law is especially vulnerable to capture by technocrats because it is a fairly narrow and specialised field,[118] the barriers to entry can be high,[119] and it necessarily draws from other technically complex subjects.[120] Values such as participation and accountability do not often appear in discussions of patent law from a more procedural perspective. They appear, instead, when external actors consider specific, substantive outcomes like access to medicine and the role of the WTO[121] – but not always in a generalised way. Starting to map tensions in patent law and the role of dispute resolution bodies through the vocabulary of administrative values enables a way of looking at

115 Benedict Kingsbury, Nico Krisch, and Patrick B Stewart, 'The Emergence of Global Administrative Law' (2005) 68(3/4) Law and Contemporary Problems 47.

116 Benedict Kingsbury, Nico Krisch, and Patrick B Stewart, 'The Emergence of Global Administrative Law' (2005) 68(3/4) Law and Contemporary Problems 47.

117 Benedict Kingsbury, Nico Krisch, and Patrick B Stewart, 'The Emergence of Global Administrative Law' (2005) 68(3/4) Law and Contemporary Problems 49.

118 Kara W Swanson, 'The Emergence of the Professional Patent Practitioner' (2009) 50(3) Technology and Culture 521.

119 Kara W Swanson, 'The Emergence of the Professional Patent Practitioner' (2009) 50(3) Technology and Culture 523, 524.

120 Banks Miller and Brett Curry, 'Expertise, Experience, and Ideology on Specialized Courts: The Case of the Court of Appeals for the Federal Circuit' (2009) 43(4) Law & Society Review 841.

121 Devi Sridhar, 'Improving Access to Essential Medicines: How Health Concerns can be Prioritised in the Global Governance System' (2008) 1(2) Public Health Ethics 83, 84.

patent law that is expansive and integrative. Focusing on participation as the ability to contribute to or modify binding provisions of an agreement renders it a fundamental value of patent law, applicable to all aspects of patents and not just when tensions manifest sufficiently as negative distributional outcomes.

In positioning the book and its approach, it is also important to recognise that administration remains only one of many potential ways of constructing the institutions and relationships of global law. The administrative vocabulary as it is deployed throughout the book, to re-describe the fundamental elements of patent law, is not intended to be a definitive or authoritative approach. The administrative lens applied to patent law is an exploration, the very start of a conversation around an alternate way of understanding and evaluating how international patent law works.

Part of the appeal of alternative conceptions is that, within global administration, the mechanisms and tools for promoting accountability or democracy within international regulation are essentially drawn from the legal systems of the Global North and thus raise questions about *who* is shaping the development of global administration.[122] The administrative vocabulary provides a way of analysing a global space in which, though there are certainly binding obligations, there is no single authoritative legislative power. Interactions between agencies, courts, and bodies are engaged in a mutual process of communication or irritation, which theoretically suggests (in the absence of a global sovereign power) a space in which any state has the capacity to generate new legal realities. Yet patent law reveals how these soft hierarchies built on dynamic interactions will work to privilege specific actors, institutions, and perspectives. The legal impact of the CJEU interpreting a provision of patent law to improve access to medicine, both within the EU and in terms of broader international reach, would be of a profoundly different character than an apex court in a developing country interpreting the same provision. There is certainly an equality in that all bodies within the global system that consider questions of patent law can work to reinterpret provisions in a way that reflects their own priorities. Yet it remains that the absence of a single legislative power does not guarantee an equality of participation in how the concepts and values of global patent law develop. This relative dynamic of authority and influence between institutions speaks again to the fundamentally interconnected nature of patent law that extends far beyond a sense of 'technical' regulation.

This type of more structural critique – one that invites a more radical reconstruction of the system rather than reform of the institutions – appears in more critical approaches to global administration. This can be found in work that adopts a Third World Approaches to International Law (TWAIL) perspective or emphasises postcolonial understandings of international law and trade. From these perspectives, simply identifying the presence of administrative principles in international institutions does not resolve the fundamental inequalities that make up the structural

122 Benedict Kingsbury, Nico Krisch, and Patrick B Stewart, 'The Emergence of Global Administrative Law' (2005) 68(3/4) Law and Contemporary Problems 51.

fabric of global governance.[123] Xavier essentially argues that designing approaches that incorporate GAL principles does nothing to address how the tribunals and institutions are created, their dominant rationale, and the politics involved in their functioning and creation.[124] Instead, these principles can be understood as working to camouflage a universalist approach to Western values that is 'embedded within the global infrastructure and creates a sense of false hope for the people of the Global South'.[125] The value of accountability or participation is then not found in what they claim to guarantee in terms of how international administration functions, but as a vocabulary through which systems of international regulation can be deconstructed. There is, again, a return to the functionalist aspects of administration, inviting the reader to look beyond the presence or absence of accountability mechanisms and to instead approach the subject more holistically. This is an expansive and deeply contextual approach that applies to both patent law and any other form of international administration. Such an approach prompts fundamental questions about patent law; in the design of the TRIPS Agreement, for example, did every participant realistically have the power to modify the content of its binding obligations? Are these provisions of an identically binding quality to all participants in practice? To what extent could the participant subvert these provisions and would they be challenged?

1.5 Linking global administration and the book's patent contexts

1.5.1 Chapter 2: Developments in European patent law

Chapter 2 explores the development of the new European Patent with Unitary Effect (EPUE) because it represents a development in European patent law, the creation of a new legal interface, and a new dispute resolution body. The EPUE demonstrates the complex dynamics of patent law, though its development necessarily reflects the process of negotiation between national and international, political and legal, and European and non-European. Central to this analysis is the development of the Unified Patent Court (UPC) and interpreting its position through the values of participation and transparency found in GAL scholarship.

While the chapter involves an investigation into the more legislative elements that establish the EPUE, the focus is very much on the procedural aspects of the EPUE implementation and the UPC court structure rather than the legislative process more generally. Institutionally, the focus centres on the role of courts in the

123 'Ultimately, the presence of procedural administrative law does not usher in greater legitimacy to the various international institutions. Rather, this argument camouflages the Western universalism embedded within the global infrastructure': Sujith Xavier, 'Top Heavy: Beyond the Global North and the Justification for Global Administrative Law' (2018) 57 Indian Journal of International Law 353.

124 Sujith Xavier, 'Top Heavy: Beyond the Global North and the Justification for Global Administrative Law' (2018) 57 Indian Journal of International Law 353.

125 Sujith Xavier, 'Top Heavy: Beyond the Global North and the Justification for Global Administrative Law' (2018) 57 Indian Journal of International Law 353.

implementation of the EPUE. Understanding the EPUE legislative progression from the perspective of GAL values presents a more critical way of interpreting the enhanced cooperation mechanism that was used to create the EPUE. This chapter develops a more expanded use of traditional GAL principles, specifically in terms of accountability and transparency, to question the legitimacy of the EPUE and its potential implications for EU law-making more generally. GAL presents an important lens for this investigation because, particularly in more critical constructions, it provides a way to problematise presumptions of validity and legitimacy which are often overlooked in European patent law. The EPUE provides an important context for this type of investigation because it has been repeatedly endorsed in terms of its legal validity by the CJEU, and yet the potential broader impact of the project – specifically for participation and accountability as legal values – presents serious systemic risks for the future of EU law-making.

1.5.2 Chapter 3: Understanding the dynamic (and existence) of the bilateral space

Chapter 3 applies GAL principles and Krisch's concept of an interface as an interactive and creative space in a less conventional context. The institutional and legal environment explored in Chapter 3 stretches the understanding of 'court' and 'dispute settlement body' as used in GAL scholarship. Part of this comes from presenting bilateral trade agreements as a legal interface and, for the promotion of GAL principles, how the particular role of dispute resolution bodies is constructed within these trade agreements.

Turning first to the application of GAL values and principles in the context of bilateral trade agreements, the focus remains generally on the EU and extends to the trade agreements that it has concluded. Particularly for analysing how these environments relate to GAL principles, it is the EU's express commitment to values such as transparency and accountability that presents an important opportunity to explore how far these commitments produce tangible outcomes in patent law. Bilateral agreements have been criticised for minimising the role of national parliaments and the degree of secrecy surrounding their negotiations more generally, but interpreting these legal developments through the prism of GAL provides a more integrated or grounded critique of transparency and accountability. GAL principles provide a more systemic perspective as to the issues with bilateral trade agreements in a way that joins together the validity and importance of values like transparency, participation, and accountability. The lack of transparency, and the resulting issues in accountability and participation in the European context, are then not individual critiques of bilateral trade agreements but are instead a more systematic failure to implement specific values from a GAL perspective in patent law. From this, the chapter tries to draw a parallel between the discussions in GAL literature as to the existence of a distinct 'global space' and explore the specific challenges and character of the 'bilateral space'.

The bilateral trade context also provides an environment to both apply and expand the theoretical understanding of dispute resolution bodies in GAL studies.

This relates to the fundamental scope of dispute settlement bodies within GAL scholarship, where the emphasis has typically been on arrangements that are not ad hoc or episodic.[126] The enforcement dimension of intellectual property provisions in bilateral trade agreements has been criticised in the literature for the dynamic it produces between developed and developing countries,[127] but this has not been connected with the GAL principles from this more systemic perspective. In doing so, dispute resolution is contextualised alongside the more structural aspects of the bilateral space in a way that shifts away from a sole focus on dispute. This chapter provides an important exploration into how GAL principles can guide conduct in the bilateral space because, as highlighted through the broad principles and undefined concepts in many agreements, these arrangements vest considerable interpretative power in fairly opaque dispute settlement bodies and present a fairly open-textured legal space.

1.5.3 Chapter 4: Multilateral initiatives and the future of global patent law

In terms of applying concepts and perspectives from global administration to the multilateral development of patent law, participation and the ability to meaningfully influence the content of binding provisions are very central concerns. Participation in this sense provides a way of interpreting not only how international patent law exists now, but enables a way of speaking about patent law dysfunctions that captures the tension of emerging dynamics. In this, understanding the functioning of global patent law through the vocabulary of autonomy and participation rather than solely through an analysis of legal provisions reveals the interconnected nature of patent law. This is particularly true when looking at COVID-19 and the legal response to the pandemic. An approach that centres the functioning of patent law provisions obviously provides an important way of understanding the current state of law. Approaching it from the perspective of meaningful participation speaks to something broader, more encompassing, about how patent law has a more general impact. Instead, it deconstructs the way in which patent provisions establish, reaffirm, and sustain relationships between participants and how they shape the scope of autonomy for developing countries. The discussion around COVID-19 is an especially effective subject for this type of deconstruction due to its complex global impact. It necessarily involves interconnected patent analysis but in a way that an audience can immediately recognise as coexisting alongside deeply social and political elements.

Applying a global administration perspective to multilateral patent law is also important for achieving the broader aim of the book, of communicating with and engaging those beyond the usual audience for patent law work. Global

126 Richard B Stewart, 'Global Standards for National Societies' in Sabino Cassese (ed), *Research Handbook on Global Administrative Law* (Edward Elgar 2016) 177.

127 Kajal Bhardwaj, 'India's Free Trade Agreements: Implications for Access to Medicines in India and the Global South' in Hans Löfgren (ed), *The Politics of the Pharmaceutical Industry and Access to Medicines: World Pharmacy and India* (Routledge 2018) 155.

administrative concepts help to situate the technical functioning of patent law alongside its socio-political dimensions and the emphasis on the *development* of global patent policy. This question on the future of global patent law and the potential for realising meaningful participation by all members can also be expressed through a global administration vocabulary. The chapter focuses on the potential of the African Union (AU) to rebalance the trajectory of global patent law though, in doing so, necessarily recognises the complexity of the global space for administration. In the absence of a single authoritative legislator, meaningful participation cannot be imposed or realised in a simply legal manner. It demonstrates that autonomy, participation, or transparency all have a fluid character that clearly shows the limits of approaching a complex subject like global patent law solely through its legal provisions.

1.6 Conclusion

Patent law is an area of law that operates across national and international spheres of regulation. Increasingly, patent law has become a prominent aspect of industrial policy in many different countries that emphasises the economic function of patents and patent law.[128] This type of economic framing of the patent disguises the fundamentally administrative character of the patent grant and limits the way in which we conceptualise the development and functioning of global patent policy. While the procedural aspects of patent law have been a feature of international agreements since the late 19th century and resulted in a solid foundation of global patent law,[129] many features of the patent system (like opposition) remain generally national.[130] Interpreting the interplay of national and global dynamics through the vocabulary of administrative values works to deconstruct (and re-describe) not just the values that produce international patent law, but also the institutions through which these values are given meaning in practice. Drawing from the broad work on global administration, the book involves posing a creative question: Can the functioning of international patent law be understood in terms of participation, accountability, and transparency? These values, though not exhaustive, are fundamental to both national and global administration work. Centring accountability specifically helps to produce a more nuanced understanding of how state power, through the operation of international patent law, is functionally restricted in the global space.

In this, the WTO and the TRIPS Agreement are central to the remaining chapters and feature to varying degrees in more conventional work on global administration. The WTO appears as an important actor in the development of values and

128 Brad Sherman, 'Towards a History of Patent Law' in Toshiko Takenaka (ed), *Intellectual Property in Common Law and Civil Law* (Edward Elgar 2013) 3.

129 Dongwook Chun, 'Patent Law Harmonization in the Age of Globalization: The Necessity and Strategy for a Pragmatic Outcome' (2011) 93(2) Journal of the Patent & Trademark Office Society 129.

130 Cynthia Ho, *Access to Medicine in the Global Economy: International Agreements on Patents and Related Rights* (OUP 2011) 234.

principles in international regulation,[131] how harmonisation can be interpreted from a more critical perspective,[132] and how administrative law principles (like accountability) can be translated into the global space.[133] While the TRIPS Agreement only appears sporadically from an administrative perspective, it is usually only discussed in relation to how technical standards function as a form of regulation and how the WTO necessarily privileges specific bodies with administrative power.[134] The lack of scholarship directly considering the regulatory dimensions of patent law and the TRIPS Agreement stands out because the creation of the WTO – and the transformation of the international trade system into a full administrative network[135] – coincided with the signing of the TRIPS Agreement at the conclusion of the Uruguay Round.[136] The typical focus on the creative potential of dispute resolution bodies in the production of global administration has also not been applied in a patent or intellectual property context.

Though the project investigates how administrative values can be used to interpret the complex position of dispute resolution bodies, it draws conceptually from the work of Krisch as a more specific development within global administration.[137] Here, the emphasis is on exploring the more interactional qualities of legal development and understanding dispute resolution contexts as interfaces in which multiple competing perspectives must be balanced.[138] Reconstructing tensions that emerge in the dispute resolution fora of international patent law through the language of administrative values helps to highlight its deeply contextual character. The development of global patent law, as well as its adjudication, necessarily extends beyond the creation of technical regulation and takes on social, political, and cultural dimensions. As such, the continued economic approach to patent law, embedded in states worldwide, provides an incomplete and misrepresentative understanding

131 Elisa D'Alterio, 'Judicial Regulation in the Global Space' in Sabino Cassese (ed), *Research Handbook on Global Administrative Law* (Edward Elgar 2016) 304.

132 On the tensions around universalising standards and the movement from values, to human rights, to universal constitutional values: Carol Harlow, 'Global Administrative law: The Quest for Principles and Values' (2006) 17(1) EJIL 206, 207.

133 Mariana Mota Prado, 'Diffusion, Reception and Transplantation' in Peter Cane, Herwig CH Hofmann, Eric C Ip, and Peter C Lindseth (eds), *The Oxford Handbook of Comparative Administrative Law* (OUP 2021) 265, 266.

134 Stefano Battini, 'The Proliferation of Global Regulatory Regimes' in Sabino Cassese (ed), *Research Handbook on Global Administrative Law* (Edward Elgar 2016) 60.

135 Particularly in the transformation from the dispute settlement system under the GATT and then under the WTO: Barbara Marchetti, 'The Enforcement of Global Decisions' in Sabino Cassese (ed), *Research Handbook on Global Administrative Law* (Edward Elgar 2016) 248, 249.

136 Roger Kampf, 'Does Intellectual Property Belong to the Trade Family?' in Christoph Herrmann, Bruno Simma, and Rudolf Streinz (eds), *Trade Policy between Law, Diplomacy and Scholarship* (Springer 2015) 92, 93.

137 In both sole-authored and co-authored works: Benedict Kingsbury, Nico Krisch, and Richard B Stewart, 'The Emergence of Global Administrative Law' (2005) 68(3/4) Law and Contemporary Problems 15, 16.

138 Nico Krisch, 'Framing Entangled Legalities Beyond the State' in Nico Krisch (ed), *Entangled Legalities Beyond the State* (CUP 2022) 21, 22.

of how patents work. Accountability and participation are ways of recasting patent law in a way that incorporates economic discussions but contextualises them alongside a more holistic and interconnected perspective. As discussed in the introduction to this book, one of the objectives of analysing international patent law in this way is to facilitate communication with audiences who may otherwise be disengaged from patent law. Reframing tensions, relationships, and issues in patent law through this lens is one way of unsettling or challenging the tendency towards technocratic isolation in this area.

Bibliography

Articles

Aman AC, 'Administrative Law in the United States: Present and Future' (1991) 16 *Queen's Law Journal* 179.

Aman AC, 'Globalization, Democracy, and the Need for a New Administrative Law' (2003) 10(1) *Indiana Journal of Global Legal Studies* 125.

Bogdandy AV, M Goldmann, and I Venzke, 'From Public International to International Public Law: Translating World Public Opinion into International Public Authority' (2017) 28(1) *European Journal of International Law* 115.

Boisson de Chazournes L, 'Changing Roles of International Organizations: Global Administrative Law and the Interplay of Legitimacies' (2009) 6(2) *International Organizations Law Review* 655.

Campbell R, 'Global Patent Law Harmonization: Benefits and Implementation' (2003) 13(2) *Indiana International & Comparative Law Review* 605.

Cassese S, 'Global Administrative Law: The State of the Art' (2015) 13(2) *International Journal of Constitutional Law* 465.

Chimni BS, 'Co-Option and Resistance: Two Faces of Global Administrative Law' (2005) 37 *NYU Journal of International Law and Politics* 799.

Chun D, 'Patent Law Harmonization in the Age of Globalization: The Necessity and Strategy for a Pragmatic Outcome' (2011) 93(2) *Journal of the Patent & Trademark Office Society* 127.

Featherstone K, 'Jean Monnet and the "Democratic Deficit" in the European Union' (1994) 32(2) *JComMarSt* 149.

Finger JM, 'Implementation and Imbalance: Dealing with Hangover From the Uruguay Round' (2007) 23(3) *Oxford Review of Economic Policy* 440.

Frost N, 'Out with the "Old", in With the "New": Challenging Dominant Regulatory Approaches in the Field of Human Rights' (2021) 32(2) *European Journal of International Law* 507.

Ghosh, S, 'Patents and the Regulatory State: Rethinking the Patent Bargain Metaphor after Eldred' (2004) 19(4) *Berkeley Technology Law Journal* 1315.

Halabi Y, 'The Expansion of Global Governance into the Third World: Altruism, Realism, or Constructivism?' (2004) 6(1) *International Studies Review* 21.

Harlow C, 'Global Administrative Law: The Quest for Principles and Values' (2006) 17(1) *European Journal of International Law* 187.

Hasson AI, 'Domestic Implementation of International Obligations: The Quest for World Patent Law Harmonization' (2002) 25 *Boston College International & Comparative Law Review* 373.

Héritier A and D Lehmkuhl, 'New Modes of Governance and Democratic Accountability' (2011) 46(1) *Government and Opposition* 126.

Kingsbury B, N Krisch, and PB Stewart, 'The Emergence of Global Administrative Law' (2005) 68(3/4) *Law and Contemporary Problems* 15.

Love R, 'Corporate Wealth or Public Health? WTO/TRIPS Flexibilities and Access to HIV/AIDS Antiretroviral Drugs by Developing Countries' (2007) 17(2) *Development in Practice* 208.

Miller B and B Curry, 'Expertise, Experience, and Ideology on Specialized Courts: The Case of the Court of Appeals for the Federal Circuit' (2009) 43(4) *Law & Society Review* 839.

Nakayama, N, 'The Enforcement of the TRIPS Agreement in Japan' (1995) 38 *Japanese Annual of International Law* 1.

Reinbothe R and A Howard, 'The State of Play in the Negotiations on TRIPS (GATT/Uruguay Round)' (1991) 13(5) *European Intellectual Property Review* 157.

Rodriguez V, 'Constructing a Unitary Title for the European Patent System' (2011) 6(8) *Journal of Intellectual Property Law & Practice* 574.

Santos A, 'Carving out Policy Autonomy for Developing Countries in the World Trade Organisation: The Experience of Brazil and Mexico' (2012) 52(3) *Virginia Journal of International Law* 551.

Shapiro M, '"Deliberative," "Independent" Technocracy v. Democratic Politics: Will the Globe Echo the E.U.?' (2005) 68(3/4) *Law and Contemporary Problems* 341.

Sridhar D, 'Improving Access to Essential Medicines: How Health Concerns can be Prioritised in the Global Governance System' (2008) 1(2) *Public Health Ethics* 83.

Stewart RB, M Ratton, and S Badin, 'The World Trade Organisation: Multiple Dimensions of Global Administrative Law' (2011) 9(3-4) *International Journal of Constitutional Law* 556.

Swanson KW, 'The Emergence of the Professional Patent Practitioner' (2009) 50(3) *Technology and Culture* 519.

Tripathi R, 'Concept of Global Administrative Law: An Overview' (2011) 67(4) *India Law Quarterly* 355.

Upreti PN, 'Eli Lilly v Government of Canada: The Tale of Promise v Expectation' (2018) 21(3) *International Arbitration Law Review* 84.

Wasserman Rajec S R, 'The Harmonization Myth in International Intellectual Property Law' (2020) 60 *Arizona Law Review* 735.

Xavier S, 'Top Heavy: Beyond the Global North and the Justification for Global Administrative Law' (2018) 57 *Indian Journal of International Law* 337.

Yu PK, 'TRIPS Enforcement and Developing Countries' (2011) 26(3) *American University International Law Review* 727.

Books

Baldan F, *Judicial Coherence in the European Patent System: Lessons from the US and Japan* (Edward Elgar 2022).

Benvenisti E, *The Law of Global Governance* (Hague Academy of International Law 2014).

Cloatre E, *Pills for the Poorest: An Exploration of TRIPS and Access to Medication in Sub-Saharan Africa* (Palgrave 2013).

Ho C, *Access to Medicine in the Global Economy: International Agreements on Patents and Related Rights* (OUP 2011).

Lea D, *Property Rights, Indigenous People and the Developing World: Issues from Aboriginal Entitlement to Intellectual Ownership Rights* (Martinus Nijhoff 2008).

Mgbeoji I, *Biopiracy: Patents, Plants, and Indigenous Knowledge* (UBC Press 2006).

Moir HVJ, *Patent Policy and Innovation: Do Legal Rules Deliver Effective Economic Outcomes?* (Edward Elgar 2013).

Okoh AS, *Oil Mortality in Post-Fossil Fuel Era Nigeria: Beyond the Oil Age* (Springer 2021).

Peukert A, *A Critique of the Ontology of Intellectual Property Law* (CUP 2021).

Ragavan S, *Patent and Trade Disparities in Developing Countries* (OUP 2012).

Chapters

Battini S, 'The Proliferation of Global Regulatory Regimes' in Sabino Cassese (ed), *Research Handbook on Global Administrative Law* (Edward Elgar 2016) 45.

Bhardwaj K, 'India's Free Trade Agreements: Implications for Access to Medicines in India and the Global South' in Hans Löfgren (ed), *The Politics of the Pharmaceutical Industry and Access to Medicines: World Pharmacy and India* (Routledge 2018) 134.

Biddulph S, 'Administrative Power' in Peter Cane, Herwig Ch Hofmann, Eric C IP, and Peter L Lindseth (eds), *Oxford Handbook of Comparative Administrative Law* (OUP 2021) 380.

Burghardt G, 'The EU/US Transatlantic Relationship: The Indispensable Partnership' in Christoph Hermann, Bruno Simma, and Rudolf Streinz (eds), *Trade Policy Between Law, Diplomacy and Scholarship* (Springer 2015) 193.

Casini L, 'The Expansion of the Material Scope of Global Law' in Sabino Cassese (ed), *Research Handbook on Global Administrative Law* (Edward Elgar 2016) 25.

D'Alterio E, 'Judicial Regulation in the Global Space' in Sabino Cassese (ed), *Research Handbook on Global Administrative Law* (Edward Elgar 2016) 303.

Della Cananea G, 'Administrative Law Beyond the State: The Influence of International and Supranational Organizations' in Peter Cane, Herwig Ch Hofmann, Eric C IP, and Peter L Lindseth (eds), *Oxford Handbook of Comparative Administrative Law* (OUP 2021) 357.

Donaldson M and B Kingsbury, 'The Global Governance of Public Law' in Cormac Mac Amhlaigh, Claudio Michelon, and Neil Walker (eds), *After Public Law* (OUP 2013) 264.

Golia AJ, 'Judicial Review, Foreign Relations and Global Administrative Law: The Administrative Function of Courts in Foreign Relations' in Helmut Philipp Aust and Thomas Kleinlein (eds), *Encounters Between Foreign Relations Law and International Law: Bridges and Boundaries* (CUP 2021) 130.

Hernandez RFU, 'Global Administrative Law and the Global South' in Sabino Cassese (ed), *Research Handbook on Global Administrative Law* (Edward Elgar 2016) 392.

Joseph S, 'Democratic Deficit, Participation and the WTO' in Sarah Joseph, David Kinley, and Jeff Waincymer (eds), *The World Trade Organization and Human Rights: Interdisciplinary Perspectives* (Edward Elgar 2009) 313.

Juszczyk G, 'Legitimacy Crisis in the World Trade Organisation Appellate Body: Other Ways than the MPIA?' in Jelena Bäumler, Christina Binder, Marc Bungenberg, Markus Krajewski, Giesela Rühl, Christian J Tams, Jörg Philipp Terhechte, and Andreas R Ziegler (eds), *European Yearbook of International Economic Law* (Springer 2022) 87.

Kampf R, 'Does Intellectual Property Belong to the Trade Family?' in Christoph Herrmann, Bruno Simma, and Rudolf Streinz (eds), *Trade Policy Between Law, Diplomacy and Scholarship* (Springer 2015) 87.

Krisch N, 'Framing Entangled Legalities Beyond the State' in Nico Krisch (ed), *Entangled Legalities Beyond the State* (CUP 2022) 1.

Madsen MR, 'Judicial Globalization: The Proliferation of International Courts' in Sabino Cassese (ed), *Research Handbook on Global Administrative Law* (Edward Elgar 2016) 282.

Marchetti B, 'The Enforcement of Global Decisions' in Sabino Cassese (ed), *Research Handbook on Global Administrative Law* (Edward Elgar 2016) 242.

Michaels R, 'Tertiary Rules' in Nico Krisch (ed), *Entangled Legalities Beyond the State* (CUP 2022) 424.

Novogrodsky NB, 'Beyond TRIPS: The Role of Non-State Actors and Access to Essential Medicines' in Thomas Pogge, Matthew Rimmer, and Kim Rubenstein (eds), *Incentives for Global Public Health: Patent Law and Access to Essential Medicines* (CUP 2010) 343.

Odagiri H, A Goto, and A Sunami, 'IPR and the Catch-Up Process in Japan' in Hiroyuki Odagiri, Akira Goto, Atsushi Sunami, and Richard R Nelson (eds), *Intellectual Property*

Rights, Development, and Catch-up: An International Comparative Study (OUP 2010) 95.
Prado MM, 'Diffusion, Reception and Transplantation' in Peter Cane, Herwig Ch Hofmann, Eric C IP, and Peter C Lindseth (eds), *The Oxford Handbook of Comparative Administrative Law* (OUP 2021) 254.
Sherman B, 'Towards a History of Patent Law' in Toshiko Takenaka (ed), *Intellectual Property in Common Law and Civil Law* (Edward Elgar 2013) 3.
Stewart RB, 'Global Standards for National Societies' in Sabino Cassese (ed), *Research Handbook on Global Administrative Law* (Edward Elgar 2016) 175.
Taggart M, 'The Province of Administrative Law Determined' in Michael Taggart (ed), *The Province of Administrative Law* (Hart 1997) 1.
Thio LI, 'Courts and Judicial Review' in Peter Cane, Herwig Ch Hofmann, Eric C IP, and Peter L Lindseth (eds), *Oxford Handbook of Comparative Administrative Law* (OUP 2021) 721.
Vesperini G, 'Europe and Global Law' in Sabino Cassese (ed), *Research Handbook on Global Administrative Law* (Edward Elgar 2016) 371.
Ziller J, 'Comparison Within Multi-Level Polities and Governance Regimes' in Peter Cane, Herwig Ch Hofmann, Eric C IP, and Peter L Lindseth (eds), *Oxford Handbook of Comparative Administrative Law* (OUP 2021) 137.
Legislation/Legal Sources
Article 27, TRIPS Agreement.
Article 27, TRIPS Agreement.
Article 33, TRIPS Agreement.

Cases

Eli Lilly and Company v The Government of Canada UNCT/14/2.

Other

WTO, 'Understanding the WTO: The Organization' (*WTO*) <https://www.wto.org/english/thewto_e/whatis_e/tif_e/org1_e.htm>.

2 Current developments in European patent law through the lens of administrative values

2.1 Introduction

The development and implementation of the European Patent with Unitary Effect (EPUE) is an important step for European patent law. At least in theory, it represents significant progress towards a more complete patent harmonisation in Europe.[1] While European patent law can be described as fragmented,[2] the reality is that this is more of a substantive fracturing of patent law than a procedural one. This is primarily due to the European Patent Convention (EPC) and other Directives on specific areas of patent law.[3] The grant of a single patent that would be valid and enforceable throughout the EU would simplify the situation for inventors and businesses over the existing administrative centralisation and subsequent involvement of national systems for enforcement. Yet despite this potential, the EPUE falls significantly short of creating a harmonised patent interface and fundamentally hampers the ability of EU Member States to participate in a meaningful and equal way. Approaching the EPUE – both from an administrative and more conventional patent perspective – is a rare opportunity to explore the creation of a contemporary harmonising patent framework. The EPUE can be used as a case study to explore the dynamic involved with the production of international patent law, yet it also provides a fairly contained legal environment before moving to less structured global contexts. The values of transparency, accountability, and participation are fundamental to the analysis of the EPUE and its legal provisions. In this, European patent law can be viewed through the lens of administrative values to

1 With the objective of creating a specialised patent jurisdiction and promoting research, development, and investment in innovation: EU Commission, 'Internal Market, Industry, Entrepreneurship, and SMEs: Unitary Patent' (*EU Commission*) <https://ec.europa.eu/growth/industry/strategy/intellectual-property/patent-protection-eu/unitary-patent_en>.

2 Specifically in terms of patent validation but also more generally: Amanda Odell-West, 'Exclusions in Patent Law as an Indirect Form of Regulation for New Health Technologies in Europe' in Mark L Flear, Anne-Maree Farrell, Tamara K Hervey, and Thérèse Murphy (eds), *European Law and New Health* Technologies (OUP 2013) 152.

3 On the complex role of the EPC in bringing together standards in patent law: Alexander Stack, *International Patent Law: Cooperation, Harmonization and an Institutional Analysis of WIPO and the WTO* (Edward Elgar 2011) 94.

DOI: 10.4324/9781003616856-3

highlight issues not only in this initial moment of creation but also how dynamics of law-making can be shifted more fundamentally.

Contextualising how the EPUE connects to transparency and accountability is crucial to exploring how the legal relationship to courts and other bodies is constructed. Fundamental to understanding the EPUE in this way is a recognition that it was produced through the enhanced cooperation process – a mechanism that allows a group of EU Member States to proceed with a legal initiative, subject to certain restrictions, when EU consensus is impossible.[4] The Unified Patent Court (UPC) Agreement created an associated court structure to deal with the enforcement of the EPUE.[5] As such, the UPC is a particularly central consideration when analysing the values of European patent law due to its influential role in dispute resolution within this new patent framework. The creation of a new patent framework and court system produces a space in which the fundamental values and priorities that drive their output are still in development or yet to emerge. As a result of this, the language of participation and transparency provides a way of looking at the legal foundation of the EPUE and UPC to anticipate potential tensions. The UPC can also be analysed in terms of both its development as a specialised patent court in Europe and representative of a more global trend towards specialisation in intellectual property dispute resolution.[6] It is in this capacity as a specialised court that it will necessarily shape the trajectory of patent law in Europe as a network of courts and judges deal with the interpretation and application of EPUE (and EPUE-adjacent) sources of law.[7] The tendency towards specialisation, if left unchecked, can contribute to a patent system that is insulated from broader legal engagement.

Patent law provides an interesting context for deconstructing the relationship between dispute resolution bodies and administrative values because the EPUE will actually coexist with several, already functioning, legal interfaces in European patent law. The result is that the EPUE, as an interface, not only involves negotiating the values and objectives of the Member States involved but also the relationship *between* patent interfaces such as the EPC and national patent systems through the UPC. This additional fracturing of patent law and its foundational elements in Europe highlights the unique framing of technical law that is enabled through the vocabulary of transparency and accountability. While the analysis remains firmly grounded in the textual provisions of the UPC Agreement (UPCA), as there has been just under two years of the court actually hearing cases, the text of the agreement outlines the powers available to the UPC and its judges. The agreement text, interpreted through the lens of participation, then, necessarily incorporates

4 Article 20, TEU.

5 Agreement on a Unified Patent Court (UPC Agreement).

6 On the increasing global attention that specialised intellectual property courts have attracted: Olga Gurgula, Maciej Padamczyk, and Noam Shemtov, 'Specialised IP Judiciary: What Are the Key Elements to Consider When Establishing or Reforming an Effective IP Court?' (2022) 71(3) GRUR International 206, 207.

7 Such as the interpretation of the EPC and national law.

elements of both substantive patent law and more procedural considerations such as compulsory licensing and *l'ordre public*.

Section 2.2 of the chapter considers the existing parallel interfaces in European patent law, while Section 2.3 analyses the development and implementation of the EPUE. Section 2.3 specifically explores the legal impact of both the EPUE and the UPC in constituting a new legal interface for patent law and how the role of a specialised dispute settlement body is important for enabling meaningful participation. Section 2.4 considers the interactions between the EPUE and specific technological contexts, focusing primarily on the relationship of *l'ordre public* exceptions and compulsory licensing to the values of participation and accountability.

2.2 Patent law in Europe: The existing interface(s)

2.2.1 Coexisting mechanisms of patent protection

2.2.1.1 The continued emphasis on territoriality in patent law and its impact

The enduring role of territoriality in patent law is a key aspect of the potential in harmonised initiatives, specifically in Europe, where the validity of a patent is tied to the jurisdiction in which it was granted.[8] The tensions in territoriality are particularly pronounced in Europe by virtue of the internal market, where patent law stands out in an environment that prioritises integration and rejects the splitting or isolation of markets. The attempts at resolving this tension in patent law have consistently encountered political difficulty,[9] resulting in less ambitious projects that emphasise a sense of administrative centralisation over true substantive harmonisation that would incorporate enforcement. The EPUE, at least on a theoretical level, addresses the negative aspects of a strictly territorial approach in Europe and meaningfully advances the harmonisation of patent law. However, this is not to understate the significance of the administrative and broad harmonisation brought by the EPC. The ability for applicants to file a single application, despite how this leads to a suite of national applications, was a major development for European patent law.[10]

Yet the impact of territoriality extends beyond the grant of a patent right and into its enforcement, where the judgment of the validity of a patent (rather than its validity alone) is strictly connected to the jurisdiction in which the decision was rendered. While this raises issues even at a global level, it is in a European context

8 Volker Michael Jänich, 'The Territorial Dimension of Intellectual Property Law' in Karl M Meessen (ed), *Economic Law as an Economic Good: Its Rule Function and Its Tool Function in the Competition of Systems* (Sellier 2009) 216, 217.

9 Even with the more technical aspects of jurisdiction under the CPC, where a number of national courts would serve as courts of first instance, several members 'designated all their courts – obviously for political and federalist reasons – to have jurisdiction at the national level': Stefan Luginbuehl, *European Patent Law: Towards a Uniform Interpretation* (Edward Elgar 2011) 20.

10 Tony Howard, 'The Legal Framework Surrounding Patents for Living Materials' in Johanna Gibson (ed), *Patenting Lives: Life Patents, Culture and Development* (Routledge 2008) 9.

that it contrasts so sharply with the freedom of establishment and the internal market. Companies and goods flow easily, yet the patent protection of any products (and the licences held by licensees) is still very much nationally focused. The territorial emphasis takes on a particular character in Europe, though, because it reflects issues common to systems dealing with complex decentralised or federalist structures. The distinguishing factor between the EU and somewhere like the US is that, in practice, the EU lacks a unifying forum for these disputes.[11] The creation of the Court of Appeals for the Federal Circuit (CAFC), in joining together the Court of Customs and Patent Appeals and the appellate division of the Court of Claims,[12] was specifically aimed at remedying the diverging approaches of different circuit courts that were damaging the user experience of the patent system.[13] The lack of a unifying forum in the European context, specifically in enforcement, is an important part of why the UPC is such an important development.

2.2.1.2 National systems of patent protection

Though Member States are broadly bound by the provisions of the TRIPS Agreement, they are generally free to develop their own approaches to elements of substantive patent law with 'considerable national autonomy over how to comply with the minimum standards'.[14] The emphasis on these national perspectives on patent law contrasts more generally with the strong trend in law towards harmonisation in Europe. Three primary outcomes of this national emphasis are considered here. These are the cost of applying to several jurisdictions for patent protection, the risk of divergent judgments in the event of a dispute, and how this positions the EU as a competitive patent jurisdiction in a global context. Turning first to the cost of applying to multiple jurisdictions within the EU, it is common practice for businesses to apply for patent protection in only a handful of jurisdictions rather than in *all* Member States.[15] Applicants are free to apply for patents with national patent offices, in a process that is more integrated with the national context and provides

11 Though the role of the CJEU and its involvement may increase with the introduction of the UPC as there will be a more direct patent basis for considering referred questions (though this is a complement to more traditional avenues such as competition law elements and the Biotech Directive): Clement Salung Petersen and Jens Schovsbo, 'Decision-Making in the Unified Patent Court: Ensuring a Balanced Approach' in Christophe Geiger, Craig Allen Nard, and Xavier Seuba (eds), *Intellectual Property and the Judiciary* (Edward Elgar 2018) 231, 238.

12 Through the Federal Courts Improvement Act 1982.

13 On the conflicting interpretations of patent principles and the eventual introduction of the CAFC: Srividhya Ragavan, *Patent and Trade Disparities in Developing Countries* (OUP 2012) 22.

14 Susy Frankel, 'The TRIPS Agreement and Cross-Retaliation' in Susy Frankel and Meredith Kolsky Lewis (eds), *Trade Agreements at the Crossroads* (Routledge 2014) 210.

15 Typically Germany, France, the UK, and the Netherlands: Dan L Burk, 'Patents and Related Rights: A Global Kaleidoscope' in Rochelle C Dreyfuss and Justine Pila (eds), *The Oxford Handbook of Intellectual Property Law* (OUP 2018) 462.

an important option for SMEs.[16] As this type of application can be more appropriate for small businesses, the process will remain a significant part of patent law in Europe even as patent cooperation initiatives continue.[17]

Despite the economic sense of this for applicants, it also produces a patent climate in which specific Member States (Western European in particular) are disproportionately influential in the overall trajectory of European patent law. While to an extent Europe still relies on these national systems of protection, there is a certain asymmetry in which European jurisdictions drive the development of patent law in practice. This immediately raises questions about the degree to which the EPUE and UPC will further privilege or entrench the interests and perspectives of the high-patent-activity jurisdictions and their legal systems. In a related sense, it questions how any patent harmonisation can be responsive to the needs of smaller jurisdictions, if at all. All of these elements raise important challenges about how responsive and accountable the EPUE will be in terms of patent stakeholders in Europe. Especially in terms of accountability, the development of the EPUE and UPC practice presents a tension around the forum in which accountability is judged. This is further complicated by the fact that this project was led by the Member States themselves rather than representing a unified EU perspective.

2.2.2 The 'European' patent system

2.2.2.1 The European Patent Convention and procedural harmonisation

The European Patent Convention (EPC) is a fundamental element of patent law in Europe because, despite not being an EU instrument, it essentially provides an international framework that provides for substantial administrative and substantive harmonisation.[18] It is precisely from this bringing together of standards that the actual impact of the EPUE would at first appear to be much more subtle. The EPC is an international convention that allows actors to submit a singular patent application to the EPO for any number of EPC signatories and provides a route towards

16 One concern that emerged in McDonagh's interview work investigating the perception of the EPUE in the UK was that, because SMEs typically only patent in a small number of jurisdictions, the cost of renewal for an EPUE may be still too high: Luke McDonagh, 'Exploring Perspectives of the Unified Patent Court and Unitary Patent Within the Business and Legal Communities' (2014) UKIPO 32, 33 <https://assets.publishing.service.gov.uk/government/uploads/system/uploads/attachment_data/file/328035/UPC_Study.pdf>.

17 'Patent applicants should remain free to obtain either a national patent, a European patent with unitary effect, a European patent taking effect in one or more of the Contracting States to the EPC, or a European patent with unitary effect validated in addition in one or more other Contracting States to the EPC which are not among the participating Member States': paragraph 26, Regulation 1257/2012.

18 Alfredo Ilardi, *The New European Patent* (Hart 2015) 10; though the EPO itself states that 'the EPC has established a single European patent procedure for the grant of patents on the basis of a single application and created a uniform body of substantive patent law designed to provide easier, cheaper and stronger protection for inventions in the contracting states.': EPO, 'European Patent Guide: 2.2' (*EPO*) <https://www.epo.org/applying/european/Guide-for-applicants/html/e/ga_c2_2.html>.

patent protection that simplifies applications covering multiple jurisdictions.[19] Yet this process does not lead to the grant of a singular patent right and, here, the fundamental administrative character of patent law becomes clear. Instead of a singular patent right, the grant of a European patent results in a patent that 'shall, in each of the Contracting States for which it is granted, have the effect of and be subject to the same conditions as a national patent granted by that State'.[20] So while the administrative centralisation of the initial filing of patent applications in Europe meaningfully facilitates applications that cover multiple jurisdictions, it also highlights how these substantive requirements of patent law must be interpreted in each national context.

The EPC is interesting because the space for interpretation and facilitating responsiveness in patent law is not produced through exceptions or limitations (like compulsory licensing or *l'ordre public* provisions). The subject matter exclusions of Article 52 can be seen as a mechanism that facilitates this type of interactive participation, as a static provision that has been extensively developed through interpretation and dispute. Though as a non-EU provision, this process of interpretation and development takes on a distinctive character compared to provisions of the ordinary legislative context. The development of Article 52 and its function as a flexibility comes from how the jurisprudence on Article 52 has predominantly developed through the Enlarged Board of Appeal (EBA) rather than through ordinary national courts.[21] Unlike compulsory licensing, which provides a space for autonomous action by the parties (empowering the signatory to act), the subject-matter exclusions allow specific actors to negotiate the meaning and impact of a binding obligation within international patent law. The developments in the EBA and national courts on the question of subject matter eligibility are obviously connected, and yet they both have the potential to shift, subtly, how this provision operates in practice. The EBA, in particular, is isolated to a degree from the pressures of a national legal context and as a non-court body that still functions quasi-judicially, reflects exactly the type of technocratic decision-making that concerns global administration. This necessarily raises issues about the accountability, transparency, and participation elements of the provisions themselves and their subsequent evolution when this process is divorced from conventional systems of accountability. Centring these administrative values reveals a context in which specialised administrative bodies, broadly shielded from general oversight, interpret

19 On discussion of the cost-saving of an EPO application (in some studies, more affordable when applying for more than four member countries) but also that the idea of international competition is skewed – more affordable costs in Japan or the US are not directly relevant because they cannot grant patents in Europe: Peter Drahos, *The Global Governance of Knowledge: Patent Offices and Their Clients* (CUP 2010) 127, 128.

20 Article 2, EPC.

21 The complex development of Article 52(3) through the Technical Board of Appeal and the Enlarged Board of Appeal in the context of computer programs: Sigrid Sterckx and Julian Cockbain, *Exclusions from Patentability: How Far Has the European Patent Office Eroded Boundaries?* (CUP 2012) 70.

and advance areas of international patent law with very little room for participation (generalist or otherwise). In this context, what options exist for stakeholders to challenge this progressive interpretation of patent provisions? From a more practical perspective, this type of deep involvement by patent actors could perhaps reflect a more nuanced experience of responsiveness in patent law. Rather than a technocratic isolation, the development of patent law in this way can be interpreted as a direct response to emerging legal challenges observed in a dispute setting.

The central role of the EBA also emphasises the influence of the European Patent Office (EPO) in the development of patent law at this broader level and how the provisions of the EPC are interpreted over time. Patent rights that are granted through this process are then subject to challenge in their own jurisdictions, the jurisprudence about patent law is still very much grounded in the national law environment. There is then a tension in the interface that the EPC creates. While the general contours of the patent as a legal instrument are fairly settled, the actual adjudication of the patent takes place in a dispute settlement context that is more responsive to priorities in the embedded national legal context. Decisions taken by the national dispute settlement body lack the more general impact on patent law that the decisions rendered by the EBA have. There is a certain dissonance where the EBA can shape the fundamentals of patent law and yet is subject to none of the ordinary institutions of a national legal system, while the actual court of a Member State can only ever have limited impact and operates strictly within a much more embedded and constraining political and social context.

2.3 The creation of a new patent interface in Europe

2.3.1 What exactly is a 'Unitary Patent'?

2.3.1.1 Establishing the contours of the European Patent with Unitary Effect

The EPUE and the UPC are constituted by a set of three agreements that deal with the structure of the court, the creation of unitary patent protection, and an agreement that specifically deals with the translation arrangements. Regulation 1257/2012 establishes the EPUE as a legal instrument and highlights the important objectives of promoting harmonisation in European patent law.[22] Early in the text, the EPUE is presented as an important development in fostering scientific development and a way of improving the functioning of the internal market.[23] The EPUE is explicitly aimed at eliminating 'costs and complexity for undertakings throughout the Union', and yet there is a tension between these broad objectives and the fundamentally compromised nature of the EPUE that appears in two contexts.[24] The first is a more specific or narrow legal perspective as to the actual qualities of the patent, and the second is how it relates to the proposed benefits of harmonising

22 Paragraph 4, Regulation 1257/2012.
23 Paragraph 4, Regulation 1257/2012.
24 Paragraph 4, Regulation 1257/2012.

European patent law. Each of these has a fundamental impact on the ability of Member States to participate meaningfully in the development of European patent law. While the Regulation highlights the role of the EPO in granting 'European' patents,[25] the EPUE Regulation does not actually deal with the grant of a unitary patent. Instead, it deals with an expansion of the territorial scope of a granted patent whereby the patent can only be limited, revoked, or transferred in all the participating states.[26] Licensing, however, retains a national focus and allows the patent to be licensed with regard to part of or an entire territory of a participating Member State.[27] Compulsory licensing also keeps this national focus and is governed by the provisions applicable in each Member State.[28] Taken together, this structure emphasises the administrative patent grant process by avoiding the direct grant of a unitary patent. Without the appropriate delegation of this power from the Member States themselves, the grant of a patent remains a national function that is exercised by specific agencies of the state.

One of the broader issues in the development of the EPUE's objectives of harmonisation and the reality of the EPUE comes from the fact that the EPUE is intended, at least through a lengthy transition period,[29] to coexist with other forms of patent protection in Europe.[30] The text of the Regulation itself highlights four possible options for patent applicants: obtaining a national patent, an EPUE, a patent that results from the EPC, and an EPUE in addition to patents from signatories to the EPC who are not part of the EPUE.[31] Exhaustion, and particularly the role of the CJEU in the jurisprudence of this area,[32] is considered explicitly in the Regulation and ensures that despite these varying options for patent applicants, at least exhaustion remains harmonised. Together, these interconnected and varying systems of patent law raise profound concerns around transparency and participation in patent law in Europe for stakeholders. Even just in terms of the complexity of options for obtaining patent protection, the existence of multiple different systems means that patent law continues to appear overly complex. The lack of a singular regime also has an impact on the ability to challenge or propose reform for European patent law simply because there is no unifying foundation. It is the overlapping nature of patent protection in Europe that obscures the accountability for how binding patent provisions are developed and weakens the link between stakeholder participation and state. European patent law, in practice, takes on a diffuse character which resists simplification and transparency.

The Regulation itself recognises the potential for a shifting scope of the EPUE territory in Article 17, establishing that the uniform protection of the EPUE shall

25 Paragraph 5, Regulation 1257/2012.
26 Article 3(2), Regulation 1257/2012.
27 Paragraph 7, Regulation 1257/2012.
28 Paragraph 10, Regulation 1257/2012.
29 Article 6, Regulation 1260/2012.
30 Paragraph 26, Regulation 1257/2012.
31 Paragraph 26, Regulation 1257/2012.
32 Paragraph 12, Regulation 1257/2012.

only extend to those participating Member States that have implemented the UPC as the court with exclusive jurisdiction over EPUEs.[33] The protean nature of the EPUE territory also affects the more administrative aspects of patent harmonisation like the development of an EPUE register established by Rule 16 of the Rules relating to Unitary Patent Protection.[34] In addition to the more ordinary aspects of patent ownership that must be entered into the register (like the date of filing for unitary effect or the date of publication of the European patent),[35] the register should have both the date of effect of the unitary protection *and* the participating Member States in which the patent has unitary effect.[36] While this type of arrangement is a necessary consequence of developing a patent regime with lengthy transition periods, it produces a system that fails to simplify the process of identifying both the scope and existence of patent rights in Europe. It creates a fundamental lack of clarity. In complicating the European patent system and creating obstacles to quickly establishing the status of a patent, the EPUE creates a more general challenge to accessibility. The lack of simplicity can potentially impair stakeholders – patent holders and industry more generally – from being able to clearly and effectively understand the legal state of patent protection in their areas.

2.3.1.2 The legal environment produced by patent harmonisation priorities

The agreements that establish the EPUE have an interesting dynamic because they rely extensively on existing sources of law, described by others as a 'hollow' piece of legislation,[37] as the EPUE is defined essentially through reference to other established legal sources like the EPC. The use of enhanced cooperation instead of the ordinary legislative procedure of the EU is directly connected to one of the major controversies with the legal status of the EPUE due to its reliance on secondary, non-EU law. One result of this is that the EPUE agreements centre on the acceptance of the 'transformation fiction' to explain how the grant of the patent actually functions.[38] The transformation fiction is intended to address existing EU principles of law and necessarily highlights the administrative foundation of patent law. The use of the transformation fiction is related to concerns over the *Meroni* doctrine that deals with the improper delegation of administrative or regulatory powers.[39] As a result, the EPUE agreements characterise the EPUE as a patent granted

33 Article 18 2 EPUE Regulation.

34 Formally *Rules relating to Regulation 1257/2012 and 1260/2012*, but EPO refers to it as 'rules relating to Unitary Patent protection'.

35 Rule 16 (1)(a) and (c), Rules relating to Regulation 1257/2012 and 1260/2012.

36 Rule 16 (1)(f) and (g), Rules relating to Regulation 1257/2012 and 1260/2012.

37 Winfried Tilmann, 'Recitals' in Winfried Tilmann and Clemens Plassmann (eds) *Unified Patent Protection in Europe: A Commentary* (OUP 2018) 83.

38 Angelos Dimopoulos, 'An Institutional Perspective II: The Role of the CJEU in the Unitary (EU) Patent System' in Justine Pila and Christopher Wadlow (eds) *The Unitary EU Patent System* (Bloomsbury 2015) 58.

39 C-9/56, C-10/56 *Meroni v High Authority* [1957/1957].

according to the existing EPC procedure that, through the sole and exclusive operation of EU law, is a national patent that is then given territorially unitary effect.[40] In avoiding the *Meroni* doctrine, the EPUE confirms tacitly that patent law's fundamental connection to the exercise of state power needs to be actively addressed in harmonisation. While the process may not lead to direct judicial review in the classic administrative sense, the provisions that restrict patentable subject matter or the patent term of the EPUE are necessarily constraints on the exercise of state power – even as they operate indirectly in explicitly recognising that the power to grant patents has not been delegated. The actual legal character of the EPUE seems almost minimised or side-lined when referred to as just a 'unitary patent' as it is distinctly *not* the grant of a unitary patent. The EPUE simply involves expanding the applicable territory of an EPC patent rather than establishing a new right in itself to specifically avoid the grant of an EU patent.

The Regulation also provides a degree of institutional entanglement that extends beyond the legislative provisions and into the substantive content of the patent. Article 14, in particular, establishes a strong relationship between the Commission and the EPO on the EPUE.[41] While Article 14 highlights the importance of cooperation on how the agreement functions, there is an economic focus to the text that centres the issue of renewal fees for the EPUE and how this impacts the budget of the EPO.[42] This type of coordinating function of the Commission extends to Article 16 because it provides for periodic reporting about the functioning of the Regulation to the European Parliament and Council.[43] Interestingly, renewal fees appear again in Article 16 with a particular emphasis on compliance with Article 12,[44] suggesting that the issue of fees will be a prominent part of the regular reporting to the European Parliament. These elements do promote a degree of transparency and accountability in the EPUE system, though the economic focus could suggest that the system will only be responsive to a narrow set of issues or concerns from stakeholders.

Chapter V of the UPC Agreement establishes the sources of law for the adjudication of the EPUE and forms a central part of the new patent interface.[45] The outlining of the applicable sources of substantive law is necessarily framed by the sections that immediately precede it, which emphasise the primacy of EU law and establish a system in which the Contracting Member States are jointly and severally liable for damages that result from breaches of EU law by the Court of Appeal.[46] Article 24 presents a clear set of legal sources that start with EU law (but specifically highlighting Regulations 1257/2012 and 1260/2012), the UPC Agreement,

40 Regulation (EU) No. 1257/2012 of the European Parliament and of the Council (2012) 1(7).

41 Article 14, Regulation 1257/2012.

42 Article 14, Regulation 1257/2012.

43 Article 16, Regulation 1257/2012.

44 Article 16(2), Regulation 1257/2012.

45 Chapter V (Articles 24–30), UPC Agreement.

46 Specifically grounding the non-contractual liability of Member States for damage caused by national courts that breach Union law: Article 22, UPC Agreement.

the EPC, other international agreements applicable to patent law, and finally, national law.[47] Subsection (2) of Article 24 explores more substantially the role of national law and again establishes what could essentially be seen as a hierarchy of applicable law.[48] The extent to which national law shall form the basis of decisions of the UPC can be decided from a set of related sources: The directly applicable EU rules on private international law;[49] international provisions that have international law rules;[50] and in the absence of either of those, the national provisions on private international law as decided by the UPC.[51] None of these provisions produce an especially reassuring understanding of the precise relationship between the different sources of law or the basis for challenging how these relationships are applied to determine cases in practice. In providing a hierarchy of legal sources that comprehensively accounts for the complexity of the EPUE, there is, again, a recurring sense that patent law is developing in an opaque and web-like way.

So, while the EPUE does not necessarily provide the harmonised application of patent law that was imagined under the failed CPC, it does succeed as a basic interface for European patent law. It succeeds in bringing together these different sources of law with at least some periodic reporting to the European Parliament and establishes a hierarchy of applicable law that (while not providing complete detail) does present a comprehensive scope of sources. Crucially for the EPUE as an interface, the bringing together of these different sources of law is backed by a court system and this means that the interactive relationship of legal sources will be shaped (and enforced) at the international rather than national level. One area of tension that emerges in the sources of law included in the UPC provisions is between the strong international emphasis (of EU law and primacy) and the more contextual mechanisms within patent law that make binding obligations more responsive to local (here, national) conditions. Mechanisms like compulsory licensing and provisions that explicitly rely on concepts of public morality are all embedded in the specific political and social context of a Member State. How can an international court manage these very different priorities in a sufficiently nuanced way that still ensures harmonisation across Europe?

The transition period provided for in the UPC Agreement is another area that impacts not only the development of the EPUE and its patent harmonisation in Europe, but meaningfully shapes how successful the EPUE is in bringing together this diverse set of legal sources in an organised and transparent way. The transition period has two main elements: a combination of a general seven-year transition period of the UPC's exclusive jurisdiction and the ability for patent owners to opt out their patents from UPC jurisdiction.[52] The seven-year transition period is provided for in Article 83(1) and allows owners of a European patent to bring

47 Article 24(1)(a)–(e), UPC Agreement.
48 Article 24(2), UPC Agreement.
49 24(2)(a), UPC Agreement.
50 24(2)(b), UPC Agreement.
51 24(2)(c), UPC Agreement.
52 Article 83, UPC Agreement.

their actions for revocation or infringement before national courts or other competent national bodies.[53] The opt-out provisions covered in subsection 3 of the same Article provide for the general ability of patent owners to opt out from the exclusive jurisdiction of the UPC,[54] as long as the patent or supplementary certificate was applied for before the end of the transition period and an action has not already been brought before the UPC.[55]

The emphasis on autonomy for patent owners and the transition period more broadly means that the EPUE, in bringing these sources of law into contact within the same framework, will involve a very long-term and perhaps uncertain project of gradual harmonisation. The objectives of the EPUE were explicitly to deal with the harmonisation of European patent law and reduce fragmentation, yet it will be a considerable time before this will be realised (even if the EPUE and UPC are actually successful). Article 83 provides for a 'broad consultation' by the Administrative Committee of the users of the patent system during this period, as well as investigating the number of patents or supplementary certificates that are still processed by national authorities.[56] Based on the results of this consultation, the transition period can be extended a further seven years and so represents perhaps an important opportunity for serious reflection on the EPUE system.[57] The interface that the EPUE creates, specifically with the UPC as essentially a manager for the broad scope of applicable law, provides some unique challenges to participation and transparency precisely because the results will not be immediate. While the relevant provisions establish hierarchies of law and the jurisdiction of the court, the reality is that the true impact of connecting different sources of patent law and whether the exact balance can ever be uniformly applied throughout Europe will only be seen in the future. Adding to this uncertainty is the fact that these sources of law, rules of the court, and advancements in patent principles will be developed not through binding legal text but through the long-term dynamic interactions of the UPC, Member States, and the CJEU.

2.3.2 *Legal challenges to the new framework*

2.3.2.1 *Foundational concerns as to the legal basis of enhanced cooperation*

Understanding how enhanced cooperation functions and how it was used to produce the EPUE is important from the perspective of administrative values because it challenges, quite profoundly, the degree to which participation and accountability are meaningfully represented within patent law. Rather than the thin conception used in some administrative work, enhanced cooperation demonstrates that participation and accountability cannot be reduced to a binary of presence and absence.

53 Article 83(1), UPC Agreement.
54 Article 83(3), UPC Agreement.
55 Article 83(3), UPC Agreement.
56 Article 84(5), UPC Agreement.
57 Article 84(5), UPC Agreement.

The impact of these values on the development of patent law is at once explicitly visible and also fundamentally embedded in every aspect of the process. The use of enhanced cooperation was the subject of several legal challenges, with the first major developments occurring in the joined cases of Spain and Italy that suggested the legal basis for enhanced cooperation had not been satisfied.[58] Beyond the actual substance of the decision that authorised enhanced cooperation, the gap of only eight months between the language proposals put forward by the Commission and the authorisation of enhanced cooperation attracted particular attention given that enhanced cooperation is explicitly constructed as a 'last resort'.[59] In fairness, while there was only a short period between these two events, it is perhaps not as radical as it would first appear. The similarities between the EPUE and the CPC, specifically on the issue of language and how controversial it continues to be, at least give some context as to how this negotiating impasse could be perceived as critical enough to allow for enhanced cooperation. Yet crucially, this short period between the proposals and the enhanced cooperation authorisation foreclosed the ability of the Member States to negotiate the issues more comprehensively. Language is a complex issue that involves culture, law, and politics while the discussions around patent harmonisation were explicitly framed in economic terms. Together, these factors suggest that negotiations would have always been extended and difficult but would correspondingly reflect a more engaged, reflective, and accountable future of harmonised European patent law.

Beyond the specific criticism that focuses on the degree to which the EPUE meets the criteria for enhanced cooperation, there has been some opposition to the use of enhanced cooperation more generally.[60] The relationship of enhanced cooperation to Article 118 Treaty on the Functioning of the European Union (TFEU) has also resulted in specific criticism, connecting intellectual property policy and the creation of centralised Union intellectual property rights with the internal market.[61] The CJEU, in *Joined Cases C-274/11 and C-295/11*, ruled that the authorisation of enhanced cooperation in pursuit of a patent right is legitimate because Article 118 empowers the creation of a system of uniform protection.[62] From this, and with the EPUE being created through enhanced cooperation, it establishes a system of uniform protection in the participating states and binds *only* the participating states.[63] Italy had argued that since Article 118 refers to EU institutions establishing European intellectual property rights and the setting up of centralised 'Union-wide' initiatives in supervision and coordination,[64] the Council had actually authorised the creation of a European right which is not valid throughout the

58 2011/167/EU Council Decision of 10 March 2011.

59 Thomas Jaeger, 'Reset and Go: The Unitary Patent System Post-Brexit' (2017) 48(3) IIC 259.

60 David Medina, 'How the Unitary Patent Will Fragment European Patent Law' (2015) 47 Arizona State Law Journal 342.

61 Article 118, TEU.

62 Paragraphs 66–68, Joined Cases C-274/11 and C-295/11.

63 Paragraphs 66–68, Joined Cases C-274/11 and C-295/11.

64 Paragraph 64, Joined Cases C-274/11 and C-295/11.

Union.[65] The parties also argued more generally under Article 326 that the internal market and social cohesion would be damaged by the creation of the EPUE through enhanced cooperation.[66]

The approach of the court has been criticised as overly formalistic and narrow,[67] but it demonstrates that there is clearly an almost singular focus on the economic potential of patent harmonisation in European patent law. Specifically on the relationship between Treaties, AG Villalón produced an opinion in Case *C-414/11* that dealt with a specific understanding of intellectual property competence post-Lisbon.[68] The Member States there argued that Lisbon did not, in fact, change the legal status of intellectual property rights in Europe as a shared competence.[69] These arguments centred on an understanding that intellectual property rights form part of the internal market under Article 4(2)(a), the more or less harmonised nature of intellectual property under Article 114, and the broader reach of Article 118.[70] Together, approaching patent law from a purely economic perspective appears to inadequately represent how it develops and functions. A more contextual perspective reveals the difficulty within the EPUE regime of understanding the interplay of different legal sources in a way that specifically centres on the exercise of state power and concerns around how sovereignty is safeguarded. In the legal challenges to the EPUE, the arguments that were raised by the parties reflect a deep tension in European law-making around the relationship between the Member States and the EU. Given the persistent use of economic objectives to discuss patent harmonisation in Europe, it is perhaps not surprising that the discussions – on competence in particular – have been framed primarily in terms of the internal market. The challenges to effective participation raised by the parties in patent law are then not unique to patent or intellectual property initiatives. Rather, they emerge at least partly from more fundamental questions on competence, the evolving relationship between the EU and Member States, and the complex ways that state power is directed or restricted in an international *cooperative* context.

The Commission in *C414/11* disagreed on the issue of competence and argued that, through the operation of the TRIPS Agreement and the similar wording between EU and WTO texts, intellectual property formed a substantial part of the common commercial policy and, therefore, formed an exclusive competence of the Union.[71] AG Villalón, somewhat unhelpfully, suggested that both the Member States *and* the Commission are correct regarding the status of intellectual property

65 Paragraph 64, Joined Cases C-274/11 and C-295/11.

66 Paragraphs 70–74, 75–78, Joined Cases C-274/11 and C-295/11.

67 Joseph Kenneth Yarsky, 'Hastening Harmonisation in EU Patent Law through a Preliminary Reference Power' (2017) 40(1) Boston College International and Comparative Law Review 176.

68 Paragraph 44, C414/11 Opinion of Advocate General Cruz Villalón.

69 Paragraph 44, C414/11 Opinion of Advocate General Cruz Villalón.

70 Paragraph 44, C414/11 Opinion of Advocate General Cruz Villalón.

71 Paragraph 43 (outlining the argument of the European Commission as to the validity of case law relevant to establishing exclusive or shared competence), C414/11.

in Europe.[72] In particular, AG Villalón highlighted the Commission's emphasis on consistency in the commercial aspects of intellectual property and the importance of intellectual property being preserved as a shared competence.[73] Though competence is a complex area and an analysis must necessarily go beyond one-sided conclusions, the result of these decisions and opinions is a sense of unsettled tension in intellectual property. Suggesting that both the Commission and the Member States were correct in their construction of patent law may reflect the nuances of the discussion, but it does little to address how these issues can be addressed in the future. Patent law is in the unenviable position of being a fairly niche area that nevertheless raises profound questions about the relationship between the EU and its Member States. We return again to the importance of political will in patent projects that, in the Europe of 2025, are unlikely to ever reach mainstream status. This is also exacerbated by the presumption of patent law as a technical and economic discipline precisely because it masks these more nuanced and interdisciplinary questions about authority, participation, and state power in an international setting.

2.3.2.2 The language regime and complex position of patent law

The second set of issues that were raised in the legal challenges to the EPUE by Italy and Spain were focused on the use of three official languages.[74] Here, they argued that the use of English, German, and French in the EPUE was discriminatory.[75] In these proceedings, Spain and Italy put forward the five language regime that is used by the European Union Intellectual Property Office (EUIPO).[76] The return of a five-language regime reflects the early proposals of the CPC and demonstrates the complex process of reconciling the cultural and legal diversity of Europe with the type of linguistic range that would produce a costly and unwieldy system for patent users. The disputes around the language regime speak to the entangled quality of international patent law as an interdisciplinary subject, where the economic function of the patent needs to be understood alongside its social, political, and cultural impact. This interconnected quality appears prominently in the challenges to enhanced cooperation because of the general use of five languages in European intellectual property. While it would have been only a small modification to the provisions to more proactively incorporate two important patent jurisdictions in the EPUE, it would have easily produced at least an image of a European patent harmonisation that is responsive to both economic and non-economic considerations and priorities.

72 Paragraph 55, C414/11 Opinion of Advocate General Cruz Villalón.

73 Paragraph 59, C414/11 Opinion of Advocate General Cruz Villalón.

74 C-274/11 *Kingdom of Spain v Council of the European Union*; C-295/11 *Italy v Council of the European Union*.

75 Regulation 1260/2012 clarifies that the language regime should build on that of the EPO as the body responsible for the grant of the patent (paragraphs 5 and 6) and therefore the official languages of the EPO are the official languages of the EPUE: Article 14(1) EPC; C-274/11 *Kingdom of Spain v Council of the European Union*; C-295/11 *Italy v Council of the European Union*.

76 Paragraphs 10–15, C-274/11 *Kingdom of Spain v Council of the European Union*; C-295/11 *Italy v Council of the European Union*.

With the CJEU endorsing this language regime and the fact that this is occurring within the framing of an enhanced cooperation project, the persistent rejection of a more nuanced understanding of patent law perhaps indicates something about the priorities of the institutions involved. Rather than a project of patent harmonisation that presents measured and sustainable development at an EU-wide level, the EPUE demonstrates clearly that the interests of major patent jurisdictions in Western Europe were (from the very start) indispensable. This raises obvious concerns about the extent to which smaller or non-Western European Member States were able to meaningfully participate in the development of European patent law. While Western European jurisdictions may be the most active areas and logically should drive (and benefit) from harmonisation, it still takes place within the EU and some weight should be given to the active incorporation of all Member States. The timing of the EPUE and the intensely political nature of language disputes are interesting when seen in the context of Brexit.[77] While it is not to suggest that the CJEU would have arrived at a different conclusion if the intended language regime was to exclude English, there is certainly something different about the character of the dispute when it readily permits the exclusion of languages that are perceived to be less important to the economic objectives of patent law.

The impact of permitting a language regime that proceeds with three choices presents an implied hierarchy of languages in European patent law while further embedding an internal market-dependent understanding of patents. It is important to recognise, however, that language regimes are not always this contentious. The language regime of the EPO has been German, French, and English since its inception and has generally avoided any controversy for this structure. The fact that these issues have emerged in the context of the EPUE then indicates that there is something materially different in how the relationship between Member States, the EU, and patent law is being configured or constructed through the enhanced cooperation process. If the objective was to provide a competitive patent framework from an international perspective, there were suggestions that English as the sole language would have been altogether less controversial.[78] There is, again, a recurring sense that the exclusion of Italian and Spanish stands out as something that would never happen to English, French, or German. The EPUE regime could have been designed around French and German and legitimately, like with Spanish and Italian, excluded English. Yet there is clearly something else in the contextual

77 Arguing that the language disputes could have been raised in relation to any EU Member State, Steve Peers, 'The Constitutional Implications of the EU Patent' (2011) 9(1) ECLR 251; arguing that only English should be used in the EPUE to minimise any potential discrimination: Ceyhun Necati Pehlivan, 'The Creation of a Single European Patent System: From Dream to (Almost) Reality' (2012) 34(7) EIPR 458.

78 'In a globalized world and a highly-integrated Union, in light of the increasing intermingling of languages, in spite of the legitimate interests of protecting Europe's individual regions and cultures, the time has come in which at least the economic and commercial sector should be run in a single language: English'. Christoph M Sielmann, *Governing Difference: Internal and External Differentiation in European Union Law* (Nomos 2019) 91.

experience of patent law development – political, legal, cultural – that suggests that the CJEU would not have endorsed a regime that excluded English. What it means for actors, in this case the EU Member States, to meaningfully participate in a legal process can therefore never be reduced simply to formalist or technical understandings of procedure. This is perhaps further obscured in patent law due to the narrow economic framing which serves to insulate these design choices from their broader social and political context.

2.3.3 Exploring the institutions of the interface: The Unified Patent Court

2.3.3.1 Establishing the court and its legal structure

The precise structure of the UPC changed throughout its drafting history, with the UPC currently representing a more moderate proposal for a specialised court that is firmly within the EU court system and subject to oversight by the CJEU.[79] The early drafts of the UPC were more radical in that it was intended to form its own closed system, which was an attempt at removing the CJEU jurisdiction in patent issues.[80] Given that one of the explicit motives for introducing a specialised court for patent law was increased efficiency,[81] concerns over CJEU jurisdiction and potential delays were understandable. The CJEU's timeline for cases and case backlog appeared to be the motivation for trying to exclude or minimise its oversight.[82] The court structure and its functioning are core elements in realising the more efficient patent climate that the EPUE was intended to create,[83] specifically connected to the current difficulties that characterise European cross-border patent litigation with the delays from torpedo litigation and *lis pendens*.[84]

The UPC Agreement was, however, modified after *Opinion 1/09* to include the CJEU as the terminal court of appeal for matters arising under the EPUE.[85] The extensive reliance on non-EU law in the EPUE agreements also raised concerns about the role (and legitimacy) of the CJEU as a final court of appeal.[86] This was reflected specifically in the issue of how the CJEU would interpret the primacy of

79 Agreement on Unified Patent Court (2013/C 175/01).

80 Alfredo Ilardi, *The New European Patent* (Bloomsbury 2015) 80.

81 Luke McDonagh, *European Patent Litigation in the Shadow of the Unified Patent Court* (Edward Elgar 2016) 167.

82 Though noting that this is no longer the case, with EU courts making serious progress with the backlog and that expansions between 2015 and 2019 should permanently address this: Nigel Foster, *EU Law Directions* (OUP 2018) 67.

83 Luke McDonagh, *European Patent Litigation in the Shadow of the Unified Patent Court* (Edward Elgar 2016) 167.

84 Defining *lis pendens* and the impact: Stefan Luginbuehl, *European Patent Law: Towards a Uniform Interpretation* (Edward Elgar 2011) 48; defining torpedo litigation and its broader impact: Marketa Trimble, *Global Patents: Limits of Transnational Enforcement* (OUP 2012) 55.

85 Paragraph 66, Opinion 1/09.

86 Joseph Kenneth Yarsky, 'Hastening Harmonisation in EU Patent Law through a Preliminary Reference Power' (2017) 40(1) Boston College International and Comparative Law Review 180.

EU law,[87] especially as the EU is a party to the EPC, which is then incorporated through the EPUE agreements.[88] The UPC, for the patents that it has jurisdiction over,[89] will decide on the validity and infringement of EPUEs in respect of the entire territory covered by the enhanced cooperation participants.[90] There are two issues with the jurisdiction of the UPC, though both are related to the boundaries of the UPC and how this positions the court moving forward. The issue of jurisdiction is important because of the transition period, prompting discussion about how this potentially relegates the UPC to the periphery as an optional court with shared jurisdiction throughout this (potentially extensive) transition.[91]

The transition period is actually an important opportunity to strengthen the standing and legitimacy of the UPC in the long term and ensure that European patent law remains responsive to the interests of varied stakeholders. The transition period represents an opportunity for the UPC to demonstrate the competence and effectiveness of the decentralised structure and build precedent, but also in more concrete legal terms through the preliminary reference system and further contribute to harmonisation in EU patent law.[92] For harmonisation specifically, the transition period is a chance for the UPC to present itself as a stable forum to ensure its success post-transition period and to generate user trust in its (almost) Pan-EU jurisdiction. Yet this question of legitimacy, effectiveness, or responsiveness to patent system users is not necessarily an issue unique to the UPC and seems common to any newly introduced court (specialised or otherwise).

There are some limitations to the use of preliminary references to promote harmonisation and ensure wider participation in the development trajectory of European patent law through the UPC.[93] And yet preliminary references cannot be the sole mechanism for ensuring a balanced development of international patent law. Preliminary references have been discussed as producing clarifications and certainty in law essentially at random,[94] the clarifications are limited to specific and

87 Though concerns about the CJEU and primacy of EU law are present outside of intellectual property, Diana-Urania Galetta, *Procedural Autonomy of EU Member States: Paradise Lost? A Study on the "Functionalized Procedural Competence" of EU Member States* (Springer 2010) 75.

88 Winfried Tilmann, 'Article 21' in Winfried Tilmann and Clemens Plassmann (eds) *Unified Patent Protection in Europe: A Commentary* (OUP 2018) 455.

89 While the jurisdiction will eventually be expansive, the opt-out potential and the transition period impact this: Article 3 (scope of application) and Article 83 (transitional regime) UPC Agreement.

90 'Consequently, a European patent with unitary effect should only be limited, transferred or revoked, or lapse, in respect of all the participating Member States'. Regulation No. 1257/2012.

91 Nicholas Fox, 'Brevets Sans Frontières: How Much Litigation Will Actually Take Place in the Unified Patent Court?' (2018) 40(2) EIPR 86.

92 On the general use of the preliminary reference procedure to gradually clarify specific areas of law, Folkert G Wilman, 'A Decade of Private Enforcement of Intellectual Property Rights under IPR Enforcement Directive 2004/48: Where Do We Stand? (And Where Might We Go?)' 42(4) ELR 530.

93 Though again, the limitations of the preliminary reference system also appear in other areas of intellectual property. See: Morten P Broberg and Niels Fenger, *Preliminary References to the European Court of Justice* (OUP 2010) 185.

94 Fabrizio Vismara, 'The Role of the Court of Justice of the European Communities in the Interpretation of Multilingual Texts' in Barbara Pozzo and Valentina Jacometti (eds) *Multilingualism and the Harmonisation of European Law* (Kluwer 2006) 63.

narrow areas,[95] and that the preliminary reference process itself can involve lengthy waiting periods.[96] Specific to the UPC, however, is that the preliminary reference system would necessarily be shaped by the more technology-specific dimensions of the EPUE (and the transition period more broadly). Here, the receptiveness of industry (or lack of receptiveness) to the untested patent environment would mean that preliminary references would likely only appear well outside this transition period and could not form part of the UPC's early competence/legitimacy building.[97] The degree to which different industries accept the EPUE would correspond with a greater or lesser potential that cases would emerge, questions of law would be raised, and preliminary references would eventually be requested. The uncertainty which is inherent to this approach of ensuring responsive and adaptive patent law also informs how much litigation the UPC system will actually see in this transition period. At least initially, the actual amount of litigation seen in the UPC was questioned in academic work and the early caseload has been fairly modest.[98] Particularly in the transition period, the moderate caseload has generally been linked to industry-specific uptake and the fact that national patents are initially not part of the UPC jurisdiction.[99]

So at least during the transition period, the apparently broad jurisdiction of the UPC is, in practice, relatively limited.[100] The limited activities of the UPC, especially with the coexisting national and international methods of patent protection, mean that the UPC has an important period of reflection during which any issues can be addressed. Though issues would remain about which stakeholders would be central in this process of reflection and how this impacts effective participation, the transition period does at least provide a space for competing values and developing an emergent institutional identity. From this, the UPC has time to further develop its relationships with other institutions and sources of law in a patent context. The scale of the EPUE means that while the transition period is an important opportunity for establishing legitimacy and effective participation, several elements of the UPC and EPUE structure suggest the potential for review during the transition period will be severely limited and may be primarily related to the permeable territorial scope of the EPUE.

95 Fabrizio Vismara, 'The Role of the Court of Justice of the European Communities in the Interpretation of Multilingual Texts' in Barbara Pozzo and Valentina Jacometti (eds) *Multilingualism and the Harmonisation of European Law* (Kluwer 2006) 63.

96 Interviews with Italian practitioners highlighted the broad concerns around speed: Stefania Bariatti, Ilaria Viarengo, Francesca C Villata, Sara Bernasconi, and Filippo Marchetti, 'Cross-Border Litigation Pattern – Empirical Data and Analysis' in Paul Beaumont, Mihail Danov, Katarina Trimmings, and Burcu Yüksel (eds) *Cross-Border Litigation in Europe* (Bloomsbury 2017) 182.

97 Nicholas Fox, 'Brevets Sans Frontières: How Much Litigation Will Actually Take Place in the Unified Patent Court?' (2018) 40(2) EIPR 85.

98 Nicholas Fox, 'Brevets Sans Frontières: How Much Litigation Will Actually Take Place in the Unified Patent Court?' (2018) 40(2) EIPR 85.

99 Nicholas Fox, 'Brevets Sans Frontières: How Much Litigation Will Actually Take Place in the Unified Patent Court?' (2018) 40(2) EIPR 85.

100 Nicholas Fox, 'Brevets Sans Frontières: How Much Litigation Will Actually Take Place in the Unified Patent Court?' (2018) 40(2) EIPR 85.

2.3.3.2 *Exploring the important role of institutional identity in the early years of the Unified Patent Court*

One of the major shortcomings in the UPC system is the role of ambitious timeframes for decisions, translations, and appeals – though they do, on the surface, appear to be an important part of trying to address the delays and inefficiencies that have typically characterised European patent litigation. The guidelines are generally considered to be roughly equivalent to existing systems in the EU,[101] though there are some unique institutional features of the UPC that mean these timescales take on a particular character within the soft law dimension of a specialised court. These time limits are important since they will shape the early litigation challenges and, subsequently, the identity of the UPC in demonstrating both the efficiency and effectiveness of their decisions. The industry-specific adoption of the EPUE will also be a core element in how this develops, with the potential to provide a broadly effective (and European) response to the threat of non-practicing entities to convince other industries that the court can competently deal with high-value patent issues.[102] The development of a robust institutional identity is also related to the legal foundation of the UPC, where Jaeger has argued that the stability could be further advanced by either modifying Article 257 TFEU to explicitly include international courts or by introducing a new subsection to the same effect.[103] This would have the immediate effect of legitimising the legal foundation of the court,[104] but it would also recast the harmonisation that the UPC brings. This consolidates the foundation of the court in a way that reflects positively on its decisions – and specifically the precedent it generates – by rejecting the legal fiction of transformation,[105] and instead founding the UPC on a legitimate basis of EU law.

There has also been an attempt to construct the UPC as a more conventional European court in the style of the Benelux courts, as a common court with a joint court of appeals that could be considered to have sufficient national ties to establish it as a legitimate court structure.[106] Equating the UPC with the Benelux court, despite their significant differences,[107] then appears as an attempt to rescue the legitimacy of the court. As it stands, the UPC seems to highlight the priority of establishing a European patent court and presenting the image of a harmonised patent over ensuring that the area as a whole is robust and legally resilient.

101 Nicholas Fox, 'Brevets Sans Frontières: How Much Litigation Will Actually Take Place in the Unified Patent Court?' (2018) 40(2) EIPR 89.

102 Specifically on the potential issue of non-practicing entities (NPEs): Daniel Krauspenhaar, *Liability Rules in Patent Law: A Legal and Economic Analysis* (Springer 2014) 84.

103 Thomas Jaeger, 'Reset and Go: The Unitary Patent System Post-Brexit' (2017) 48(3) IIC 280.

104 Thomas Jaeger, 'Reset and Go: The Unitary Patent System Post-Brexit' (2017) 48(3) IIC 280.

105 Paragraph 66, Opinion 1/09.

106 Thomas Jaeger, 'Reset and Go: The Unitary Patent System Post-Brexit' (2017) 48(3) IIC 281.

107 'The legal construction of the UPC according to the UPCA in its final form follows the legal construction of the Benelux Court': Andreas von Falck and Stephan Dorn, 'Article 34' in Clemens Plassman and Winfried Tilmann (eds), *Unified Patent Protection in Europe: A Commentary* (OUP 2018) 677.

One of the more abstract shortcomings of the UPC comes from the tensions in its institutional structure and the difficulties of harmonising substantive patent law within Europe. While there are provisions to ensure that there are a variety of judges that hear cases throughout the UPC structure,[108] this necessarily entails a variable set of perspectives on issues of patent law on an essentially ad hoc basis. Fundamentally, the geographic scope of the UPC and its approach to judge selection introduces some significant concerns about the transparency of European patent law as it becomes applied in the practice of the UPC. The judges hearing cases within the UPC are expected to apply, somehow consistently across the effective territory of the EPUE, a mixture of national and international law with no transparent indications as to how this would be achieved. Perhaps more concerning is that this precise mix of national and international law could not be known to the users of the patent system before the legal proceedings take place. Relying extensively on sources of law outside of an agreement is not a significant problem per se, but it does appear more contentious when this extensive referencing is combined with the unusual legal foundation of the EPUE, the difficulties in ensuring consistency throughout a changing territory,[109] and the inevitable difficulties that will face the CJEU in interpreting this to questions of law. A primary law basis, despite how difficult this would have been in negotiations, would have at least addressed these questions of legal certainty even as it would have delayed the implementation of a true EU patent even further. The CJEU will eventually be called upon to interpret the agreement (both the UPC and the EPUE), raising difficult questions about the priority (and however this is eventually reflected in actual UPC practice) of sources of law within the agreement and the need to preserve the primacy of EU law.[110] Underlying this complexity are serious concerns about the consistency of UPC jurisprudence and the transparency of how each court will construct the specific relationship between different spheres of law.

The tension here is that either outcome – whether the judges succeed in applying a specific mix of patent law appropriately and create a functioning harmonised enforcement process or fail and thus further fragment patent law in Europe – has a negative aspect to it. The impact of further fragmentation, specifically within a forum intended to address fragmentation, would have a clearly negative impact. Yet there is also the 'flattening' effect of a successful harmonisation that is perhaps just as concerning for patent law's responsiveness and representativeness. Imagining a successful harmonisation of law through the EPUE and the UPC necessarily risks a concretisation of patent norms at the international level that is unresponsive to the diversity of EU Member States and their patent environments. This dynamic mirrors the discussions that emerged around international human rights

108 Article 15, UPC Agreement.

109 Highlighted specifically in the definitions provided in the text that the coverage is those Participating Member States that have ratified the agreements at the time of grant: Article 2(a), Regulation 1257/2012.

110 Thomas Jaeger, 'Reset and Go: The Unitary Patent System Post-Brexit' (2017) 48(3) IIC 261.

law, where accepted treaties have the potential to solidify norms and reduce the flexibility available to states.[111]

The concern here is that the more resources that are put into addressing any potential fragmentation with the EPUE and the UPC, the resulting patent system moves further away from what could have been a true successor to the Community patent. Europe could have developed a system that would not have been founded on a process that marginalises Member States and privileges a handful and instead could have encouraged a more responsive and long-term development of European patent law rather than an 'emergency patchwork'.[112] This type of tension in the long-term development of European patent law reflects some more conventional discussions around the capture of courts by repeat players.[113] There needs to be a balance between the accessibility of the court and the risk that it becomes used predominantly by a specific type of patent actor located in specific Member States. Yet the retained element of national law in the EPUE and the potential for regional divisions of the UPC represent significant challenges to ensuring a degree of uniformity and responsiveness in the practice and content of European patent law. As the national law of the patent is an essential part of EPUE adjudication, the actors that make use of the UPC will be an important factor in how the jurisprudence of the UPC develops and thereby incorporate many of the same problematic elements that are also present with the preliminary reference system.

This creates something of a dissonance between the objectives of the EPUE in harmonising and simplifying European patent law with a system that encourages broad and meaningful participation. This is because it would enable distinctions in the applicable national law based on the nationality of the actor, presenting a risk that only the largest jurisdictions (with repeat players) will drive the understanding of the role of national law in the EPUE through their participation in the UPC. More generally, participation by actors from specific jurisdictions will necessarily contribute to how national law should feature in the UPC as the precise relationship between different sources of law is left essentially unclear in the UPC Agreement.[114] Just as the provisions of the EPUE appear to be more responsive to the needs of the largest patent jurisdictions, relying on adjudication to provide actual meaning as to the role of national law will result in an approach that contextually reflects

111 Laurence R Helfer, 'Intellectual Property and Human Rights: Mapping an Evolving and Contested Relationship' in Rochelle C Dreyfuss and Justine Pila (eds) *The Oxford Handbook of Intellectual Property Law* (OUP 2018) 142.

112 Thomas Jaeger, 'Reset and Go: The Unitary Patent System Post-Brexit' (2017) 48(3) IIC 284.

113 That in patent law, 'repeat players and larger firms have certain advantages in managing IP enforcement costs' that are related to portfolio size and even their *reputation* as repeat players: Ben Depoorter, 'Intellectual Property Enforcement Costs' in Ben Depoorter and Peter S Menell (eds), *Research Handbook on the Economics of Intellectual Property Law* (Vol 1, Edward Elgar 2019) 412.

114 Article 24 of the UPC Agreement provides the applicable sources of law but provides no real indications as to how these can be used to make decisions. The text states that the court will 'base its decisions on' these sources but this would appear to invite a flexible understanding of the proper role of, for example, national law.

the interests of specific EU Member States that become entrenched as principles of 'European' patent law.

2.3.4 *Permanently shifting the foundational values of new legal initiatives in Europe: Contextualising the use of enhanced cooperation*

2.3.4.1 *Issues with enhanced cooperation in producing new legal environments*

As discussed previously, the process of enhanced cooperation is outlined in Article 2 TEU and allows a minimum of nine Member States to proceed together with their own legislative projects as a last resort to overcome a complete stalling in negotiations.[115] These projects must not prejudice the rights of non-participating states.[116] The EPUE is a particular example of how enhanced cooperation projects can impact or undermine values like accountability and responsiveness, narrowing which states have the capacity to meaningfully participate in designing the content of binding obligations. Enhanced cooperation can be specifically approached from the perspective of its participants to interpret how, and to what extent, smaller Member States can effectively articulate their concerns within that process. The expansion of applicable territory to produce the EPUE effect stands out as a very particular use of enhanced cooperation, given that its previous uses have been in managing the complications of international divorces and the proposed financial transaction tax.[117] The EPUE, in contrast, results in essentially an approximation of a property right that is specifically designed to avoid the unlawful delegation of administrative or regulatory power. In terms of scope, the EPUE is a concerning expansion of the enhanced cooperation mechanism.

Rather than a niche area of cooperation that requires technical or specialist cooperation between a small number of Member States, the development of the EPUE presents a much more exclusionary model of law-making that centres the interests of the largest economic stakeholders. It is significant in this context that the UK leaving the EU was considered a fundamental threat to the project because of its market size and innovation output.[118] On the other hand, EU Member States that had actually challenged the workings of the agreement had little leverage to meaningfully change parts of the EPUE. This lack of capacity to amend the legal structure of the EPUE means that their participation or non-participation was irrelevant as long as the largest patent jurisdictions supported it. This is magnified when considering how significantly the unitary patent enhanced cooperation diverges from the earlier examples. This is not the minimum nine states required by Article 20

115 Article 20, TEU.
116 Article 20, TEU.
117 On divorce: Jan-Jaap Kuipers, 'The Law Applicable to Divorce as Test Ground for Enhanced Cooperation' (2012) 18(2) ELJ 202; on the proposed financial transactions tax: Joachim Englisch, John Vella, and Anzhela Yevgenyeva, 'The Financial Transaction Tax Proposal Under the Enhanced Cooperation Procedure: Legal and Practical Considerations' (2013) 2 British Tax Review 224.
118 Aisling McMahon, 'Brexit and the Unitary Patent Package: A Further Compromised Future?' (2018) 15(2) Scripted 181.

and nor is the 15 states involved in the divorce cooperation. The EPUE is all but two Member States, creating a legal regime that necessarily affects the functioning of the internal market and thereby has some influence on all Member States regardless of whether they participate or not.

It is important to recognise that, from an institutional perspective, the structure of the UPC does at least attempt to integrate the interests of all the participating Member States. It does this by establishing specialist divisions and regional divisions in a geographically distributed way.[119] Brexit, and the UK leaving the EU, fundamentally impacted the implementation of the EPUE since London was to be the host of a technical division.[120] This was further undermined by significant concerns about the legal basis on which the UK could participate in enhanced cooperation, given that they were no longer a Member State.[121] But even in this attempt at a distributed approach, the Central Divisions are located in – as they should be – the states most connected to these industries. Nevertheless, this does demonstrate clearly who the key stakeholders are in European patent law and who is important for the trajectory of European patent law.[122] Here, there is a particular tension between a patent system that maximises the economic potential of industry (and is directly embedded in the industry context) and one which provides an appropriately inclusive environment that is both accountable and responsive to the needs of all participants.

The cultural dimensions of the legal challenges around languages have been criticised as irrelevant to the actual functioning of patent law,[123] though patents have a particular relationship to text and textual documents that highlights the distinct importance of machine translations within the EPUE system.[124] The issue here is not simply that language was the flashpoint in the negotiation of the EPUE and then (legally) resolved, but that there is a continued lack of attention as to how the use of language within the EPUE serves to further establish a sense of centre and periphery in European patent law that is overlooked by an economic-focused analysis. The patent specification is the primary way in which the protected innovation is demarcated, and so the modes and uses of language are fundamentally connected

119 Annex II, Agreement on a Unified Patent Court. Available at <https://www.unified-patent-court.org/sites/default/files/upc-agreement.pdf>.

120 ibid; though discussed briefly in the context of patent litigation volume: Jorge L Contreras, Fabian Gaessler, Christian Helmers, and Brian J Love, 'Litigation of Standards-Essential Patents in Europe' (2017) 32(4) Berkeley Technology Law Journal 1467.

121 Edwin Parks, 'The European Unified Patent Court and UK Assumptions on Its Post-Brexit Patent Litigation' in Prinz von Sachsen Gessaphe, Karl August, Juan J Garcia Blesa, and Nils Szuka (eds), *Legal Implications of Brexit* (MV Wissenschaft 2018) 257.

122 Paragraphs 28 and 29, C-147/13 *Spain v Council* 2015.

123 The suggestion has been made that the argument that a narrower language regime is discriminatory could equally be applied to any EU language *outside* of Spain and Italy's proposed five languages: Steve Peers, 'The Constitutional Implications of the EU Patent' (2011) 9(1) ECLR 255.

124 See generally: Siva Thambisetty, 'The Construction of Legitimacy in European Patent Law' (2017) 3 IPQ 221, 222.

to the cultural and social background of the invention.[125] Writing patent specifications is difficult enough in a native language,[126] especially in certain industries like software development,[127] because it requires an inventor to accurately and concisely describe what exactly the invention is. By relying on machine translations and only producing human translations when infringement is alleged,[128] smaller businesses (and in particular SMEs) within those territories are profoundly disadvantaged because they have additional barriers to establishing a clear image of the state of the art. This is exacerbated by the concerns around exploitative litigation as seen in the US,[129] and in the context of the EU could lead to companies in smaller states receiving notifications of infringement and pressure to licence. With only a machine translation as to the actual scope of the patent in their language, the business or individual would have to commence legal proceedings to then have access to a true, human-translated version of the patent unless they proactively pay for a translation themselves.

The efficiency of a single application to cover the majority of the territory is certainly challenged if the result is a much more convoluted enforcement system that opens itself to the type of aggressive patent litigation that has characterised the US market for some time.[130] The concern here is not simply that the reliance on machine translation merely defers the cost to a later stage of the patent lifecycle, but that it specifically disadvantages smaller EU Member States in a way that is not the case with Western European Member States. In these spaces, innovators must rely on machine translations when investing and producing a product in an area of law that is so specifically reliant on the actual text (and associated

125 On the central importance of the patent specification (as well as its limits in specific industries such as software): Julie E Cohen and Mark A Lemley, 'Patent Scope and Innovation in the Software Industry' (2001) 89(1) California Law Review 24, 25.

126 Hanns Ullrich, 'National, European and Community Patent Protection: Time for Reconsideration' (2006) EUI Working Papers, No 2006/41. 36. < https://ideas.repec.org/p/erp/euilaw/p0070.html>.

127 Notorious for difficulties in enablement and disclosure: Andrew Chin, 'Computational Complexity and the Scope of Software Patents' (1998) 39(1) Jurimetrics 26.

128 Emphasising that after a transition period, machine translations are expected to be of sufficient quality to be used generally: Aline A Larroyed, 'Machine Translation and Disclosure of Patent Information' (2018) 49 IIC 763, 777; with reimbursements for limited classes of applicants for translations produced in the registering of a patent: Article 5, Council Regulation No. 1260/2012; and provisions for either the court or the defendant to request a translation of the patent into either the language of the place of alleged infringement or the domicile of the defendant: Article 4.1, 4.2 Council Regulation No. 1260/2012.

129 Jiaqing Lu, 'The Myths and Facts of Patent Troll and Excessive Payment: Have Non-Practicing Entities (NPEs) Been Overcompensated?' (2012) 47(4) Business Economics 234.

130 The issue was highlighted as a potential in the report commissioned by the UK Intellectual Property Office: Luke McDonagh, 'Exploring Perspectives of the Unified Patent Court and the Unitary Patent Within the Business and Legal Communities' (2014) UKIPO 5, 26. <https://assets.publishing.service.gov.uk/government/uploads/system/uploads/attachment_data/file/328035/UPC_Study.pdf>; the different 'styles' of patent drafting internationally can also influence the ease with which it can be translated accurately by machines: Aline A Larroyed, 'Machine Translation and Disclosure of Patent Information' (2018) 49 IIC 763, 780.

conventions of specification writing) of a document.[131] There is also the issue of the machine translations themselves. Despite the understanding that they would be fully operational in time for the implementation of the EPUE, the quality remains extremely variable.[132] The issue is that patent law requires comprehensive understanding and accurate translation because it is the foundation of a property claim. Even in English, if a reader only understood 90% of the terms found in the specification (much higher than the three out of ten rating the Hungarian translation was given by some researchers),[133] the full disclosure of the working of the invention is impaired at best and, at worst, the understanding of what the invention is at all could become impossible.

This sense of marginalisation and how the EPUE centres the interests of specific Member States requires a more critical investigation into the EPUE as a legal interface. Crucially, this type of perspective is not reflected in the way that patent harmonisation is discussed in Europe. It is through the vocabulary of participation and transparency that these tensions become clear and allow them to be distinctly articulated. More than this, the EPUE and UPC can be seen as an unfortunate turning point in European law and very clearly mark a break in the character of legal projects undertaken through the enhanced cooperation mechanism and what this could mean for the EU in the long term. The resulting European patent law is then, in the course of its development, producing a framework that is less responsive to the needs of specific Member States and yet legitimises exactly this type of negotiating dynamic.

2.3.4.2 Distinguishing the use of enhanced cooperation in a patent law context

What is concerning about how the EPUE minimises the ability for smaller states to have meaningful input in the substantive design of the patent is that this is a fundamental feature of enhanced cooperation. It is important to recognise that participation is an issue in many systems of law, and even the ordinary legislative procedure in the EU does not require unanimous voting.[134] Yet enhanced cooperation presents a slightly different negotiating dynamic. The use of enhanced cooperation to address a negotiating impasse has been used a handful of times (including the EPUE),[135] though it is this emphasis on this mechanism as a last resort that distinguishes

131 Siva Thambisetty, 'The Construction of Legitimacy in European Patent Law' (2017) 3 IPQ 223.

132 Specifically on the low quality of translation from Czech and Finnish: Kluwer Patent Blog, 'Translating the Unitary Patent I: "Laminated Jealous Glass"' (*Wolters Kluwer*, 18 December 2014) <http://patentblog.kluweriplaw.com/2014/12/18/translating-the-unitary-patent-i-laminated-jealous-glass/>.

133 Kluwer Patent Blog, 'Translating the Unitary Patent I: "Laminated Jealous Glass"' (Wolters Kluwer, 18 December 2014) <http://patentblog.kluweriplaw.com/2014/12/18/translating-the-unitary-patent-i-laminated-jealous-glass/>.

134 On the qualified majority required in the European Parliament (though specifically in the context of environmental issues): Christian Zuidema, *Decentralization in Environmental Governance: A Post-Contingency Approach* (Routledge 2017) 167.

135 Bernd Martenczuk, 'Enhanced Cooperation: The Practice of Ad Hoc Differentiation in the EU Since the Lisbon Treaty' (2013) 66(3) Studia Diplomatica 86.

these participation concerns from the more general ordinary legislative process. Enhanced cooperation is intended to produce a specific cooperation between participating states without prejudicing the interests of non-participating states. Yet, with the EPUE, the impact on substantive patent law more fundamentally will necessarily extend beyond the participating states. This is also implicitly recognised in the transition period and provides a sense that the EPUE *is* the future of European patent law. The expectations in the ordinary legislative process are at least more clearly communicated, where a two-thirds majority means that Member States who are not part of this majority will inevitably be affected. However, enhanced cooperation is explicitly presented as a mechanism that must not prejudice the interests of non-participating states, of a 'coming together' of like-minded Member States, which is very much not the expectation in the ordinary EU law-making process.

Enhanced cooperation was first used in the context of divorce, a cooperation of states to facilitate the treatment of international divorces in 2010 that responds to the specific legal dimensions of marriages and property that have an international character.[136] The focus here is the individual and minimising the difficulties of resolving cross-border issues between individuals. The legal impact of the enhanced cooperation in the context of divorce is, therefore, from a broader perspective, relatively contained with very defined boundaries and generally limited in its structural impact on the EU legal environment it operates within. While there is great diversity in the states as to their approach to divorce,[137] it is not an issue of national economic scale.

The proposed financial transaction tax is another enhanced cooperation project specifically aimed at ensuring the proper taxation of financial services across the EU.[138] The lack of a harmonised approach to a financial transaction tax, at both an economic and conceptual level,[139] highlights the benefits of a novel cooperation between a small number of states to facilitate experimentation on complex cross-border issues. This is reinforced by the diversity of how the proposed financial transaction tax would function amongst EU Member States.[140] The structural impact of the enhanced cooperation is fairly limited in this context, though it does provide a model of how a closer (and more experimental) cooperation between states could serve as a foundation for later EU-level implementation that involves

136 Katharina Boele-Woelki, 'To Be, or Not to Be: Enhanced Cooperation in International Divorce Law Within the European Union' (2008) 39 Victoria University of Wellington Law Review 779, 782.

137 Specifically on the more accessible or more restrictive approaches found between different countries: Daniela A Kroll and Dirk Leuffen, 'Enhanced Cooperation in Practice: An Analysis of Differentiated Integration in EU Secondary Law' (2015) 22(3) Journal of European Public Policy 359.

138 For a broad overview of the progress of enhanced cooperation in this context: Caroline Heber, *Enhanced Cooperation and European Tax Law* (OUP 2021) 63.

139 Specifically discussing Macron postponing discussions regarding the financial transaction tax until after Brexit to prevent a huge move of businesses to London: Caroline Heber, *Enhanced Cooperation and European Tax Law* (OUP 2021) 63.

140 Robert Böttner, *The Constitutional Framework for Enhanced Cooperation in EU Law* (Brill 2021) 56.

all EU Member States. There is also, at a more abstract level, a sense that a financial transaction tax is conceptually specific and targeted with a clear motivation and a straightforward means of implementation.

In contrast, the EPUE is both wider in its structural impact on the broader EU environment and its focus is decidedly much more conceptually broad. The financial transaction tax certainly demonstrates the potential of greater cooperation and a more harmonised approach in terms of achieving a specific objective, yet the EPUE differs somewhat here too. The EPUE appears to skip this testing or experimentation of cooperation on a smaller scale and instead moves straight towards fundamental structural changes in the functioning of patent law in the EU. It represents a successful example of law-making in which the interests of small dissenting states can be overlooked as long as the states with the largest economic interests agree. As such, at a structural and procedural level, the development of the EPUE is distinctly unresponsive to the needs of EU Member States beyond a small group of economically important, Western European, countries. Even in terms of implementation, the legal structure of an instrument to deal with international divorces or a financial transaction tax appears to be relatively straightforward. The EPUE, however, lacks this type of immediately identifiable legal instrument – or rather, the obvious legal instrument for the creation of a property right would be a treaty instead of an ersatz patent that is enlarged (but not granted) by an agreement.

The key to the enhanced cooperation process is that the legal projects arising from it should not prejudice the rights and interests of non-participating states and remain open for participation from the non-participating states.[141] While there is an ongoing debate and a variety of opinions regarding the prejudicing of non-participating states,[142] the significance of the EPUE project must carry with it a higher standard when assessing whether it prejudices the rights of non-participating states. The EPUE moves so clearly beyond the scope of the other enhanced cooperation projects and fundamentally impacts the internal market itself, producing a dissonance between states which do and do not have the ability to meaningfully influence the legal content of these obligations. It is, therefore, appropriate that we assess the impact on non-participating states more critically, particularly from a more participative perspective, than that which would be employed with more niche or individual cooperations between states (though it is apparent that the CJEU does not agree with such a differentiated standard as discussed in the context of the Spanish and Italian legal challenges).

Allowing Member States to cooperate in areas that touch competences of the EU and shape the internal market finds clear parallels in the international multilateral context.[143] One example would be the description of 'country club' multilateralism

141 Alfredo Ilardi, *The New European Patent* (Hart 2015) 30.

142 The CJEU concluded that enhanced cooperation did not breach Article 326 TFEU that requires that enhanced cooperation does not undermine the internal market or economic, social, and political cohesion between Member States: C-274/11 *Spain & Italy v Council*.

143 Peers, concluding that the CJEU was appropriately placed to authorise enhanced cooperation because intellectual property is an internal market area (and is therefore a shared competence)

which refers to like-minded states that cooperate internationally.[144] While this is presented as states with similar interests cooperating, the impact on smaller countries becomes clear as they are increasingly pressured to accept higher standards and the approaches of larger economies to make gains in international trade.[145] The impact of enhanced cooperation in this context similarly works to reshape the dynamic of patent law in Europe to fit the interests of the largest economic actors of the EU without requiring, or encouraging, the participation of smaller states.

2.3.4.3 Fundamental shifts in the law-making process and impaired participation

The issue with centring the requirement that enhanced cooperation be a 'last resort' is that the EPUE presents an example of law-making that undermines the fundamental mission of the EU that has distinguished it from other multilateral projects.[146] By requiring a complete impasse and yet authorising the EPUE, enhanced cooperation essentially becomes a mechanism that can be used to overcome negotiating difficulties in the ordinary course of legislative development rather than an exceptional response to a complete breakdown in communication. This distorts the fundamental essence of the enhanced cooperation mechanism. It sets an example for future negotiations that objections, in particular those by smaller states, can be overlooked as enhanced cooperation provides a ready alternative, a different forum, to press their objectives. The very existence of this alternative and its use in the EPUE has been discussed as potentially impacting the character of EU legal development,[147] and could affect the readiness with which the smaller Member States try to articulate their concerns within these processes.

Particularly with projects that involve larger Member States, the departure of the EPUE from the previous enhanced cooperation projects (even just in terms of the number of parties involved) means that the EPUE's design continued relatively unimpaired despite these initial legal challenges. It is important to recognise that the impact of the EPUE in enhanced cooperation can be seen not just from a volume perspective in the number of parties, but also from a disciplinary perspective

that also falls outside the exclusive scope of the Common Commercial Policy: Steve Peers, 'The Constitutional Implications of the EU Patent' (2011) 9(1) ECLR 251.

144 On the development of a 'country club' approach in multilateralism though specifically in the context of intellectual property: Peter K Yu, 'ACTA and Its Complex Politics' (2011) 3 WIPOJ 1.

145 One understanding of small states through realism theory is that they are best functioning essentially as satellite states to larger states: Abelraouf Mostafa Galal, 'External Behavior of Small States in Light of Theories of International Relations' (2019) 5(1) Review of Economics and Political Science 38, 39.

146 On the enduring role of consensus in European legislation (as well as the increasing conflicts that provoke a more majoritarian dimension): Stéphanie Novak, Olivier Rozenberg, and Selma Bendjaballah 'Enduring the Consensus: Why the EU Legislative Process Stays the Same' (2020) 43 Journal of European Integration 475.

147 That the use of enhanced cooperation in this coercive manner 'tilts the EU away from solidaristic norms and practices': Matthias Lamping, 'Enhanced Cooperation: A Proper Approach to Market Reintegration in the Field of Unitary Patent Protection?' (2011) 42(8) IIC 879.

as well. Future EU legislation and the ways in which smaller Member States participate will necessarily be conducted in the shadow of the expansive disciplinary approach that has been signalled with the EPUE. In endorsing the EPUE package, the EU institutions have expanded the scope of projects that can be implemented using enhanced cooperation and legitimised projects that have a more complex relationship to the functioning of the internal market. A perhaps more interesting question would be, given the fact that the EPUE considers an intellectual property right, which disciplines would actually be disallowed in an enhanced cooperation project?

This expansive approach to enhanced cooperation also does not clearly distinguish between participating and non-participating states in the practical impact of the EPUE. This means that the issue of participation is so one-sided that the non-participating states are impacted regardless of their position within the system. This is not a small number of states creating a specialised solution to a specific legal problem but is, instead, a majority of states that are legitimised by their economic size establishing what is essentially a new property right. The development of the EPUE will necessarily impact Poland's innovation environment in a variety of direct and indirect ways.[148] Not participating in the EPUE (though joining the EPUE, Poland has not ratified the court structure and, therefore, the means to enforce these patents) does little to meaningfully shape or help create a more responsive EPUE. Likewise, joining the EPUE leaves little scope for shaping its functioning because the objectives have already been clearly defined by the largest patent jurisdictions in Europe. Exploring the EPUE and its development from a perspective that centres participation rather than the potential gains of harmonisation has been an experience with a recurring sense of inevitability. That somehow, the EPUE simply makes visible a more fundamental dissonance between the political and legal autonomy of larger and smaller Member States.

The difficulties in articulating the interests of smaller states are not simply occurring in the context of intellectual property and the issues within the EPUE. Instead, they reflect the broader climate of the EU in 2025. This involves sustained criticism, specifically about the relationship between the EU institutions and smaller states,[149] but also a threat to the EU itself that is represented (though not totally

148 As far back as the 1970s, the economic risk for smaller states from the unitary patent driving out innovative activity has been discussed (notably both Czechia and Poland): Aurora Plomer, 'The Unified Patent Court and the Transformation of the European Patent System' (2020) 51 IIC 794, 795; though also specifically Poland's political climate is not conducive to the unitary patent project (with 'protection of Polish economy, strong Euroscepticism'): Bird & Bird, 'The Unitary Patent and the Unified Patent Court – Poland' (*Bird & Bird*) <https://www.twobirds.com/en/in-focus/unitary-patents-and-the-unified-patent-court/up-and-upc-interactive-map/poland>.

149 Specifically Hungary, though discussing more broadly Central European states and constitutionalism: Michel Rosenfeld, Wojciech Sadurski, and Roberto Toniatti, 'Central and Eastern European Constitutionalism a Quarter Century After the Fall of the Berlin Wall: Introduction to the Symposium' (2015) 13 (1) ICON 119, 121.

captured) by Brexit.[150] There is a legal tension between what is seen as a Western European bias in the EU from the smaller Central or Eastern states that has resulted in a variety of conflicts.[151] In the context of intellectual property and the EPUE, what is significant is that the tension is not being played out in the more open forum of the ordinary EU legislative process but instead through a more convoluted and closed process that minimises the interests of smaller Member States.

Hungary and Poland are two clear examples of this broader tension with the value of participation in international patent law. While Poland is not participating in the EPUE, Hungary was the host of the training program for the judges of the UPC.[152] Both of these countries have a complex relationship with the EU that involves a financial dimension and has generally centred on challenges to the social, rather than economic, objectives of the EU.[153] The conflict in Ukraine has added to the complex positioning of specific EU Member States as it has both reinforced the importance of European solidarity and enabled an additional avenue for political alignment (in rhetoric, if not practice).[154] The geographically distributed nature of the UPC is one way of trying to address this more political aspect of intellectual property harmonisation, of an expansive and inclusive scope, particularly with the capacity for developing regional divisions. Yet the reality is that certain regional divisions (if they are even established) will be significantly underused compared with those in Western Europe and will necessarily occupy a more peripheral role in the overall development of EPUE jurisprudence. As a result, the EPUE will remain resistant to interests from outside the major patent jurisdictions and minimise the opportunities for participation from smaller EU Member States.

2.4 Conclusion

The EPUE is an important development for Europe because it represents the next level of patent cooperation and harmonisation, intended to essentially bring patents within the same functional scope as trademarks and copyright. Patent rights and intellectual property more generally have been highlighted by the EU as an

150 On the broader challenges of sustaining the EU project: Leonardo Scuira, 'Brexit Beyond Borders: Beginning of the EU Collapse and Return to Nationalism' (2017) 70(2) Journal of International Affairs 115.

151 Tomáš Valášek, 'Why Can't the EU's West and East Work as One?' Carnegie Europe 1–2. <https://carnegieendowment.org/files/10-8-19_Valasek_EU_East_West.pdf>.

152 Edward Nodder, 'Training Centre for UPC Judges Opens in Budapest' (*Bristows*) <https://www.bristowsupc.com/latest-news/Training-Centre-for-UPC-judges-opens-in-Budapest/>.

153 One particular example is the EU negotiations over asylum seekers: John Chalmers and Gabriela Baczynska 'Hungary's Orban Rejects Criticism Over Rule of Law, Says He Is a "Freedom Fighter"' (*Reuters*, 25 September 2020) <https://www.reuters.com/article/us-hungary-orban-interview-idUSKCN26G26Q>.

154 Lisa O'Carroll, 'EU Agrees €50bn Package for Ukraine as Victor Orbán Bows to Pressure' (*The Guardian*, 1 February 2024) <https://www.theguardian.com/world/2024/feb/01/eu-agrees-50bn-package-for-ukraine-as-viktor-orban-bows-to-pressure>.

important element in the future economic growth of the region[155] – particularly in light of the negative economic consequences of the COVID-19 pandemic.[156] A significant part of the EPUE, as well as the earlier CPC and the developed harmonisation of the EPC, has been improving the competitiveness of both the European patent system and the position of SMEs specifically.[157] Fragmentation within the European patent system and the difficulty of substantively harmonising the enforcement of national patent rights have consistently distinguished the European approach to patents from that of other major jurisdictions like the US and Japan.[158] Yet the EPUE also has a broader importance beyond what it provides in the discussion of harmonisation in European patent law. The legal structure of the EPUE reinforces the administrative nature of patent law by being specifically designed to avoid the *Meroni* doctrine. From a perspective that emphasises the administrative foundation of patent law, the chapter has developed an analysis that draws on values that typically appear in administrative law scholarship. Specifically for the development of the EPUE, the chapter focused on how participation – and how the system supports or impairs – features in European patent law. These values manifest in the development of patent law, the structure and capacity of the specialised court, and the construction of specific patent law mechanisms. The EPUE represents the creation of a new interface in patent law, bringing together various national interests and actors in the pursuit of a harmonised legal framework.

The broader legal context also highlights the usefulness of considering the EPUE from a perspective that emphasises the interactive qualities of legal frameworks. This is because, particularly in the European context, patent law is constituted from several overlapping interfaces. The creation of a new interface within this overlapping environment highlights the importance of these contextual interactions, precisely because the existing interfaces are a mix of national and international, European and global. It is in this overlap that values such as participation and accountability are useful tools of interpretation. The significance of the national elements of the EPUE in the broader legal context is unusual due to the way that the EPUE was developed. The development of the EPUE has been driven by the

155 EPO, 'Unitary Patent Expected to Boost Trade and Investment in the EU, New Study Shows' (14 November 2017, *EPO*) <https://www.epo.org/news-events/news/2017/20171114_fr.html>.

156 Carolina Arias Burgos and Nathan Wajsman, 'Economic Impact of COVID-19 Crisis in IPR-Intensive Industries' (May 2021, EUIPO Discussion Paper) <https://euipo.europa.eu/tunnel-web/secure/webdav/guest/document_library/observatory/documents/reports/2021_Economic_Impact_COVID19/2021_Economic_impact_of_COVID19_crisis_in_IPR_intensive_industries_study_FullR_en.pdf>.

157 EU Commission, 'Internal Market, Industry, Entrepreneurship and SMEs: Unitary Patent' (*EU Commission*) <https://ec.europa.eu/growth/industry/strategy/intellectual-property/patent-protection-eu/unitary-patent_en>.

158 Specifically highlighting the cost of patent protection in the US and Japan compared to the proposed EPUE fees: Thierry Breton, 'Intellectual Property: Statement by EU Internal Market Commissioner Thierry Breton Welcoming the Provisional Application of the Unitary Patent' (19 January 2022, *EU Commission*) <https://ec.europa.eu/commission/presscorner/detail/en/STATEMENT_22_426>.

Member States and has been implemented through the enhanced cooperation procedure rather than the ordinary legislative process of the EU institutions. There is a specific relationship between the use of the enhanced cooperation mechanism and the more political aspects of legislative cooperation, interesting since it was precisely due to the political difficulty of harmonisation that led to enhanced cooperation. As a result, the EPUE provides a unique example of a patent project that is framed by, but not necessarily constrained by, the EU legislative apparatus and centres the value of participation in European patent law. It provides a very visible, contemporary example of actors coming together from different patent histories and traditions with the aim of advancing the substantive harmonisation of patent law – though the chapter has interpreted these developments through the lens of administrative values, and for the EPUE specifically, in terms of effective participation.

Bibliography

Articles

Boele-Woelki K, 'To Be, or Not to Be: Enhanced Cooperation in International Divorce Law Within the European Union' (2008) 39 *Victoria University of Wellington Law Review* 779.

Chin A, 'Computational Complexity and the Scope of Software Patents' (1998) 39(1) *Jurimetrics* 17.

Cohen JE and MA Lemley, 'Patent Scope and Innovation in the Software Industry' (2001) 89(1) *California Law Review* 1.

Contreras JL, F Gaessler, C Helmers, and BJ Love, 'Litigation of Standards-Essential Patents in Europe' (2017) 32(4) *Berkeley Technology Law Journal* 1457.

Englisch J, J Vella and A Yevgenyeva, 'The Financial Transaction Tax Proposal Under the Enhanced Cooperation Procedure: Legal and Practical Considerations' (2013) 2 *British Tax Review* 223.

Fox N, 'Brevets Sans Frontières: How Much Litigation Will Actually Take Place in the Unified Patent Court?' (2018) 40(2) *European Intellectual Property Review* 85.

Galal AM, 'External Behavior of Small States in Light of Theories of International Relations' (2019) 5(1) *Review of Economics and Political Science* 38.

Gurgula O, M Padamczyk, and N Shemtov, 'Specialised IP Judiciary: What are the Key Elements to Consider when Establishing or Reforming an Effective IP Court?' (2022) 71(3) *GRUR International* 206.

Jaeger T, 'Reset and Go: The Unitary Patent System Post-Brexit' (2017) 48(3) *International Review of Intellectual Property and Competition Law* 254.

Kroll DA and D Leuffen, 'Enhanced Cooperation in Practice: An Analysis of Differentiated Integration in EU Secondary Law' (2015) 22(3) *Journal of European Public Policy* 353.

Kuipers JJ, 'The Law Applicable to Divorce as Test Ground for Enhanced Cooperation' (2012) 18(2) *European Law Journal* 201.

Lamping M, 'Enhanced Cooperation: A Proper Approach to Market Reintegration in the Field of Unitary Patent Protection?' (2011) 42(8) *International Review of Intellectual Property and Competition Law* 879.

Larroyed AA, 'Machine Translation and Disclosure of Patent Information' (2018) 49 *International Review of Intellectual Property and Competition Law* 763.

Lu J, 'The Myths and Facts of Patent Troll and Excessive Payment: Have Nonpracticing Entities (NPEs) Been Overcompensated?' (2012) 47(4) *Business Economics* 234.

Martenczuk B, 'Enhanced Cooperation: The Practice of Ad Hoc Differentiation in the EU Since the Lisbon Treaty' (2013) 66(3) *Studia Diplomatica* 83.
McMahon A, 'Brexit and the Unitary Patent Package: A Further Compromised Future?' (2018) 15(2) *SCRIPT-ed* 175.
Medina D, 'How the Unitary Patent Will Fragment European Patent Law' (2015) 47 *Arizona State Law Journal* 319.
Novak S, O Rozenberg, and S Bendjaballah, 'Enduring the Consensus: Why the EU Legislative Process Stays the Same' (2020) 43 *Journal of European Integration* 475.
Peers S, 'The Constitutional Implications of the EU Patent' (2011) 9(1) *European Constitutional Law Review* 229.
Pehlivan CN, 'The Creation of a Single European Patent System: From Dream to (Almost) Reality' (2012) 34(7) *European Intellectual Property Review* 453.
Plomer A, 'The Unified Patent Court and the Transformation of the European Patent System' (2020) 51 *International Review of Intellectual Property and Competition Law* 791.
Rosenfeld M, W Sadurski, and R Toniatti, 'Central and Eastern European Constitutionalism a Quarter Century After the Fall of the Berlin Wall: Introduction to the Symposium' (2015) 13(1) *International Journal of Constitutional Law* 119.
Scuira L, 'Brexit Beyond Borders: Beginning of the EU Collapse and Return to Nationalism' (2017) 70(2) *Journal of International Affairs* 109.
Thambisetty S, 'The Construction of Legitimacy in European Patent Law' (2017) 3 *Indian Philosophical Quarterly* 221.
Wilman F, 'A Decade of Private Enforcement of Intellectual Property Rights under IPR Enforcement Directive 2004/48: Where Do We Stand? (And Where Might We Go?) 42(4) *European Law Review* 509.
Yarsky JK, 'Hastening Harmonisation in EU Patent Law Through a Preliminary Reference Power' (2017) 40(1) *Boston College International and Comparative Law Review* 167.
Yu PK, 'ACTA and Its Complex Politics' (2011) 3 *WIPOJ Journal* 1.

Books

Böttner R, *The Constitutional Framework for Enhanced Cooperation in EU Law* (Brill 2021).
Broberg MP and N Fenger, *Preliminary References to the European Court of Justice* (OUP 2010).
Drahos P, *The Global Governance of Knowledge: Patent Offices and Their Clients* (CUP 2010).
Foster N, *EU Law Directions* (OUP 2018).
Galetta DU, *Procedural Autonomy of EU Member States: Paradise Lost? A Study on the "Functionalised Procedural Competence" of EU Member States* (Springer 2010).
Granieri M and A Renda, *Innovation Law and Policy in the European Union* (Springer 2012).
Heber C, *Enhanced Cooperation and European Tax Law* (OUP 2021).
Ilardi A, *The New European Patent* (Hart 2015).
Krauspenhaar D, *Liability Rules in Patent Law: A Legal and Economic Analysis* (Springer 2014).
Luginbuehl S, *European Patent Law: Towards a Uniform Interpretation* (Edward Elgar 2011).
McDonagh L, *European Patent Litigation in the Shadow of the Unified Patent Court* (Edward Elgar 2016).
Ragavan S, *Patent and Trade Disparities in Developing Countries* (OUP 2012).
Sielmann CM, *Governing Difference: Internal and External Differentiation in European Union Law* (Nomos 2019).

Stack A, *International Patent Law: Cooperation, Harmonization and an Institutional Analysis of WIPO and the WTO* (Edward Elgar 2011).

Sterckx S and J Cockbain, *Exclusions from Patentability: How Far Has the European Patent Office Eroded Boundaries?* (CUP 2012).

Trimble M, *Global Patents: Limits of Transnational Enforcement* (OUP 2012).

Zuidema C, *Decentralization in Environmental Governance: A Post-Contingency Approach* (Routledge 2017).

Chapters

Bariatti S, I Viarengo, FC Villata, S Bernasconi, and F Marchetti, 'Cross-Border Litigation Pattern - Empirical Data and Analysis' in Paul Beaumont, Mihail Danov, Katarina Trimmings, and Burcu Yüksel (eds) *Cross-Border Litigation in Europe* (Bloomsbury 2017) 169.

Burk DL, 'Patents and Related Rights: A Global Kaleidoscope' in Rochelle C Dreyfuss and Justine Pila (eds), *The Oxford Handbook of Intellectual Property Law* (OUP 2018) 461.

Depoorter B, 'Intellectual Property Enforcement Costs' in Ben Depoorter and Peter S Menell (eds), *Research Handbook on the Economics of Intellectual Property Law* (Vol 1, Edward Elgar 2019) 407.

Dimopoulos A, 'An Institutional Perspective II: The Role of the CJEU in the Unitary (EU) Patent System' in Justine Pila and Christopher Wadlow (eds) *The Unitary EU Patent System* (Bloomsbury 2015) 57.

Eeckhout P, 'The Emperor has no Clothes: Brexit and the UK Constitution' in Benjamin Martill and Uta Staiger (eds), *Brexit and Beyond: Rethinking the Futures of Europe* (UCL Press 2018) 165.

Frankel S, 'The TRIPS Agreement and Cross-Retaliation' in Susy Frankel and Meredith Kolsky Lewis (eds), *Trade Agreements at the Crossroads* (Routledge 2014) 208.

Helfer LR, 'Intellectual Property and Human Rights: Mapping an Evolving and Contested Relationship' in Rochelle C Dreyfuss and Justine Pila (eds) *The Oxford Handbook of Intellectual Property Law* (OUP 2018) 117.

Howard T, 'The Legal Framework Surrounding Patents for Living Materials' in Johanna Gibson (ed), *Patenting Lives: Life Patents, Culture and Development* (Routledge 2008) 7.

Jänich VM, 'The Territorial Dimension of Intellectual Property Law' in Karl M Meessen (ed), *Economic Law as an Economic Good: Its Rule Function and its Tool Function in the Competition of Systems* (Sellier 2009) 213.

Odell-West A, 'Exclusions in Patent Law as an Indirect Form of Regulation for New Health Technologies in Europe' in Mark L Flear, Anne-Maree Farrell, Tamara K Hervey, and Thérèse Murphy (eds), *European Law and New Health* Technologies (OUP 2013) 148.

Parks E, 'The European Unified Patent Court and UK Assumptions on its Post-Brexit Patent Litigation' in Prinz von Sachsen Gessaphe, Karl August, Juan J Garcia Blesa, and Nils Szuka (eds), *Legal Implications of Brexit* (MV Wissenschaft 2018) 245.

Petersen CS and J Schovsbo, 'Decision-Making in the Unified Patent Court: Ensuring a Balanced Approach' in Christophe Geiger, Craig Allen Nard, and Xavier Seuba (eds), *Intellectual Property and the Judiciary* (Edward Elgar 2018) 231.

Tilmann W, 'Recitals' in Winfried Tilmann and Clemens Plassmann (eds) *Unified Patent Protection in Europe: A Commentary* (OUP 2018) 83.

Tilmann W, 'Article 21' in Winfried Tilmann and Clemens Plassmann (eds) *Unified Patent Protection in Europe: A Commentary* (OUP 2018).

von Falck A and S Dorn, 'Article 34' in Clemens Plassman and Winfried Tilmann (eds), *Unified Patent Protection in Europe: A Commentary* (OUP 2018) 578.

Vismara F, 'The Role of the Court of Justice of the European Communities in the Interpretation of Multilingual Texts' in Barbara Pozzo and Valentina Jacometti (eds) *Multilingualism and the Harmonisation of European Law* (Kluwer 2006) 61.

Legislation

Agreement on a Unified Patent Court.
Article 20 TEU.
Community Patent Convention 76/76/EEC.
EPUE Regulation
European Patent Convention.
Federal Courts Improvement Act 1982.
Regulation 1257/2012.
Regulation 1260/2012.
Rules Relating to Regulation 1257 and 1260/2012.
UPC Agreement.

Cases

2011/167/EU Council Decision of 10 March 2011.
C-9/56, C-10/56 *Meroni v High Authority* [1957/1957].
C-274/11 *Kingdom of Spain v Council of the European Union.*
C-295/11 *Italy v Council of the European Union.*
C414/11.
Joined Cases C-274/11 and C-295/11.
Opinion 1/09

Other

Bird&Bird, 'The Unitary Patent and the Unified Patent Court – Poland' (*Bird&Bird*) <https://www.twobirds.com/en/in-focus/unitary-patents-and-the-unified-patent-court/up-and-upc-interactive-map/poland>.

Breton T, 'Intellectual Property: Statement by EU Internal Market Commissioner Thierry Breton Welcoming the Provisional Application of the Unitary Patent' (19 January 2022, *EU Commission*) <https://ec.europa.eu/commission/presscorner/detail/en/STATEMENT_22_426>.

Burgos CA and N Wajsman, 'Economic Impact of COVID-19 Crisis in IPR-Intensive Industries' (EUIPO Discussion Paper, May 2021) <https://euipo.europa.eu/tunnel-web/secure/webdav/guest/document_library/observatory/documents/reports/2021_Economic_Impact_COVID19/2021_Economic_impact_of_COVID19_crisis_in_IPR_intensive_industries_study_FullR_en.pdf>.

C414/11 Opinion of Advocate General Cruz Villalón.

Chalmers J and G Baczynska, 'Hungary's Orban Rejects Criticism Over Rule of Law, Says He is a "Freedom Fighter"' (*Reuters*, 25 September 2020) <https://www.reuters.com/article/us-hungary-orban-interview-idUSKCN26G26Q>.

EPO, 'European Patent Guide: 2.2' (*EPO*) <https://www.epo.org/applying/european/Guide-for-applicants/html/e/ga_c2_2.html>.

EPO, 'Unitary Patent Expected to Boost Trade and Investment in the EU, New Study Shows' (*EPO*, 14 November 2017) <https://www.epo.org/news-events/news/2017/20171114_fr.html>.

EU Commission, 'Internal Market, Industry, Entrepreneurship, and SMEs: Unitary Patent' (*EU Commission*) <https://ec.europa.eu/growth/industry/strategy/intellectual-property/patent-protection-eu/unitary-patent_en>.

Kluwer Patent Blog, 'Translating the Unitary Patent I: "Laminated Jealous Glass"' (*Wolters Kluwer*, 18 December 2014) <http://patentblog.kluweriplaw.com/2014/12/18/translating-the-unitary-patent-i-laminated-jealous-glass/>.

McDonagh L, 'Exploring Perspectives of the Unified Patent Court and Unitary Patent Within the Business and Legal Communities' (UKIPO 2014) 32 <https://assets.publishing.service.gov.uk/government/uploads/system/uploads/attachment_data/file/328035/UPC_Study.pdf>.

Nodder E, 'Training Centre for UPC Judges Opens in Budapest' (*Bristows*) <https://www.bristowsupc.com/latest-news/Training-Centre-for-UPC-judges-opens-in-Budapest/>.

O'Carroll L, 'EU Agrees €50bn Package for Ukraine as Victor Orbán Bows to Pressure' (*The Guardian*, 1 February 2024) <https://www.theguardian.com/world/2024/feb/01/eu-agrees-50bn-package-for-ukraine-as-viktor-orban-bows-to-pressure>.

Ullrich H, 'National, European and Community Patent Protection: Time for Reconsideration' (EUI Working Papers, No 2006/41, 2006) 36. <https://ideas.repec.org/p/erp/euilaw/p0070.html>.

Valášek T, 'Why Can't the EU's West and East Work as One?' Carnegie Europe 1–2. <https://carnegieendowment.org/files/10-8-19_Valasek_EU_East_West.pdf>.

3 Applying administrative values to bilateral trade agreements in patent law and beyond

Identifying a distinct 'bilateral space'

3.1 Introduction

Bilateral agreements have become an increasingly prominent aspect of the international trade environment and contribute significantly to the global trade relationships between countries.[1] Particularly with the criticisms around both the multilateral process more generally and the speed at which bilateral projects can be concluded,[2] bilateral trade agreements have been an important element in sustaining trade and cooperation between countries. Bilateralism of recent decades – specifically that which preceded the conclusion of the Uruguay Round and the crisis in multilateralism post-Cancún[3] – may have resulted in significant developments in international trade but are a continuation of a long history of bilateral agreements.[4]

Bilateral trade agreements produce a legal context in which disputes and negotiations are necessarily diffuse, emerging from context-specific legal arrangements that reflect more localised characteristics of these agreements. As such, approaching the development of modern bilateralism and the challenges of dispute settlement presents an opportunity to explore these relationships through the lens of administrative values and to question how distinct this 'bilateral space' is. What appears when analysing bilateral trade agreements from the perspective of transparency, participation, and accountability is a sense that not only are these values fundamentally interconnected, but they also remain somewhat isolated from the

1 On the sharp growth of trade agreements since the 1990s: Silvia Sopranzetti, 'Overlapping Free Trade Agreements and International Trade: A Network Approach' (2018) 41(6) The World Economy 1549.

2 'The institutional machinery of the GATT/WTO system is cumbersome and slow. Multilateral rounds take many years to negotiate, and tend to address issues agreed upon by the parties at the inception of each round.': Thomas R Howell, 'The Multilateral Trading System and Transnational Competition in Advanced Technologies: The Limits of Existing Disciplines' in Göran Marklund, Nicholas S Vonortas, and Charles W Wessner (eds), *The Innovation Imperative: National Innovation Strategies in the Global Economy* (Edward Elgar 2009) 52.

3 On the subversive impact of preferential trade agreements on the GATT obligations before Uruguay: Marcelo de Paiva Abreu, 'Developing Countries and the Uruguay Round of Trade Negotiations' (1990) Proceedings of the World Bank Annual Conference on Development Economics 1989 28.

4 On the long history of bilateral agreements (as well as the more general trends of liberalism and protectionism over time): Olivier Cattaneo, 'The Political Economy of PTAs' in Simon Lester, Bryan Mercurio, and Lorand Bartels (eds), *Bilateral and Regional Trade Agreements: Commentary and Analysis* (CUP 2015) 31.

DOI: 10.4324/9781003616856-4

same values in a multilateral context. Though the artificial separation of these values was discussed previously, agreements in the bilateral space are so grounded in their own specific legal and political context that the overlaps between the values in practice are much more prominent. Taking transparency as an example, weaknesses of transparency in a bilateral trade agreement are at once enabled by, and also produce, deficiencies in participation and accountability. The diffuse character of dispute resolution bodies in this unsettled bilateral space means that their role in bringing substantive meaning to these values is both pervasive and yet fundamentally isolated in reach.

The chapter emphasises how administrative values can be used to understand the complex structure of (and interactions within) bilateral space and how this relates to the idea of a distinct global space described in global administration.[5] This sense of contextual responsiveness also influences how, though fundamentally similar in content, the bilateral and multilateral expression of values like transparency and participation are effectively isolated in their normative impact. When meaningful participation is realised at the more systemic or multilateral level, this has a clear and presumptive impact on how patent law will develop in the broadest sense. Yet as this chapter will discuss, advancements (or more commonly, challenges) to these values in the bilateral context have an isolating effect that undermines these rare gains at the multilateral level. Though the scale of negotiation and cooperation is very different from a multilateral agreement, the way participation is supported or undermined in the bilateral context both impacts the immediate parties to the agreement and (perhaps counterintuitively) represents a more fundamental challenge to this value globally. In this, viewing these relationships and dynamic interactions through the lens of administrative values appears to complement narratives in international trade on the increasing atomisation of international trade law,[6] emphasising that trade regulation is nevertheless normative and impacted by deeply contextual, individualised relationships between states.

For a significant period of time, bilateral trade agreements considered intellectual property in a relatively general way that emphasised references to major agreements over the adoption of specific legal standards.[7] This lack of attention to intellectual property and patent law in bilateral trade mirrors the more general

5 Elisa D'Alterio, 'Judicial Regulation in the Global Space' in Sabino Cassese (ed), *Research Handbook on Global Administrative Law* (Edward Elgar 2016) 321.

6 Though in reference to international investment law, Hamdani specifically discusses the negative impact of a patchwork of individual treaties between trade partners: Khalil Hamdani, 'Panel: Process and Value of Uniform Commercial Law – Proceedings of the Congress of the United Nations Commission on International Trade Law Held on the Occasion of the Fortieth Session of the Commission' (2007) 25 <https://uncitral.un.org/sites/uncitral.un.org/files/media-documents/uncitral/en/09-83930_ebook.pdf>.

7 One more recent example would be the agreement between the Central American Association Agreement where Article 78(g) refers simply to a commitment to 'the adequate and effective protection of intellectual property rights, in accordance with international obligations in force between the parties': Article 78(g) Agreement Establishing an Association between the European Union and Its Member States, On the One Hand, and Central America on the Other; while Title VI of the same agreement

sense pre-TRIPS to these areas as the 'domain of specialists'.[8] The rapid shift from general disinterest, even in legal circles, to public protests about the provisions of specific agreements like ACTA signals that, in the right circumstances, intellectual property can reach public attention. This increase in public discussion has occurred in a context in which major trade actors like the EU increasingly conclude bilateral agreements with elaborate chapters on the treatment of intellectual property and provide very specific binding obligations. The typical critical reception of these agreements, particularly in academia, has highlighted the way in which they subject (specifically developing) countries to inappropriate standards of patent protection.[9] The question raised about these agreements is: Why would partners accept these prohibitively stringent standards in intellectual property? The obvious answer is that these agreements offer some other benefit that is being traded for and the country lacks the capacity to aggressively negotiate on content.

But what is it about the bilateral space that enables such an impairment in the ability of weaker trade partners to resist these higher standards in patent law? And this fundamentally comes down to the isolated and highly contextualised space produced by bilateral negotiations, as well as the legitimising function of a thin presumption of consent. The bilateral space presents all areas of trade as potentially the subject of regulation *and* strategic negotiation. From this, understanding how patent law is developing through bilateral agreements necessarily involves analysing how it mirrors, diverges, or is connected to the other subjects of regulation within those agreements and intellectual property more specifically. The lack of institutional safeguards in this process of development means there is no formal procedure that can be used to problematise the negotiating dynamic and its impact on the consent of each party. In the absence of strong institutional standards, the presumption that each country is a sovereign state voluntarily entering into a trade agreement that prejudices its own interests is enough to legitimise that agreement. This is not to suggest that developing countries are unable to consent to international trade agreements. Rather, the point of the chapter is to add more nuance to how we understand the process of bilateral development in a way that questions and perhaps qualifies how countries generate consent in this context. In practice, it is the isolating effect of bilateral trade that produces an entanglement of issues in transparency, accountability, and participation. There are additional concerns when considering a more institutional perspective because, even with state participation, the negotiations are conducted by a very limited range of actors and present fundamental tensions for more responsive or reflective understandings of law.

(that deals with intellectual property) simply reaffirms the binding nature of the TRIPS Agreement in Article 229.

8 Arguing that prior to the introduction of the TRIPS Agreement, intellectual property 'was still the domain of specialists and intellectual property right producers': Wenwei Guan, 'Diversified FRAND Enforcement and TRIPS Integrity' (2018) 17(1) WTR 111.

9 Muhammad Zaheer Abbas, 'India's Distinct but Opposing Patent Model Is Under Pressure: Prospects and Challenges in the Global Arena' (2024) 80(1) India Quarterly 121, 122.

This also relates to the development of 'TRIPS-Plus' and 'WTO-Plus' disciplines and their incorporation within bilateral trade agreements.[10] The WTO Agreements, while they certainly frame these agreements at a more fundamental level,[11] are still limited in the subject matter that they can cover. The tension in the bilateral space is that it involves the creation of multiple, discipline-specific interfaces that have a varying relationship to the broader framing provided by the multilateral instrument. This presents a challenge to transparency in a more abstract sense than that which appeared in Chapter 2. Rather than the formalist transparency of precisely what provisions are binding or the geographical scope of a right in practice, the type of transparency undermined in bilateral trade agreements is more closely linked to the *trajectory* of development. Bilateral trade agreements emerge from complex legal and political relationships where, in practice, it is not clear what provisions were the result of this strategic trading.[12] Bilateral agreements represent a large number of trade agreements and have been an important part of justifying global consensus for higher standards in intellectual property.[13] Yet with the lack of transparency in bilateral trade agreements,[14] this means that the values and principles that drive the process by which global consensus is legitimised become fundamentally obscured.

Section 3.2 considers how the EU strategy towards bilateral trade agreements has shifted, transitioning from an emphasis on general provisions in intellectual property towards one that requires the implementation of specific standards. Section 3.3 explores the issue of enforcement in these bilateral trade agreements, analysing how the process of dispute resolution can be a mechanism for modulating accountability and how this impacts both transparency and participation. Section 3.4 looks

10 Though WTO-Plus provisions, because of the standards in the application of Article XXIV GATT and Article V GATS, necessarily have somewhat of an unclear or flexible nature and make it more difficult to concretely define: Gary Clyde Hufbauer and Sherry Stephenson, 'The Free Trade Area of the Americas: How Deep an Integration in the Western Hemisphere?' in Hadi Soesastro and Christopher Findlay (eds), *Reshaping the Asia Pacific Economic Order* (Routledge 2006) 130, 148.

11 On the growth of preferential trade agreements that are explicitly formed from the provisions of the WTO and GATT (though specifically highlighting goods with Article XXIV): Pravin Krishna, 'The Economics of PTAs' in Simon Lester, Bryan Mercurio, and Lorand Bartels (eds), *Bilateral and Regional Trade Agreements: Commentary and Analysis* (2nd edn, CUP 2015) 11.

12 One multilateral example of this type of strategic trading of standards can be found in the Uruguay Round, with the dynamic between increased intellectual property standards and the possibility of greater market access in textiles and agriculture for developing countries: JH Reichman, 'The TRIPS Component of the GATT's Uruguay Round: Competitive Prospects for Intellectual Property Owners in an Integrated World Market' (1993) 4 Fordham Intellectual Property, Media & Entertainment Law Journal 178.

13 Or less than *justifying* a global consensus, and just in practice producing the minimum standards applicable to intellectual property: Rohan Kariyawasam, *International Economic Law and the Digital Divide: A New Silk Road?* (Edward Elgar 2007) 239.

14 Though with more effective presumptions of transparency after *Council v Sophie In't Veld* EU:C:2014:2039: Chris Kimura and Fernanda G Nicola, 'The Negotiating Capital of Trade Experts: Transparency in EU–Asian Free Trade Agreements' in Emilia Korekea-Ago and Päivi Leino-Sandberg (eds), *Law, Legal Expertise and EU Policy-Making* (CUP 2022) 176, 177.

at problematic areas within bilateral relationships and focuses on the potential for international overlap as a challenge to the transparency of patent law obligations. It also considers the tensions in transparency and participation that emerge from an increasingly expansive construction of trade liberalisation.

3.2 The EU and the shift towards bilateralism

3.2.1 Exploring the increased attention to bilateral negotiations

3.2.1.1 Resurgent bilateralism after the Uruguay Round

Intellectual property at the international level has clear cyclical elements that contribute to increasing standards,[15] of a repeating process of multilateral consensus, with bilateral or regional agreements introducing higher standards that are then consolidated in subsequent multilateral instruments as the new consensus.[16] Bilateral agreements, approached optimistically, can be interpreted as allowing new approaches to emerge as experimental smaller-scale projects that, if successful enough, are then consolidated at the multilateral level. Unlike the previous rounds of multilateral and bilateral development, the concerning progression of policy through bilateral agreements amounts much more explicitly to a substitution of multilateral consensus building rather than a complement. For the broader realisation of meaningful participation and transparency in international patent law, this (in the opinion of this book, fundamental) shift is concerning because it further localises and atomises the relationships between actors. In these more specific contexts, values such as transparency or accountability take on an especially local character that is subject to contextual interpretation rather than general or widely developed norms.

As the Doha Development Round stalled,[17] the EU shifted towards bilateral and regional free trade agreements to pursue the same agricultural aspects of the Doha Round but in a bilateral setting.[18] The Doha Round and its troubled progress are the start of the modern dynamic of the global ratchet in intellectual property, though it is also what fundamentally distinguishes the current arrangement from that of previous multilateral consolidations. While the WTO had been involved in

15 Peter Drahos, 'Doing Deals with Al Capone: Paying Protection Money for Intellectual Property in the Global Knowledge Economy' in Peter K Yu (ed), *Intellectual Property and Information Wealth: Issues and Practices in the Digital Age* (Greenwood 2007) 50; Anke Dahrendorf, 'Global Proliferation of Bilateral and Regional Trade Agreements: A Threat for the World Trade Organisation and/or for Developing Countries?' in Jana Hertwig and Sylvia Maus (eds), *Global Risks: Constructing World Order through Law, Politics and Economics* (Peter Lang 2010) 50.

16 Bryan Mercurio, 'TRIPS-Plus Provisions in FTAs: Recent Trends' in Lorand Bartels and Federico Ortino (eds), *Regional Trade Agreements and the WTO Legal System* (OUP 2006) 235.

17 Tesh W Dagne, 'The Narrowing Transatlantic Divide: Geographical Indications in Canada's Trade Agreements (2016) 10 EIPR 598.

18 Chad E Hart and John C Beghin, 'Rethinking Agricultural Domestic Support under the World Trade Organization' in Kym Anderson and Will Martin (eds), *Agricultural Trade Reform and the Doha Development Agenda* (World Bank Publications 2005) 238.

controversy previously, Seattle and Cancún in particular,[19] the cycle of the global ratchet has never occurred in a political and trade context in which major international trade actors have so forcefully denied the legitimacy of multilateral institutions as we experience now. COVID-19 has certainly contributed to this in a more general sense with the WHO,[20] but it is the issues of vaccine accessibility and intellectual property that have brought engagement with the WTO into more ordinary public life with a sense of urgency. The diversity of responses to COVID-19 found in WTO discussions (as well as the perceived lack of progress) highlights the lack of speed or, perhaps more critically, lack of capacity for political responsiveness in the multilateral apparatus.

3.2.1.2 Exploring the global dynamics of the global ratchet

The global ratchet provides an interesting perspective for understanding how a distinct bilateral space is created between trade partners as the emphasis has typically been on the distributional outcomes of these higher standards.[21] The critique is generally founded on a perceived mismatch between the intellectual property standards and the trade partner's economic development or how these elaborated standards create some negative outcomes.[22] Yet from a more systemic perspective, the global ratchet highlights the potential of using the value of participation to understand how international patent law is developing. Increasing standards of protection through the global ratchet can be interpreted from a variety of perspectives: as collaboration towards more specific objectives within intellectual

19 On the negative result of Cancún: Olivier Cattaneo, 'The Political Economy of PTAs' in Simon Lester and Bryan Mercurio, *Bilateral and Regional Trade Agreements; Commentary and Issues* (CUP 2009) 37; Patricia Garcia-Duran, Montserrat Millet, and Jan Orbie, 'EU Trade Policy Reaction to the BIC: From Accommodation to Entrenchment' in Esther Barbé, Oriol Costa, and Robert Kissack (eds), *EU Policy Responses to a Shifting Multilateral System* (Macmillan 2016) 93.

20 Gonca Oguz Gok and Radiye Funda Karadeniz, 'The UN's Legitimacy in Global Governance and the COVID-19 Pandemic' in Gonca Oguz Gok and Hakan Mehmetcik (eds), *The Crises of Legitimacy in Global Governance* (Routledge 2022) 78.

21 That this upward ratcheting is particularly acute in the pharmaceuticals and its relationship to incremental innovation: Mario Cimoli, Giovanni Dosi, Roberto Mazzoleni, and Bhaven N Sampat, 'Innovation, Technical Change, and Patents in the Development Process: A Long-Term View' in Mario Cimoli, Giovanni Dosi, Keith E Maskus, Ruth L Okediji, Jerome H Reichman, and Joseph E Stiglitz (eds), *Intellectual Property Rights: Legal and Economic Challenges for Development* (OUP 2014) 81.

22 That this upward ratcheting is particularly acute in the pharmaceuticals and its relationship to incremental innovation: Mario Cimoli, Giovanni Dosi, Roberto Mazzoleni, and Bhaven N Sampat, 'Innovation, Technical Change, and Patents in the Development Process: A Long-Term View' in Mario Cimoli, Giovanni Dosi, Keith E Maskus, Ruth L Okediji, Jerome H Reichman, and Joseph E Stiglitz (eds), *Intellectual Property Rights: Legal and Economic Challenges for Development* (OUP 2014) 81.

property,[23] as a critical marginalising of developing countries,[24] or as a problem of political bargaining power between global actors.[25] Yet an approach that draws on global administration connects and integrates each of these perspectives. This is because it recognises both the importance of participation in developing these increased standards (as participation) but balances it by questioning the degree to which these provisions are always binding (accountability and transparency). The book has centred Europe throughout, but implicit in the way in which patent law has been approached is the role of context and how it inflects technical regulation. Something that appeared in considering Europe and the value of participation was that it became difficult to imagine which other global actors would be able to successfully interpret or develop binding obligations in the way that the EU has. From this perspective, there is a practical dissonance or unsettling asymmetry between the way the EU experiences international patent law (and international law more generally) and the way developing countries do. The EU's experience of the bilateral space in intellectual property, though especially in the way they experience participation (and accountability for) in the design of binding obligations, is representative of a more fundamental warping of these values that changes how the largest economic states function in these contexts.

Exceptions and flexibilities in patent law then take on a particular importance in this bilateral space, as discussed in Chapter 2, because they represent an opportunity to flexibly modulate the binding quality of a trade obligation. In combination with transparency and participation, the values of global administration reveal tensions in the development of international patent law that are overlooked by a strict focus on legal regulation. It presents the interaction of bilateral and legal initiatives in patent law as producing a flexible system in which each actor experiences accountability, transparency, and participation in a distinct way that necessarily impacts the content and form of legal provisions, their binding quality, and the role of dispute settlement bodies.

23 Australian bilateral trade agreements with TRIPS-Plus provisions have been discussed in promoting the ratification of the WIPO internet treaties, Madrid Protocol and the Singapore Treaty related to trademarks: Christoph Antons and Reto M Hilty, 'Introduction: IP and the Asia–Pacific "Spaghetti Bowl" of Free Trade Agreements' in Christoph Antons and Reto M Hilty (eds), *Intellectual Property and Free Trade Agreements in the Asia–Pacific Region* (Springer 2015) 20.

24 Where '[j]ust when these emerging economies started to benefit from TRIPS Standards and just when other smaller developing countries were contemplating similar strategies, developed countries once again pushed for higher intellectual property standards': Peter K Yu, 'Development Bridge Over Troubled Intellectual Property Water' in Carlos Correa and Xavier Seuba (eds), *Intellectual Property and Development: Understanding the Interfaces* (Springer 2019) 98.

25 'Even if developing countries possess the relevant intellectual property expertise they have little real bargaining power in a negotiation in which they are seeking access to the U.S. or European markets (especially if they wish to become members of the European Community or NAFTA). Almost certainly, developing country negotiators are acquiescing to the intellectual property norms in BIPs as part of the "standard deal" they have to accept as the price for gaining access to the entry to the lucrative markets of Europe and the United States': Peter Drahos, 'BITs and BIPs: Bilateralism in Intellectual Property' (2001) 4 JWIP 805.

From a more abstract perspective that centres meaningful participation, there is certainly no inherent problem with countries coming together to pursue specific trade interests or develop higher standards of intellectual property protection.[26] This 'country club' approach to bilateral agreements is an optimistic view of what is happening in international trade, but it certainly does describe some specific examples of bilateral agenda-setting. Deals involving Australia,[27] for example, have typically incorporated more stringent intellectual property enforcement mechanisms, while both South Korea and Japan have favoured strong enforcement mechanisms in agreements with other industrialised countries.[28] Tension arises when there is a prominent asymmetry between trade partners in terms of market, economy, or resources and particularly between agreements involving developed and developing countries. In this context, the use of bilateral agreements to increase standards in intellectual property is perhaps most problematic and demonstrates how the bilateral space takes a specific character distinct from multilateralism. Consent, sovereignty, and participation are then not absolute values in the bilateral space but instead exist in a variety of modulated or inflected forms. The lens of participation helps to deconstruct this further – something that is essential in bilateral trade since the very system itself reinforces a formalist and procedural understanding of autonomy that masks when values or interests come into conflict.

Transparency emerges as a central concern in the global ratchet, though given the complex nature of bilateral legal development, it also impacts how the states involved experience accountability and participation. The global ratchet fundamentally obscures the values that drive legal development in a way that does not occur in either national or global contexts. Decentralised and atomised negotiations between partners are an essential part of international regulation that, in concert, produce fragments of a future potential international standard.[29] However, in doing

26 The TRIPS Agreement does not mirror the Paris or Berne Conventions in their guidance as to the relationship with subsequent agreements, though the relationship with 'special agreements' and essentially an endorsement by the Appellate Body as to the priority of these specific provisions over general Vienna Convention principles as a *lex specialis*: Henning Grosse Ruse-Khan, 'From TRIPS to FTAS and Back: Re-Conceptualising the Role of a Multilateral IP Framework in a TRIPS-Plus World' (2018) Netherlands Yearbook of International Law 57.

27 While Australia is a developed country with a robust intellectual property framework, in the AUS-FTA, both copyright and enforcement standards were raised – a benefit to the US as Australia is a net importer of intellectual property: Andrew D Mitchell and Tania Voon, 'Australia–United States Free Trade Agreement' in Simon Lester and Bryan Mercurio (eds), *Bilateral and Regional Trade Agreements: Case Studies* (CUP 2009) 31.

28 From the late 1980s, South Korea saw a domestic strengthening of intellectual property standards: Alan Gutterman and Bentley J Anderson, *Intellectual Property in Global Markets* (Springer 1997) 299; also on the important regional position that Japan and South Korea occupy (and more recently, China) as the beneficiaries of increased intellectual property standards in the context of ASEAN and the Regional Comprehensive Economic Partnership Agreement: Anupam Chander and Madhavi Sunder, 'The Battle to Define Asia's Intellectual Property Law: From TPP to RCEP' (2018) 8 UC Irvine Law Review 331, 337.

29 Sarah R Wasserman Rajec, 'The Harmonization Myth in International Intellectual Property Law' (2020) 62 Arizona Law Review 762; though see also the discussion on the role of non-multilateral

so, the actual formation of this accepted international standard and its normative framing, context, and content is hidden. The bilateral space lacks the type of clear and identifiable legal processes that a national piece of legislation would be subject to, while it also facilitates an obscuring of what actors are actually producing the global standards in international patent law (and perhaps more importantly, their normative objectives and values). This is not to say that we cannot identify the major actors that drive international consensus in the context of the global ratchet, where it is very clear that the EU (and the US) have been important in driving this process of expansion.[30] Rather, from the perspective of a substantive sense of transparency and accountability over narrow formalism, this way of producing international consensus cannot be more sharply or cleanly separated out into distinct legal processes in a way that national law can. The signing of trade agreements is perhaps the only part of this bilateral consensus-building process that provides a marked point in its development, but it necessarily represents only one (limited) indication of formal agreement on legal provisions and minimises the contextual elements of negotiation, priorities, and objectives that produced it.

The first step of the global ratchet that Drahos put forward is that the standard-setting objectives need to be shifted away from a forum where there are negotiating difficulties and into a forum more open to realising the trade objectives.[31] One of the clearest examples of forum shifting in this style was, at least in the context of intellectual property, the move away from WIPO towards the WTO.[32] The second step takes this multilateral foundation and uses bilateral or regional trade agreements to coordinate intellectual property interests, driving standards above the established international minimums.[33] The final step of the ratchet is where these higher international standards are then consolidated in a multilateral instrument and form the new international minimum.[34]

---

agreements as templates and providing a 'specific vision of economic ordering' (also raised by Rajec, 763): Rochelle C Dreyfuss, 'Harmonization: Top Down, Bottom Up – and Now Sideways?: The Impact of the IP Provisions of Megaregional Agreements on Third Party States' in Benedict Kingsbury, David M Malone, Paul Mertenskötter, Richard B Stewart, Thomas Streinz, and Atsushi Sunami (eds), *Megaregulation Contested: Global Economic Ordering After TPP* (OUP 2019) 345, 346.

30 Where the EU and the US regularly appear as central actors in the upward trajectory of standards in intellectual property protection: Susan Sell, 'The Global IP Upward Ratchet, Anti-Counterfeiting and Piracy Enforcement Efforts: The State of Play' (2010) PIJIP Research Paper 15, 4, 5 <https://digitalcommons.wcl.american.edu/research/15/>.

31 Peter Drahos, 'BITs and BIPs: Bilateralism in Intellectual Property' (2001) 4 JWIP 798.

32 Though complaints remain as to the effectiveness of WIPO for developing countries, an important element of the WTO–WIPO interface is the 1995 agreement that covered the provision of technical assistance to developing countries in their TRIPS implementation: Carolyn Deere Birkbeck, 'WIPO's Assistance to Developing Countries: The Evolution of Debate and Current Challenges' in Xavier Seuba and Carlos Correa (eds), *Intellectual Property and Development: Understanding the Interfaces* (Springer 2019) 142.

33 Peter Drahos, 'BITs and BIPs: Bilateralism in Intellectual Property' (2001) 4 JWIP 798.

34 Peter Drahos, 'BITs and BIPs: Bilateralism in Intellectual Property' (2001) 4 JWIP 798.

While much emphasis has been placed on how bilateral and regional trade agreements have developed, the broader multilateral context significantly impacts how these bilateral standards are actually consolidated.[35] The use of bilateral agreements as a tool for developed countries to achieve specific objectives has long been identified as an important element in the bilateral dynamic.[36] The consensus that these agreements help to produce necessarily reflects these complex drivers of cooperation, but the trade agreement text itself (outside of extreme examples) resists a disentangling of the exact source of its provisions.[37] The consensus proper comes into existence at the point of multilateral recognition and consolidation, but there is, again, a degree of obfuscation of the origins (and producers) of this consensus as it emerges from a diffuse and isolated bilateral space(s). The consolidation stage has been where the Global North/South divide can be most clearly identified because it necessarily produces a singular, authoritative framing of international trade that embodies a particular normative understanding or vision.[38] Despite the critiques as to the quality or character of the multilateral consolidation,[39] the multilateral space is still procedurally inflected by very visible elements of participation and transparency that encourage compromise, negotiation, and moderation.

But when considered from the perspective of the major economies of the world (and the EU in particular), what does the EU gain from submitting to the multilateral process? Which strategic objectives (trade or otherwise) cannot be achieved through bilateral agreements? It is from this uncertainty around the eventual consolidation stage, with the struggles of multilateral organisations and cooperation, that these bilateral agreements become a central driver of international patent law. From this perspective, bilateral agreements and the dispute settlement systems they create facilitate a type of localised modulation of global patent law. Yet the creative potential and flexibility of the bilateral are joined by serious challenges to transparency and participation. The EU, though this is also applicable to other major

35 Bryan Mercurio, 'TRIPS-Plus Provisions in FTAs: Recent Trends' in Lorand Bartels and Federico Ortino (eds), *Regional Trade Agreements and the WTO Legal System* (OUP 2006) 236.

36 Jan Wouters, Sanderign Duquet, and Nicolas Hachez, 'International Investment Law: The Perpetual Search for Consensus' in Olivier de Schutter, Johan FM Swinnen, and Jan Wouters (eds), *Foreign Direct Investment and Human Development: The Law and Economics of International Investment Agreements* (Routledge 2013) 26.

37 One example would be where the text of specific provisions is directly taken from one of the trade partners.

38 The tension between the Global North and South in a multilateral context is not new or reserved for intellectual property. Of particular importance is the idea of the G20 as a 'bridge' between these groups, but questions regarding how representative the G20 actually is continue: Amitav Acharya, 'Global Governance in a Multiplex World' (2017) RSCAS Working Paper 2017/29 5.

39 The reality is that participation in the Uruguay Round was enabled directly through state autonomy and sovereignty. Though there are tensions as to the precise balance between 'the imperative of trade liberalization and respect for state sovereignty' in the WTO Agreements: Anne Orford, 'Theorizing Free Trade' in Anne Orford and Florian Hoffmann (eds), *The Oxford Handbook of the Theory of International Law* (OUP 2016) 733.

economies,[40] has the market size and international presence that enables a relative freedom in designing these bilateral interfaces. It is this scale and global presence which empowers the contextual flexibility of accountability and transparency in the bilateral space. Though, more optimistically, it also reflects the potential of the EU to support the reform and strengthening of these values in international patent law and its bilateral negotiations. Rather than increasing the substantive protection of patent law in these agreements, they could be used to entrench standards and expectations around transparency and meaningful participation. This normative development reflects the creative aspects of the bilateral space – as experimental initiatives for these values considering they eventually provide the foundational elements of a global consensus around patent law, intellectual property, and trade regulation more broadly.

3.2.1.3 Contextualising the role of bilateral trade agreements in global trade

The structure that encourages this type of differential treatment stems from the precursor to the TRIPS Agreement, the GATT, where tariff-based trade liberalisation and broad welfare gains were central priorities.[41] Not only was the focus very much on barriers to trade, but it was also couched in neoliberal discussions of 'unmitigated welfare gains' that helped establish a system in which commitments to tariff reductions were a major tool of liberalisation.[42] This emphasis on barriers to trade is also reflected in the relatively simple design of flexibilities and exceptions since the disciplinary focus was narrow and easily defined. Deconstructing the development of international trade through the lens of administrative values provides a more nuanced understanding of how trade liberalisation, as a concept, evolved and impacts the dynamic relationships between trade partners. At a very basic level, the early scope of trade liberalisation and barriers to trade provided a transparent sense of what was being negotiated and the consequences of accepting such binding provisions. And yet this transparency and specific scope of trade discipline does not mean that all agreements were perfectly balanced, demonstrating that these values require a more contextual approach. In this, the entangling of legal and economic systems of different countries could be pursued effectively as there was a clear correspondence between the provisions, the objectives of the trade partners, and limited avenues for conflicting interpretations of these provisions.

40 The trade agreements pursued by the EU and US are not uniform and respond to the capacity of their trading partners: Jayashree Watal, 'Is TRIPS a Balanced Agreement from the Perspective of Recent Free Trade Agreements?' in Josef Drexl, Henning Grosse Ruse-Khan, and Souheir Nadde-Phlix (eds), *EU Bilateral Trade Agreements and Intellectual Property: For Better or Worse?* (Springer 2014) 48.

41 Rochelle C Dreyfuss, 'TRIPS-Round II: Should Users Strike Back?' (2004) 71 University of Chicago Law Review 21.

42 Rochelle C Dreyfuss, 'TRIPS-Round II: Should Users Strike Back?' (2004) 71 University of Chicago Law Review 21; that a minimum framework flows from the 'unmitigated welfare gains': Laurence R Helfer and Graeme W Austin, *Human Rights and Intellectual Property: Mapping the Global Interface* (CUP 2011) 34.

The difficulty in balancing the broader integrity of a system that encourages more specific agreements within a framework of minimum obligations is that, from the early economic framing and rationale around liberalisation, it is difficult to justify going below these standards for non-economic reasons.[43]

In such a system, members are entirely free to go beyond the minimum obligations but, as we see in the context of TRIPS flexibilities,[44] become extremely risk-averse with provisions that could *suggest* their legal treatment of intellectual property falls below this minimum standard.[45] Particularly concerning in this type of arrangement is that the process of dispute resolution is increasingly detached from that of the WTO and instead filters into an arbitration process. This raises many concerns about transparency,[46] but it is also framed by the fact that these dispute resolution mechanisms are constructed on a per-agreement basis and further contribute to the atomisation of dispute resolution. Here, the focus on dispute resolution bodies identified in earlier chapters (and in global administration more generally) shifts into something more hazy and indistinct, where the dispute resolution bodies themselves take on a very different character from the conventional courts of global administration.[47] It is perhaps the very contextual construction of dispute resolution bodies emerging from bilateral agreements that contribute to the complex (and often unclear) relationship between the meaningful realisation of administrative values, organisational structure, and distinctions between the substantive and procedural. These dispute settlement bodies are produced from these agreements and effectively dissolve the distinction between substantive and procedural values in practice. The dispute settlement bodies are then both the subject and the object of these trade agreements, produced from a legal framework that reflects specific embedded values and priorities, which are then judged by that very dispute settlement body.

While bilateral and regional agreements develop rules that apply to specific regions or specific countries, they are an essential part of the process of developing

43 Raj Bhala, *Modern GATT Law: A Treatise on the General Agreement on Tariffs and Trade* (Sweet & Maxwell 2005) 619.

44 Particularly in the context of African states, the lack of usage of the compulsory licensing mechanism is not because there is an absence of epidemics but rather the fear of economic repercussions: Olufemi Soyeju and Joshua Wabwire, 'The WTO-TRIPS Flexibilities on Public Health: A Critical Appraisal of the East African Community Regional Framework' (2018) 17(1) WTR 166.

45 Laurence R Helfer and Graeme W Austin, *Human Rights and Intellectual Property: Mapping the Global Interface* (CUP 2011) 34; that members who go below these standards are subject to dispute settlement: Rochelle C Dreyfuss, 'TRIPS-Round II: Should Users Strike Back?' (2004) 71 University of Chicago Law Review 21.

46 With the increasing complexity of choice of forum and law for dispute resolution: Frederick M Abbott, 'A New Dominant Trade Species: Is Bilateralism a Threat?' (2007) 10(3) JIEL 571, 577.

47 GAL scholarship features prominent international dispute resolution bodies (like the ICJ) throughout: Jan Wouters, 'Government by Negotiation' in Sabino Cassese (ed), *Research Handbook on Global Administrative Law* (Edward Elgar 2016) 208; though see also Alberto do Amaral Júnior and Cynthia Kramer, 'WTO as a Self-Limited Regime: The Case of Article XX GATT' in Alberto do Amaral Júnior, Luciana Maria de Oliveira Sá Pires, and Cristiane Lucena Carneiro (eds), *The WTO Dispute Settlement Mechanisms: A Developing Country Perspective* (Springer 2019) 70.

international consensus.[48] When enough of these more specific trade agreements have been negotiated and implemented, they form a strong basis for recognising certain principles or practices as forming part of the multilateral consensus.[49] The development of intellectual property rights in this context must be understood in the broader history of intellectual property. Patent law has maintained a strong foundation of territoriality, but intellectual property as a distinct policy area involves balancing different legal, regulatory, and economic factors more generally. This national emphasis presents a tension when these disciplines are incorporated into bilateral agreements because it broadens the relevant factors for balancing. Instead of industrial policy being balanced against a domestic set of factors, patent law in a bilateral context becomes one of many legal elements up for negotiation. As opposed to the single undertaking in the WTO that reduces the scope for substantial asymmetries,[50] the bilateral context allows (and even facilitates) the trading of intellectual property standards for trade gains in other areas. The result is that while the bilateral space broadens the scope of relevant disciplines for trade gains, the mechanisms and flexibilities within specific disciplines like intellectual property are restricted in return for market access or other economic incentives. The result is a system of law in which the origins of its values, principles, and objectives can never be reliably identified. Though some cases may present obvious indications about what exactly was 'traded',[51] the absence of more developed mechanisms that enable transparency (and thus broader participation) presents several risks. It means that patent law produced in these environments has a complete lack of normative transparency, which is masked by the substantive provisions themselves. The visibility of the trade agreement provisions distracts the viewer as it draws on the conventional understanding of law as technical rules and regulations, obscuring the fact that they are being presented with none of the political, social, or cultural contexts of their production.

48 Bob Reinalda, *Routledge History of International Organisations: From 1815 to the Present Day* (Routledge 2009) 636.

49 Bryan Mercurio, 'TRIPS-Plus Provisions in FTAs: Recent Trends' in Lorand Bartels and Federico Ortino (eds), *Regional Trade Agreements and the WTO Legal System* (OUP 2006) 236.

50 Though Wolfe concludes that the single undertaking, rather than producing an outcome in negotiation, instead shapes the possibility of an outcome: Robert Wolfe, 'The WTO Single Undertaking as Negotiating Technique and Constitutive Metaphor' (2009) 12(4) JIEL 835, 836.

51 As in the Uruguay Round in areas like textiles and agriculture: JH Reichman, 'The TRIPS Component of the GATT's Uruguay Round: Competitive Prospects for Intellectual Property Owners in an Integrated World Market' (1993) 4 Fordham Intellectual Property, Media & Entertainment Law Journal 178.

3.2.2 *Modulating binding obligations in the bilateral space: National autonomy and policy space as flexibilities*

3.2.2.1 *Policy space, autonomy, and developing countries*

The use of bilateral agreements in pursuit of trade liberalisation is not inherently problematic, but it further distinguishes the current generation of as-yet unconsolidated bilateral standards from the global ratchet of previous decades. It is also important to recognise that the EU is not the only jurisdiction using bilateral agreements in a way that restricts TRIPS flexibilities, with the US also promoting similar agreements.[52] Developing countries occupy a specific position in this environment since they necessarily have a more fraught task balancing between maximising national autonomy (and a nationally responsive intellectual property policy) and securing valuable market access.[53]

An important element of the TRIPS Agreement is that it preserved a degree of policy space for WTO Members that can be used to moderate the relationship between the multilateral and national spheres to empower actors.[54] The TRIPS Agreement has a complex relationship to policy space because, by reserving some space for national autonomy, it enables both the freedom to trade away this autonomy for strategic trade gains *and* the flexibility to interpret TRIPS obligations from a specific perspective. Within this global framework, the WTO Members are not only using the remaining policy space to work towards their national objectives, but they are also using this lateral movement to create new interfaces between trade partners that may either build on the TRIPS Agreement (TRIPS-Plus) or entangle other, non-WTO disciplines (WTO-Plus).[55] The scope of national policy space is then tied to the national intellectual property environment and highlights how, in the bilateral space, the qualities or character of the legal agreements may

52 Alvaro Santos, 'Carving Out Policy Autonomy for Developing Countries in the World Trade Organisation: The Experience of Brazil and Mexico' in David M Trubek, Helena Alviar Garcia, Diogo R Coutinho, and Alvaro Santos (eds), *Law and the New Developmental State: The Brazilian Experience in Latin American Context* (CUP 2013) 204.

53 Where '… resistance to demands for higher levels of protection might be based on concepts of good governance and political responsibility towards citizens': Frederick M Abbott, 'The Future of IPRs in the Multilateral Trading System' in Christophe Bellmann and Ricardo Melendez-Ortiz (eds), *Trading in Knowledge: Development Perspectives on TRIPS, Trade and Sustainability* (Routledge 2013) 44.

54 The TRIPS Agreement preserved a degree of national autonomy, this policy space can be used to implement standards that are still fully consistent with TRIPS: Keith E Maskus, 'Policy Space in Intellectual Property Rights and Technology Transfer: A New Economic Research Agenda' in Xavier Seuba and Carlos Correa (eds), *Intellectual Property and Development: Understanding the Interfaces* (Springer 2019) 13.

55 On WTO-Plus provisions: Knut Brünjes and Milena Weldenfeller, 'Multilateral Trade Policy Is Back' in Christoph Herrmann, Bruno Simma, and Rudolf Streinz (eds), *Trade Policy between Law, Diplomacy and Scholarship* (Springer 2015) 51; on TRIPS-Plus provisions: Marco M Aleman, 'Impact of TRIPS-Plus Obligations in Economic Partnership and Free Trade Agreements on International IP Law' in Josef Drexl, Henning Grosse Ruse-Khan, and Souheir Nadde-Phlix (eds), *EU Bilateral Trade Agreements and Intellectual Property: For Better or Worse?* (Springer 2014) 63.

not be generalisable. The values and processes that drive these cooperations, and thus the resulting legal relationship, may indeed reflect substantive transparency and accountability. Yet since they are produced from specific interactions with very minimal procedural requirements or oversight, there is a sense in which they embody a more contextual transparency, or a more contained accountability, that may be different to how these values function in a multilateral agreement. Considerations such as industry size, industry type, and export market size all impact what exactly can be traded to secure greater protection for patent law and create a unique profile for each country and prospective trading partner.[56]

The push towards bilateralism, and the space that enables this type of legal development, comes from the inherent character of multilateral initiatives. While the gains from multilateral consensus-building are impressive from a political perspective, they necessarily represent the absolute minimum of commonality and are very rarely radical developments.[57] This process of consensus building is especially complex in the WTO because of its expansive membership. Yet it is precisely this broad membership that also brings with it a greater transparency and participation in terms of what is proposed, negotiated, and accepted – though there are obviously issues with how non-official activities and relationships between actors within the WTO framework affect the *process* of negotiation.[58] The impact of relationships between different actors and the broader sense of institutional dynamics are, however, not unique to the WTO.[59] Nevertheless, the procedural safeguards and emphasis on participation embedded in the WTO system also impact not only the speed of negotiations but their long-term future more generally. There is a sense in which, in a perhaps optimistic reading of WTO development, that it is precisely the challenges and drawn-out or failed negotiations that solidify the WTO's legitimacy in international trade. In an era of political volatility and reactionary policy, the WTO operates almost in opposition to those forces. Speed has been presented as one of the benefits of bilateral agreements over multilateral rounds of negotiation (as well as potentially greater freedom in subject matter),[60] but a shift in tone in

56 Despite the linguistic isolation of Japanese and Korean, both of these markets have significant cultural exports. Anime, for example, in the US was worth around $2.7 billion in 2009: Nissim Kadosh Otmazgin, *Regionalizing Culture: The Political Economy of Japanese Popular Culture in Asia* (University of Hawaii Press 2013) 74.

57 Alex F McCalla and John D Nash, *Reforming Agricultural Trade for Developing Countries: Quantifying the Impact of Multilateral Trade Reform* (World Bank Publications 2007) 29.

58 See generally the work of Tommaso Soave, *The Everyday Makers of International Law: From Great Halls to Back Rooms* (CUP 2022).

59 Jeffrey J Rachlinski and Andrew J Wistrich, 'Judging the Judiciary by the Numbers: Empirical Research on Judges' (2017) 13 Annual Review of Law and Social Science 203, 204.

60 One particular example would be the rapid pace of negotiation and conclusion for the US and Korea trade agreement, though important counterexamples of the AUSFTA and ACTA that experienced much longer timelines but due primarily to the extensive criticism rather than the bilateral mode: Andrew D Mitchell and Tania Voon, 'Australia–United States Free Trade Agreement' in Simon Lester and Bryan Mercurio (eds), *Bilateral and Regional Trade Agreements: Case Studies* (CUP 2009) 11.

recent years has undermined this idea of bilateral agreements as the quicker route to trade liberalisation. In the European context, the development of CETA and ACTA were not only protracted negotiations simply due to the complexity of the provisions themselves,[61] but from the growing political opposition that contributed to the drawn-out process and eventual failure.[62]

The extensive use of exceptions and options in multilateral agreements also highlighted the potential of the bilateral space where trade gains can be more directly responsive to the specific trading relationship between countries.[63] This quality of multilateral agreements to provide (and sustain) space for exceptions demonstrates that a strong focus on participation (and, by extension, transparency) does not necessarily prevent or remove flexibility. Instead, it provides a space for, essentially, a more transparent exercise of flexibilities. In this, flexibilities are essential not just in the development of intellectual property but in how they shape the dynamic of bilateral agreements more generally. Intellectual property standards are still bound up with other areas of trade in bilateral agreements in a way that works to minimise flexibilities and incentivise the adoption of higher standards in exchange for gains elsewhere.[64] Multilateral agreements almost require exceptions and opt-out clauses because of the political nature of the process, and this implicitly works to recognise the importance of these mechanisms in sustaining the distinct global space. Without allowing for some member autonomy, the risk would be that a country that disagrees with a specifically onerous provision would entirely withdraw from an agreement that they would otherwise stand to benefit from. By providing space for these tensions and divergences, the increased flexibility has the potential to simultaneously undermine accountability through opt-outs, while at the same time promoting a much more visible indication as to the state of the binding obligations. In doing so, these divergent values and expectations are recognised,

61 The economic significance and degree of rule-making contrast markedly with the absolute lack of transparency in developing the CETA text: Panagiotis Delimatsis, 'TTIP, CETA, TISA Behind Closed Doors: Transparency in the EU Trade Policy' (2016) TILEC Discussion Paper 2016-020 12.

62 The opposition to ACTA and CETA appeared in both civil and governmental contexts. On the widespread online coverage and in-person protests at the leaked texts: Peter K Yu, 'Development Bridge Over Troubled Intellectual Property Water' in Xavier Seuba and Carlos Correa (eds), *Intellectual Property and Development: Understanding the Interfaces* (Springer 2019) 112. The withdrawal of US support from TPP is perhaps another example of a failure to conclude inspiring the remaining members to form a different agreement with similar provisions (Comprehensive and Progressive Agreement for Trans-Pacific Partnership): Peter K Yu, 'Development Bridge Over Troubled Intellectual Property Water' in Xavier Seuba and Carlos Correa (eds), *Intellectual Property and Development: Understanding the Interfaces* (Springer 2019) 108.

63 Pierre Latrille, 'Services Rules in Regional Trade Agreements: How Diverse or Creative Are They Compared to the Multilateral Rules?' in Rohini Acharya (ed), *Regional Trade Agreements and the Multilateral Trading System* (CUP 2016) 460.

64 On the single undertaking approach in FTAs that joins together trade and intellectual property to incentivise partners, particularly developing countries, to accede to agreements with TRIPS-Plus provisions: Pedro Roffe, 'Intellectual Property Chapters in Free Trade Agreements: Their Significance and Systemic Implications' in Josef Drexl, Henning Grosse Ruse-Khan, and Souheir Nadde-Phlix (eds), *EU Bilateral Trade Agreements and Intellectual Property: For Better or Worse?* (Springer 2014) 24.

brought within the multilateral system, and legitimised. The bilateral space itself exists in the shadow of multilateral, compromise-driven decision-making that is in the process of constant balance between progress and flexibility.

3.2.2.2 The global growth of bilateral trade agreements and systemic tensions

The use of bilateral agreements to supplement (rather than as an alternative to) multilateral standards is not unique to the post-TRIPS legal environment. Both the US and EU had used bilateral agreements to further their trade interests in the period even leading up to the Uruguay Round.[65] Though what is significant about the shift of the Global Europe strategy in 2006 is not that it was a return to bilateralism but, as Araujo argues, that it destabilised the distinction between internal EU intellectual property policy and recast it as an element of external trade policy.[66] The degree to which intellectual property policy and patent law reflect high standards of transparency and accountability is then of particular importance because bilateral agreements become a vehicle through which EU approaches are disseminated globally. The Global Europe strategy presents a transformation from an EU that had been engaged in bilateralism into an EU that recognises a more instrumentalist understanding of the potential of bilateralism and the unique qualities of the bilateral space. A more critical perspective would be that it represents a turning point in EU external relations that deploys bilateral agreements to reflect and reproduce domestic standards and domestic arrangements. Here, the inherent qualities of bilateral negotiations and their highly specific dynamics become relevant again. The EU has strong commitments to transparency and so,[67] in theory, the more conscious usage of bilateral agreements could be a positive shift for strong administrative values in the design of international patent law. The reality is that, whatever current criticism of the EU and its bilateral trade agreements, the EU is completely free to go beyond the legal minimums provided for by the WTO. In doing so, the EU could give actual meaning to its commitments on transparency and accountability whilst essentially enshrining these values in the evolving international patent law space (though this would eventually impact the norms of international trade law either directly or indirectly). This shift in perspective on the potential of bilateral agreements is distinct from previous cycles of multilateral development precisely because of the political climate that led to the Global Europe initiative to begin with. It combines the use of bilateralism as an instrument with a political landscape that persistently questions the value of multilateral institutions, revealing the context-specific and almost insulated quality of bilateral space as the most effective tool for achieving trade objectives.

65 Billy AM Araujo, *The EU Deep Trade Agenda* (OUP 2016) 141.
66 Billy AM Araujo, *The EU Deep Trade Agenda* (OUP 2016) 142.
67 EU Commission, 'Transparency in EU Trade Negotiations' <https://policy.trade.ec.europa.eu/eu-trade-relationships-country-and-region/transparency-eu-trade-negotiations_en>.

3.3 On the enforcement dimension of bilateral agreements

3.3.1 Europe and the EU Global Strategy

3.3.1.1 Bilateral trade and the emergence of areas of 'particular strategic interest'

The EU has followed the direction of the US in negotiating trade agreements after adopting the Global Europe Strategy,[68] incorporating comprehensive chapters on patent term extension, genetic resources, and most interestingly as of recently, enforcement.[69] Two specific areas of intellectual property have been particularly important for the EU, highlighted as instances of 'particular strategic interest' and define the current trajectory of EU identity in bilateral negotiations.[70] These are the enforcement of intellectual property rights and the continued expansion of Geographical Indications (GIs).[71] Though these areas extend far beyond the specific issue of patent law, these agreements place alongside all forms of intellectual property. The fact that their regulation exists in an interconnected single text means that approaching these agreements requires a more expansive approach to understand the way in which the subjects are positioned. Rather than simply considering how patent law is constructed or affected by the specific patent provisions, understanding the dynamic of the agreement asks the reader to analyse where tensions are different, problems emerge, or text is identical across the entire scope of intellectual property within the agreement. This type of expansive approach at once mirrors and also picks at the superficial unity of the agreement – that the text stands as a complete whole, rather than a series of intellectual property agreements.

The Global Europe shift saw this emphasis on enforcement of intellectual property rights and GIs increase, with GIs in particular becoming the de facto way of protecting specific cultural products in many countries due to the strict insistence of the EU in negotiations.[72] Understood in the context of the global ratchet, this presents another dimension to the process of forum-shifting. The EU has obtained most of its gains in terms of the substantive requirements of patents and is now in line with their post-2006 'deep trade integration' direction,[73] using bilateral agreements or preferential trade agreements to regulate areas that had been rejected from inclusion at the WTO level. These bilateral interfaces are then a subversion of

68 Richard Schaffer, Filiberto Agusti, and Lucien J Dhooge, *International Business Law and Its Environment* (Cengage 2017) 575.

69 One example is the EU–South Korea trade agreement that covers all of these issues: Article 10.40 (genetic resources), Section C (enforcement), and Article 10.35 (patent term extension) KOREU FTA.

70 Billy AM Araujo, *The EU Deep Trade Agenda* (OUP 2016) 143.

71 Billy AM Araujo, *The EU Deep Trade Agenda* (OUP 2016) 143.

72 That the EU's traditional focus has been on making protection for GIs more robust internationally: Jayashree Watal, 'Is TRIPS a Balanced Agreement from the Perspective of Recent Free Trade Agreements?' in Josef Drexl, Henning Grosse Ruse-Khan, and Souheir Nadde-Phlix (eds), *EU Bilateral Trade Agreements and Intellectual Property: For Better or Worse?* (Springer 2014) 42.

73 Billy AM Araujo, *The EU Deep Trade Agenda* (OUP 2016) 13.

the WTO, both in terms of the legal impact of the agreements and the implicit restrictions to autonomy that are occurring through the adoption of specific forms of legal protection such as GIs. Yet despite the enthusiasm with which the EU has focused on using bilateral agreements to develop intellectual property standards, it is unclear in a post-Global Europe context whether the EU perceives these agreements as policy alternatives to multilateralism or if it is merely preparation for an eventual consolidation in multilateral form.[74] This perhaps raises some fundamental questions about how transparency and accountability take on a specific character in a multilateral space – would a successful multilateral trade round in patent law remedy the impaired transparency and participation that has been so central in the bilateral agreements of recent years? Or does consolidation simply legitimise, as is discussed in global administration,[75] the output of an impaired system with little shift in status quo?

3.3.1.2 The potential for subverting stability in the multilateral environment

What is important in understanding this subversion of the multilateral environment is, rather than addressing the concerns around the expansion of trade disciplines and sustainably committing to progress at the multilateral level,[76] the EU bilateral agreements are themselves an expansion. They incorporate additional regulatory areas, promote the EU legal construction of these fields, and thereby contribute to the type of breakdown between internal and external (as well as substantive and procedural). What is occurring here is not, as others have argued,[77] that the bilateral context is a direct precursor to a multilateral consensus in which bilateral agreements are used to pressure the inclusion of similar trade provisions multilaterally.[78] Instead, the position of bilateral agreements relative to the multilateral space is much more contextually sensitive. The process of compromise in terms of intellectual property protection in a multilateral context is discussed at length elsewhere and explores how lengthy negotiations lead, inevitably, to a final text that

74 Tesh W Dagne, 'The Narrowing Transatlantic Divide: Geographical Indications in Canada's Trade Agreements' (2016) 10 EIPR 598, 603; Klaus Meyer and Mike W Peng, *International Business* (Cengage 2016) 265.

75 Sujith Xavier, 'Top Heavy: Beyond the Global North and the Justification for Global Administrative Law' (2018) 57 Indian Journal of International Law 353.

76 Something that is particularly apparent in the EU's environmental approach in the absence of a multilateral consensus, building from a bottom-up approach in a more decentralised way: Elisa Morgera, 'The EU and Environmental Multilateralism: The Case of Access and Benefit-Sharing and the Need for a Good-Faith Test' (2014) 16 Cambridge Yearbook of European Legal Studies 109.

77 Kent Jones, *Reconstructing the World Trade Organisation for the 21st Century: An Institutional Approach* (OUP 2015) 186.

78 That regional trade agreements do not automatically lead to a global consensus that can be used for multilateral reinforcement, instead requiring a concerted effort to broaden the membership of these regional agreements and to raise these issues at the level of the WTO for it to be truly consolidated: Kent Jones, *Reconstructing the World Trade Organisation for the 21st Century: An Institutional Approach* (OUP 2015) 186.

represents significant compromises between the parties.[79] But do current attitudes to multilateral and political cooperation in 2025 have the structural integrity to support not only the agreement, but the process of compromise? Economically powerful countries can simply choose not to interact with this process of compromise or progressively reduce its practical scope through strategic bilateral agreements. The EU no longer has to pressure the inclusion of new trade disciplines at the multilateral level because of the systemic weakness of the WTO and the lack of tangible benefits in accepting a slower or more compromise-driven negotiation strategy. We return to a question raised earlier: What kind of trade objectives would require the EU to engage in multilateral cooperation that cannot be reasonably achieved through bilateral or targeted agreements?

In this context, the subversive quality of bilateral interfaces is magnified when the trade agreements being negotiated cover wide areas of trade between the partners.[80] As discussed previously, these agreements position intellectual property alongside other disciplines and risk the adoption of specific modes of intellectual property protection in exchange for trade access.[81] While the multilateral trade environment also allows countries to strategically offer access to specific markets in order to secure concessions from the other trade partners, the bilateral context makes this approach much more effective because it atomises the relationship and allows for more differentiated negotiations. From this perspective, transparency takes on a localised character and is impaired or promoted within these atomised legal relationships. This is concerning in terms of the agreements themselves, though they also represent additional tensions in fragmentation of international patent law that undermine the prospect of more consistent transparency in future multilateral initiatives.

Specifically for intellectual property, the interactions between potentially competing frames of reference (like in the context of pharmaceuticals and human rights) can be difficult enough to manage at a national level since they involve many different policy levers. As with the process of bilateral cooperation discussed previously, this presents a significant challenge for transparency because it obscures the precise way in which competing objectives are balanced, how dominant actors approach areas of priority, and how compromise is negotiated around sensitive or politically important issues. The bilateral context opens this balancing exercise up to a greater number of factors, externalising – from a disciplinary perspective – the assessment of trade-offs to be made. A trading partner must weigh entirely distinct regulatory approaches within intellectual property against areas such as agricultural

79 Sam Ricketson, 'Implementing Treaty Obligations at the National Level' in Niklas Bruun, Graeme B Dinwoodie, Marianne Levin, and Ansgar Ohly (eds), *Transition and Coherence in Intellectual Property Law* (CUP 2021) 108.

80 Thomas Cottier, Dannie Jost, and Michelle Schupp, 'The Prospects of TRIPS-Plus Protection in Future Mega-Regionals' in Thilo Rensmann (ed), *Mega-Regional Trade Agreements* (Springer 2017) 193.

81 Thomas Cottier, Dannie Jost, and Michelle Schupp, 'The Prospects of TRIPS-Plus Protection in Future Mega-Regionals' in Thilo Rensmann (ed), *Mega-Regional Trade Agreements* (Springer 2017) 191.

access, state subsidies, and foreign direct investment.[82] Patent law and intellectual property policy that flow from this type of exercise are somewhat disconnected in that they represent the product of a very contextually specific interaction that is neither global nor national. These provisions contribute to the creation of a legal space that differs in character from either national or multilateral interfaces and is crucially presented to the world with none of that contextual information.

Returning to the distinction between TRIPS-Plus and WTO-Plus provisions, there is a fundamental tension in the EU strategy of 'deep trade integration' since it is not clear that the potential for overlapping spheres of regulation is a prominent concern.[83] Effective accountability and transparency are at the centre of this interconnected (and yet isolated) network of bilateral agreements. Part of the shift towards deep trade integration has been the move beyond border measures or import tariffs and into more complex forms of regulation,[84] where issues like technical standards and internal regulatory policies are considered. One of the difficulties with this area is defining what exactly constitutes 'deep' integration, but it has been approached flexibly as going beyond import tariff measures and often into competition policy, sanitary and phytosanitary standards (SPS), government procurement, and transport standards.[85] One example of this transition towards deeper integration can be seen in the work on the Partnership and Cooperation Agreement with Ukraine from 1994 and the 2014 Cooperation Agreement, where academic work deconstructed the spectrum of cooperation between deep and simple.[86] What is notable about this shift towards 'deep' integration is that they appear to overwhelmingly be issues of administration. Even more than patent law, concerns about how these agreements protect and support transparency, accountability, and participation are not optional considerations. They are fundamental values that are central in managing how rules are made and how the interconnected national/international/global influence impacts the content of these rules.

82 On the tense relationship between bilateral agreements and their practical (and symbolic) relationship to agricultural developments in the WTO: Ellis S Krauss, 'The United States in APEC's EVSL Negotiations' in Ellis S Krauss and TJ Pempel (eds), *Beyond Bilateralism: US–Japan Relations in the New Asia–Pacific* (Stanford University Press 2004) 287.

83 On the process and substance of deep trade integration: Bernard Hoekman and Denise Eby Konan, 'Deep Integration, Discrimination, and Euro-Mediterranean Free Trade' in Jürgen von Hagen and Mika Widgren (eds), *Regionalism in Europe: Geometries and Strategies After 2000* (Springer 2012) 171; James H Mathis, 'Regional Trade Agreements and Domestic Regulation: What Reach for "Other Restrictive Regulations of Commerce"?' in Lorand Bartels and Federico Ortino (eds), *Regional Trade Agreements and the WTO Legal System* (OUP 2006) 100.

84 Bregt Natens, *Regulatory Autonomy and International Trade in Services: The EU under GATS and RTAS* (Edward Elgar 2016) 147.

85 Michael Emerson, T Huw Edwards, Ildar Gazizullin, Matthias Lücke, Daniel Müller-Jentsch, Vira Nanivska, Valeriy Pyatnytskiy, Andreas Schneider, Rainer Schweickert, Olexandr Shevtsov, and Olga Shumylo, *The Prospect of Deep Free Trade between the European Union and Ukraine* (CEPS 2006) 8, 9.

86 Michael Emerson, T Huw Edwards, Ildar Gazizullin, Matthias Lücke, Daniel Müller-Jentsch, Vira Nanivska, Valeriy Pyatnytskiy, Andreas Schneider, Rainer Schweickert, Olexandr Shevtsov, and Olga Shumylo, *The Prospect of Deep Free Trade between the European Union and Ukraine* (CEPS 2006) 7, 8.

Yet the move towards more explicit regulatory processes and away from simpler border provisions also emphasises the importance of flexibilities as they provide some way of mitigating the tensions in multiple, potentially overlapping, regulatory obligations created by different bilateral agreements. From a more systemic perspective, this type of overlapping regulation can be understood as an issue of transparency since it presents an obscuring of precisely which obligations are binding and in which contexts. It is only in dispute that these overlapping obligations begin to be disentangled, where their binding quality is interpreted to produce a workable system of law in practice. The start of dispute proceedings collapses the network of binding obligations into a position of (at least provisional) certainty as to their relationship to the actors involved. The potential for dramatically incoherent policy stemming directly from tariff measures is limited because tariffs represent only minimal cooperation with a legal actor and involve a relatively manageable resource burden (especially relevant for developing countries).[87] Explicit regulation in this deep trade integration sense raises the same type of issues but with a dramatically increased risk for conflict between regulatory regimes. Managing this type of regulatory integration also requires a much greater degree of administrative support and, again, centres the role of contextually positioned dispute resolution bodies in producing a workable understanding of complex trade obligations. Together, the potential for overlap demonstrates some of the limits of procedural transparency as a standard for interpreting bilateral trade agreements. Each agreement explicitly states its provisions and is available for anyone to read. And yet it is in practice, particularly when this practice breaks down and results in a dispute, that demonstrates how such a thin expectation of transparency is very unstable. It is not a fundamental representation of transparency but, instead, a compromised and limited form.

The tensions between different regulatory approaches, specifically in intellectual property, are directly relevant to the EU's more recent focus on enforcement since they have the greatest potential for (actual or perceived) grievances regarding compliance. As the regulatory dimensions of trade in these agreements become more widespread, the emphasis will shift to the ever-increasing mechanisms for dispute resolution in these agreements.[88] These issues are magnified for developing countries with which the EU concludes trade agreements because, in a bilateral space, the EU is only one of many potential trade partners. It is unlikely that a country would seek to only conclude a trade agreement with the EU and not seek

87 Even in the context of ACTA, the provisions concerned border seizures, which while expansive in their reach (applying even if the destination of the goods was one in which no intellectual property rights were violated), were not particularly legally disruptive. On the impact of ACTA and border measures: Olasupo Owoeye, 'Access to Medicines and Parallel Trade in Patented Pharmaceuticals' (2015) 37(6) EPIR 359, 366.

88 On the problematic trajectory of ever-stronger dispute resolution mechanisms that could lead to trade restrictiveness: James H Mathis, 'Regional Trade Agreements and Domestic Regulation: What Reach for "Other Restrictive Regulations of Commerce"?' in Lorand Bartels and Federico Ortino (eds), *Regional Trade Agreements and the WTO Legal System* (OUP 2006) 108.

out similar agreements with China or the US (though this also does not take into account geographic drivers of cooperation and integration, as with the ASEAN countries or close neighbours). In this context, countries must invest the resources necessary to actively manage these potentially competing (or at the very least, different) regimes or face dispute proceedings for breaching the terms of the trade agreement. The continued attention to regulatory systems highlights the difficulty of managing the relationship between different bilateral interfaces, which, depending on the agreement, intersect differently in terms of discipline, scope of the obligations, and impact on transparency in regulation.

3.4 Lessons from the EU and its bilateral expansion

3.4.1 Moving beyond narrow understandings of trade liberalisation

3.4.1.1 The shifting focus of international cooperation: Patent law and the next frontier

Trade liberalisation and the removal of barriers to trade have been the main methods of integration for the Members of the WTO, representing the primary method by which markets are opened and trade relations between countries are improved.[89] Bilateral agreements and Preferential Trade Agreements (PTAs) are, compared with the more substantially impactful method of multilateral instruments, considered the 'second-best' option for trade policy.[90] Multilateralism as a way of promoting trade liberalisation has also been shaped by the shifting priorities of the international trade environment.[91] It is a trade context that, in recent decades, has moved from simpler issues of cross-border trade towards more contentious deep trade disciplines with noticeable opposition.[92] The increase in complexity in how legal regimes are connected highlights the need for an appropriately developed understanding of not only how these connections are formed but also to analyse the quality, character, and dynamic of these relationships. This shift towards more complex representations of international trade demonstrates the importance of, if not the administrative values of transparency and participation, the use of guiding values as a lens through which to view these configurations. Tariff-based trade liberalisation presents clear and delineated factors within international trade that, in

89 Ernst-Ulrich Petersmann, 'The WTO and Regional Trade Agreements as Competing Fora for Constitutional Reforms: Trade and Human Rights' in Lorand Bartels and Federico Ortino (eds), *Regional Trade Agreements and the WTO Legal System* (OUP 2006) 282.

90 On trade liberalisation as primarily the elimination of trade discrimination, regional agreements as a second-best policy: Ernst-Ulrich Petersmann, 'The WTO and Regional Trade Agreements as Competing Fora for Constitutional Reforms: Trade and Human Rights' in Lorand Bartels and Federico Ortino (eds), *Regional Trade Agreements and the WTO Legal System* (OUP 2006) 282.

91 'Moreover, deeper integration is always much easier at the regional level than it is at the multilateral level. As we know from previous experience, multilateral negotiations take a very long time and are very complex, whereas RTAs move much faster.': Rafael Leal-Arcas, *Climate Change and International Trade (*Edward Elgar 2013) 371.

92 That the shift from regulating cross-border trade in goods to more integrated regulation is so difficult that it has successfully happened at the multilateral level: Billy AM Araujo, *The EU Deep Trade Agenda* (OUP 2016) 22.

terms of binding obligations, appear to inherently reflect a more substantive sense of transparency. As with bilateral trade agreements discussed previously, however, this obviously does not necessarily speak to the actual empowerment of participation or transparency in the *process* of producing tariff-based liberalisation.[93] Yet at least in terms of what the binding obligation entails, the resulting provisions are clear in terms of the legal effect that they produce.

While there are more and more regional trade agreements being negotiated and implemented, the fact is that they are increasingly moving from trade liberalisation to a more explicit approach of *coordination* in terms of domestic policy and foreign policy.[94] One example of this shift would be the EU, though this has been suggested to be a feature of customs unions rather than the EU per se.[95] Customs unions obviously involve explicit coordination between the members that constitute the union, though some features are particular to the EU. What separates the EU from the nascent customs unions around the world,[96] currently emerging in a variety of institutional and political contexts, is that the EU has a developed apparatus that manages its international representation. Considered from a more critical perspective, the EU is not necessarily a manifestation of 'coordination' between its constituting members in domestic and foreign policy but rather a more fundamental breaking down of the distinction between internal and external, national and international, and substantive and procedural. And yet what further distinguishes these developments from earlier periods in international trade history is that all of this is occurring in a trade context where the viability of multilateral consolidation is fundamentally in question.

The EU's position regarding the externalisation of its regulatory environment and eagerness to participate in the international trade environment can be seen to emanate from the central position that the internal market holds in Europe.

93 On the political economy dimensions of tariff-based trade liberalization and environmental protection: Per G Fredriksson, 'The Political Economy of Trade Liberalization and Environmental Policy' (1999) 65(3) Southern Economic Journal 513, 514.

94 The shift towards domestic policy coordination and foreign policy coordination away from simple trade liberalisation is particularly pronounced for customs unions like the EU: Ernst-Ulrich Petersmann, 'The WTO and Regional Trade Agreements as Competing Fora for Constitutional Reforms: Trade and Human Rights' in Lorand Bartels and Federico Ortino (eds), *Regional Trade Agreements and the WTO Legal System* (OUP 2006) 282.

95 Ernst-Ulrich Petersmann, 'The WTO and Regional Trade Agreements as Competing Fora for Constitutional Reforms: Trade and Human Rights' in Lorand Bartels and Federico Ortino (eds), *Regional Trade Agreements and the WTO Legal System* (OUP 2006) 282.

96 The rise of customs unions is a global phenomenon that promotes greater integration and trade at a regional and subregional level, with the aspirational development of the African Union, the successful customs unions of the East African Community (EAC), the West African Economic and Monetary Union (UEMOA), Central African Economic and Monetary Union (CEMAC), and the Southern African Customs Union (SACU) all prominent examples just within the African continent: Anna-Luise Chané and Magnus Killander, 'The EU and Africa' in Ramses A Wessel and Jed Odermatt (eds), *Research Handbook on the European Union and International Organisations* (Edward Elgar 2019) 594; though cf. the analysis that customs unions are actually a second-best policy option if the objective is free trade, that membership rules and other factors mean that customs unions stop short of a complete trade liberalisation: Karl Farmer and Matthias Schelnast, *Growth and International Trade: An Introduction to the Overlapping Generations Approach* (Springer 2013) 297.

Externalising some regulatory principles is required to not subject European producers to different regulatory schemes in foreign markets.[97] In embracing deeper trade integration through these bilateral and regional interfaces, the EU is preserving its own policy space (by not being subject to multilateral compromise) and progressively reshaping the bilateral spaces with its trade partners to reflect its priorities and the regulatory needs of European producers.[98] There is also a more neutral understanding of the spread of European regulatory approaches, specifically in new and emerging disciplines, where it is the quality, robustness, or prestige that leads other countries to adopt.[99] This appears prominently in the development of data protection regimes and extends even to other developed countries,[100] yet the distinction here is that regulatory convergence is being promoted through trade agreements rather than an independent adoption of the standards. While the outcome is the same, there is something in the dynamic between the EU and developing countries, in the asymmetry, that suggests a less neutral process of sharing or a more explicit exporting of standards. All of this has a profound impact on the dynamic between potential trade partners, in particular when looking from the perspective of meaningful participation. This normative power of the EU, whether expressed in a bilateral or more unilateral context, minimises the ability for smaller trade actors to participate as equals in practice. This is not to say that all agreements from the EU are inherent threats to standards of transparency and participation, but rather that even high procedural standards for these values within trade agreements cannot necessarily address the practical, more political relationship between the actors involved. Robust commitments to transparency and participation would be a positive development, though the degree of asymmetry in economic power renders these values as always somehow qualified in character.

The rate with which these regional agreements are being negotiated – notably post-2003 Seattle Ministerial[101] – has been put forward as evidence that the Members

97 That regulatory externalisation is required to not disadvantage European producers in a global marketplace: Sangeeta Khorana and W Gregory Voss, 'The Digital Single Market: Move from Traditional to Digital?' In Sangeeta Khorana and Maria Garcia (eds), *Handbook on the EU and International Trade* (Edward Elgar 2018) 389.

98 Integration inevitably leads to a loss of policy space and regulatory autonomy: Brendan Vickers, 'Sub-Regions First: The Role and Evolution of Regional Economic Communities in Africa' in Giovanni Carbone (ed), *A Vision for Africa's Future: Mapping Change, Transformation and Trajectories Towards 2030* (Ledizioni 2018) 80.

99 On the diffusion of competition law models in Asia from Europe (though crucially these transplants were modified slightly to meet local expectations, like creating a competition authority that is not independent from the government): Tony Prosser, 'Competition Law and the Role of the State in East Asia' in Michael W Dowdle, John Gillespie, and Imelda Maher (eds), *Asian Capitalism and the Regulation of Competition: Towards a Regulatory Geography of Global Competition Law* (CUP 2013) 253.

100 Even before the GDPR, the Data Protection Directive has been highlighted as a prominent influence in the data protection laws of Asian countries from the 1990s onwards: Graham Greenleaf, *Asian Data Privacy Laws: Trade and Human Rights Perspectives* (OUP 2014) 12.

101 The surge in regional agreements after the failed Ministerial: Tubagus Feridhanusetyawan, 'Preferential Trade Agreements in the Asia–Pacific Region' (2005) (IMF Working Paper) 13.

of the WTO do not perceive such agreements to supplement the WTO framework and are rather intended to supplant it.[102] These agreements also have a significant focus on enforcement in relation to these regulatory issues, specifically in terms of which disputes can be submitted to the enforcement apparatus created by the trade agreement. The EU is particularly interesting in the context of dispute resolution in such Regional Trade Agreements (RTAs) as they have tended to focus on implementing exclusive mechanisms of dispute resolution.[103] The diversion of disputes away from the transparent dispute settlement of the WTO and into specialised and exclusive mechanisms established by the agreement introduces a significant element of differential treatment into the international environment. The tension here is that, as mentioned earlier, the paralysis of the WTO DSB has severely impacted the functioning of the multilateral trading system.[104] Yet exclusive dispute settlement mechanisms in these agreements are not the only option for dealing with this dysfunction, with the Multi-Party Interim Appeal Arbitration Arrangement (MPIA) demonstrating that there is still at least some vitality in multilateral dispute settlement. This shift in dispute settlement context also presents its own challenges to the use of flexibilities and exceptions, because their operation is then further individualised and their exercise is constructed relatively within each trade agreement.

Specifically for understanding the impact on transparency and participation in the international patent system, the shift towards exclusive dispute settlement would be minimal if it were confined to technically ambitious or complex agreements. This type of response would mirror the development of other specialised dispute mechanisms,[105] yet the rate and scope of agreements concluded provide what is essentially a parallel system of dispute resolution. In this context, it renders the WTO dispute settlement system an exception but also has the potential to impact the future trajectory of the WTO more generally. The disruption to the DSB

102 With a number of around 60, WTO Members clearly see bilateralism or regionalism at least somewhat as a replacement for multilateralism: Tubagus Feridhanusetyawan, 'Preferential Trade Agreements in the Asia–Pacific Region' (2005) (IMF Working Paper) 13.

103 On the emphasis on (exclusive) dispute settlement mechanisms in the EU regional trade agreements and excluding substantive topics from ordinary WTO dispute settlement process: Claude Chase, Alan Yanovich, Jo-Ann Crawford, and Pamela Ugaz, 'Mapping of Dispute Settlement Mechanisms in Regional Trade Agreements: Innovative or Variations on a Theme?' in Rohini Acharya (ed), *Regional Trade Agreements and the Multilateral Trading System* (CUP 2016) 636.

104 Imogen Saunders, 'Populism, Backlash and the Ongoing Use of the World Trade Organization Dispute Settlement System: State Responses to the Appellate Body Crisis' (2021) 35(1) Maryland Journal of International Law 172, 173.

105 The rise of specialisation across intellectual property and at a global level: intellectual property courts in Japan, South Korea, and China: Kyle Pietari, 'An Overview and Comparison of US and Japanese Patent Litigation' (2016) 98 Journal of the Patent and Trademark Office Society 540, 542; Duncan Matthews, 'Intellectual Property Courts in China' in Spyros Maniatis, Ioannis Kokkoris, and Wang Xiaoye (eds), *Competition Law and Intellectual Property in China and the ASEAN* (OUP 2019) 76; increased specialisation within Portugal for family and juvenile courts: *OECD Economic Surveys: Portugal 2019* (OECD 2019) 121; and the efficiency of court specialisation of the Tel Aviv District Court: Yifat Aran and Moran Ofir, 'The Effects of Specialised Courts over Time' in Sofia Ranchordás and Yaniv Roznai (eds), *Time, Law, and Change: An Interdisciplinary Study* (Bloomsbury 2020) 186.

Appellate Body has been significant and the MPIA does represent at least some positive response to these challenges. Yet the continued proliferation of agreements with their own dispute settlement mechanisms gives no positive indication that major economies like the EU will want to (or now, *need* to) engage with the work necessary to address the DSB Appellate Body problem. The entanglement that occurs here between actors in the bilateral space is taking place *within* the WTO framework and yet operates in a way that emphasises these more discrete points of contact contained in the specific agreements between countries. Such an inversion has been identified in the evolution of the Most-Favoured Nation (MFN) principle whereby the WTO framework has instead become representative of the 'least-favoured nation'.[106] And so, too, with dispute settlement – the WTO apparatus and institutions become not only the baseline, but the very bare minimum afforded to parties as a formal obligation. This sense of a minimum or baseline applicable standard also impacts how transparency and accountability function in this context. The relegation of multilateral values as a minimum standard undermines any attempt at developing more responsive or nuanced understandings of transparency and participation at the systemic multilateral level. Instead, values are advanced (or undermined) in the more limited and isolated contexts of discrete dispute resolution bodies as formalist constructions. Even if a specific dispute body was to provide a strong interpretation of these values in practice,[107] there is only a limited impact on the generalised role of transparency or accountability since it comes from such a contextually inflected environment. This is exacerbated by broader limitations of transparency in arbitral proceedings that further restrict the information available about how the dispute proceeded and the dynamic of its participants.

3.4.1.2 The emergence of European priorities in bilateral negotiations and their impact on patent law

The main focus of the EU in its bilateral agreements before the implementation of the Global Europe Strategy had typically been the protection of GIs and generally did not consider intellectual property as a discrete discipline.[108] The emphasis on GIs was an early priority for the EU for two main reasons, the first of which is that as a geographically and culturally diverse region, the EU (more than most inter-

106 Least favoured nation as it relates to discriminatory international trade as a subversion of MFN tariffs: Jagdish Bhagwati, *Termites in the Trading System: How Preferential Trading Agreements Undermine Free Trade* (OUP 2008) 14.

107 Such as a broader construction of participation in WTO disputes: Richard B Stewart, Michelle Ratton, and Sanchez Badin, 'The World Trade Organisation: Multiple Dimensions of Global Administrative Law' (2011) 9(3–4) ICON 564.

108 David Vivas Eugui and Christoph Spennemann, 'The Treatment of Geographical Indications in Recent Regional and Bilateral Free Trade Agreements' in Meir Perez Pugatch (ed), *The Intellectual Property Debate: Perspectives from Law, Economics, and Political Economy* (Edward Elgar 2006) 317.

national actors) had the most to gain from ensuring the products of its producers were protected in a manner that reflected the standard of protection domestically.[109] As discussed previously, an important consideration when looking at the treatment of patent law in the bilateral space is that it appears alongside other forms of intellectual property. Obligations covering GIs are generally only a single chapter of a trade agreement, which also covers elements from all forms of intellectual property. Understanding how GIs are constructed in these chapters is potentially important for patent law because the shift towards patent law provisions as a discrete subject was a later development. GIs, therefore, present a model of how the EU approaches, negotiates, and elaborates on provisions in a trade agreement that could be instructive for imagining the future of bilateral patent law and potential challenges to transparency, accountability, and participation.

Ensuring the protection of GIs – even by using the language of GIs – was important due to the fact that TRIPS requires countries to ensure the protection of these assets but not necessarily to incorporate the GI system as it emerged in Europe. The bilateral context became a central forum in exporting this mechanism of protection for GIs, though the majority of this 'exporting' was done in the context of developing countries that either lacked a robust enough existing system or were willing to adopt the EU standard to secure market access.[110] It is striking in its homogenising impact on developing countries because two of the largest economies – the US and Japan – do not protect GIs in the same manner as the EU. Both have distinct histories of cultural heritage and distinguished products that GIs typically protect, but neither have adopted the exact EU vocabulary.[111] The legislative provisions in both jurisdictions result in very similar levels of protection in practice to that provided under the GI system in Europe, and the unwillingness to harmonise the language of GIs suggests that there is a certain degree of conscious (conceptual if not practical) distancing going on.

109 With an estimated sales value of over 77 billion Euros in 2017: EU Commission, 'Study on Economic Value of EU Quality Schemes, Geographical Indications (GIs) and Traditional Specialities Guaranteed (TSGs)' (2021) <https://op.europa.eu/en/publication-detail/-/publication/a7281794-7ebe-11ea-aea8-01aa75ed71a1>.

110 The majority of the EU–Colombia–Peru FTA, as it concerns the protection of GIs, is essentially a set of demands from the EU side and covers an expanded scope of protection for instances that do not confuse a customer and terms that are considered generic or semi-generic in many other countries: Keith E Maskus, 'Assessing the Development Promise of IP Provisions in EU Economic Partnership Agreements' in Josef Drexl, Henning Grosse Ruse-Khan, and Souheir Nadde-Phlix (eds), *EU Bilateral Trade Agreements and Intellectual Property: For Better or Worse?* (Springer 2014) 179.

111 Despite lacking a geographical indications system, discussing the active involvement of the US government in promoting competition through a system of certification marks: Yogesh Pai and Tania Singla, '"Vanity GIs": India's Legislation on Geographical Indications and the Missing Regulatory Framework' in Irene Calboli and Ng-Loy Wee Loon (eds), *Geographical Indications at the Crossroads of Trade, Development, and Culture* (CUP 2017) 343; on the transition in Japan from regional collective trademarks to the current GI system: Greg de St Maurice, 'Savoring the Kyoto Brand' in Nancy K Stalker (ed), *Devouring Japan: Global Perspectives on Japanese Culinary Identity* (OUP 2018) 155.

In terms of how these different systems of protection coexist, the cultural and economic significance of the subject matter has the potential to meaningfully subvert future multilateral consensus. While the threat of multiple regulatory blocs has been raised in the context of broader trade regulation, GIs are politically and culturally sensitive enough that it would be a remarkable development for a major market actor such as the US or Japan to abandon their existing domestic principles and adopt the EU framework in a multilateral forum. As stated previously, the protection in each of these jurisdictions is very similar in practice but the language and precise structures are distinct to each.

In a process that would also come to define the development of the EPUE, the bilateral agreements that were concluded before 2006 would typically incorporate international agreements by reference.[112] This means that these agreements would typically not outline distinct provisions that would bind the parties and instead include an obligation to respect specific international agreements.[113] Incorporation by reference reflects the tension between the substantive and formal understandings of GAL values, where transparency has the potential to legitimise a lack of participatory impact. In this context, there is a transparency as to where the provisions come from and their legal effect, yet because of their mode of incorporation, trade partners have no real way of challenging these provisions or adapting them to their own needs. How would a partner have a meaningful input on the provisions of an obligation that are not even part of the agreement under negotiation?

This emphasis on broad principles and general themes changed with the Global Europe strategy in 2006. From this point, bilateral agreements included extensive intellectual property chapters and provisions to bind the parties involved to specific, generally more stringent, standards.[114] These chapters that govern intellectual property are also more specialised in the sense that they consider each intellectual property right separately[115] – something that has been highlighted as contributing significantly to the increasing length, scope, and specificity of these intellectual property sections.[116] The negotiation of each intellectual property right as a distinct regulatory sphere has a distinct impact on the character of the resulting agreement, primarily from a domestic perspective and more specifically in the case of developing countries. It represents an additional layer of complexity in the balancing

112 Tilman Krüger, 'Shaping the WTO's Institutional Evolution: The EU as a Strategic Litigant in the WTO' in Dimitry Kochenov and Fabian Amtenbrink (eds), *The European Union's Shaping of the International Order* (CUP 2014) 174.

113 Tilman Krüger, 'Shaping the WTO's Institutional Evolution: The EU as a Strategic Litigant in the WTO' in Dimitry Kochenov and Fabian Amtenbrink (eds), *The European Union's Shaping of the International Order* (CUP 2014) 174.

114 Thitapha Wattanapruttipaisan, 'The Topology of ASEAN FTAs, with Special Reference to IP-Related Provisions' in Christoph Antons and Reto M Hilty (eds), *Intellectual Property and Free Trade Agreements in the Asia–Pacific Region* (Springer 2014) 137, 138.

115 Anke Moerland, 'Do Developing Countries Have a Say? Bilateral and Regional Intellectual Property Negotiations with the EU' (2017) 48 IIC 760, 763.

116 Michael Handler and Bryan Mercurio, 'Intellectual Property' in Simon Lester, Bryan Mercurio, and Lorand Bartels (eds), *Bilateral and Regional Trade Agreements: Commentary and Analysis* (CUP 2015) 363.

of intellectual property rights for trade partners, criticised earlier in the book for widening the scope of relevant factors when balancing an appropriate intellectual property policy to considerations not just outside of intellectual property, but also to the macroeconomic features of another international actor. This type of shift in strategy also raises the same type of tensions in which this more diffuse and individualised approach to trade agreements works to obscure the values and principles driving the development of international trade law.

The individualised intellectual property provisions of the EU's intellectual property chapters push this further, with trade partners assessing trade-offs and compromises to their autonomy to set their own intellectual property policy on an industry-specific basis. This allows the EU to extract specific concessions in terms of intellectual property standards that maximise the benefits to its domestic producers, while also presenting an increasingly disciplinary-specific relationship between actors. This type of arrangement also highlights the multilevel impact of atomisation that is going on in international trade agreements. Rather than presenting a generalised lack of transparency (though this is also a concern),[117] the deficiencies themselves become localised and discipline-specific. One example would be in Chapter 10 of the South Korea-EU (KOREU) Agreement that deals with intellectual property broadly, but it is the comprehensive scope of the agreement that is perhaps indicative of the general developments in bilateral trade agreements. While it deals with substantive elements of patent law – even the controversial introduction of criminal sanctions for infringement[118] – it also regulates more specific or niche considerations such as the publication of judicial decisions,[119] legal costs and who bears the cost of proceedings,[120] and the protection of data submitted for plant protection products.[121] Taken together, the intellectual property provisions of KOREU are interesting because they represent the conclusion of a text which could easily be a standalone agreement in terms of scope. The agreement reflects the expansiveness of the bilateral agreements being concluded and the challenge of balancing between trade gains, autonomy, and increased standards in intellectual property in a way that empowers participants and promotes transparency – particularly when the agreements are operating at such a scope and scale.

3.4.1.3 Deconstructing how responsiveness and autonomy are minimised in the bilateral space

One of the major features of EU trade agreements with developing countries is that rather than providing for specific exceptions to the enhanced intellectual property

117 'After all, trade negotiations under the multilateral trading system are more open and transparent than in any bilateral or plurilateral trade agreements': Michelle Limenta, 'Open Trade Negotiations as Opposed to Secret Trade Negotiations: From Transparency to Public Participation' (2012) 10 New Zealand Yearbook of International Law 84.

118 Subsection B, Chapter 10 – Criminal Enforcement: KOREU Agreement.

119 Article 10.52, KOREU Agreement.

120 Article 10.51, KOREU Agreement.

121 Article 10.37, KOREU Agreement.

standards, there are typically only general statements about the trade partner's retained access to the flexibilities offered under TRIPS.[122] One example can be found in the KOREU Agreement which demonstrates the typically asymmetric approach. While all of Chapter 10 of the KOREU Agreement deals with intellectual property, there are essentially two explicit references to flexibilities in this sense and, therefore, provide an indication as to how the agreement meaningfully restricts, by omission, the autonomy of partners. Before considering these references to potential flexibilities in the text, it is important to recognise just how uneven the attention is in the agreement for issues of intellectual property. Flexibilities that deal with public health can be found in Article 10.34 – and yet there are entire subsections to the agreement that deal with different intellectual property rights.[123] The agreement is also indicative of how bilateral agreements are developing in terms of scope because the KOREU Agreement, in subsection D of Chapter 10, deals with the protection of design rights. The agreements are not just targeted cooperation in high-value areas like patent law or trademark, but instead represent quite comprehensive intellectual property agreements on their own. Article 10.34 purports to deal with the relationship between patents and public health, and yet it consists of two paragraphs. One of these paragraphs appears to merely outline the fact that the Doha Round produced the paragraph 6 system and parties should respect that,[124] and the other requires that the parties should recognise the importance of the TRIPS Agreement and Doha Declaration.[125]

Given the difficulties with which developing countries have had in successfully using the Doha Declaration or TRIPS flexibilities,[126] these agreements clearly demonstrate the fundamental asymmetry in legal obligation and autonomy for trade partners.[127] While the developing country adopts higher standards (specifically in enforcement) that generally reflect the legal approach of the EU, there is no corresponding increase or advance in flexibilities or options for lawfully derogating the obligations of the trade agreement in specific circumstances. In these agreements, what is lost is not just the overall structure of negotiations in a multilateral context, but also the institutional mechanisms and values that mitigate obvious imbalances between WTO members. One example would be the role of third parties

122 Billy AM Araujo, *The EU Deep Trade Agenda* (OUP 2016) 167.

123 Subsection C of Chapter 10 would be one example which deals with how liability for ISPs should be constructed.

124 Article 10.34(1), KOREU Agreement.

125 Article 10.34(1), KOREU Agreement.

126 '… the difficulties that may exist for developing countries to establish and maintain the political conditions which they can make a concrete use of TRIPS flexibilities.': Gaëlle Krikorian, 'The Politics of Patents: Conditions of Implementation of Public Health Policy in Thailand' in Sebastian Haunss and Kenneth C Shadlen (eds), *Politics of Intellectual Property: Contestation Over the Ownership, Use and Control of Knowledge and Information* (Edward Elgar 2009) 49.

127 On the difficulties of developing countries making use of the flexibilities in TRIPS: Ernias Tekeste Biadgleng, 'The Development–Balance of the TRIPS Agreement and Enforcement of Intellectual Property Rights' in Justin Malbon and Charles Lawson (eds), *Interpreting and Implementing the TRIPS Agreement: Is it Fair?* (Edward Elgar 2008) 110.

in WTO procedures,[128] falling short of the type of formal amicus system in other legal arrangements but still enabling a wider scope of participation and minimising information asymmetries. This emphasis on participation is essential to reducing great asymmetries (and contributing to the legitimacy of an initiative overall), and yet cannot be easily transplanted to the bilateral space. More generally, however, these concerns around participation and transparency are taking place in an environment where there have been persistent calls to allow for NGOs or other civil society contributions to EU and WTO Agreements.[129]

References to specific flexibilities also appear when the EU is negotiating the implementation of enforcement obligations, though this has typically taken the form of provisions lifted almost identically from the Enforcement Directive in the EU that permit some manoeuvrability in the process of domestic implementation.[130] Rather than suggesting an EU focused on mitigating the negative impact of its trade rules, these inconsistencies speak to a bilateral trade policy constituted from discrete and somewhat disconnected legal interfaces. The KOREU Agreement, in particular, represents an experimentalist approach to trade agreements that will set the foundation for future trade agreements. In the context of these references to flexibilities in trade agreements, even a very generous reading of those interpretations into the trade agreements cannot overcome the fact that these are agreements that have been negotiated outside of the multilateral trade environment and are, by their nature, TRIPS-Plus and implement more restrictive obligations. These provisions do not modify the underlying multilateral framework, and therefore, without the explicit and concerted development of flexibilities within these agreements, there is little hope that these trading partners could rely securely on a provision that merely references an aspirational objective of food security or research.[131] Developing countries in particular have struggled to make use of the explicit flexibilities of the TRIPS Agreement – for a variety of legal and political reasons[132]

128 For academic commentary: Marc L Busch and Eric Reinhardt, 'Three's a Crowd: Third Parties and WTO Dispute Settlement' (2006) 58(3) World Politics 446.

129 On the contested perspectives on NGO involvement (or 'global civil society' more generally) in the WTO: Matthew D Stephen, 'Contestation Overshoot: Rising Powers, NGOs, and the Failure of the WTO Doha Round' in Matthew D Stephen and Michael Zürn (eds), *Contested World Orders: Rising Powers, Non-Governmental Organizations, and the Politics of Authority Beyond the Nation–State* (OUP 2019) 43.

130 Thomas Jaeger, 'IP Enforcement Provisions in EU Economic Partnership Agreements' in Josef Drexl, Henning Grosse Ruse-Khan, and Souheir Nadde-Phlix (eds), *EU Bilateral Trade Agreements and Intellectual Property: For Better or Worse?* (Springer 2014) 192.

131 One notable example is the side letters the US included in its FTA with Peru, Colombia, and Panama that state the importance of the trade agreement signatories to protect public health, though the legal status of these letters is concerning not least because they do not form part of the actual trade agreement text and provide difficulties in the terminology they use (such as 'TRIPS health solution'): Michael Handler and Bryan Mercurio, 'Intellectual Property' in Simon Lester and Bryan Mercurio (eds), *Bilateral and Regional Trade Agreements: Commentary and Issues* (CUP 2009) 337.

132 On the political elements of bilateral agreements that balance the economic sense of an agreement: Olivier Cattaneo, 'The Political Economy of PTAs' in Simon Lester and Bryan Mercurio (eds), *Bilateral and Regional Trade Agreements: Commentary and Issues* (CUP 2009) 30.

– which would also question the value of the legal status of a side document or underdeveloped provision in a bilateral trade agreement.[133]

The KOREU Agreement, in Article 10.34, provides something similar in terms of an aspirational mechanism. In contrast to the elaborate subchapters devoted to each specific type of intellectual property, Article 10.34 merely states that the parties are entitled to rely on the Doha Declaration. A fundamental element of this agreement, however, is that it is an agreement between two industrialised countries and this necessarily impacts the scope of provisions that are included (or not included). Yet the KOREU Agreement is significant even in how clearly it demonstrates what is essentially non-content in the part dealing with public health. The KOREU Agreement reflects a more general trend that, within these broader trade agreements, a comprehensive, standalone intellectual property agreement is also being concluded in parallel.

KOREU, as controversial as it is in the development of criminal enforcement, can also be read as the first step into a cautious new stage of policy development at the level of bilateral agreements and an increasingly comprehensive approach to these initiatives. Beyond the criticisms of policy laundering and the expansive Commission mandate, its significance extends far beyond this because it highlights the importance of interpretation in constructing legal meaning. By failing to provide an appropriate level of transparency as to how policy and provisions were produced, accountability as to how those provisions are then interpreted is also impacted. As a result, a limited set of actors empowered to interpret or create meaning from broad trade provisions benefit from the combined failings in transparency, accountability, and participation in the bilateral space. Though its rules on criminal enforcement may be extensive, the KOREU text does not, in fact, define what is to be considered 'commercial scale' infringement and, therefore, retains the relatively open definition in TRIPS and provides scope for interpretative development.[134] Crucially, the interpretation of what constitutes 'commercial scale', if it emerged from a dispute over KOREU provisions, would reflect the process of increasingly specific frames of reference for these interfaces and essentially produce a definition of 'commercial scale' applicable only to the unique context of the KOREU relationship. This is perhaps not, as Araujo argues, evidence that the parties were not willing to incorporate controversial TRIPS-Plus language into the KOREU Agreement,[135] and instead can be read more as an exercise in caution. The KOREU Agreement is controversial enough since it covers criminal enforcement at all. To then include a specific (and presumably, expansive) definition of what commercial scale is, even though TRIPS fails to provide one, is unlikely to have fundamentally hindered the conclusion of the agreement.

133 Michael Handler and Bryan Mercurio, 'Intellectual Property' in Simon Lester and Bryan Mercurio (eds), *Bilateral and Regional Trade Agreements: Commentary and Issues* (CUP 2009) 337.

134 Xavier Seuba, *The Global Regime for the Enforcement of Intellectual Property Rights* (CUP 2017) 391.

135 Billy AM Araujo, *The EU Deep Trade Agenda* (OUP 2016) 174.

The accusations of policy laundering stand out when one considers the development of enforcement provisions within the EU framework and suggests a subversion of the legislative process by the Commission.[136] When criminal enforcement measures were proposed in the EU, there were important human rights considerations that were raised by the European Parliament to balance the expansiveness of the provisions.[137] These safeguards are not incorporated into Association agreement between the EU and Central America (EU-CA) or the KOREU trade agreement and, therefore, rely on the general TRIPS exceptions to protect non-trade human rights concerns.[138] This is the defining characteristic of the EU's strategy in new trade agreements: a post-Global Europe strategy of minimising the internal and external boundaries in law that creates increasingly contextualised legal arrangements that minimise transparency, accountability, and participation. In this, the lack of correspondingly developed flexibilities to the expanded obligations is not simply a minimising of flexibilities but a symptom of a broader approach that prioritises expansion over balanced development. This is not to argue that the EU has become a sinister actor that intentionally sets out to hamper the autonomy of developing countries. Rather, it should instead be taken as evidence that the concepts of transparency, accountability, and participation are not prominent considerations – or at least the vocabulary of these values is not – when developing international trade policy and intellectual property more specifically. It also speaks to the broader importance of the approach used in this book, where perhaps an analysis of international trade that focuses on understanding it from an inclusive or expansive perspective could reveal these currently invisible tensions in an accessible vocabulary. Though not to the same extent as patent law, this type of framing works to highlight the interconnected nature of trade and facilitate communication and engagement with those outside of a conventional international trade audience.

3.5 Conclusion

Bilateral and free trade agreements have emerged as some of the most important elements in the trade relationship between international actors and have contributed significantly to the growth of global trade. Bilateral agreements promote cooperation between partners across a variety of disciplines in a way that provides tangible trade gains at a (potentially, and not always) quicker pace than when negotiating in the multilateral environment. They also provide a unique perspective for exploring how administrative values such as accountability, participation, and transparency function in a more contextually sensitive and localised trade environment. While

136 On the Commission forcing internal regulatory reform by stealth: Billy AM Araujo, *The EU Deep Trade Agenda* (OUP 2016) 174.

137 George Cumming, Mirjam Freudenthal, and Ruth Janal, *Enforcement of Intellectual Property Rights in Dutch, English, and German Civil Procedure* (Kluwer 2008) 57.

138 Peter K Yu, 'EU Economic Partnership Agreements and International Human Rights' in Josef Drexl, Henning Grosse Ruse-Khan, and Souheir Nadde-Phlix (eds), *EU Bilateral Trade Agreements and Intellectual Property: For Better or Worse?* (Springer 2014) 126.

there are periods in recent decades where multilateralism would appear to falter and bilateralism emerges in response, the more recent proliferation of bilateral agreements (particularly with the EU) reflects a much broader history of alternating cycles of multilateralism and bilateralism.

The creation of these new relationships is then a fundamental part of the development of 'TRIPS-Plus' and 'WTO-Plus' provisions that have emerged as a significant discussion in bilateral agreements in recent decades. Though the WTO agreements necessarily provide a broad framing for legal interfaces that deal with trade because of their expansive nature, there are still disciplines outside the scope of the WTO. The tension in the bilateral context comes from the fact that it does not involve the creation of a singular legal interface. Instead, the bilateral space involves the creation of multiple, increasingly specific, legal interfaces that produce their own relationship to transparency and accountability. The chapter emphasised not only how the administrative values can be used to interpret these trade relationships, but how they can also contribute to our understanding of a distinct bilateral space more fundamentally.[139] At this level, each IP chapter that is developed in each specific trade relationship provides a localised interpretation of the values that drive legal developments in intellectual property. This presents bilateral trade agreements as being both disciplinary-specific and specific to the trade partners in a way that is not necessarily generalisable. This also extends to the use of mechanisms such as exceptions or flexibilities to navigate these interfaces, highlighting that both the interface itself and the tools it provides are context-specific. Evidence of transparency or accountability in specific bilateral trade agreements is not necessarily identical in quality or character, even when similar provisions exist in other bilateral agreements that cover similar subject matter.

Beyond this, the more general dynamic of these bilateral interfaces to the broader instrument will necessarily be influenced by whether or not they are elaborating on existing obligations (TRIPS-Plus) or are incorporating disciplines that are not currently regulated in a multilateral instrument (WTO-Plus). The 'global ratchet' of ever-increasing standards in intellectual property highlights the tensions in the relationship between the multilateral and bilateral modes of law-making as it has a restrictive effect on how multilateral consensus forms and negotiations function. These higher standards and elaborated constructions of TRIPS provisions have become a central part of the debate around contemporary issues in patent law like access to medicine. The concerns around the global ratchet have been explored throughout this chapter from the perspective of transparency as to the development of intellectual property.

The issue for transparency here is not only the lack of transparency as to the binding quality of provisions, but a more fundamental lack of transparency around the trajectory of international intellectual property law itself. Bilateral trade agreements have been used as evidence for global consensus and advancing higher

139 Drawing on earlier discussions in global administration as to the existence of a distinct 'global space': Elisa D'Alterio, 'Judicial Regulation in the Global Space' in Sabino Cassese (ed), *Research Handbook on Global Administrative Law* (Edward Elgar 2016) 321.

global standards, yet they emerge from the increasing atomisation of modern trade agreements in the bilateral space. These concerns are compounded because of the lack of transparency and participation that frame bilateral trade agreements, where the role of state actors appears to be minimised. For participation, it is a narrow class of actors that are responsible for the negotiation and development of bilateral agreements in a way that resists general oversight or engagement. Taken together, there is a dissonance between the clear textual provisions and its contextual development process. The values and principles that informed the negotiations, as well as the political process of 'trading' standards in areas of strategic interest, are obscured and produce a concerning lack of transparency as to the future development of international patent law.

Bibliography

Articles

Abbas MZ, 'India's Distinct but Opposing Patent Model is Under Pressure: Prospects and Challenges in the Global Arena' (2024) 80(1) *India Quarterly* 117.

Abbott FM, 'A New Dominant Trade Species: Is Bilateralism a Threat?' (2007) 10(3) *Journal of International Economic Law* 571.

Busch ML and E Reinhardt, 'Three's a Crowd: Third Parties and WTO Dispute Settlement' (2006) 58(3) *World Politics* 446.

Chander A and M Sunder, 'The Battle to Define Asia's Intellectual Property Law: From TPP to RCEP' (2018) 8 *UC Irvine Law Review* 331.

Dagne TW, 'The Narrowing Transatlantic Divide: Geographical Indications in Canada's Trade Agreements' (2016) 10 *European Review of Intellectual Property Law* 598.

Drahos P, 'BITs and BIPs: Bilateralism in Intellectual Property' (2001) 4 *The Journal of World Intellectual Property* 791.

Dreyfuss RC, 'TRIPS-Round II: Should Users Strike Back?' (2004) 71 *University of Chicago Law Review* 21.

Fredriksson PG, 'The Political Economy of Trade Liberalization and Environmental Policy' (1999) 65(3) *Southern Economic Journal* 513.

Guan W, 'Diversified FRAND Enforcement and TRIPS Integrity' (2018) 17(1) *World Trade Review* 91.

Limenta M, 'Open Trade Negotiations as Opposed to Secret Trade Negotiations: From Transparency to Public Participation' (2012) 10 *New Zealand Yearbook of International Law* 73.

Moerland A, 'Do Developing Countries Have a Say? Bilateral and Regional Intellectual Property Negotiations with the EU' (2017) 48 *International Review of Intellectual Property and Competition Law* 760.

Morgera E, 'The EU and Environmental Multilateralism: The Case of Access and Benefit-Sharing and the Need for a Good-Faith Test' (2014) 16 *Cambridge Yearbook of European Legal Studies* 109.

Owoeye O, 'Access to Medicines and Parallel Trade in Patented Pharmaceuticals' (2015) 37(6) *European Review of Intellectual Property Law* 359.

Pietari K, 'An Overview and Comparison of US and Japanese Patent Litigation' (2016) 98 *Journal of the Patent and Trademark Office Society* 540.

Rachlinski JJ and AJ Wistrich, 'Judging the Judiciary by the Numbers: Empirical Research on Judges' (2017) 13 *Annual Review of Law and Social Science* 203.

Rajec SRW, 'The Harmonization Myth in International Intellectual Property Law' (2020) 62 *Arizona Law Review* 735.

Reichman JH, 'The TRIPS Component of the GATT's Uruguay Round: Competitive Prospects for Intellectual Property Owners in an Integrated World Market' (1993) 4 *Fordham Intellectual Property, Media & Entertainment Law Journal* 171.
Ruse-Khan HG, 'From TRIPS to FTAS and Back: Re-Conceptualising the Role of a Multilateral IP Framework in a TRIPS-Plus World' in *Netherlands Yearbook of International Law* (2018) 57.
Saunders I, 'Populism, Backlash and the Ongoing Use of the World Trade Organization Dispute Settlement System: State Responses to the Appellate Body Crisis' (2021) 35(1) *Maryland Journal of International Law* 172.
Sopranzetti S, 'Overlapping Free Trade Agreements and International Trade: A Network Approach' (2018) 41(6) *The World Economy* 1549.
Soyeju O and J Wabwire, 'The WTO-TRIPS Flexibilities on Public Health: A Critical Appraisal of the East African Community Regional Framework' (2018) 17(1) *World Trade Review* 145.
Stewart RB, M Ratton, and S Badin, 'The World Trade Organisation: Multiple Dimensions of Global Administrative Law' (2011) 9(3–4) *International Journal of Constitutional Law* 556.
Wolfe R, 'The WTO Single Undertaking as Negotiating Technique and Constitutive Metaphor' (2009) 12(4) *Journal of International Economic Law* 835.
Xavier S, 'Top Heavy: Beyond the Global North and the Justification for Global Administrative Law' (2018) 57 *Indian Journal of International Law* 337.

Books

Araujo BAM, *The EU Deep Trade Agenda* (OUP 2016).
Bhagwati J, *Termites in the Trading System: How Preferential Trading Agreements Undermine Free Trade* (OUP 2008).
Bhala R, *Modern GATT Law: A Treatise on the General Agreement on Tariffs and Trade* (Sweet & Maxwell 2005).
Cumming G, M Freudenthal, and R Janal, *Enforcement of Intellectual Property Rights in Dutch, English, and German Civil Procedure* (Kluwer 2008).
Emerson M, TH Edwards, I Gazizullin, M Lücke, D Müller-Jentsch, V Nanivska, V Pyatnytskiy, A Schneider, R Schweickert, O Shevstov, and O Shumylo, *The Prospect of Deep Free Trade Between the European Union and Ukraine* (CEPS 2006).
Eugui DV and C Spennemann, 'The Treatment of Geographical Indications in Recent Regional and Bilateral Free Trade Agreements' in Meir Perez Pugatch (ed), *The Intellectual Property Debate: Perspectives from Law, Economics, and Political Economy* (Edward Elgar 2006) 317.
Farmer K and M Schelnast, *Growth and International Trade: An Introduction to the Overlapping Generations Approach* (Springer 2013).
Greenleaf G, *Asian Data Privacy Laws: Trade and Human Rights Perspectives* (OUP 2014).
Gutterman A and BJ Anderson, *Intellectual Property in Global Markets* (Springer 1997).
Helfer LR and GW Austin, *Human Rights and Intellectual Property: Mapping the Global Interface* (CUP 2011).
Jones K, *Reconstructing the World Trade Organisation for the 21st Century: An Institutional Approach* (OUP 2015) 186.
Kariyawasam R, *International Economic Law and the Digital Divide: A New Silk Road?* (Edward Elgar 2007).
Leal-Arcas R, *Climate Change and International Trade* (Edward Elgar 2013).
McCalla AF and JD Nash, *Reforming Agricultural Trade for Developing Countries: Quantifying the Impact of Multilateral Trade Reform* (World Bank Publications 2007).

Natens B, *Regulatory Autonomy and International Trade in Services: The EU under GATS and RTAS* (Edward Elgar 2016).
Otmazgin NK, *Regionalizing Culture; The Political Economy of Japanese Popular Culture in Asia* (University of Hawaii Press 2013).
Reinalda B, *Routledge History of International Organisations: From 1815 to the Present Day* (Routledge 2009).
Seuba X, *The Global Regime for the Enforcement of Intellectual Property Rights* (CUP 2017).
Schaffer R, F Agusti, and LJ Dhooge, *International Business Law and Its Environment* (Cengage 2017).

Chapters

Abbott FM, 'The Future of IPRs in the Multilateral Trading System' in Christophe Bellmann and Ricardo Melendez-Ortiz (eds), *Trading in Knowledge: Development Perspectives on TRIPS, Trade and Sustainability* (Routledge 2013) 36.
Aleman MM, 'Impact of TRIPS-Plus Obligations in Economic Partnership- and Free Trade Agreements on International IP Law' in Josef Drexl, Henning Grosse Ruse-Khan, and Souheir Nadde-Phlix (eds), *EU Bilateral Trade Agreements and Intellectual Property: For Better or Worse?* (Springer 2014) 61.
Amaral Júnior AD and C Kramer, 'WTO as a Self-Limited Regime: The Case of Article XX GATT' in Alberto do Amaral Júnior, Luciana Maria de Oliveira Sá Pires, and Cristiane Lucena Carneiro (eds), *The WTO Dispute Settlement Mechanisms: A Developing Country Perspective* (Springer 2019) 69.
Antons C and RM Hilty, 'Introduction: IP and the Asia–Pacific "Spaghetti Bowl" of Free Trade Agreements' in Christoph Antons and Reto M Hilty (eds), *Intellectual Property and Free Trade Agreements in the Asia–Pacific Region* (Springer 2015) 1.
Aran Y and M Ofir, 'The Effects of Specialised Courts over Time' in Sofia Ranchordás and Yaniv Roznai (eds), *Time, Law, and Change: An Interdisciplinary Study* (Bloomsbury 2020) 167.
Biadgleng ET, 'The Development-Balance of the TRIPS Agreement and Enforcement of Intellectual Property Rights' in Justin Malbon and Charles Lawson (eds), *Interpreting and Implementing the TRIPS Agreement: Is it Fair?* (Edward Elgar 2008) 97.
Birkbeck CD, 'WIPO's Assistance to Developing Countries: The Evolution of Debate and Current Challenges' in Xavier Seuba and Carlos Correa (eds), *Intellectual Property and Development: Understanding the Interfaces* (Springer 2019) 137.
Brünjes K and M Weidenfeller, 'Multilateral Trade Policy is Back' in Christoph Herrmann, Bruno Simma, and Rudolf Streinz (eds), *Trade Policy Between Law, Diplomacy and Scholarship* (Springer 2015) 47.
Cattaneo O, 'The Political Economy of PTAs' in Simon Lester, Bryan Mercurio, and Lorand Bartels (eds), *Bilateral and Regional Trade Agreements: Commentary and Analysis* (CUP 2015) 28.
Chané AL and M Killander, 'The EU and Africa' in Ramses A Wessel and Jed Odermatt (eds), *Research Handbook on the European Union and International Organisations* (Edward Elgar 2019) 587.
Chase C, A Yanovich, JA Crawford, and P Ugaz, 'Mapping of Dispute Settlement Mechanisms in Regional Trade Agreements: Innovative or Variations on a Theme?' in Rohini Acharya (ed), *Regional Trade Agreements and the Multilateral Trading System* (CUP 2016) 608.
Cimoli M, G Dosi, R Mazzoleni, and BN Sampat, 'Innovation, Technical Change, and Patents in the Development Process: A Long-Term View' in Mario Cimoli, Giovanni Dosi, Keith E Maskus, Ruth L Okediji, Jerome H Reichman, and Joseph E Stiglitz (eds),

Intellectual Property Rights: Legal and Economic Challenges for Development (OUP 2014) 57.

Cottier T, D Jost, and M Schupp, 'The Prospects of TRIPS-Plus Protection in Future Mega-Regionals' in Thilo Rensmann (ed), *Mega-Regional Trade Agreements* (Springer 2017) 191.

D'Alterio E, 'Judicial Regulation in the Global Space' in Sabino Cassese (ed), *Research Handbook on Global Administrative Law* (Edward Elgar 2016) 303.

Dahrendorf A, 'Global Proliferation of Bilateral and Regional Trade Agreements: A Threat for the World Trade Organisation and/or for Developing Countries?' in Jana Hertwig and Sylvia Maus (eds), *Global Risks: Constructing World Order Through Law, Politics and Economics* (Peter Lang 2010) 39.

Drahos P, 'Doing Deals with Al Capone: Paying Protection Money for Intellectual Property in the Global Knowledge Economy' in Peter K Yu (ed), *Intellectual Property and Information Wealth: Issues and Practices in the Digital Age* (Greenwood 2007) 41.

Dreyfuss RC, 'Harmonization: Top Down, Bottom Up–and Now Sideways?: The Impact of the IP Provisions of Megaregional Agreements on Third Party States' in Benedict Kingsbury, David M Malone, Paul Mertenskötter, Richard B Stewart, Thomas Streinz, and Atsushi Sunami (eds), *Megaregulation Contested: Global Economic Ordering After TPP* (OUP 2019) 345.

Garcia-Duran P, M Millet, and J Orbie, 'EU Trade Policy Reaction to the BIC: From Accommodation to Entrenchment' in Esther Barbé, Oriol Costa, and Robert Kissack (eds), *EU Policy Responses to a Shifting Multilateral System* (Macmillan 2016) 93.

Gok GO and RF Karadeniz, 'The UN's Legitimacy in Global Governance and the COVID-19 Pandemic' in Gonca Oguz Gok and Hakan Mehmetcik (eds), *The Crises of Legitimacy in Global Governance* (Routledge 2022) 72.

Handler M and B Mercurio, 'Intellectual Property' in Simon Lester, Bryan Mercurio, and Lorand Bartels (eds), *Bilateral and Regional Trade Agreements: Commentary and Analysis* (CUP 2015) 324.

Hart CE and JC Beghin, 'Rethinking Agricultural Domestic Support under the World Trade Organization' in Kym Anderson and Will Martin (eds), *Agricultural Trade Reform and the Doha Development Agenda* (World Bank Publications 2005) 221.

Hoekman B and DE Konan, 'Deep Integration, Discrimination, and Euro-Mediterranean Free Trade' in Jürgen von Hagen and Mika Widgren (eds), *Regionalism in Europe: Geometries and Strategies After 2000* (Springer 2012) 171.

Howell TR, 'The Multilateral Trading System and Transnational Competition in Advanced Technologies: The Limits of Existing Disciplines' in Göran Marklund, Nicholas S Vonortas, and Charles W Wessner (eds), *The Innovation Imperative: National Innovation Strategies in the Global Economy* (Edward Elgar 2009) 50.

Hufbauer GC and S Stephenson, 'The Free Trade Area of the Americas: How Deep an Integration in the Western Hemisphere?' in Hadi Soesastro and Christopher Findlay (eds), *Reshaping the Asia Pacific Economic Order* (Routledge 2006) 130.

Jaeger T, 'IP Enforcement Provisions in EU Economic Partnership Agreements' in Josef Drexl, Henning Grosse Ruse-Khan, and Souheir Nadde-Phlix (eds), *EU Bilateral Trade Agreements and Intellectual Property: For Better or Worse?* (Springer 2014) 189.

Khorana S and WG Voss, 'The Digital Single Market: Move from Traditional to Digital?' In Sangeeta Khorana and Maria Garcia (eds), *Handbook on the EU and International Trade* (Edward Elgar 2018) 384.

Kimura C and FG Nicola, 'The Negotiating Capital of Trade Experts: Transparency in EU-Asian Free Trade Agreements' in Emilia Korekea-Ago and Päivi Leino-Sandberg (eds), *Law, Legal Expertise and EU Policy-Making* (CUP 2022) 173.

Krauss ES, 'The United States in APEC's EVSL Negotiations' in Ellis S Krauss and T J Pempel (eds), *Beyond Bilateralism: US-Japan Relations in the New Asia–Pacific* (Stanford University Press 2004) 272.

Krikorian G, 'The Politics of Patents: Conditions of Implementation of Public Health Policy in Thailand' in Sebastian Haunss and Kenneth C Shadlen (eds), *Politics of Intellectual Property: Contestation Over the Ownership, Use and Control of Knowledge and Information* (Edward Elgar 2009) 29.

Krishna P, 'The Economics of PTAs' in Simon Lester, Bryan Mercurio, and Lorand Bartels (eds), *Bilateral and Regional Trade Agreements: Commentary and Analysis* (2nd edn, CUP 2015) 11.

Krüger T, 'Shaping the WTO's Institutional Evolution: The EU as a Strategic Litigant in the WTO' in Dimitry Kochenov and Fabian Amtenbrink (eds), *The European Union's Shaping of the International Order* (CUP 2014) 169.

Latrille P, 'Services Rules in Regional Trade Agreements: How Diverse or Creative are they Compared to the Multilateral Rules?' in Rohini Acharya (ed), *Regional Trade Agreements and the Multilateral Trading System* (CUP 2016) 421.

Maskus KE, 'Assessing the Development Promise of IP Provisions in EU Economic Partnership Agreements' in Josef Drexl, Henning Grosse Ruse-Khan, and Souheir Nadde-Phlix (eds), *EU Bilateral Trade Agreements and Intellectual Property: For Better or Worse?* (Springer 2014) 171.

Maskus KE, 'Policy Space in Intellectual Property Rights and Technology Transfer: A New Economic Research Agenda' in Xavier Seuba and Carlos Correa (eds), *Intellectual Property and Development: Understanding the Interfaces* (Springer 2019) 3.

Mathis JH, 'Regional Trade Agreements and Domestic Regulation: What Reach for "Other Restrictive Regulations of Commerce"?' in Lorand Bartels and Federico Ortino (eds), *Regional Trade Agreements and the WTO Legal System* (OUP 2006) 79.

Matthews D, 'Intellectual Property Courts in China' in Spyros Maniatis, Ioannis Kokkoris, and Wang Xiaoye (eds), *Competition Law and Intellectual Property in China and the ASEAN* (OUP 2019) 76.

Mercurio B, 'TRIPS-Plus Provisions in FTAs: Recent Trends' in Lorand Bartels and Federico Ortino (eds), *Regional Trade Agreements and the WTO Legal System* (OUP 2006) 215.

Mitchell AD and T Voon, 'Australia-United States Free Trade Agreement' in Simon Lester and Bryan Mercurio (eds), *Bilateral and Regional Trade Agreements: Case Studies* (CUP 2009) 6.

Orford A, 'Theorizing Free Trade' in Anne Orford and Florian Hoffmann (eds), *The Oxford Handbook of the Theory of International Law* (OUP 2016) 701.

Pai Y and T Singla, '"Vanity GIs": India's Legislation on Geographical Indications and the Missing Regulatory Framework' in Irene Calboli and Ng-Loy Wee Loon (eds), *Geographical Indications at the Crossroads of Trade, Development, and Culture* (CUP 2017) 333.

Petersmann EU, 'The WTO and Regional Trade Agreements as Competing Fora for Constitutional Reforms: Trade and Human Rights' in Lorand Bartels and Federico Ortino (eds), *Regional Trade Agreements and the WTO Legal System* (OUP 2006) 281.

Prosser T, 'Competition Law and the Role of the State in East Asia' in Michael W Dowdle, John Gillespie, and Imelda Maher (eds), *Asian Capitalism and the Regulation of Competition: Towards a Regulatory Geography of Global Competition Law* (CUP 2013) 228.

Ricketson S, 'Implementing Treaty Obligations at the National Level' in Niklas Bruun, Graeme B Dinwoodie, Marianne Levin, and Ansgar Ohly (eds), *Transition and Coherence in Intellectual Property Law* (CUP 2021) 107.

Roffe P, 'Intellectual Property Chapters in Free Trade Agreements: Their Significance and Systemic Implications' in Josef Drexl, Henning Grosse Ruse-Khan, and Souheir Nadde-Phlix (eds), *EU Bilateral Trade Agreements and Intellectual Property: For Better or Worse?* (Springer 2014) 17.

Santos A, 'Carving Out Policy Autonomy for Developing Countries in the World Trade Organisation: The Experience of Brazil and Mexico' in David M Trubek, Helena Alviar

Garcia, Diogo R Coutinho, and Alvaro Santos (eds), *Law and the New Developmental State: The Brazilian Experience in Latin American Context* (CUP 2013) 167.
de St Maurice G, 'Savoring the Kyoto Brand' in Nancy K Stalker (ed), *Devouring Japan: Global Perspectives on Japanese Culinary Identity* (OUP 2018) 153.
Stephen MD, 'Contestation Overshoot: Rising Powers, NGOs, and the Failure of the WTO Doha Round' in Matthew D Stephen and Michael Zürn (eds), *Contested World Orders: Rising Powers, Non-Governmental Organizations, and the Politics of Authority Beyond the Nation-State* (OUP 2019) 39.
Vickers B, 'Sub-Regions First: The Role and Evolution of Regional Economic Communities in Africa' in Giovanni Carbone (ed), *A Vision for Africa's Future: Mapping Change, Transformation and Trajectories Towards 2030* (Ledizioni 2018) 69.
Watal J, 'Is TRIPS a Balanced Agreement from the Perspective of Recent Free Trade Agreements?' in Josef Drexl, Henning Grosse Ruse-Khan, and Souheir Nadde-Phlix (eds), *EU Bilateral Trade Agreements and Intellectual Property: For Better or Worse?* (Springer 2014) 41.
Wattanapruttipaisan T, 'The Topology of ASEAN FTAs, with Special Reference to IP-Related Provisions' in Christoph Antons and Reto M Hilty (eds), *Intellectual Property and Free Trade Agreements in the Asia–Pacific Region* (Springer 2014) 109.
Wouters J, 'Government by Negotiation' in Sabino Cassese (ed), *Research Handbook on Global Administrative Law* (Edward Elgar 2016) 296.
Wouters J, S Duquet, and N Hachez, 'International Investment Law: The Perpetual Search for Consensus' in Olivier de Schutter, Johan F M Swinnen, and Jan Wouters (eds), *Foreign Direct Investment and Human Development: The Law and Economics of International Investment Agreements* (Routledge 2013) 25.
Yu PK, 'Development Bridge Over Troubled Intellectual Property Water' in Carlos Correa and Xavier Seuba (eds), *Intellectual Property and Development: Understanding the Interfaces* (Springer 2019) 97.
Yu PK, 'EU Economic Partnership Agreements and International Human Rights' in Josef Drexl, Henning Grosse Ruse-Khan, and Souheir Nadde-Phlix (eds), *EU Bilateral Trade Agreements and Intellectual Property: For Better or Worse?* (Springer 2014) 109.

Legislation

Article 78 Agreement Establishing an Association between the European Union and its Member States, On the One Hand, and Central America on the Other.
Article 229 TRIPS Agreement.
Article XXIV GATT 1947.
Article XXIV GATT 1994.
KOREU Agreement.

Cases

Council v Sophie In't Veld EU:C:2014:2039.

Other

Acharya A, 'Global Governance in a Multiplex World' (RSCAS Working Paper 2017/29 2017) 5.
Delimatsis P, 'TTIP, CETA, TISA Behind Closed Doors: Transparency in the EU Trade Policy' (2016) TILEC Discussion Paper 2016-020.

EU Commission, 'Study on Economic Value of EU Quality Schemes, Geographical Indications (GIs) and Traditional Specialities Guaranteed (TSGs)' (2021) <https://op.europa.eu/en/publication-detail/-/publication/a7281794-7ebe-11ea-aea8-01aa75ed71a1>.
EU Commission, 'Transparency in EU Trade Negotiations' <https://policy.trade.ec.europa.eu/eu-trade-relationships-country-and-region/transparency-eu-trade-negotiations_en>.
Feridhanusetyawan T, 'Preferential Trade Agreements in the Asia–Pacific Region' (IMF Working Paper 2005).
Hamdani K, 'Panel: Process and Value of Uniform Commercial Law: Proceedings of the Congress of the United Nations Commission on International Trade Law Held on the Occasion of the Fortieth Session of the Commission' (2007) 25.
OECD, *OECD Economic Surveys: Portugal 2019* (OECD 2019)
de Paiva Abreu M, 'Developing Countries and the Uruguay Round of Trade Negotiations' in *Proceedings of the World Bank Annual Conference on Development Economics 1989* (1990) 28 <https://uncitral.un.org/sites/uncitral.un.org/files/media-documents/uncitral/en/09-83930_ebook.pdf>.
Sell S, 'The Global IP Upward Ratchet, Anti-Counterfeiting and Piracy Enforcement Efforts: The State of Play' (PIJIP Research Paper 2010) 15, 4, 5 <https://digitalcommons.wcl.american.edu/research/15/>.

4 Multilateral tensions and the future of international patent law

Using the language of global administration to interpret modern developments and challenges

4.1 Introduction

Multilateralism is an important element in understanding how different actors participate in the development of intellectual property since it is from the TRIPS Agreement that the very foundations of the international environment are created. The global impact of TRIPS in harmonising the general contours of the patent as a legal instrument was significant as it not only provided the global reach of a multilateral agreement but also acted as a consolidation of previous bilateral trade agreements.[1] Yet it is also at this multilateral level, or overarching level, that problems with the treatment of patent law have emerged.[2] This chapter reinterprets the progression of multilateral initiatives in patent law not only through their substantive legal content but instead reconstructs them through the language of participation, accountability, and transparency.

The multilateral environment of patent law provides a particular way of analysing the autonomy of participants in practice because, with an overt COVID-19 framing later in the chapter, the TRIPS Agreement provides the fundamental elements of compulsory licensing and *l'ordre public* mechanisms.[3] It is precisely at this global level that autonomy (and lack of it) becomes very apparent. The exercise of these mechanisms is deeply contextual and grounded in the local conditions – political, legal, and social – of the participant. And yet their multilateral framing is necessarily somewhat decontextualised and generalised, requiring an inherently flexible approach to their use. The reality is that, despite this flexibility, these provisions to adapt binding obligations in patent law remain underused.[4] This

1 Peter K Yu, 'The Non-Multilateral Approach to International Intellectual Property Normsetting' in Daniel J Gervais (ed), *International Intellectual Property: A Handbook of Contemporary Research* (Edward Elgar 2015) 89.

2 Like the norm-setting dynamic more broadly, but also whether a balance between objectives is actually achievable in the current political context of the WTO: Sergio Napolitano, 'From TRIPS to Access to Medicines: What's There in Between?' in Srividhya Ragavan and Amaka Vanni (eds), *Intellectual Property Law and Access to Medicines: TRIPS Agreement, Health, and Pharmaceuticals* (Routledge 2021) 74.

3 Articles 31 and 27(2), TRIPS Agreement.

4 On the narrow scope of actors actually making use of compulsory licensing, though particularly the underuse of the Paragraph 6 system: Eduardo Urias and Shyama V Ramani, 'Access to Medicines

DOI: 10.4324/9781003616856-5

raises profound questions not only about the legal provisions themselves but also the relationship *between* actors in the global space. Each member of the WTO has voluntarily entered into the organisation and demonstrated at least a baseline of autonomy. What is it about the multilateral space that continues to create situations in which patent rights directly contrast with the health and social needs of a WTO Member? Is it a fundamental restriction of autonomy? Or, given the sovereign autonomy exercised in joining the WTO, is it a more nuanced restriction or impairment to the ability of a WTO Member to meaningfully participate in the development of binding obligations in patent law?

Investigating this relationship between autonomy and meaningful participation is central to understanding how the WTO functions and how international patent law develops. This is because the global space, in the global administrative imagination and beyond, has a profound relationship with the actors that constitute it. This is particularly the case with the WTO because it is very much the members who create, sustain, and advance the framework.[5] While the chapter incorporates some analysis of the EU as a major actor within the WTO framework, it also draws on the more critical perspectives to the TRIPS Agreement like decolonisation and the right to health.[6] As with the discussion of the TRIPS Agreement itself, this focus on actors is to help further map how different participants experience the administrative values of transparency, accountability, and participation – and which actors have the potential to disrupt existing configurations of power in participation as powerful counternarratives. In this, the development of the African Union (AU) represents a potentially significant actor in the WTO framework for two particular reasons. The first is that one area of emphasis in conventional critical work has focused on exploring how systemic imbalances are responsible for developing country inequalities in patent law.[7] This systemic approach, then, highlights the importance of consensus-building between developing and middle-income countries.[8] Framing patents through the lens of participation emphasises the systemic quality of contemporary issues in patent law that disproportionately affect developing countries. Access to medicine, genetic resources, and benefit sharing should not be seen as discrete issues but as fundamental impairments to meaningful participation in the development of global patent law. An appropriately developed AU would represent an important actor for this type of reorientation of the trade

after TRIPS: Is Compulsory Licensing an Effective Mechanism to Lower Drug Prices? A Review of the Existing Evidence' (2020) 3 Journal of International Business Policy 367, 377.

5 Chang-Fa Lo, 'A Proper Balance Between WTO's Members-Driven Nature and the Appellate Body's Role as an Adjudicator – Careful Exercise of Judicial Activism' in Chang-Fa Lo, Junji Nakagawa, and Tsai-fang Chen (eds), *The Appellate Body of the WTO and Its Reform* (Springer 2020) 132.

6 See specifically Chapter 7 (TRIPS and the Right to Health) in Sarah Joseph, *Blame it on the WTO?* (OUP 2011) 214.

7 Belinda Townsend, 'Defending Access to Medicines in Regional Trade Agreements: Lessons from the Regional Comprehensive Economic Partnership – A Qualitative Study of Policy Actors' Views' (2021) 17 Globalization and Health 4.

8 Belinda Townsend, 'Defending Access to Medicines in Regional Trade Agreements: Lessons from the Regional Comprehensive Economic Partnership – A Qualitative Study of Policy Actors' Views' (2021) 17 Globalization and Health 4.

environment, specifically in producing consensus on the interaction and impact of health and intellectual property and provide a different (though not necessarily counter) perspective to that of the EU and the US. The second reason that the AU is central to a potential shift in the ability to meaningfully participate at a more foundational level is that it demonstrates the potential of an integrated reinterpretation of flexibilities within patent law to enhance autonomy. Consensus as to the use and contours of mechanisms like compulsory licensing and *l'ordre public* would extend beyond the immediate health crisis contexts that are often considered in flashpoints of discourse and could instead be seen as more permanently shifting how values, objectives, and priorities are reflected in the development of global patent law.[9]

The chapter first considers the development and conclusion of the Uruguay Round, exploring how the TRIPS Agreement sublated (rather than resolved) tensions in meaningful participation in patent law. This part of the chapter focuses on more critical perspectives to intellectual property and applying these to the process of multilateral development and the TRIPS Agreement more specifically. Section 4.2 explores the emergence of COVID-19 and how this reveals the limited potential of patent mechanisms in times of crisis. However, the multilateral response to COVID-19 and vaccinations also work to emphasise the interconnected nature of patent law and the importance of a more contextual approach. Participation and autonomy frame COVID-19 in a way that demonstrates the linkages between compulsory licensing shortcomings, the Doha Health Declaration, and the complex role of vaccine donations in constructing our understanding of autonomy in practice. Section 4.3 considers the future development of global patent law and provides some areas that will require particular attention in the coming years.

4.2 The WTO and intellectual property

4.2.1 The joining of intellectual property and trade

4.2.1.1 Tensions from the incomplete merge of patent law and trade

The signing of TRIPS is one of the most important trade agreements in recent times, establishing a global minimum framework that standardised a level of protection in intellectual property that establishes a common perspective of intellectual property (importantly, though not exclusively, in terms of its economic significance

9 Specifically on the potential of developing subregional legal infrastructures for compulsory licensing in the face of increasing standards from bilateral trade agreements: Thaddeus Manu, 'Assessing the Potential Impact of Intellectual Property Standards in EU and US Bilateral Trade Agreements on Compulsory Licensing for Essential Medicines in West African States' (2015) 23(2) AJICL 248, 249; on the potential of African nations in recognizing the 'practical, political and legal benefits of developing common African positions and approaches regarding genetic resources', though also on benefit-sharing more broadly: Patrick Agejo Ageh, 'Ethical Dilemma with Respect to CBD Regulations in Genetic Modification of Biological Resources in Cameroon' (2017) 25(4) AJICL 508, 509.

to global trade).[10] TRIPS, as an international intellectual property agreement, retains a strong resemblance to the industrial property-focused Paris Convention in that it does not significantly depart from its provisions.[11] The TRIPS Agreement is fundamentally important to deconstructing the multilateral space through the lens of participation as it explicitly presented the 'joining' of intellectual property and trade. This has been discussed extensively in terms of its impact on intellectual property as a discipline and incorporating it within the global system of trade, and yet it produces a complex conceptual shift in how we view patent law. As discussed throughout this book, the technocratic view of patent law works to isolate it from generalist critique and centres the authority of experts. Patent law takes on a regulatory character, a sense of technical regulation, that presents it as somehow neutral or disembodied. And yet the bringing together of intellectual property and trade fundamentally reveals this artifice. Patent law has always been political, but in rendering it a trade subject and bringing it within the scope of a diplomatically inflected institution (the WTO), it becomes explicitly entangled with these additional dimensions. The joining of intellectual property and trade in the TRIPS Agreement at once recognises the multifaceted character of patent law and essentially renders those additional qualities functionally invisible. The TRIPS Agreement provides the conceptual space to approach patent law not only as a technical subject of regulation, but also as one with a distinct political, social, and cultural impact. While the TRIPS Agreement carries the fundamental characteristics of the Paris Convention, one of the most notable reconstructions has been the treatment of exclusions within patent law. This can be seen specifically in terms of conditions for compulsory licences as they were incorporated within the WTO framework. The flexibilities that are provided for in the TRIPS Agreement are significant since they represent textual avenues for the exercise of autonomy and meaningful participation. Compulsory licensing, particularly in this global space, has an inherent flexibility to be applied to both economic and patent law objectives in a way that is responsive to national or local conditions.

The compulsory licensing provisions demonstrate the level of conceptual standardisation that the TRIPS Agreement supports and can be identified at two levels. The first is at the level of innovation policy more broadly, that the 'Objectives' section of TRIPS is framed as bringing together a common patent policy and therefore establishes the 'real' 'purpose' of patent law; whereas the second level appears more in a standardisation in scope of specific mechanisms within patent law.[12] The push for standardisation at the international level through a deeper level of substantive integration is one of the defining successes of the WTO, where TRIPS is a clear

10 Florence Shu-Acquaye, 'The Decline of HIV/AIDS: A New Paradigm in Sub-Saharan Africa?' (2016) AJICL 375.

11 Chris Dent, 'The Purpose of Patents for Invention: Regulation of Exchange Versus Incentive' (2017) 3 IPQ 249.

12 Chris Dent, 'The Purpose of Patents for Invention: Regulation of Exchange Versus Incentive' (2017) 3 IPQ 253.

manifestation of the potential reach of a legal framework.[13] The use of multilateral mechanisms to secure progress in an area that has been typically defined by strict territoriality is a valuable development,[14] though in consolidating the international standards around intellectual property it should also bring with it a conceptual coherence of its exceptions and flexibilities. While the TRIPS Agreement succeeds in establishing a benchmark of international functional coherence, specifically in areas like the length of a patent and patent subject eligibility rules, it lacks a conceptual coherence that would provide a more integrated relationship between intellectual property and its impact on human health or technology transfer. The TRIPS Agreement possesses the core elements of conceptual coherence by incorporating provisions on compulsory licensing or *l'ordre public* exceptions, and yet it fails to support their actual exercise in practice. These provisions especially require a focus on the extent to which members can participate in their use because, as exceptions, their usage needs to negotiate between areas of legitimate concern or crisis and the more general underpinning of the patent law framework. In this, *l'ordre public* could function as an important tool for actors navigating the binding provisions of global patent law but, as with national policy space, requires additional support within and beyond the text.

In terms of functional coherence of intellectual property, an important development that TRIPS brought was the minimum standards in terms of the patentable subject matter, requiring signatories to provide patents for all fields of technology in a manner that stood in contrast to the domestic regimes of some WTO Members at the time.[15] This expansive understanding of the appropriate scope of patent protection is balanced in TRIPS by the flexibilities and exceptions to patentability,[16] intended to reserve a degree of policy space for Members to pursue legitimate policy objectives without undermining the broader WTO framework in intellectual property. As with the issue of compulsory licensing, the disconnect between the existence of these exceptions and the degree to which nations have actually made use of them has meant that their impact in balancing the expansive patent eligibility provisions has been extremely limited. Article 27(2) of TRIPS is key to establishing the Member States' ability to flexibly regulate exceptions to the pat-

13 Of TRIPS as the evidence that the WTO achieved a paradigm shift in international trade: Billy AM Araujo, *The EU Deep Trade Agenda: Law and Policy* (OUP 2016) 15.

14 Henning Grosse Ruse-Khan, 'IP and Trade in a Post-TRIPS Environment' in Hanns Ullrich, Reto M Hilty, Matthias Lamping, and Josef Drexl (eds), *TRIPS Plus 20: From Trade Rules to Market Principles* (Springer 2016) 165.

15 The expansive nature of patent subject protection has been described as a 'radical shift': Sylvestre Yamthieu, 'The Search for a Balance between the Legitimacy of Industrial Property Rights and the Need for Food Security' (2016) 38 EIPR 556; the tone around compulsory licensing can be particularly pointed in the context of some US authors and the impact to US innovation: 'Many LDCs have simply refused to grant or recognise patents for pharmaceuticals and agrichemical inventions for dubious public policy reasons. In addition, in the past, many LDCs and some industrialised nations, e.g. Canada and New Zealand, have used "compulsory licensing" regimes to effectively expropriate the rights to sell these products': Orrin G Hatch, *Pharmaceutical Patent Issues* (DIANE 2000) 259.

16 Justin Malbon, Charles Lawson, and Mark Davison, *The WTO Agreement on Trade-Related Aspects of Intellectual Property Rights: A Commentary* (Edward Elgar 2014) 434.

ent provisions since it permits them to exclude inventions based on public order or protecting plant or animal life,[17] providing some counterbalance that can reflect a country's cultural and political perspectives in a relatively limited way. It is important to recognise that this exception to patentability is not an exception that arises from trade considerations, and by incorporating an aspect of social policy into the central objectives of economic protection and intellectual property harmonisation, the TRIPS Agreement presents the possibility of providing balance to intellectual property from a multidisciplinary perspective.[18]

Incorporating a compulsory licensing mechanism also adds a (superficial or conventional) competition law dimension to these balancing elements for intellectual property to be managed or controlled, extending to situations in which a patent has already been granted. As such, compulsory licensing can only address welfare issues from that point forward – whether they concern health, development, or some other objective.[19] Global patent law, and TRIPS as its foundational interface, is inherently a multidisciplinary subject that is only reflected in fragments with the flexibilities and exceptions provided for in the text. As a text produced within the WTO and the original guiding principle of trade liberalisation, the provisions of TRIPS are explicitly framed by conventional international trade attitudes that establish acceptable minimum standards. It does also allow its Members to establish higher standards that reflect their own national objectives or approaches.[20] In pursuing these national objectives, however, WTO Members are still bound by the general obligation of non-discrimination outlined in Article 27(1),[21] but the distinction between regimes that are considered differential and those that are discriminatory is valuable.[22] It is here that there is some sense of an asymmetry between a legitimate exercise of autonomy or participation, and an illegitimate one. The ability to articulate, defend, and effectively challenge these actions in global patent law (or global trade more generally) requires a significant degree of economic, political, and legal resources. Just as in Chapter 3, there is an intuitive understanding of the distinction between actors and their exercise of autonomy but which defies exact legal identification. The US essentially paralysed the WTO AB

17 TRIPS, Article 27(2); On the central nature of Article 27(2) to the flexibilities enjoyed by WTO signatories: Asanka Perera and Paul Sugden, 'Myriad Genetics Inc: Patenting of Isolated Human DNA – A Missed Policy Opportunity or Judicial Interpretation Supporting a Judicial Minimalist Status Quo (Part I)' (2017) EIPR 340.

18 This exception allows the incorporation of social policy objectives into the central objectives of economic protection and patent harmonisation: Asanka Perera and Paul Sugden, 'Myriad Genetics Inc: Patenting of Isolated Human DNA – A Missed Policy Opportunity or Judicial Interpretation Supporting a Judicial Minimalist Status Quo (Part I)' (2017) EIPR 340.

19 Ty Thanh Nguyen, *Competition Law, Technology Transfer and the TRIPS Agreement; Implications for Developing Countries* (Edward Elgar 2010) 2.

20 Patrick Low and Arvind Subramanian, *TRIMS in the Uruguay Round: An Unfinished Business?* (World Bank 1995) 429; Pedro Henrique D Batista, Dennis Byrski, Matthias Lamping, and Roberto Romandini, 'IP-Based Incentives Against Microbial Crisis: A European Perspective' (2019) IIC 46.

21 Article 27(1), TRIPS Agreement.

22 William J Davey, *Non-Discrimination in the World Trade Organisation: The Rules and Exceptions* (Martinus Nijhoff 2012) 108.

single-handedly,[23] resisting pressure from the international community. This raises a fairly straightforward question – the problems raised by the US in terms of WTO DSB and AB authority are not unique, but would a developing country have been able to politically commit to the same course of action? We return to the joining of intellectual property and trade which, just as the undermining of the WTO AB, both recognises explicitly the multidimensional character of international trade and in the same moment somehow minimises it in practice. It is clear that a developing country rejecting the operation of the WTO AB would not solely be a trade issue but would instead be a refraction of multidimensional political, economic, and legal concerns. It is this interconnected character that starts to highlight how important the autonomy and participation framing is within the context of global trade, reflecting a contextual experience that differs vastly between actors (even with an identical textual foundation).

Returning to the distinction between discrimination and differential treatment, provided that objective differences can be identified, then a regime that incorporates different standards is then a legitimate differential regime.[24] Central to this is the ability to successfully frame the issue under consideration and, therefore, represents a nuanced exercise of autonomy from within a legal framework. This is the distinction that was put forward in the *EC v Canada* panel dispute,[25] supporting broadly a differential/discriminatory dichotomy.[26] The proviso of Article 27 is that exceptions to the principle of non-discrimination must not be discriminate as to the field of technology of the invention, where the invention was created, or whether the production was domestic or imported.[27] These represent strong examples of a system in which exceptions to take account of national perspectives and contexts are limited and sharply outlined, though in this situation, this sharper delineation was the result of a dispute and not the original TRIPS framing. It speaks to an actor that was willing and able to bear the risk of dispute resolution proceedings being filed against them, as well as the resources to be mobilised in response to this legal challenge. It presents an autonomy in designing *potentially* incompatible trade provisions that can only be exercised by those able to bear potential legal action. The chilling effect of 'potentially' infringing trade policy was previously described in the context of bilateral trade agreements and flexibilities, but a similar dynamic

23 Victor Crochet and Weihuan Zhou, 'Critical Insecurities? The European Union's Strategy for a Stable Supply of Minerals' (2024) 27(1) JIEL 153.

24 Pedro Henrique D Batista, Dennis Byrski, Matthias Lamping, and Roberto Romandini, 'IP-Based Incentives Against Microbial Crisis: A European Perspective' (2019) IIC 46.

25 WTO *Canada – Continued Suspension of Obligations in the EC – Hormones Dispute* (16 October 2008) DS321.

26 Elaborating on the significance of the distinction proposed by Canada as to treatment which is differential and that which is discriminatory: Zhiqian Wan and Samuel Meng, 'A Case for a Limited Breeding Exemption from Patent Protection' (2018) IIC 274.

27 Article 27(1), TRIPS Agreement; Graham B Dinwoodie and Rochelle C Dreyfuss, *A Neofederalist Vision of TRIPS: The Resilience of the International Intellectual Property Regime* (OUP 2012) 106.

emerges here in the ability to meaningfully engage with a negotiation of legal distinctions (here, between discrimination and differentiation).

In preventing discrimination as to the field of technology, the TRIPS Agreement then requires Member States to offer patents in controversial areas such as genes (as well as the processes that lead to their invention).[28] Some areas are especially controversial, not simply in the incorporation of genetic material but also plant resources.[29] Here, the expansion of protection to processes of extraction and transformation essentially means that a successful applicant has control over the entity as a whole (as opposed to the individual, patented gene).[30] The gene cannot be meaningfully dislocated from the entity in which it is embodied and therefore, the legal right therefore displaces practical reality because it is the right that is the basis for ownership, for enforcement, for sale. These concerns are contentious from the perspective of the developing countries and the obligations they took on post-TRIPS, though it is in this area that the split conventionally identified between the developed and developing countries does not necessarily describe (accurately) the alignment of views regarding the patent protection of seeds. India was prominent among the developing countries as it broadly supported protection for seeds and plant varieties because of their expertise in new variety creation,[31] where this provision matched international provisions with domestic objectives. Beyond the concerns of the dynamic between process and product specifically in the contexts of plant varieties and genes, the TRIPS Agreement provided a valuable consolidation in terms of conceptual coherence. These provisions essentially stopped discussion as to whether these forms of technology should be subject to intellectual property protection at all.[32] Nevertheless, TRIPS Article 27.3(b) contains a requirement for protection for plant varieties with the potential for some exercise of state autonomy.[33] The provision allows Member States to decide whether it will be an

28 Hans Morten Haugen, *The Right to Food and the TRIPS Agreement: With a Particular Emphasis on Developing Countries' Measures for Food Production and Distribution* (Brill 2007) 241.

29 Sylvestre Yamthieu, 'The Search for a Balance Between the Legitimacy of Industrial Property Rights and the Need for Food Security' (2016) 38 EIPR 558.

30 Under the pretext of protecting the transformation or extraction process of a gene, how rights holders come to appropriate the entire plant: Sylvestre Yamthieu, 'The Search for a Balance Between the Legitimacy of Industrial Property Rights and the Need for Food Security' (2016) 38 EIPR 558; the most concerning manifestations have occurred in systems with strong enforcement systems that have seen controversial decisions by multinationals like Monsanto: Michael Blakeney, 'DNA Patenting' in Harikesh B Singh, Alok Jha, and Chetan Keswani (eds), *Intellectual Property Issues in Biotechnology* (CABI 2016) 132.

31 Contrasting with India's proficiency with generics production: Mario Cimoli, Giovanni Dosi, Roberto Mazzoleni, and Bhaven N Sampat, 'Innovation, Technical Change, and Patents in the Development Process: A Long-Term View' in Mario Cimoli, Giovanni Dosi, Keith E Maskus, Ruth L Okediji, Jerome H Reichman, and Joseph E Stiglitz (eds), *Intellectual Property Rights: Legal and Economic Challenges for Development* (OUP 2014) 69.

32 Reflecting a broader debate on whether plants and other living things should be protected by intellectual property at all: Anne Saab, 'An International Law Approach to Food Regime Theory' (2018) 31(2) LJIL 264.

33 Article 27(3)(b), TRIPS Agreement.

intellectual property-based system or a *sui generis* system,[34] preserving at least some policy space at the national level. However, in returning to Chapter 3 and the impact of bilateral agreements, the practical potential of this autonomy has subsequently been eroded by the EU's insistence on specific forms of protection in its bilateral trade agenda.

The protection of plant varieties is one of the specific areas in which the TRIPS Agreement provides some very early foundational elements of a functional and conceptual coherence, which is subsequently undermined by the failure to more concretely support the exercise of autonomy in reserved policy space. This is exacerbated specifically in the case of plant rights and its interaction with patent law, where there is no endorsement of any *sui generis* system in particular (or any guidance offered for the development of *sui generis* rights).[35] TRIPS, as an Agreement of the WTO, is especially important in the context of plant varieties because non-compliance is backed by WTO dispute settlement and sanctions.[36] This leads to an environment in which Members are, at least in principle, free to choose the most appropriate method of protection for a particular form of technology. And yet in practice, this choice disproportionately impacts developing countries that lack the resources to, in the event of a dispute as to the effectiveness of the measures, adequately defend them in dispute settlement. Moving on from the living/non-living distinction in the context of patent eligibility, recent decades have focused on how plant genetic material is constructed in a globalised trade environment.[37] Genetic material in the global space has undergone a significant transition in terms of how it moves through space. Previously, genetic material was traded internationally without a significant degree of restriction and is now subject to complex regulation.[38] The Convention on Biological Diversity (CBD) was a response to the expansion in international trade brought by TRIPS, in particular the context of developing countries, where the issue of plant genetic material had become increasingly fraught and represented one of their remaining comparative advantages.[39] The interconnected

34 Boniface Guwa Chidyausiku, 'Plant Variety Protection and Patents on Life Forms' in Christophe Bellmann, Graham Dutfield, and Ricardo Meléndez-Ortiz (eds), *Trading in Knowledge: Development Perspectives on TRIPS, Trade and Sustainability* (Earthscan 2003) 104.

35 Tom Kabau and Angela Mutema, 'Implementation of International Obligations on Plant Breeders' Rights in Kenya: Pitfalls and Prospects' (2018) 26(4) AJICL 620; Regine Andersen, *Governing Agrobiodiversity: Plant Genetics and Developing Countries* (Routledge 2016) 165.

36 The protection of plant varieties is significant because it is backed by the system of WTO sanctions if a member is non-compliant: Tom Kabau and Angela Mutema, 'Implementation of International Obligations on Plant Breeders' Rights in Kenya: Pitfalls and Prospects' (2018) AJICL 637.

37 On the substantial shift that has occurred in how plant genetic material is perceived, from a freely traded common heritage towards a more private property ownership understanding: Prashant Reddy Thikkavarapu, 'Access to Plant Genetic Resources and Benefit Sharing: Has India Lost the Plot?' [2018] 3 IPQ 181.

38 Antony Taubman, 'Genetic Resources' in Silke von Lewinski (ed), *Indigenous Heritage and Intellectual Property: Genetic Resources, Traditional Knowledge and Folklore* (Kluwer 2008) 250.

39 Prashant Reddy Thikkavarapu, 'Access to Plant Genetic Resources and Benefit Sharing: Has India Lost the Plot?' (2018) 3 IPQ 181.

quality of the TRIPS Agreement raised earlier, particularly in how it relates to agreements outside of intellectual property, is also reflected here. The number of formalised agreements on the treatment of genetic materials beyond intellectual property provides evidence of an expansive (if somewhat unclear) practical relationship between overlapping regimes in quite complex subject matters.

But it is the TRIPS Agreement and the incorporation of intellectual property as an aspect of trade that has opened, notably in the context of bilateral agreements, the possibility of an intellectual property-based claim under Investor–State Dispute Resolution.[40] One of the early interactions of intellectual property and investment in a dispute context was in Canada,[41] where a dispute over pharmaceuticals highlighted not only the importance of intellectual property as an investment but also reflected its increasingly prominent role internationally.[42] The expansion towards intellectual property as the subject of investor–state dispute resolution is concerning but not simply from the perspective of the legitimacy of investor–state tribunals themselves or the degree to which intellectual property should rightly be considered a form of actionable investment in this context.[43] It is concerning because, specifically drawing from the experience in *Eli Lilly*, it has proven difficult to properly and effectively define the relationship between patent rights, pharmaceuticals, and access concerns even as they currently stand. Incorporating the further dimension of potential investor–state dispute enforcement presents a situation in which it is even more difficult to establish a balance of interests between these elements, particularly so because it filters disputes out of the WTO apparatus. Decisions resulting from these disputes not only raise the economic risk to smaller states, but they also contribute to the individualisation of both the process and the outcome. This dynamic impacts not only the national level, though it is certainly a prominent concern. The extension of investor–state concerns presents a potential constraint to national autonomy and the ability to establish their objectives in intellectual property (whether these are distributional or ideological) and affects the international level of intellectual property specifically in terms of compulsory licensing. Compulsory licensing has remained an underused mechanism in the international framework for a variety of contextual political or economic factors,[44] but treating

40 Pratyush Nath Upreti, 'Eli Lilly v Government of Canada: The Tale of Promise v Expectation' (2018) 21(3) Int ALR 84.

41 ICSID, *Eli Lilly and Company v The Government of Canada*, UNCITRAL Case No. UNCT/14/2.

42 Eli Lilly was significant not just because of its reference to intellectual property within an investment dispute, but because it specifically concerned pharmaceuticals: Pratyush Nath Upreti, 'Eli Lilly v Government of Canada: The Tale of Promise v Expectation' (2018) 21(3) Int ALR 84.

43 On the accusations that investor–state tribunals disproportionately favour the state, as well as the expansive approach that these tribunals take as to the scope of their role: Tanjina Sharmin, *Application of Most-Favoured-Nation Clauses by Investor–State Arbitral Tribunals: Implications for the Developing Countries* (Springer 2020) 17.

44 On the underuse of compulsory licensing specifically, but of TRIPS flexibilities more generally: Kanchana Kariyawasam and Matthew Tsai, 'Intellectual Property, Climate Change and Technology Transfer in South Asia' in Matthew Rimmer (ed), *Intellectual Property and Clean Energy: The Paris Agreement and Climate Justice* (Springer 2018) 228.

intellectual property as an actionable investment means that there are additional concerns for (primarily but not exclusively) developing countries choosing to make use of these legitimate flexibilities. It is from this perspective that we see the greatest impact on the ability of developing countries to participate meaningfully in developing the content of global patent law and exercising their autonomy. This is due to the fact that, like in the compulsory licensing provisions themselves, the TRIPS Agreement simply provides for the foundation of these mechanisms. The terms of how these frameworks actually function are essentially determined in practice by a group of economically powerful countries that increasingly work to minimise the safeguards and flexibilities of other WTO Members. The issue is not whether treating intellectual property as a form of investment will materially lead to more frequent disputes, but instead whether there is an intense disconnect between the objectives and provisions contained in the TRIPS Agreement and the actual functioning of this system. This means that even the *possibility* of investor–state disputes would disincentivise the legitimate exercise of TRIPS flexibilities. In this sense, the restriction to participation and exercise of state autonomy in the functioning of patent law becomes implicit, highlighting the limitations of focusing too closely on the textual provisions alone.

The WTO itself has expressed concern over the balance between intellectual property rights and public policy, specifically referencing the impact on health technologies and their accessibility to ordinary citizens.[45] While this is important, these concerns lack substantive impact in the absence of a more engaged multilateral community. The concerns specifically about accessibility in health and the impact of intellectual property signal the difficult position that TRIPS occupies internationally,[46] given its success in bringing intellectual property harmonisation to a global level but where its functioning extends beyond technical regulation and takes on an almost explicitly political dimension. For pharmaceuticals, this has manifested as a tension between accessibility and the restrictiveness of intellectual property rights, but the access to medicine debate is symptomatic of a far larger problem with the WTO. The issue with incorporating intellectual property under the WTO umbrella is that, as with the provisions for the abandoned ITO and predecessor GATT, the paradigm of trade liberalisation fundamentally shaped the structure and objectives at the multilateral level. The WTO as an international forum started from a perspective of trade liberalisation and the reduction of trade tariffs, though through its subsequent development and expansion, this has come to include an increasing variety of disciplines that shift (in a limited way) the original focus of the institution. The expansion of appropriate scope at the multilateral level is not a problem in itself, but the difficulties in balancing intellectual property around concerns other than variations on trade restrictiveness originate from

45 Tomruk Üstünkaya, 'A Counterfeit Catastrophe: Considerations of Illegal Prescription Drugs Produced by 3D-Printing Technology' (2018) 40(6) EIPR 378.

46 Sumner La Croix and Ming Lui, 'Patents and Access to Essential Medicines' in Keith E Maskus (ed), *Intellectual Property, Growth and Trade* (Emerald Group 2007) 440.

this difficult process of expansion and shifting of organisational focus. This also comes at a potential cost to the coherence between different subjects of regulation because, as with the expansion of investment to intellectual property, the multilateral provisions are not only balanced against an additional factor to be considered but incorporate a radically different *type* of factor to be balanced.

4.3 Patent law and the transition between pre- and post-Doha Declaration

4.3.1 Exploring the fluid character of autonomy and meaningful participation

4.3.1.1 Access to medicine, the Doha Declaration, and autonomy pre-COVID-19

The issue of benefit sharing in patent law is related to the consistent struggles in international intellectual property law to not only strike an appropriate balance of interests in terms of the patent holder and other entities in that field but also in the relationship between the benefit to the patent holder versus that of broader public interest.[47] Concerns around the distributional impact of intellectual property provisions in terms of public and private have a long history in intellectual property, though it was in response to the TRIPS Agreement that the language around benefit sharing – and a reinforcement of the intellectual property's distributional dimension – became more explicit in its attempts to balance the functioning of intellectual property through the lens of equity and fairness.[48] While benefit sharing in an abstract sense should be a fully integrated objective of the intellectual property interface,[49] it was in the tension between economically developed countries and the markets of developing countries that the idea of benefit-sharing took on a distinctly human dimension with the continued prevalence of HIV/AIDS. The lens that was turned to intellectual property policy itself was expansive, emphasising that both the result of the research (the product) and the underlying knowledge should be available more widely.[50]

The HIV/AIDS epidemic in the context of Africa put the issue of affordable treatments for the condition into sharp relief with the high prices of medication and the prominent role that patent law played in the context of medicine. Yet it is also significant in terms of understanding how the transformation of patent law in a

47 Prashant Reddy Thikkavarapu, 'Access to Plant Genetic Resources and Benefit Sharing: Has India Lost the Plot?' (2018) IPQ 181.

48 Prashant Reddy Thikkavarapu, 'Access to Plant Genetic Resources and Benefit Sharing: Has India Lost the Plot?' (2018) IPQ 189.

49 Specifically in patent law, disclosure is a fundamental aspect of the system: Joachim Weyand and Heiko Haase, 'Patenting Computer Programs: New Challenges' (2005) 36(6) IIC 655.

50 Not only research outcomes but the research itself: Prashant Reddy Thikkavarapu, 'Access to Plant Genetic Resources and Benefit Sharing: Has India Lost the Plot?' (2018) IPQ 189; though cf. on the difficulty of defining 'open science' and 'open access': Fernando Loizides, Barrou Diallo, Andrew Pollard, and Aekaterini Mavri, 'Increasing the Discovery and Use of Non-Patent Literature (NPL): Scientific Publications in Patent Examination' in Leslie Chan and Fernando Loizides (eds), *Expanding Perspectives on Open Science: Communities, Cultures and Diversity in Concepts and Practices: Proceedings of the 21st International Conference on Electronic Publishing* (IOS 2017) 218.

global space has fundamental limits in terms of its textual flexibilities for developing countries. The health crisis of HIV/AIDS propelled the stagnating multilateral environment towards the conclusion of the Doha Round and the subsequent Doha Health Declaration,[51] presenting what was essentially a restatement of the flexibilities of those already available under TRIPS and a clarification of the legal status of medicine produced under compulsory licensing but intended for a different market.[52] While the Doha Declaration and the subsequent amendment of the TRIPS Agreement have been positive developments, particularly that it occurred at the multilateral level given the difficulty of other Doha Round issues,[53] there are some fundamental issues. In particular, there is a significant tension between the legal regulation of an appropriate 'health crisis' and the timeframe that this implies with the exercise of compulsory licensing.

In the context of more limited epidemics,[54] the ability for a country to declare that there is an extreme health crisis and, as a last resort,[55] to compel a licence for the production of a patented medicine to aid in its treatment appears to be an appropriate mechanism. Compulsory licensing – or the issuance of a compulsory licence – is a process provided for both in the TRIPS Agreement and in many national jurisdictions that allows after satisfying a series of administrative requirements,[56] a licence to be granted for a patented invention without the patent owner's permission.[57] Compulsory licensing has a long history in intellectual property, even internationally,[58] and in recent decades has taken on particular significance when

51 J Janewa OseiTutu, 'Prioritising Human Development in African Intellectual Property Law' (2016) WIPOJ 25.

52 Highlighting the importance of public health without amending the TRIPS Agreement: Owais H Shaikh, *Access to Medicine Versus Test Data Exclusivity: Safeguarding Flexibilities Under International Law* (Springer 2016) 58.

53 Rafael Leal-Arcas, 'How Will the EU Approach the BRIC Countries? Future Trade Challenges' (2008) 2 ICL 243.

54 Limited in a medical sense in that they represent individual or acute medical events that can be addressed with vaccines or other short-term treatments, specifically discussion of season high-incidence conditions: Pedro Henrique D Batista, Dennis Byrski, Matthias Lamping, and Roberto Romandini, 'IP-Based Incentives Against Microbial Crisis: A European Perspective' (2019) IIC 37.

55 Ordinarily contacting the patent owner to use the threat of compulsory licensing to incentivise lower prices: Bryan Mercurio, 'TRIPS-Plus Provisions in FTAs: Recent Trends' in Lorand Bartels and Federico Ortino (eds), *Regional Trade Agreements and the WTO Legal System* (OUP 2006) 237.

56 Discussing the procedural context: Elizabeth Siew-Kuan Ng, 'Global Health and Development: Patents and Public Interest' in Thomas Pogge, Matthew Rimmer, and Kim Rubenstein (eds), *Incentives for Global Public Health: Patent Law and Access to Essential Medicines* (Cambridge University Press 2010) 121.

57 Tomoko Miyamoto, 'International Treaties and Patent Law Harmonization: Today and Beyond' in Toshiko Takenaka (ed), *Patent Law and Theory: A Handbook of Contemporary Research* (Edward Elgar 2008) 172.

58 Specifically with the Paris Convention and an early emphasis on local working as a condition for compulsory licensing: Althaf Marsoof, 'Local Working of Patents: The Perspective of Developing Countries' in Ashish Bharadwaj, Vishwas H Devaiah, and Indranath Gupta (eds), *Multi-dimensional Approaches Towards New Technology: Insights on Innovation, Patents, and Competition* (Springer 2018) 324.

looking at the accessibility of medicine.[59] This connection with medicine is a dramatic example of the tensions in patent law because it can enable the broader manufacture of patented medicines and, therefore, provide them at a lower cost than from the patent owner or licensee. Yet in doing so, it necessarily comes into conflict with the traditional justifications of the patent system that present the patent as a way of incentivising investment and preventing third parties from 'free-riding' on those developments.[60]

Through this, the benefits of research and production are, even if only for a limited time and in response to extreme human need, rebalanced against the economic qualities of patent law. The issue in this context is that the particular nature of HIV/AIDS – though these qualities are not exclusive to these conditions[61] – means the Doha Declaration and its clarification of compulsory licensing can only ever be of limited impact to both human health and a broader rebalancing of benefit-sharing between developed and developing countries. This is because HIV/AIDS cannot be addressed through the type of time-limited or acute intervention that is required by the TRIPS Agreement,[62] further demonstrating evidence of a more fundamental tension inherent to the relationship of global law and national context. The treatment of HIV/AIDS requires a lifelong course of treatment, which itself is an issue that has prominently raised issues of evergreening and reformulation of antiretroviral treatments.[63] The treatment and potential of compulsory licensing are then clearly of a radically different quality to a health crisis in the context of measles or yellow fever that require only a single treatment. The irony in the success of the Doha Declaration is that the condition that sparked the return back towards multilateral cooperation for possible resolution can only partially benefit from the reaffirmed flexibilities of the TRIPS Agreement.

The balancing of interests in intellectual property through these interface mechanisms is a difficult prospect, though markedly so when narrowed to a nebulous frame of reference such as 'benefit sharing'. Given the human health impact of HIV/AIDS, as well as the many other conditions that represent dangerous epidemics worldwide, a restatement of the flexibilities is at least a positive conceptual development for patent law in terms of rebalancing who benefits from advancements in

59 That eventually led to the Doha Health Declaration and its incorporation into the TRIPS Agreement: Roger Kampf, 'Does Intellectual Property Belong to the Trade Family?' in Christoph Herrmann, Bruno Simma, and Rudolph Streinz (eds), *Trade Policy between Law, Diplomacy and Scholarship* (Springer 2015) 101.

60 On the 'free-riding' discourse in patent law: James Bessen and Michael J Meurer, *Patent Failure: How Judges, Bureaucrats, and Lawyers Put Innovators at Risk* (Princeton University Press 2008) 88.

61 With developing countries pushing the boundaries of what constitutes a 'health crisis' to cover conditions like heart disease and liver cancer: Phoebe H Li, 'Rights and Responsibilities in Patents: A Precautionary Patent Framework in WTO Law' (2013) 35(9) EIPR 523, 524.

62 On the requirement for the scope and duration of the licence be limited to the purpose for which it was authorized: TRIPS Agreement, Article 31(c).

63 Phoebe H Li, 'Rights and Responsibilities in Patents: A Precautionary Patent Framework in WTO Law' (2013) 35(9) EIPR 520.

technology. The issue is that HIV/AIDS represent their own polycentric frameworks and the complex legal and cultural framing of the conditions is one of the reasons that the issue reached the multilateral level at all.[64] The Doha Declaration could have gone further in its substantive scope or promoted additional mechanisms for enabling WTO Members to actually make use of the flexibilities. Yet, in the long-term understanding of global patent law, it is at least promising that even the small gain of a restatement has led to some successes in managing the spread of HIV with compulsory licensing.[65]

Whatever the impact on the distributional dimension of health, the Doha Declaration suffered at a broader, more structural level in terms of its potential scope as countries were wary that it would be a repeat of the Uruguay Round.[66] This led not only to a situation in which the EU's pursuit of expanded WTO disciplines was rejected,[67] but this rejection was compounded by the perceived failings of the WTO as a multilateral forum and institution.[68] The impact of compulsory licensing in the context of medicine and developing countries has had notable successes, though it is important to consider the potential distortions that it introduces at both the level of intellectual property rights as legal rights themselves and the incentives they generate in future pharmaceutical research. Part of this tension between intellectual property rights and compulsory licensing fundamentally comes from the framing of compulsory licensing as an exception to the ordinary functioning of intellectual property rights. Suggestions have been made about reframing this mechanism instead as a right, facilitating a shift in perspective (and burden of proof) and promote a more proactive compulsory licensing procedure.[69] This again reflects the difficulty in managing the outcomes of patent law through 'external' frames of reference, but more fundamentally demonstrates the power of the neutral or technical framing of patent law. From this perspective, the exercise of autonomy in compulsory licence proceedings is premised on a derogation from, a distortion of, the ordinary function of a normatively neutral patent law.

The distinctly national reach of a compulsory licensing process also highlights the diversity of approach between WTO Members, ranging from extensive use of compulsory licensing to implementations that rely on a broader human rights

64 The global reach of HIV/AIDS as a pandemic is significant, though the political and legal response in the US demonstrated that the issues of stigma and health reach extend beyond just developing countries: with a '… homophobic silence by national media and political establishment' in the US: Jennifer Brier, *Infectious Ideas: U.S. Political Responses to the AIDS Crisis* (University of North Carolina Press 2009) 5.

65 Examples such as the use of compulsory licensing by countries like Zimbabwe in their efforts to manage the HIV/AIDS crisis: Florence Shu-Acquaye, 'The Decline of HIV/AIDS: A New Paradigm in Sub-Saharan Africa?' (2016) AJICL 375.

66 Billy AM Araujo, *The EU Deep Trade Agenda: Law and Policy* (OUP 2016) 22.

67 Billy AM Araujo, *The EU Deep Trade Agenda: Law and Policy* (OUP 2016) 22.

68 Billy AM Araujo, *The EU Deep Trade Agenda: Law and Policy* (OUP 2016) 22.

69 Phoebe Li, 'Intellectual Property and Development: Patents, Mass Innovation and the Xiaokang Society' (2016) 8 WIPOJ 98.

perspective.[70] Considered specifically in terms of maintaining a balance in how the system functions, the implementation of harmonised standards of intellectual property in the global space then remains somewhat disconnected from the distinctly national approaches to compulsory licensing that emerge through practice.[71] As part of the logical extreme of accessibility in medicine and its relationship to intellectual property, the potential of removing patent protection for pharmaceutical products and their processes appears occasionally in academic discourse.[72] When considering the premise of removing patent protection for an industry that relies so extensively on their existence,[73] it is important to remember that pharmaceutical products as ineligible for patent protection was the case in a number of jurisdictions pre-TRIPS.[74] It may appear to be a radical proposal now, yet this reflects the pervasive naturalisation of patent rights that is facilitated by multilateral instruments and the overt trade framing. Discussed elsewhere, a central consideration when looking at patent law from a more critical ontological perspective is that nothing in patent law is natural, inherent, or inevitable.[75] More significant than the existence of jurisdictions in which pharmaceuticals were unpatentable is the fact that these jurisdictions did not exclusively consist of developing countries – the most notable of which in a European context was France.[76] In this, the decision to remove pharmaceutical compounds as eligible subject matter is, therefore, not necessarily a completely radical or reactionary countermove to balance the dynamic of the TRIPS Agreement but instead one that has a significant historical foundation. The prospect of removing patent protection for pharmaceuticals would undoubtedly destabilise industry worldwide and is unlikely to be a net positive. It is, however, a reminder of the inherent flexibility of patent law and encourages engagement with its social, cultural, and political impact as well as its economic character.

The most significant issue with the removal of patent protection is not the impact on wealthy multinationals but the potentially negative impact this would have on national generic producers and, by extension, the health of citizens. A lack of patent protection for pharmaceuticals at an isolated, national level would present the opportunity for pharmaceutical manufacturers to focus on profiting from exports and could introduce shortages domestically that raise the price of

70 Florence Shu-Acquaye, 'The Decline of HIV/AIDS: A New Paradigm in Sub-Saharan Africa?' (2016) AJICL 375.

71 On the degree of domestic legal reform required for TRIPS compliance on the African continent: Florence Shu-Acquaye, 'The Decline of HIV/AIDS: A New Paradigm in Sub-Saharan Africa?' (2016) AJICL 374.

72 Milton M Silverman and Philip R Lee, *Pills, Profits, and Politics* (University of California Press 1974) 43.

73 Jay P Kesan, 'Taking Stock and Looking Ahead: The Future of U.S. Patent Law' in Ryo Shimanami (ed), *The Future of the Patent System* (Edward Elgar 2012) 159.

74 Such as India: PM Rao and Joseph A Klein, *Strategies for High-Tech Firms: Marketing, Economic, and Legal Issues* (Routledge 2013) 201.

75 See generally: David Tilt, 'Camp and Patent Law' (2025) 15(1) QMJIP.

76 Sumner La Croix and Ming Liu, 'Patents and Access to Essential Medicines' in Keith E Maskus (ed), *Intellectual Property, Growth and Trade* (Elsevier 2007) 438.

accessible medications.[77] Specifically in the case of HIV/AIDS and other complex conditions, the lack of patent protection could push local pharmaceutical producers towards short-term profit objectives rather than investing in the R&D necessary to manufacture the complex compounds required for treatment and negatively impact the national health of the country. This is the logical complement of the national character of compulsory licensing, where an exercise of autonomy by a state potentially threatens private, rather than state, consequences. A core element throughout the participation framing has been the capacity to meaningfully impact the content of binding obligations in patent law. In this, the national decision to use the compulsory licence mechanism is both an exercise of autonomy and a contribution to the substantive content of compulsory licensing through practice. This can result in legal challenges, but it still represents a process of filling the decontextualised multilateral provision with particular objectives, values, and priorities. Pharmaceuticals appear to be especially vulnerable to this negative impact on incentive due to the degree to which pharmaceutical companies rely on them to protect expensive investments and the accuracy with which they can be replicated through the patent specification.[78]

4.3.1.2 Compulsory licensing, autonomy, and COVID-19

The COVID-19 pandemic has been a globally disruptive event, highlighting tensions in a variety of contexts – healthcare asymmetries, the economic impact, and human rights[79] – that are all important in understanding how the recovery from COVID-19 can create a society with a more equitable understanding of participation. This is particularly the case for Africa and the promotion of vaccine accessibility as it is fundamentally connected to the relationship between patents and healthcare.[80] The emergence of COVID-19 and the legal discourse reflected many of the complex political, economic, and legal tensions that were solidified in the Uruguay Round and only incrementally improved by the Doha Health Declaration.[81] In combination with extensive bilateral trade agreements that already minimise the existing international flexibilities that can facilitate access to medicine in times of national need,[82] effective autonomy and participation in global patent law are key concepts.

77 M Monirul Azam, 'The Impact of TRIPS on the Pharmaceutical Regulation and Pricing of Drugs in Bangladesh: In Search of Policy Decisions' (2017) Int JLM 390.

78 Involving costs of market approval and demonstrating human safety that all contribute to high costs in development and not a linear path from new chemical compound to successful medical treatment: Stuart O Schweitzer, *Pharmaceutical Economics and Policy* (2nd edn, OUP 2007) 29.

79 Juan Pablo Bohoslavsky, 'COVID-19 Economy vs Human Rights: A Misleading Dichotomy' (2020) 22(1) Health and Human Rights 383, 384.

80 Philippe Cullet, 'Patents and Medicines: The Relationship between TRIPS and the Human Right to Health' (2003) 79(1) International Affairs 139.

81 Andrew Law, *Patents and Public Health: Legalising the Policy Thoughts in the Doha Declaration* (Nomos 2008) 156.

82 Roy Love, 'Corporate Wealth or Public Health? WTO/TRIPS Flexibilities and Access to HIV/AIDS Antiretroviral Drugs by Developing Countries' (2007) 17(2) Development in Practice 216.

They are central to interpreting not only the immediate stages of the COVID-19 pandemic but also ensuring that, in the future, countries with more limited financial resources can act quickly and assertively in protecting their national populations through contextual adaptations of patent law through practice.

The focus here is on compulsory licensing, as well as its limitations, because it not only represents a mechanism with the potential to meaningfully address concerns around accessibility and patent law but it has also taken a very central role in international discussions around COVID-19. A more sustainable approach to the negative impacts of intellectual property on health depends on a greater emphasis on regional cooperation to support effective participation.[83] In an African context, this builds on the work of the African Union (AU), the African Regional Intellectual Property Office (ARIPO) and the *Organisation Africaine de la Propriété Intellectuelle* (OAPI) to help articulate more responsive modalities of intellectual property that reflect the needs of African countries and represent these effectively to the international community.[84] COVID-19, in this context, is an opportunity to more permanently reframe the functioning of patent law that takes a more complete view of the societal impact of these rights and centres participation as a core function. Doing so involves an analysis that moves beyond the Doha Declaration's centring of the patent right (and the limitations of the compulsory licensing process) and instead into the complex interactions of development, state autonomy, and health that have been consistently neglected by these international instruments in the African context.[85]

Regional initiatives and regional common practice are important avenues for supporting a more responsive construction of intellectual property law. This is because, despite the difficulty in sustaining these types of coalitions,[86] the alternatives of COVID-19 Vaccines Global Access (COVAX) donations, temporary waivers, and compulsory licensing[87] are profoundly limited. They are not only limited in both substantive scope and actual impact, but they further conceptually restrict the autonomy of African states to the goodwill of wealthy states and their particular construction of how patent law *should* function. An important part of understanding how compulsory licensing interacts with autonomy in the context of intellectual property (and crucially, outside of a narrow patent focus) is the contin-

83 Nitsan Chorev and Kenneth C Shadlen, 'Intellectual Property, Access to Medicines, and Health: New Research Horizons' (2015) 50(2) Studies in Comparative International Development 147.

84 As well as their broader importance in the context of Pan-Africanism: Caroline B Ncube, 'Three Centuries and Counting: The Emergence and Development of Intellectual Property Law in Africa' in Rochelle Dreyfuss and Justine Pila (eds), *The Oxford Handbook of Intellectual Property Law* (OUP 2018) 414, 415.

85 Poku Adusei, 'Regulatory Diversity as Key to the "Myth" of Drug Patenting of Sub-Saharan Africa' (2010) 54(1) Journal of African Law 32, 33.

86 Nitsan Chorev and Kenneth C Shadlen, 'Intellectual Property, Access to Medicines, and Health: New Research Horizons' (2015) 50(2) Studies in Comparative International Development 147.

87 WHO, 'COVAX Joint Statement: Call to Action to Equip COVAX to Deliver 2 Billion Doses in 2021' (*WHO*, 27 May 2021) <https://www.who.int/news/item/27-05-2021-covax-joint-statement-call-to-action-to-equip-covax-to-deliver-2-billion-doses-in-2021>.

uing scholarship on decolonisation.[88] Beyond the trade aspects of the multilateral patent waiver that was discussed at the WTO,[89] intellectual property is a complex area because it creates a system that balances different objectives and values. This process of balancing, and the actor performing this balancing, is necessarily involved in renegotiating or reconstructing the relationships between a variety of different actors that range from private businesses and universities to government funding agencies and ordinary citizens. This is present in more explicit regards with transitions of intellectual property regimes in decolonisation,[90] but continues to highlight the creative potential that autonomy can (or should) have for ensuring that states can adapt patent law in ways that are responsive to national conditions.

The process of decolonisation, for both patent law substantively and the actual teaching of legal curricula,[91] is an important lens for exploring the dynamic of vaccine equity in COVID-19 precisely because it focuses on the autonomy of the participants. The pandemic has been characterised by a series of connected incidents where a clear disparity – in power, autonomy, or money – has created a distinctly asymmetric relationship between rich countries and the rest of the world. Though it is considered here in terms of compulsory licensing and the legal capacity to make use of this mechanism, this disparity has also taken more covert forms. The emphasis on donations rather than sustainable solutions,[92] the active undermining of initiatives to support developing countries in vaccine accessibility,[93] and the subsequent legal *status* of successful initiatives are all framed by the power dynamic

88 Caroline B Ncube, 'Decolonising Intellectual Property Law in Pursuit of Africa's Development' (2016) 8(1) WIPOJ 35.

89 On the broader impact of intellectual property rights in 'facilitating investment and innovation in medical development' that 'should not be discounted in the rush to alleviate the health, economic, and social devastation and uncertainty brought about by COVID-19': Bryan Mercurio, 'WTO Waiver from Intellectual Property Protection for COVID-19 Vaccines and Treatments: A Critical Review' (2021) 62 Virginia Journal of International Law Online 16.

90 Primarily because of the colonial exportation of intellectual property systems that cemented a specific orientation, but also in how different African countries' intellectual property systems were reconstructed through decolonisation: Tshimanga Kongolo, 'History of Intellectual Property in Africa' (2017) 39 EIPR 428, 437.

91 Specifically on the importance of decolonising IP curricula: Caroline B Ncube, 'Decolonising Intellectual Property Law in Pursuit of Africa's Development' (2016) 8(1) WIPOJ 35, 37.

92 Jessica Elgot, 'UK's Covid Vaccine Donations Alongside Move to Block Waiver "Shameful"' (*The Guardian*, 28 July 2021) <https://www.theguardian.com/politics/2021/jul/28/uks-covid-vaccine-donations-alongside-move-to-block-waiver-shameful>.

93 On the increasing tension between the EU Commission and European Parliament, and the pressure for a more comprehensive approach to addressing COVID-19 globally: European Parliament, 'Parliament Calls for Temporary COVID-19 Vaccine Patent Waiver' (*EU Parliament*, 10 June 2021) <https://www.europarl.europa.eu/news/en/press-room/20210604IPR05514/parliament-calls-for-temporary-covid-19-vaccine-patent-waiver>; EU, 'Communication from the European Union to the Council for TRIPS: Urgent Trade Policy Responses to the COVID-19 Crisis: Intellectual Property' (4 June 2021) <https://trade.ec.europa.eu/doclib/docs/2021/june/tradoc_159606.pdf>.

that necessarily centres the interests of rich countries and minimises the autonomy of others.[94]

There exists a dissonance in the international functioning of intellectual property that must exist somewhere beyond the text, given that the international framework appears to have a tool for addressing exactly these crisis situations and lack of accessibility. It is startling that, years into a pandemic, the explicit mechanism for issuing a time-limited compulsory license with adequate remuneration has not been used. Part of this tension comes from the multifaceted relationship between patent protection and pharmaceuticals, where the conventional language we use around patent law is very responsive to the profit aspect of medicine rather than its accessibility. Pharmaceuticals also appear to be more susceptible to this type of 'strong' patent impact because of the nature of patent protection in this field. Chemical compounds or dosing regimes are easy to convey graphically in a patent specification,[95] while industries like software or artificial intelligence have known issues with the clarity of disclosure in the patent specification and have a potentially more ambiguous scope.[96] The imbalance that appears here, specifically in the contrast between the profits of pharmaceutical companies and the health cost of medicine inaccessibility, is further complicated by the territorial emphasis in patent law.[97] COVID-19 highlighted the advances in science and communication that allowed scientists to share information on a global scale and easily collaborate across borders.[98] And yet the modes of protecting these outputs, the patents and other forms of intellectual property, are distinctly territorial and hamper the type of global cooperative response that a highly infectious pandemic needs. The territorial nature of patent law is certainly not a new observation, though it is in its stark contrast to the organic spread of disease that its scope (and the need for extensive cooperation) appears impaired and somehow antiquated.

94 One example is the status of vaccines produced under licence by the Serum Institute of India, which subsequently was not included in the EU vaccine passport for international travel: Hasit Shah, 'The Vaccine Most Widely Used in Africa and India Isn't Part of Europe's Vaccine Passport' (*Quartz*, 29 June 2021) <https://qz.com/2026656/the-eu-digital-covid-certificate-excludes-the-covishield-vaccine/>.

95 One relevant example is one of the US vaccine-related patents held by Moderna, in which the chemical structure of the claimed invention (as well as the prior art) is presented graphically: Moderna, 'United States Patent No. 10,703,789 B2' (7 July 2020) 2–5 <https://www.modernatx.com/sites/default/files/US10703789.pdf>.

96 Ajeet P Pai, 'The Low Written Description Bar for Software Inventions' (2008) 94(2) Virginia Law Review 485.

97 Timothy A Cook, 'Courts as Diplomats: Encouraging an International Patent Enforcement Treaty through Extraterritorial Constructions of the Patent Act' (2011) 97(5) Virginia Law Review 1181.

98 Qi Zhou, 'International Collaboration for Global Accessibility of COVID-19 Vaccines' (2020) 7(8) National Science Review 1269.

4.3.1.3 Deconstructing the global patent response to the pandemic

Discussions around how to navigate the intellectual property surrounding the COVID-19 vaccine were a significant element of the pandemic, with countries worldwide exploring the intellectual property-related options to maximise vaccine deployment.[99] Two main proposals have emerged from these discussions, each of which would have a limited impact in isolation and without the more fundamental changes to the international intellectual property context. Aside from their patent law characteristics, they also involve profound concerns as to the autonomy and empowerment of meaningful participation for developing countries. The first is that of a patent waiver, considered seriously by states through the WTO and involving a temporary waiver of the intellectual property rights covering the vaccine. This would allow countries worldwide to manufacture the vaccine without inviting patent infringement litigation.[100] The language in the national discussions in the WTO context involves a certain degree of ambiguity that has yet to be properly deconstructed. While 'patent' waiver is often used, the language coming from the US, for example, speaks more of a waiver of the intellectual property.[101]

The issue is important as so much of vaccine accessibility, or any pharmaceutical, is not simply the chemical structure of the product but the know-how and the tacit knowledge that is involved in producing a product that is suitable for distribution.[102] A waiver of the patent right is significant, but without the associated knowledge – which itself may be a trade secret or simply uncodified tacit knowledge of a workplace[103] – is of limited use.[104] This also speaks to the weaknesses of compulsory licensing which, with the objective of a more *responsive* system to promote accessibility, the notification requirements and lengthy consultation periods with the patent holder can represent unacceptable delays for public health.[105]

99 Rogelio Mayta, KK Shailaja, and Anyang' Nyong'o, 'Vaccine Nationalism is Killing Us. We Need an Internationalist Approach' (*The Guardian*, 17 June 2021) <https://www.theguardian.com/commentisfree/2021/jun/17/covid-vaccine-nationalism-internationalist-approach>.

100 WTO, 'TRIPS Council to Continue to Discuss Temporary IP Waiver, Revised Proposal Expected in May' (*WTO*, 30 April 2021) <https://www.wto.org/english/news_e/news21_e/trip_30apr21_e.htm>.

101 Ambassador Katherine Tai in the US, for example, refers to the 'Biden–Harris Administration's support for waiving intellectual property protection for COVID-19 vaccines': Katherine Tai, 'Statement from Ambassador Katherine Tai on the Covid-19 TRIPS Waiver' (5 May 2021) <https://ustr.gov/about-us/policy-offices/press-office/press-releases/2021/may/statement-ambassador-katherine-tai-covid-19-trips-waiver>.

102 Margaret McInerney, 'Tacit Knowledge Transfer with Patent Law: Exploring Clean Technology Transfers' (2011) 21(2) Fordham Intellectual Property, Media and Entertainment Law Journal 453.

103 Siva Thambisetty, Aisling McMahon, Luke McDonagh, Hyo Yoon Kang, and Graham Dutfield, 'The TRIPS Intellectual Property Waiver Proposal: Creating the Right Incentives in Patent Law and Politics to End the COVID-19 Pandemic' (*LSE Legal Studies Working Paper*, 2021) 21. Available on SSRN at: <https://papers.ssrn.com/sol3/papers.cfm?abstract_id=3851737>.

104 Siva Thambisetty, Aisling McMahon, Luke McDonagh, Hyo Yoon Kang, and Graham Dutfield, 'The TRIPS Intellectual Property Waiver Proposal: Creating the Right Incentives in Patent Law and Politics to End the COVID-19 Pandemic' (LSE Legal Studies Working Paper, 2021) 22. Available on SSRN at: <https://papers.ssrn.com/sol3/papers.cfm?abstract_id=3851737>.

105 Emily Ng and Jillian Clare Kohler, 'Finding Flaws: The Limitations of Compulsory Licensing for Improving Access to Medicines – An International Comparison' (2008) 16 Health Law Journal 154.

The second perspective on vaccine accessibility that has emerged in pandemic discourse is that of voluntary initiatives to promote accessibility, specifically for developing countries.[106] This has been supported by international organisations such as the World Health Organisation (WHO)'s COVAX initiative that purchases vaccine doses for donation and also private actors who have also committed to non-enforcement of their patents while the pandemic is ongoing.[107] The donation of vaccine doses will no doubt have a positive impact on the countries that need them most and cannot acquire them, but it does nothing to address the dynamics that facilitated such an inequality in the first place (and indeed, considering the international manufacturing reliance, reinforces the political decision-making around exports and production).[108] The balance here, in looking back at the height of the pandemic, is that the need for vaccine doses immediately was clear. Donations and other private initiatives undoubtedly aided, to some degree, in the saving of lives around the world. The concern is that whatever the effectiveness, a global health response focused on donations completely decentres the receiving country and its autonomy. Donations can never operate at the scale which COVID-19 requires, with the need to vaccinate entire populations. There is also an additional sense of tension that extends beyond patent law and even ordinary politics that limits any response that is not positive to the donations. Politically or even socially, how could a developing country complain about the number of doses or their physical condition when they are a donation, a gift, that has been graciously given? A similar dynamic emerged with the donation of personal protective equipment (PPE) during the peak of infection and resulted, especially between China and African countries, in claims that large amounts of donated items were faulty (and therefore unusable in a medical context).[109] The donation aspect fundamentally impacts the dynamic between the donator and the recipient that is at once political, social, and cultural in how it shapes the autonomy of those involved.

The reason that these developed countries have so many additional doses to donate is that early in the pandemic they acquired many more than needed and

106 Pfizer is providing doses at a not-for-profit price to the US government that are then to be shared with 'low- and lower middle-income countries and organizations that support them': Pfizer, 'Pfizer and Biontech to Provide 500 Million Doses of COVID-19 Vaccine to U.S. Government for Donation to Poorest Nations' (*Pfizer*, 10 June 2021) <https://www.pfizer.com/news/press-release/press-release-detail/pfizer-and-biontech-provide-500-million-doses-covid-19>.

107 Ann Danaiya Usher, 'A Beautiful Idea: How COVAX Has Fallen Short' (2021) 397 The Lancet 2322.

108 Siva Thambisetty, Aisling McMahon, Luke McDonagh, Hyo Yoon Kang, and Graham Dutfield, 'The TRIPS Intellectual Property Waiver Proposal: Creating the Right Incentives in Patent Law and Politics to End the COVID-19 Pandemic' (*LSE Legal Studies Working Paper*, 2021) 9. Available on SSRN at: <https://papers.ssrn.com/sol3/papers.cfm?abstract_id=3851737>.

109 Though in the case of masks from China to Kenya, the masks were a mix of imported and donated: Jevans Nyaiage, 'Could Quality Problems Unravel China's Coronavirus Mask Diplomacy in Africa?' (*South China Morning Post*, 11 August 2020) <https://www.scmp.com/news/china/diplomacy/article/3096908/africa-chinas-mask-diplomacy-will-rise-or-fall-quality-those>.

essentially froze out other countries.[110] The US and the UK are two prominent examples of this, with a variety of incidents that demonstrate the tone surrounding vaccine acquisition. Political representations of the positive role of 'greed' in vaccine development and acquisition, the success of capitalism, and former President Trump's acquisition of the global supply of hydroxychloroquine, which later had its emergency FDA approval rescinded, were all prominent elements of public discussion.[111] Taken in context, the idea of relying on the voluntary donation of doses from countries that themselves acquired these pharmaceuticals by excluding others is not the foundation of a long-term health response, but instead highlights the importance (and need) of a more systemic realignment between patent law and health. It demonstrates that even with the existing flexibilities and rhetoric of international solidarity,[112] the economically developed countries will act in their own self-interest to the detriment of those most vulnerable in the world in times of crisis. COVID-19 is, though perhaps was, a unique opportunity for such a systemic reframing. While it is a pandemic and the death toll has been significant, its deadliness compared to what could have emerged is actually relatively low and has remained fairly responsive to treatment.[113] The task of dealing with the inequalities of accessibility through COVID-19 is therefore an opportunity not simply to address the existing inequalities but to fundamentally reshape how the system functions to empower all nations to make use of the available flexibilities and minimise nationalist health protectionism.

110 Oxfam, 'Small Group of Rich Nations Have Bought Up More Than Half the Future Supply of Leading COVID-19 Vaccine Contenders' (*Oxfam*, 17 September 2020) <https://www.oxfam.org/en/press-releases/small-group-rich-nations-have-bought-more-half-future-supply-leading-covid-19>.

111 Laura Kuenssberg, '"Greed" and "Capitalism" Helped UK's Vaccines Success, Says PM' (*BBC News*, 24 March 2021) <https://www.bbc.co.uk/news/uk-politics-56504546>; Elizabeth Cohen and Wesley Bruer, 'US Stockpile Stuck with 63 Million Doses of Hydroxychloroquine' (*CNN Health*, 18 June 2020) <https://edition.cnn.com/2020/06/17/health/hydroxychloroquine-national-stockpile/index.html>.

112 EU Council, 'Infographic – COVID-19: The EU's Contribution to Global Vaccine Solidarity' (*EU Council*, 18 June 2021) <https://www.consilium.europa.eu/en/infographics/covid-covax-global-vaccine-solidarity/>.

113 Such as the level 3 emergency of Ebola in the context of the 2018 outbreak: WHO, 'Ebola Outbreak in the Democratic Republic of the Congo Declared a Public Health Emergency of International Concern' (*WHO*, 17 July 2019) <https://www.who.int/news/item/17-07-2019-ebola-outbreak-in-the-democratic-republic-of-the-congo-declared-a-public-health-emergency-of-international-concern>.

4.4 Coalitions, consensus, and the potential for fundamental reinterpretation

4.4.1 Contextualising the challenges and opportunities of rebalancing global patent law in Africa

4.4.1.1 Specific African dynamics in the reframing of patent law

The territorial emphasis in intellectual property rights increases the complexity of the international framework, but it is especially dramatic when considered in developing countries with emerging regional cooperation. Within the AU, for example, there are countries that represent a variety of intellectual property perspectives, histories, and industries that interact across diverse economic and political contexts.[114] The colonial reframing of intellectual property is one common force across much of Africa,[115] but the actual dynamics of African countries and their innovative industries are very much nationally focused and tied to specific physical spaces. These strong national areas of expertise represent, if consolidated along common needs, a great potential to articulate a more responsive 'African' quality to intellectual property policy for COVID-19 and future health crises.[116] African countries have a long history of trying to mediate the tensions between trade, intellectual property rights, and human health that reached a significant point in the mid-2000s with the Doha Health Declaration and the global response to HIV/AIDS.[117] The Doha Health Declaration specifically reaffirmed the sovereign right for states to compel compulsory licenses for patented medicines in national emergencies and rules for those lacking manufacturing capacity, though it was the international experience of HIV/AIDS that fundamentally shaped the discussions in this area.[118]

It is certainly significant that South Africa was one of the countries proposing the broad intellectual property waiver for COVID-19 accessibility in late 2020 (yet very little manufacturing of the vaccine has taken place in Africa),[119] setting

114 Y Mupangavanhu, 'African Union Rising to the Need for Continental IP Protection? The Establishment of the Pan-African Intellectual Property Organization' (2015) 59(1) Journal of African Law 21.

115 Ruth L Okediji, 'The International Relations of Intellectual Property: Narratives of Developing Country Participation in the Global Intellectual Property System' (2003) 7 Singapore Journal of International & Comparative Law 316.

116 Francis Gurry, 'Intellectual Property for an Emerging Africa' (*WIPO Magazine*, October 2015) <https://www.wipo.int/wipo_magazine/en/2015/si/article_0001.html>.

117 It was also an important opportunity to reframe the relationship between intellectual property and health by using the Doha Health Declaration as a basis: Peter Drahos, 'Making and Keeping Negotiating Gains: Lessons for the Weak from the Negotiations Over Intellectual Property Rights and Access to Medicines' in Larry Crump and S Javed Maswood (eds), *Developing Countries and Global Trade Negotiations* (Routledge 2007) 107.

118 Peter Drahos, 'Making and Keeping Negotiating Gains: Lessons for the Weak from the Negotiations Over Intellectual Property Rights and Access to Medicines' in Larry Crump and S Javed Maswood (eds), *Developing Countries and Global Trade Negotiations* (Routledge 2007) 107.

119 Ann Danaiya Usher, 'South Africa and India Push for COVID-19 Patents Ban' (2020) 396 *The Lancet* 1790; On the notable lack of manufacturing taking place in Africa: Siva Thambisetty, Aisling McMahon, Luke McDonagh, Hyo Yoon Kang, and Graham Dutfield, 'The TRIPS Intellec-

the tone for the global discussions that followed. Compulsory licensing has been raised as a way of addressing vaccine inequality in the COVID-19 pandemic, and it is correct that this mechanism has remained a tool with great potential for the health of *some* African people.[120] Despite the great success of using the threat of compulsory licenses seen most prominently in Rwanda, Zambia, Zimbabwe, and South Africa,[121] the Doha Declaration did not lead to the kind of wide-ranging accessibility that is required to permanently address HIV/AIDS. Understood in the context of a pandemic or health crisis, compulsory licensing shows an extreme asymmetry in the countries that benefit from both its availability and its usage, highlighting three particular issues for autonomy and meaningful participation in international patent law.

Firstly, there is an asymmetry in the domestic willingness to interact with the compulsory licensing process given the contentious position it occupies internationally (and the litigation that it can invite),[122] lending itself particularly to countries with more comprehensive regimes like South Africa and its approach to anti-competitive practices.[123] The second asymmetry operates at a legislative level. Despite the fact that compulsory licensing has led to some significant health outcomes and benefited populations, there are still a very small number of African countries that lack elaborated compulsory licensing frameworks.[124] Perhaps more concerning is the great diversity in associated legislation. This includes states that consider limitations on patent evergreening (Namibia, Rwanda, and Zambia) and the 12 that have provisions that cover the Bolar exemption.[125] Each represents a tension between the textual existence of a flexibility and the resources, legal

tual Property Waiver Proposal: Creating the Right Incentives in Patent Law and Politics to End the COVID-19 Pandemic' (*LSE Legal Studies Working Paper*, 2021) 9. Available on SSRN at: <https://papers.ssrn.com/sol3/papers.cfm?abstract_id=3851737>.

120 Olasupo Ayodeji Owoeye, 'Compulsory Patent Licensing and Local Drug Manufacturing Capacity in Africa' (2014) 92(3) World Health Organization Bulletin 215.

121 Heinz Klug, 'Access to Medicines and the Transformation of the South African State: Exploring the Interactions of Legal and Policy Changes in Health, Intellectual Property, Trade, and Competition Law in the Context of South Africa's HIV/AIDS Pandemic' (2012) 37(2) Law & Social Inquiry 310; Hilary Wong, 'The Case for Compulsory Licensing during COVID-19' (2020) 10(1) Journal of Global Health 2.

122 Evident in the hesitancy of states taking the step to exercise the TRIPS flexibilities: Mishka Glaser and Ann Marie Murphy, 'Patients Versus Patents: Thailand and the Politics of Access to Pharmaceutical Products' (2010) 27(1) Journal of Third World Studies 219.

123 Patrick L Osewe, Yvonne K Nkrumah, and Emmanuel K Sackey, *Improving Access to HIV/AIDS Medicines in Africa: Trade-Related Aspects of Intellectual Property Rights Flexibilities* (World Bank 2008) 16.

124 Marion Motari, Jean-Baptiste Nikiema, Ossy MJ Kasilo, Stanislav Kniazkov, Andre Loua, Aissatou Sougou, and Prosper Tumusiime, 'The Role of Intellectual Property Rights on Access to Medicines in the WHO African Region: 25 Years After the TRIPS Agreement' (2021) 21 BMC Public Health 9.

125 Marion Motari, Jean-Baptiste Nikiema, Ossy MJ Kasilo, Stanislav Kniazkov, Andre Loua, Aissatou Sougou, and Prosper Tumusiime, 'The Role of Intellectual Property Rights on Access to Medicines in the WHO African Region: 25 Years After the TRIPS Agreement' (2021) 21 BMC Public Health 9.

or otherwise, to actually make use of it. And yet this underuse also shapes the potential of the flexibilities and the role of developing countries in elaborating the substantive and normative content of these provisions. Demonstrating through the practice of these provisions is a way of adding to their normative content, providing an example of what objectives compulsory licensing *should* be used for and in which ways. Even in dispute, the legal challenge provides a creative forum in which a decision must be reached as to the configuration of patent law rules, public health, and the specific health context under consideration. These all represent ways in which, however indirectly, developing countries can participate in the trajectory of international intellectual property without negotiating further multilateral instruments or revising the actual text of the TRIPS Agreement. It is inherently riskier to proactively engage with compulsory licensing and potentially face trade violation proceedings, but the stagnation of global patent law requires moments of creative conflict to create momentum.

The global discussions around COVID-19 vaccine accessibility and compulsory licensing overlook the great deal of domestic or internal reform required for international cooperation to reach (meaningfully) beyond simple donations from one state to another. The contagious nature of the COVID-19 pandemic demonstrates that a concerted, global response needed to be more responsive and more sustainable than compulsory licensing can be.[126] Taking the successful example of Mozambique in the context of *lamivudine*, *stavudine*, and *nevirapine*,[127] the negotiations were ongoing but the cost of raw materials meant that production was not possible. By their very nature, pandemics require a high degree of coverage that is somehow in tension with the conceptual operation of compulsory licensing. Compulsory licensing specifically envisages a health crisis of such severity and scope that it justifies modifying the treatment of patent rights, and yet the time-limited expectation in the TRIPS Agreement and practical elements are completely at odds with our global experience of pandemic as something more amorphous.

This also highlights that the approaches to COVID-19 should have been focused on sustainable responses rather than discrete reactions to individual events. From this perspective, the pandemic's rapidly evolving nature was of particular concern. A narrow focus on intellectual property, of patents to a specific vaccine or set of vaccines, does nothing to prepare African states for the inevitable emergence of variants that are resistant to current vaccines.[128] In such a case, the compulsory licensing of a single patent does little to help sustainably respond to a resurgence as it would require initiating new discussions with manufacturers on access to a new patented

126 On the importance of scale in COVID-19 response: Tom Kibasi, 'The Global Scale of the Coronavirus Disaster Demands a Global Response' (*The Guardian*, 22 September 2020) <https://www.theguardian.com/commentisfree/2020/sep/22/coronavirus-global-novel-virus-world-health>.

127 Patrick L Osewe, Yvonne K Nkrumah, and Emmanuel K Sackey, *Improving Access to HIV/AIDS Medicines in Africa: Trade-Related Aspects of Intellectual Property Rights Flexibilities* (World Bank 2008) 17.

128 James Gallagher, 'Covid: Is There a Limit to How Much Worse Variants Can Get?' (*BBC News*, 12 June 2021) <https://www.bbc.co.uk/news/health-57431420>.

vaccine. Which, when the lengthy delays that are involved with the required negotiations with the patent holders are considered and may also be the subject of legal challenge,[129] still present an inappropriate gap between the start of the health emergency and when patients actually start being treated. For African countries specifically, this establishes a very clear relationship between the patent owners of Europe or North America and a sense of centre and periphery of both global patent law and global health. Instead of a sustainable reframing of intellectual property, a cooperative emphasis on health and patent law, or the promotion of real technology transfer and rapid scaling-up,[130] this arrangement entrenches a continual and cyclical reliance on multinational actors. It works to firmly establish an experience of state autonomy where the most important interests and those with the capacity to participate are vested and centred *outside* of Africa (and developing countries more generally).

4.4.1.2 The voluntary quality of fundamental values in times of crisis: Administrative and beyond

One of the positive developments for accessibility, however limited, is that of the vaccine manufacturers and their relatively permissive approach to the vaccine patents during the pandemic.[131] Even though there are a variety of modalities to this approach to intellectual property rights that range from what is essentially a commitment to non-profit production to the non-enforcement of patent rights during the pandemic,[132] together they also lack the type of long-term approach that is required of an international pandemic response. This also raises many of the same issues as vaccine donations, though in some ways it is a more pernicious development given that it relies on the generosity of a private entity designed explicitly to produce profit. The first issue that appears to be unique to the voluntary commitment of businesses is that they have generally committed to the non-enforcement of their patent rights over the vaccine *while* COVID-19 remains a pandemic.[133] An immediate

129 Aisling McMahon, 'Global Equitable Access to Vaccines, Medicines and Diagnostics for COVID-19: The Role of Patents as Private Governance' (2021) 47 Journal of Medical Ethics 148.

130 Siva Thambisetty, Aisling McMahon, Luke McDonagh, Hyo Yoon Kang, and Graham Dutfield, 'The TRIPS Intellectual Property Waiver Proposal: Creating the Right Incentives in Patent Law and Politics to End the COVID-19 Pandemic' (*LSE Legal Studies Working Paper*, 2021) 20. Available on SSRN at: <https://papers.ssrn.com/sol3/papers.cfm?abstract_id=3851737>.

131 Unsurprisingly, the chairman of Pfizer opposes intellectual property waivers and argues that it will impact vaccine production for developing countries: Albert Bourla, 'An Open Letter from Pfizer Chairman and CEO to Colleagues' (*Pfizer*, 2021) <https://www.pfizer.com/news/hot-topics/why_pfizer_opposes_the_trips_intellectual_property_waiver_for_covid_19_vaccines>.

132 AstraZeneca has essentially foregone £14.5bn by not profiting from the vaccine so far: Simon Jack, 'AstraZeneca Vaccine – Was it Really Worth It?' (*BBC News*, 30 March 2021) <https://www.bbc.com/news/business-56570364>; while Moderna committed to non-enforcement of patents during the pandemic: Moderna, 'Statement by Moderna on Intellectual Property Matters during the COVID-19 Pandemic' (*Moderna*, 8 October 2020) <https://investors.modernatx.com/news-releases/news-release-details/statement-moderna-intellectual-property-matters-during-covid-19>.

133 Though AstraZeneca is notable because their commitment to cost price for developing countries does not include Zimbabwe, and their ability to declare the pandemic to be over: Michael Safi,

concern emerges here that affects both the treatment of COVID-19 and also the response to future health crises. Voluntary non-enforcement facilitates a situation in which, while the developed countries purchase bulk amounts of vaccines and essentially freeze out other countries in need, the number of vaccinated people in those countries will bring down cases and COVID-19 will no longer be considered a pandemic.[134] AstraZeneca, for example, has established what is essentially a right of self-determination in declaring when the pandemic is over, and this raises significant concerns as to the actual impact on public health from such voluntary arrangements.[135] This is particularly the case because, unlike donations, a business's choice not to strictly enforce their intellectual property rights is essentially an omission – it does not require them to do something that contributes to public health but rather to refrain from starting legal proceedings against manufacturers. This may seem like a minor distinction, but taken together with the broader elements of corporate discussion of the pandemic, highlights how cautious we should be of relying on (to any major degree) the actions of a for-profit organisation.

The commitment not to profit from the vaccine while it remains a pandemic first appears as a generous move from an intellectual property rights holder that is prioritising public health in an industry that heavily relies on these rights,[136] when, in fact, it is essentially a commitment by a private business to profit from the poorest countries once the wealthiest have been sufficiently vaccinated. Even in terms of acquisition, due to the purchasing power and the bilateral relationships between countries, the developing countries (but specifically within Africa) were already paying greater costs per dose than most European countries.[137] And most concerning of all is that this was happening *during* the pandemic. The early price differentiation set a concerning tone for future negotiations with developing countries as the pandemic continued to evolve, new variants emerged, and attention turned to their large populations of potential consumers.

The voluntary nature of this response is also concerning for developing countries in Africa since it produces (non-legal) intellectual property policy that is temporary and represents an unavoidably inconsistent approach in how it constructs

---

'AstraZeneca Vaccine Price Pledge Omits Some Poor Countries, Contract Shows' (*The Guardian*, 17 June 2021) <https://www.theguardian.com/world/2021/jun/17/astrazeneca-vaccine-price-pledge-omits-some-poor-countries-contract-shows>.

134 Siva Thambisetty, Aisling McMahon, Luke McDonagh, Hyo Yoon Kang, and Graham Dutfield, 'The TRIPS Intellectual Property Waiver Proposal: Creating the Right Incentives in Patent Law and Politics to End the COVID-19 Pandemic' (*LSE Legal Studies Working Paper*, 2021) 13. Available on SSRN at: <https://papers.ssrn.com/sol3/papers.cfm?abstract_id=3851737>.

135 Provisionally under contract to declare the pandemic over by July 2021: Donato Paolo Mancini, 'AstraZeneca Vaccine Document Shows Limit of No-Profit Pledge' (*Financial Times*, 7 October 2020) <https://www.ft.com/content/c474f9e1-8807-4e57-9c79-6f4af145b686>.

136 Olga Gurgula, 'Strategic Patenting by Pharmaceutical Companies – Should Competition Law Intervene?' (2020) 51 IIC 1066.

137 Helen Sullivan, 'South Africa Paying More Than Double EU Price for Oxford Vaccine' (*The Guardian*, 22 January 2021) <https://www.theguardian.com/world/2021/jan/22/south-africa-paying-more-than-double-eu-price-for-oxford-astrazeneca-vaccine>.

enforcement. This not only affects the national autonomy of a state in a general sense, but also does not allow for the crucial element of planning for future policy in a way that is sufficiently flexible or sufficiently transparent as to industry conditions. In the African context, with the existing foundation of regional cooperation and regional initiatives, the reliance on the goodwill of private companies provides an improper basis for an autonomous African policy approach. Placing the power, the autonomy to enforce or promote accessibility, distinctly *within* Africa – whether or not it is strictly incorporated within the AU or a more regional institutionalisation specifically framed as intellectual property policy – presents a clearer commitment to the prioritisation of African health over the profiteering of wealthy corporations.

4.4.1.3 Pandemic patents and the potential of regionalism to support meaningful participation

In recent years, intellectual property has taken on an increasing regional emphasis that can be seen worldwide, as discussed in Chapter 3. This has emerged not only in the proliferation of bilateral trade agreements with intellectual property chapters but also in the constellations *around* these agreements such as Mercosur, the ASEAN countries, or indeed the AU.[138] Given the highly asymmetric impact of COVID-19,[139] a greater regional emphasis on the precise contours of the vaccine waiver or coordinated solution is key to ensuring that the mechanism effectively addresses the national and regional specificities of African countries rather than a blanket or undifferentiated mechanism.[140] There are elements of this type of responsive or integrated cooperation that were reflected in the context of the Doha Declaration that permitted non-profit manufacturing of medicines to be exported to countries that lack manufacturing capacity themselves,[141] but the difficulties specifically for African countries were in successfully utilising this process. The issue of vaccine accessibility, for both COVID-19 and any eventual variants that may develop from incomplete vaccine distribution, can be articulated much more effectively through

138 Edward D Mansfield and Helen V Milner, 'The New Wave of Regionalism' (1999) 53(3) International Organizations 589.

139 Khurram Shehzad, Umer Zaman, Xiaoxing Liu, Jarosław Górecki, and Carlo Pugnetti, 'Examining the Asymmetric Impact of COVID-19 Pandemic and Global Financial Crisis on Dow Jones and Oil Price Shock' (2021) 13(9) Sustainability 4688.

140 An example of this type of undifferentiated mechanism is in the Doha Health Declaration, where the only real success case was Canada producing medicine for Rwanda and not achieving widespread implementation: Jillian C Cohen-Kohler, Laura C Esmail, and Andre Perez Cosio, 'Canada's Implementation of the Paragraph 6 Decision: Is It Sustainable Public Policy?' (2007) 3(12) Globalization and Health 2; also on the reluctance of the Canadian company involved to repeat the process: Gabriele Spina Ali, 'The Sound of Silence: International Treaties and Data Exclusivity as a Limit to Compulsory Licensing' (2016) 38 EIPR 748.

141 Frederick M Abbott and Jerome H Reichman, 'The Doha Round's Public Health Legacy: Strategies for the Production and Diffusion of Patented Medicines Under the Amended TRIPS Provisions' (2007) 10(4) JIEL 939.

a local African lens that also forms part of a broader process of greater regional integration. Considering the issues of intellectual property and vaccine accessibility as discrete regional problems can facilitate consensus-building within Africa. This is an important aspect of empowering participation in the normative and substantive content of patent law mechanisms, especially in recent years, since the AU has seen some obstacles in realising harmonious integration.[142]

African countries are in a globally unique position to promote regional and differentiated intellectual property responses to vaccine accessibility because of the existing architecture that operates in this context. Despite their limitations, the development of ARIPO and OAPI are key elements that could help support the transformation of the AU into a complete institutional setup. These would be key institutions to link public health, patent law, and market functioning with a more differentiated understanding of binding global obligations and present a consolidated African voice at the international level.[143] There is a great deal of expertise in the intellectual property offices of Africa that can be used to more comprehensively articulate the intellectual property issues that affect African countries.[144] The task is, however, to discover how this expertise can be mobilised to clearly outline the needs of Africa as the international community and also inform the actual negotiation of the precise contours of a waiver or other mechanism. This sense of articulation and exploiting the African combination of regional, national, and supranational institutional arrangement is of central importance in patent law and meaningful participation. Other major actors in the international accessibility discussion already place emphasis on this kind of solidarity when negotiating global provisions in patent law and beyond.[145]

The regional potential and diversity of perspectives in the African context do come somewhat into conflict with the broader multilateral framing of intellectual property under the TRIPS Agreement, though. Aside from the extensive net of bilateral trade agreements,[146] this multilateral framework provides an explicitly economic rationale that creates a perceived emphasis on 'marketization rather

142 Sophie Wingate, 'Politicians Scuffle at African Union Parliament in Row over How to Elect New President' (*The Independent*, 1 June 2021) <https://www.independent.co.uk/tv/news/politicians-scuffle-at-african-union-parliament-in-row-over-how-to-elect-new-president-va25a294d>.

143 Emphasised by the agreed cooperation between ARIPO and OAPI for a four-year initiative to work on harmonisation, capacity building, and 'taking common positions on major IP issues affecting the Member States of the two organizations at continental and international levels': ARIPO, 'OAPI and ARIPO Sign New Cooperation Agreement' (*ARIPO*, 9 February 2017) <https://www.aripo.org/oapi-and-aripo-sign-new-cooperation-agreement>.

144 Seen in a more international context with the AU Commission and the EU Intellectual Property Organisation (EUIPO): AfrIPI, 'AfrIPI Endorses Intellectual Property Cooperation Plan in Africa' (*AfrIPI*, 7 September 2020) <https://internationalipcooperation.eu/en/afripi/news/afripi-endorses-intellectual-property-cooperation-plan-africa>.

145 Sophie Meunier, 'What Single Voice? European Institutions and EU–U.S. Trade Negotiations' (2000) 54(1) International Organizations 103.

146 Sanusha Naidu and Brendan Vickers, *South Africa, Africa, and International Investment Agreements (Centre for Conflict Resolution: Policy Advisory Group Seminar Report, 1 July 2014)* 16.

than African-ness'.[147] The result is a sense of isolation or a disconnect between trade members as they each pursue their own national economic objectives seen through the prism of progressive trade liberalisation and international trade.[148] In such a context, it is again difficult for smaller trade partners to resist the demands of larger trade partners and restrictive interpretations of multilateral mechanisms.[149] Regional coalitions have been proposed as a potential way of correcting this imbalance for developing countries,[150] but takes on a particular significance in the context of Africa and COVID-19 for two distinct reasons. The first relates to the potential of African countries and the AU to be the strongest example of regional coalitions of developing countries. This emerges from the physical close positioning of African countries with similar levels of economic development and common power dynamics with non-African trade partners (at the moment, specifically China but also more broadly speaking).[151] There is a sense of physical proximity and interconnectedness of a large number of states that is not necessarily as present with other coalitions of developing countries. The potential for close physical, economic, and political engagements is important for producing, specifically considering the pandemic experience, an African approach to policy and policy-building that firmly establishes the content of global patent law obligations as *responsive to* (rather than *responsible for*) African health.

The second is that COVID-19 is an opportunity to start a more fundamental reframing of intellectual property, its history, and its objectives as an African area of law. This has already been proposed specifically in the context of access to medicine and the potential benefits of regional coalitions as providing a legitimate normative basis for a reinterpretation of WTO practice,[152] but COVID-19 is perhaps more fundamental in this reframing because of its widespread impact. The economic and health dimensions of COVID-19 have impacted both developing and developed countries, bringing unprecedented global attention to the issue of non-economic aspects of patent rights and how they can exacerbate the accessibility of life-saving medicines. The broader issue of considering a mechanism for greater accessibility of the COVID-19 vaccine is that it is filtered through the political dimension of international intellectual property negotiation and institutions

147 Luwam Dirar, 'Norms of Solidarity and Regionalism: Theorizing State Behavior Among Southern African States' (2016) 24(3) Michigan State International Law Review 689.

148 Samuel MacIsaac and Buck C Duclos, 'Trade and Conflict: Trends in Economic Nationalism, Unilateralism and Protectionism' (2020) 26(1) Canadian Foreign Policy Journal 2.

149 Debora J Halbert, 'The Curious Case of Monopoly Rights as Free Trade: The TPP and Intellectual Property and Why it Still Matters' (2017) 7 Journal of Information Policy 212.

150 Sonia E Rolland, 'Developing Country Coalitions at the WTO: In Search of Legal Support' (2007) 48(2) Harvard International Law Journal 483.

151 David A Gantz, *Liberalizing International Trade after Doha: Multilateral, Plurilateral, Regional, and Unilateral Initiatives* (CUP 2013) 266.

152 With an emphasis on building coalitions 'with local, continental, and global civil society and business networks': Brendan Vickers, 'Africa and the Rising Powers: Bargaining for the "Marginalized Many"' (2013) 89(3) International Affairs 676.

of global trade.[153] This has typically hampered sustainable progress – and indeed, continued to do so long into the vaccine discussions (in particular, with Germany and the UK)[154] – but it is precisely this political dimension of widespread public awareness that can push forward discussions in this area when they are presented with a unified African voice.

4.4.2 Administrative values and the future of multilateral patent cooperation

4.4.2.1 Intellectual property and human development in the global space

While the objective of a more equitable outcome from the multilateral operation of patent law has been identified, the issue remains whether the multilateral framework itself requires a subsequent consolidation or whether its provisions can be sustainably interpreted to more prominently empower autonomy and participation. The question here is, what steps need to be taken to reimagine the multilateral structure of patent law and whether this is a creative task (of a new agreement) or an interpretative one (reshaping the normative and substantive content through the practice of existing instruments). The reality is that, specifically in developing countries, national practice is already shifting towards a closer relationship between human rights and patent law and it is the multilateral framing of these issues that lags behind. As such, a multilateral revision may not be necessary, aside from the political likelihood of such a development, if this consensus of interpretation and practice becomes widespread enough to empower smaller countries to deploy this type of interpretative approach. An emphasis on practice as a basis for an informal widespread consensus suffers in terms of lacking an explicit legal foundation for its justification, though a multilateral revision similarly would struggle with incorporating these perspectives through an appropriate mechanism. As discussed earlier, the modern multilateral context means that the implementation of flexibilities or exceptions has taken on a completely different dynamic than it did pre-TRIPS and operates in a more diffuse environment of bilateral negotiations with no guarantee of consolidation.

Part of this integration of human rights concerns into the construction of a national patent policy involves a reframing of broader national objectives, prioritising a robust understanding of development and establishing its promotion at a national level that is currently in its early stages across Africa.[155] It is important in this reframing of intellectual property policy to recognise that the promotion of human development and the fundamental aspects of intellectual property are not necessarily or inherently opposing forces. Intellectual property, and specifically

153 Sebastian Haunss, 'The Politicisation of Intellectual Property: IP Conflicts and Social Change' (2011) 3(1) WIPOJ 130.

154 Dharshini David, 'Covid: Germany Rejects US-Backed Proposal to Waive Vaccine Patents' (*BBC News*, 6 May 2021) <https://www.bbc.co.uk/news/world-europe-57013096>.

155 J Janewa OseiTutu, 'Prioritising Human Development in African Intellectual Property Law' [2016] WIPOJ 33.

patent law within that, is related to the promotion of innovation and economic development,[156] as well as individual autonomy and ownership.[157] The justification of intellectual property as rooted in 'purely Western' values of ownership and labour theory unhelpfully simplify the complex national histories of developing countries, not just on the African continent but across the world.[158] It is a task that fundamentally speaks to the empowerment of a state, whatever its state of economic development, to contribute meaningfully to the way in which patent law functions at the national and international levels. The basis upon which patent rights are justified is not, in the turn towards human development as a national priority, a crucial element in the full integration of development as a legitimate component of patent policy. Instead, the emphasis should be on the actual functioning of these rights and not their conceptual justification, promoting an approach by which patent obligations at the international level *can* be interpreted through the lens of human development.[159] The focus on practice and the physical impact of patent rights again shifts the emphasis away from technocratic language and looks instead to the reality of these states.

The development of the AU positions African countries as important for this reimagining of the multilateral functioning of patent rights, specifically as they relate to intellectual property as complementary to human development rather than as fundamentally in conflict with it.[160] A developed AU would parallel some of the strengths that the EU enjoys, even just in a negotiating context due to the size of the market that it represents and meaningfully empower African participation in a way that has rarely been seen in global patent law. But it would also have a prominent role in modelling the integration of human rights in intellectual property that mirrors some of the developments already seen at the national level in Africa.[161] Within

156 J Janewa OseiTutu, 'Prioritising Human Development in African Intellectual Property Law' [2016] WIPOJ 29.

157 Phoebe Li, 'Intellectual Property and Development: Patents, Mass Innovation and the Xiaokang Society' (2016) 8 WIPOJ 97.

158 The classic Western justification for IP rooted in '... *purely Western values of labour theory, individual ownership, personality right theory, economic and utilitarian ownership.*': Phoebe Li, 'Intellectual Property and Development: Patents, Mass Innovation and the Xiaokang Society' (2016) 8 WIPOJ 97; though cf. the experience of Tokugawa Japan, important precisely because it predates the series of legal transplants that defined Japan's modern constitutional structure in which the *nakama* system involved payment of taxes to central government to police membership and an almost trademark-like system that prevented passing off. While these systems did not use the vocabulary of modern property, they were nevertheless fundamentally connected to the ideas of individual ownership and the economic dimensions of ownership. On the *nakama* system: Kevin Cunningham Jr, 'Two's Company: The Rise in Chinese PCT Participation and What it Means for Japan' (2017) 99 Journal of the Patent & Trademark Office Society 677.

159 J Janewa OseiTutu, 'Prioritising Human Development in African Intellectual Property Law' (2016) WIPOJ 31.

160 J Janewa OseiTutu, 'Prioritising Human Development in African Intellectual Property Law' (2016) WIPOJ 30.

161 Africa, as a customs union, presents enormous economic significance: Mukhisa Kituyi, 'The $2.5 Trillion African Economy: Why a Borderless Africa Offers Best Hope for Unleashing the Continent's Potential' (UNCTAD December 2019) <https://unctad.org/news/25-trillion-african

the AU initiative, the Innovation Strategy is a Pan-African approach that considers the development of intellectual property that could be used to align elements of intellectual property with human development objectives. In the future, however, this perhaps builds more significantly towards a form of preliminary consolidation of an African approach to patent law and human rights. In this, the AU mirrors the political position of states in a post-Doha multilateral space. Just as with the EU in the current state of multilateralism, the AU would not necessarily need to seek (or require) a multilateral consolidation to improve the legal treatment of important domestic industries. An AU that promotes a Pan-African development-centred construction of patent rights would, through conscious consensus building and practice, not necessarily require a multilateral revision or consolidation to be effective. More ambitiously, the AU could extend this approach further and strategically employ bilateral agreements to further entrench African participation as to the content and function of patent rights in the global space.

One possible way of promoting this change initially at the national level would be for African countries to adopt national legislation that explicitly outlines the objectives of patent law provisions specifically in reference to human development or development maximisation objectives.[162] While Osei-Tutu suggests that this should not take the form of language in the style of the US Constitution and instead should be realised through express statements as to the purpose of intellectual property in human development, the practical utility of provisions raises some concerns.[163] For national courts and other developing countries pursuing similar objectives, concrete and highly legalised provisions on the relationship between patent law and human development are key to the practice of these provisions in a dispute settlement context. Again, we return to the creative potential of dispute resolution bodies not only in deciding on conflicts, but also in providing a flexible environment in which the normative and practical dimensions of obligations are (re)negotiated. This presents a practical set of tools through which the binding obligations of patent law can be modulated, but in a way that does not depend solely on explicit mechanisms or exceptions. Though their impact is undeniable, a continued focus on the language of exceptions continues to suggest that human development or health crises are in conflict with patent law but which are somehow justified through their extreme quality. However, the issue with relying on court practice to normatively fill out the function of patents is that potential welfare inequalities have already occurred. This approach also assumes, in the global space, that a government has sufficient resources and legal expertise to successfully challenge non-compliance with a mere national example of interconnected human development and patent law as support. The interdisciplinary nature of patent policy here

-economy-why-borderless-africa-offers-best-hope-unleashing-continents; specifically, the Kenyan approach, which while it stops short of an explicit linking of intellectual property and development, supports the interpretative use of development in intellectual property: J Janewa OseiTutu, 'Prioritising Human Development in African Intellectual Property Law' (2016) WIPOJ 32.

162 J Janewa OseiTutu, 'Prioritising Human Development in African Intellectual Property Law' (2016) WIPOJ 32.

163 J Janewa OseiTutu, 'Prioritising Human Development in African Intellectual Property Law' (2016) WIPOJ 32.

becomes especially clear because it highlights, even at the national level, that this system also relies on a functioning court system – 'functioning' considered both in terms of actual functional efficiency and also in the degree of political separation or impartiality. This remains a challenge in many developing (and some developed) countries and compounds the broader empowerment of the state to act with autonomy.[164]

The use of dispute resolution bodies as a primary vehicle for empowering state participation in patent law suffers in the sense that decisions and human rights advancements in patent law can only ever be patchwork in their progress. While it avoids the individualisation or singularisation highlighted earlier with bilateral dispute systems, it still presents issues within patent law as discrete tensions rather than systemic conflicts. It relies on specific types of disputes successfully navigating the court structure and, even if successfully interpreted in terms of a human development lens, represents an individual and highly specific set of facts. This has limited use, specifically in international dispute resolution, that can only ever really serve as a deterrent for addressing other patent-related welfare inequalities and not a more systematic rebalancing. The potential in the widespread adoption of such a reframing is,[165] however, important to not only addressing welfare inequalities caused by patent law but also in promoting the type of increased regional collaboration that is essential in advancing bargaining power and meaningful participation.[166] The reinterpreting of binding obligations is interesting here since it is not only state actors that are involved in negotiating the relationship between patent law and human development. Instead, it becomes a mosaic process with input from dispute resolution bodies, national actors, and other states in a way that emphasises the important element of participation that is so key to effective consensus building.

4.4.2.2 Addressing participation and the legacy of colonial force

Part of the reframing of patent law objectives in Africa and managing its national polycentricity is dealing with the cross-disciplinary impact of colonialism on intellectual property. Colonialism on the African continent pervades the entire legal context, shaping the legal autonomy of African countries, the implementation of foreign standards and sources of law, to the very language used in political and

164 While observed specifically in the context of human rights abuses when the state has an interest (such as in a military context), it is not difficult to extend this reasoning to a financial or investment context: Romola Adeola, Ademola Oluborode Jegede, and Asikia Karibi-Whyte, 'Restructuring Nigeria's Federalism Post-1999: How Should Nigeria Federate and Share Resources?' in Romola Adeola and Ademola Oluborode Jegede (eds), *Governance in Nigeria Post-1999: Revisiting the Democratic 'New Dawn' of the Fourth Republic* (Pretoria University Law Press 2019) 145.

165 As the basis of a claim of regional practice: J. Janewa OseiTutu, 'Prioritising Human Development in African Intellectual Property Law' (2016) WIPOJ 32.

166 Specifically, at the intersection of developing economies and decolonisation, the strengthening of existing coalitions and a more connected approach to the multilateral by developing countries will help promote decolonisation: Caroline B Ncube, 'Decolonising Intellectual Property in Pursuit of Africa's Development' (2016) WIPOJ 38.

legal settings.[167] The type of reinterpretation or reshaping that can be used to normatively reshape the binding multilateral obligations in a more responsive way must address the lasting impact of colonialism in intellectual property and patent law more specifically. Without addressing the specific relationship of intellectual property and the propagation of colonial interests, any resulting consensus at the national and international level is fundamentally absent the contextual specificity that has been rightly criticised in the TRIPS Agreement and the promotion of a one-size-fits-all approach to intellectual property.[168]

In this context, it is important to distinguish that the decolonisation of intellectual property and patent law, at both a disciplinary level and a functional, practical level, is not necessarily decolonisation in its strictest sense. In a narrow interpretation, decolonisation would refer solely to the removal of direct colonial rule at a broad state level.[169] In the context of patent law, however, the decolonisation sought by many is not necessarily the return to a pre-colonial legal context but the recentring of the national framework and the empowerment of national autonomy to realise national objectives.[170] Ncube suggests that since the domestic calibration of regulatory space with national objectives is often insufficient to be effective,[171] the space for multilateral and international negotiations is secured by ensuring that there is an appropriate degree of policy space in the minimum standards of the multilateral text that can be adapted to domestic economic and developmental needs.[172] This process of making use of the policy space built into multilateral provisions necessarily touches on the issue of participation and the ability, in practice, for states to exercise their autonomy. Unfortunately, this emphasis on the capacity for domestic calibration in the context of multilateral standards also requires a greater shift away from the language of exceptions to patent obligations to enable a more sustainable and long-term recalibration of autonomy. Centring state participation and autonomy is an important objective, but framing them in relation to

167 Toyin Falola, *Colonialism and Violence in Nigeria* (Indiana University Press 2009) 139; specifically in the dimension of language: Thomas Stolz and Ingo H Warnke, 'From Missionary Linguistics to Colonial Linguistics' in Klaus Zimmermann and Birte Kellermeier-Rehbein (eds), *Colonialism and Missionary Linguistics* (de Gruyter 2015) 3.

168 On the economic necessity of a 'customised' intellectual property regime, aiding the transition from 'elite corporate innovation' to a more diffuse innovation in a way that promotes equality and enhances public access to science: Phoebe Li, 'Intellectual Property and Development: Patents, Mass Innovation and the Xiaokang Society' (2016) 8 WIPOJ 99.

169 Caroline B Ncube, 'Decolonising Intellectual Property in Pursuit of Africa's Development' (2016) WIPOJ 38.

170 Though cf. more generally on the role of customary law as '... retaining and indeed reviving customary law is seen as an important part of reclaiming the African heritage lost to colonialism.': Fareda Banda, 'Namibia' in *The International Survey of Family Law 1996* (Martinus Nijhoff 1996) 268; On the process of centring Africa's development objectives as crucial to successful decolonisation: Caroline B Ncube, 'Decolonising Intellectual Property in Pursuit of Africa's Development' (2016) WIPOJ 39.

171 Caroline B Ncube, 'Decolonising Intellectual Property in Pursuit of Africa's Development' (2016) WIPOJ 38.

172 Caroline B Ncube, 'Decolonising Intellectual Property in Pursuit of Africa's Development' (2016) WIPOJ 38.

the exercise of flexibilities or exceptions to the multilateral standard has a sense of downgrading the legitimacy of policy space for differentiated objectives. It also works to further entrench the conventional trade focus and language of the WTO in a way that minimises the human development dimension – which is precisely why national participation and autonomy are so important to begin with.

The promotion of policy space to enable domestic calibration also does not address the broader experiences of specifically African countries in making use of the existing flexibilities in TRIPS. The reality is that just because a flexibility is legally provided for in the agreement does not mean that even those who would benefit substantially from it would utilise it. The same can also be said for any method of flexibly adapting the binding provisions of global patent law, whether they are formally enshrined as exceptions or not. The political economy factors that shape the decision-making process in compulsory licensing are unlikely to change substantially when translated into a different vocabulary of patent flexibility. TRIPS, as an international agreement, has protected policy space that its signatories can use to more closely meet their national objectives, but this unstructured space has gradually minimised the utility of having these flexibilities at all. Addressing the dysfunctional interactions that restrict developing countries by more comprehensively meeting the challenges of participation in a polycentric environment is a more sustainable way of integrating human development with patent law. This would also work to address issues of autonomy and participation rather than creating an additional environment in which policy space is again progressively reinterpreted and restricted.

Ncube importantly suggests that the very act of states creating or modifying existing intellectual property law is an engagement with the process of decolonisation,[173] though it is not necessarily the state level at which the process of decolonisation should be focused. Individual states and their successes in reframing patent obligations are important, but the benefits of a more consistent approach based on common standards among developing countries should be a more concrete objective. The legitimacy, normative content, and respect for national autonomy and participation are strongest when built through a gradual establishment of Pan-African consensus on the significance of human development in patent law. This type of collaborative approach between partners could also be important in promoting a consistent interpretation of their intellectual property obligations, extending to both national and international representations. An approach that does not rely on or emphasise the role of individual state experimentation in intellectual property through decolonisation presents a stronger foundation for reinterpreting the nature of the multilateral space, but also helps to emphasise a more equitable relationship between countries in developing the provisions of global patent law.

173 The process of doing so, in itself, is a rejection of the 'one-size-fits-all' approach to intellectual property: Caroline B Ncube, 'Decolonising Intellectual Property in Pursuit of Africa's Development' (2016) WIPOJ 38.

4.5 Conclusion

COVID-19, now looking at it almost as a past event, demonstrated that significant work is still required to properly address the complex issues of health equality and legal autonomy. The tensions in these areas as they relate to the health outcomes of citizens take on a distinct character when considered in the context of African countries because they reflect disputes between fundamental values at the intersection of intellectual property, health, and national autonomy. In doing so, the limitations of an approach that focuses on patents in addressing *systemic* health inequality issues become clear. The debate is centred on patents and how they can represent a significant barrier to accessibility for developing countries in securing vaccine doses,[174] yet they are only one aspect of a broader international system of trade that impairs meaningful participation and equality of autonomy between rich countries and the rest of the world.

And so despite these limitations in compulsory licensing as an individual legal mechanism – as well as the more specific administrative and political difficulties of actually making use of it[175] – the reality is that current (political) attention remains attached to the idea of a multilateral patent waiver to promote improved accessibility to the vaccine. A patent waiver can only ever represent a narrow or incomplete response to the pandemic, but the tensions that must be addressed in exploring the exact contours of a waiver are fundamental for deconstructing the power dynamic that shaped (and continues to shape) relationships between countries. African countries have a particular position in this global dynamic as the institutional arrangements provide at least the building blocks needed to reconfigure the experience of autonomy in patent law and global health in a way that is difficult to achieve as an individual country. Regional cooperation and the emphasis on building regional consensus within Africa has an international dimension in that it helps improve relationships with other actors,[176] while at the same time, it builds on the intellectual property-specific cooperative work and initiatives that OAPI and ARIPO have supported.

Initiatives that address or otherwise seek to mitigate the imbalance in autonomy – whether this is political, legal, or medical autonomy – are fundamentally connected to the ongoing project of decolonisation and the use of decolonisation as a lens through which the power relationships of the international community can be interpreted. Decolonisation appears prominently in patent analysis outside of

174 Bryan Mercurio, 'WTO Waiver from Intellectual Property Protection for COVID-19 Vaccines and Treatments: A Critical Review' (2021) 62 Virginia Journal of International Law Online 11.

175 Olufemi Soyeju and Joshua Wabwire, 'The WTO-TRIPS Flexibilities on Public Health: A Critical Appraisal of the East African Community Regional Framework' (2017) 17(1) World Trade Review 166.

176 Though also on the importance of promoting consensus within Africa, particularly given the 'often divergent national interests': Charles Mutasa, 'Inspirations and Hesitations in Africa's Relations with External Actors' in Dawn Nagar and Charles Mutasa (eds), *Africa and the World: Bilateral and Multilateral International Diplomacy* (Palgrave 2018) 6, 16.

a pandemic context,[177] though the international response to COVID-19 has provided some new and particularly concrete expressions of this power dynamic in patent law and trade. The purchasing of large numbers of vaccine doses or potential medications,[178] the emphasis on donation schemes that either go unfulfilled or providing vaccines on the verge of expiration,[179] and the active undermining of initiatives in African countries that attempt to address manufacturing all contribute to the enduring power dynamic between Africa and developed countries in the West.[180] Crucially, this is an issue not exclusive to patent law, but instead is a reflection of a continued impairment in the ability to meaningfully contribute to the legal content of the global space. Autonomy for developing countries, especially through the COVID-19 experience, has continually centred on the ability of the richest countries to approach the pandemic with very few practical restrictions. The emphasis on donations and voluntary non-enforcement establishes a clear sense of centre and periphery in terms of autonomy and which states are important or influential. Addressing accessibility specifically through the lens of intellectual property and patent law will not transform this relationship wholesale but instead represents a small step in the recentring of human health internationally – in crisis and beyond. It supports a more critical engagement with how the international community continues to minimise the autonomy of developing countries, especially in times of emergency.

Bibliography

Articles

Abbott FM and JH Reichman, 'The Doha Round's Public Health Legacy: Strategies for the Production and Diffusion of Patented Medicines Under the Amended TRIPS Provisions' (2007) 10(4) *Journal of International Economic Law* 921.

Adusei P, 'Regulatory Diversity as Key to the "Myth" of Drug Patenting of Sub-Saharan Africa' (2010) 54(1) *Journal of African Law* 26.

Ageh PA, 'Ethical Dilemma with Respect to CBD Regulations in Genetic Modification of Biological Resources in Cameroon' (2017) 25(4) *African Journal of International and Comparative Law* 507.

177 Akin Olla, 'Welcome to the New Colonialism: Rich Countries Sitting on Surplus Vaccines' (*The Guardian*, 14 April 2021) <https://www.theguardian.com/commentisfree/2021/apr/14/rich-countries-surplus-covid-vaccines>; Matiangai Sirleaf, 'Disposable Lives: COVID-19, Vaccines, and the Uprising' (2021) 121 Columbia Law Review Forum 71, 72.

178 Laura Hughes, Hannah Kuchler, Donato Paolo Mancini, and Oliver Barnes, 'UK Purchases Additional 11m Coronavirus Vaccine Doses' (*FT*, 1 December 2021) <https://www.ft.com/content/b809c6e5-baa5-43d2-b666-6067d90ad3ed>.

179 Sarah Newey, '"Trojan Horse": Bulk of UK Vaccine Donations to Poor Countries Set to Expire in September' (*The Telegraph*, 28 July 2021) <https://www.telegraph.co.uk/global-health/science-and-disease/trojan-horse-bulk-uk-vaccine-donations-poor-countries-set-expire/>.

180 Particularly those that are exporters of intellectual property: David G Legge and Sun Kim, 'Equitable Access to COVID-19 Vaccines: Cooperation around Research and Production Capacity is Critical' (2021) 4(S1) Journal for Peace and Nuclear Disarmament 73, 112.

Ali GS, 'The Sound of Silence: International Treaties and Data Exclusivity as a Limit to Compulsory Licensing' (2016) 38 *European Intellectual Property Review* 744.

Azam MM, 'The Impact of TRIPS on the Pharmaceutical Regulation and Pricing of Drugs in Bangladesh: In Search of Policy Decisions' (2017) 59 *International Journal of Law and Management* 376.

Batista PHD, D Byrski, M Lamping, and R Romandini, 'IP-Based Incentives Against Microbial Crisis: A European Perspective' (2019) 50 *International Review of Intellectual Property and Competition Law* 30.

Boholavsky JP, 'COVID-19 Economy vs Human Rights: A Misleading Dichotomy' (2020) 22(1) *Health and Human Rights* 383.

Chorev N and KC Shadlen, 'Intellectual Property, Access to Medicines, and Health: New Research Horizons' (2015) 50(2) *Studies in Comparative International Development* 143.

Cohen-Kohler JC, LC Esmail, and AP Cosio, 'Canada's Implementation of the Paragraph 6 Decision: Is It Sustainable Public Policy?' (2007) 3(12) *Globalization and Health* 1.

Cook TA, 'Courts as Diplomats: Encouraging an International Patent Enforcement Treaty Through Extraterritorial Constructions of the Patent Act' (2011) 97(5) *Virginia Law Review* 1181.

Crochet V and W Zhou, 'Critical Insecurities? The European Union's Strategy for a Stable Supply of Minerals' (2024) 27(1) *Journal of International Economic Law* 147.

Cullet P, 'Patents and Medicines: The Relationship Between TRIPS and the Human Right to Health' (2003) 79(1) *International Affairs* 139.

Cunningham Jr K, 'Two's Company: The Rise in Chinese PCT Participation and What it Means for Japan' (2017) 99 *Journal of the Patent & Trademark Office Society* 670.

Dent C, 'The Purpose of Patents for Invention: Regulation of Exchange Versus Incentive' (2017) 3 *Intellectual Property Quarterly* 245.

Dirar L, 'Norms of Solidarity and Regionalism: Theorizing State Behavior Among Southern African States' (2016) 24(3) *Michigan State International Law Review* 667.

Glaser M and AM Murphy, 'Patients Versus Patents: Thailand and the Politics of Access to Pharmaceutical Products' (2010) 27(1) *Journal of Third World Studies* 215.

Gurgula O, 'Strategic Patenting by Pharmaceutical Companies – Should Competition Law Intervene?' (2020) 51 *International Review of Intellectual Property and Competition Law* 1062.

Halbert DJ, 'The Curious Case of Monopoly Rights as Free Trade: The TPP and Intellectual Property and Why it Still Matters' (2017) 7 *Journal of Information Policy* 204.

Haunss S, 'The Politicisation of Intellectual Property: IP Conflicts and Social Change' (2011) 3(1) *WIPOJ Journal* 129.

Kabau T and A Mutema, 'Implementation of International Obligations on Plant Breeders' Rights in Kenya: Pitfalls and Prospects' (2018) 26(4) *African Journal of International and Comparative Law* 616.

Klug H, 'Access to Medicines and the Transformation of the South African State: Exploring the Interactions of Legal and Policy Changes in Health, Intellectual Property, Trade, and Competition Law in the Context of South Africa's HIV/AIDS Pandemic' (2012) 37(2) *Law & Social Inquiry* 297.

Kongolo T, 'History of Intellectual Property in Africa' (2017) 39 *European Intellectual Property Review* 428.

Leal-Arcas R, 'How Will the EU Approach the BRIC Countries? Future Trade Challenges' (2008) 2 *ICL Journal* 235.

Legge DG and S Kim, 'Equitable Access to COVID-19 Vaccines: Cooperation around Research and Production Capacity is Critical' (2021) 4(S1) *Journal for Peace and Nuclear Disarmament* 73.

Li P, 'Intellectual Property and Development: Patents, Mass Innovation and the Xiaokang Society' (2016) 8 *WIPOJ Journal* 97.

Li PH, 'Rights and Responsibilities in Patents: A Precautionary Patent Framework in WTO Law' (2013) 35(9) *European Intellectual Property Review* 516.
Love R, 'Corporate Wealth or Public Health? WTO/TRIPS Flexibilities and Access to HIV/AIDS Antiretroviral Drugs by Developing Countries' (2007) 17(2) *Development in Practice* 208.
MacIsaac S and BC Duclos, 'Trade and Conflict: Trends in Economic Nationalism, Unilateralism and Protectionism' (2020) 26(1) *Canadian Foreign Policy Journal* 1.
Mansfield ED and HV Milner, 'The New Wave of Regionalism' (1999) 53(3) *International Organizations* 589.
Manu T, 'Assessing the Potential Impact of Intellectual Property Standards in EU and US Bilateral Trade Agreements on Compulsory Licensing for Essential Medicines in West African States' (2015) 23(2) *African Journal of International and Comparative Law* 226.
McInerney M, 'Tacit Knowledge Transfer with Patent Law: Exploring Clean Technology Transfers' (2011) 21(2) *Fordham Intellectual Property, Media and Entertainment Law Journal* 449.
McMahon A, 'Global Equitable Access to Vaccines, Medicines and Diagnostics for COVID-19: The Role of Patents as Private Governance' (2021) 47 *Journal of Medical Ethics* 142.
Mercurio B, 'WTO Waiver from Intellectual Property Protection for COVID-19 Vaccines and Treatments: A Critical Review' (2021) 62 *Virginia Journal of International Law Online* 9.
Meunier S, 'What Single Voice? European Institutions and EU–U.S. Trade Negotiations' (2000) 54(1) *International Organizations* 103.
Motari M, JB Nikiema, OMJ Kasilo, S Kniazkov, A Loua, A Sougou, and P Tumusiime, 'The Role of Intellectual Property Rights on Access to Medicines in the WHO African Region: 25 Years After the TRIPS Agreement' (2021) 21 *BMC Public Health* 1.
Mupangavanhu Y, 'African Union Rising to the Need for Continental IP Protection? The Establishment of the Pan-African Intellectual Property Organization' (2015) 59(1) *Journal of African Law* 1.
Ncube CB, 'Decolonising Intellectual Property Law in Pursuit of Africa's Development' (2016) 8(1) *WIPOJ Journal* 34.
Ng E and JC Kohler, 'Finding Flaws: The Limitations of Compulsory Licensing for Improving Access to Medicines – An International Comparison' (2008) 16 *Health Law Journal* 143.
Okediji RL, 'The International Relations of Intellectual Property: Narratives of Developing Country Participation in the Global Intellectual Property System' (2003) 7 *Singapore Journal of International & Comparative Law* 315.
OseiTutu JJ, 'Prioritising Human Development in African Intellectual Property Law' (2016) 8 *WIPOJ Journal* 23.
Owoeye OA, 'Compulsory Patent Licensing and Local Drug Manufacturing Capacity in Africa' (2014) 92(3) *World Health Organization Bulletin* 214.
Pai AP, 'The Low Written Description Bar for Software Inventions' (2008) 94(2) *Virginia Law Review* 457.
Perera A and P Sugden, 'Myriad Genetics Inc: Patenting of Isolated Human DNA - A Missed Policy Opportunity or Judicial Interpretation Supporting a Judicial Minimalist Status Quo (Part I)' (2017) *European Intellectual Property Review* 334.
Rolland SE, 'Developing Country Coalitions at the WTO: In Search of Legal Support' (2007) 48(2) *Harvard International Law Journal* 483.
Saab A, 'An International Law Approach to Food Regime Theory' (2018) 31(2) *Leiden Journal of International Law* 251.
Shehzad K, U Zaman, X Liu, J Górecki, and C Pugnetti, 'Examining the Asymmetric Impact of COVID-19 Pandemic and Global Financial Crisis on Dow Jones and Oil Price Shock' (2021) 13(9) *Sustainability* 4688.

Shu-Acquaye F, 'The Decline of HIV/AIDS: A New Paradigm in Sub-Saharan Africa?' (2016) 24(3) *African Journal of International and Comparative Law* 362.
Sirleaf M, 'Disposable Lives: COVID-19, Vaccines, and the Uprising' (2021) 121 *Columbia Law Review Forum* 71.
Soyeju O and J Wabwire, 'The WTO-TRIPS Flexibilities on Public Health: A Critical Appraisal of the East African Community Regional Framework' (2017) 17(1) *World Trade Review* 145.
Thikkavarapu PR, 'Access to Plant Genetic Resources and Benefit Sharing: Has India Lost the Plot?' (2018) 3 *Intellectual Property Quarterly* 181.
Tilt D, 'Camp and Patent Law' (forthcoming 2025) 15 *Queen Mary Journal of Intellectual Property*.
Townsend B, 'Defending Access to Medicines in Regional Trade Agreements: Lessons from the Regional Comprehensive Economic Partnership – A Qualitative Study of Policy Actors' Views' (2021) 17 *Globalization and Health* 1.
Upreti PN, 'Eli Lilly v Government of Canada: The Tale of Promise v Expectation' (2018) 21(3) *International Arbitration Law Review* 84.
Urias E and SV Ramani, 'Access to Medicines after TRIPS: Is Compulsory Licensing an Effective Mechanism to Lower Drug Prices? A Review of the Existing Evidence' (2020) 3 *Journal of International Business Policy* 367.
Usher AD, 'A Beautiful Idea: How COVAX Has Fallen Short' (2021) 397 *The Lancet* 2322.
Üstünkaya T, 'A Counterfeit Catastrophe: Considerations of Illegal Prescription Drugs Produced by 3D-Printing Technology' (2018) 40(6) *European Intellectual Property Review* 374.
Vickers B, 'Africa and the Rising Powers: Bargaining for the "Marginalized Many"' (2013) 89(3) *International Affairs* 673.
Wan Z and S Meng, 'A Case for a Limited Breeding Exemption from Patent Protection' (2018) 50 *International Review of Intellectual Property and Competition Law* 274.
Weyand J and H Haase, 'Patenting Computer Programs: New Challenges' (2005) 36(6) *International Review of Intellectual Property and Competition Law* 655.
Yamthieu S, 'The Search for a Balance Between the Legitimacy of Industrial Property Rights and the Need for Food Security' (2016) 38 *European Intellectual Property Review* 551.
Zhou Q, 'International Collaboration for Global Accessibility of COVID-19 Vaccines' (2020) 7(8) *National Science Review* 1269.

Books

Andersen R, *Governing Agrobiodiversity: Plant Genetics and Developing Countries* (Routledge 2016).
Araujo BAM, *The EU Deep Trade Agenda: Law and Policy* (OUP 2016).
Banda F, 'Namibia' in *The International Survey of Family Law 1996* (Martinus Nijhoff 1996).
Bessen J and MJ Meurer, *Patent Failure: How Judges, Bureaucrats, and Lawyers Put Innovators at Risk* (Princeton University press 2008).
Brier J, *Infectious Ideas: U.S. Political Responses to the AIDS Crisis* (University of North Carolina Press 2009).
Davey WJ, *Non-Discrimination in the World Trade Organisation: The Rules and Exceptions* (Martinus Nijhoff 2012).
Dinwoodie GB and RC Dreyfuss, *A Neofederalist Vision of TRIPS: The Resilience of the International Intellectual Property Regime* (OUP 2012).
Falola T, *Colonialism and Violence in Nigeria* (Indiana University Press 2009) 139; specifically in the dimension of language: Thomas Stolz and Ingo H Warnke, 'From Missionary Linguistics to Colonial Linguistics' in Klaus Zimmermann and Birte

Kellermeier-Rehbein (eds), *Colonialism and Missionary Linguistics* (de Gruyter 2015) 3.
Gantz DA, *Liberalizing International Trade after Doha: Multilateral, Plurilateral, Regional, and Unilateral Initiatives* (CUP 2013).
Hatch OG, *Pharmaceutical Patent Issues* (DIANE 2000).
Haugen HM, *The Right to Food and the TRIPS Agreement: With a Particular Emphasis on Developing Countries' Measures for Food Production and Distribution* (Brill 2007).
Joseph S, *Blame it on the WTO?* (OUP 2011).
Low P and A Subramanian, *TRIMS in the Uruguay Round: An Unfinished Business?* (World Bank 1995).
Malbon J, C Lawson, and M Davison, *The WTO Agreement on Trade-Related Aspects of Intellectual Property Rights: A Commentary* (Edward Elgar 2014).
Mandeville T, *Understanding Novelty: Information, Technology Change and the Patent System* (Greenwood 1996).
Nguyen TT, *Competition Law, Technology Transfer and the TRIPS Agreement; Implications for Developing Countries* (Edward Elgar 2010).
Osewe PL, YK Nkrumah, and EK Sackey, *Improving Access to HIV/AIDS Medicines in Africa: Trade-Related Aspects of Intellectual Property Rights Flexibilities* (World Bank 2008).
Rao PM and JA Klein, *Strategies for High-Tech Firms: Marketing, Economic, and Legal Issues* (Routledge 2013).
Schweitzer SO, *Pharmaceutical Economics and Policy* (2nd edn, OUP 2007).
Sender MP, *Cross-Border Enforcement of Patent Rights: An Analysis of the Interface Between Intellectual Property and Private International Law* (OUP 2002).
Shaikh OH, *Access to Medicine Versus Test Data Exclusivity: Safeguarding Flexibilities Under International Law* (Springer 2016).
Sharmin T, *Application of Most-Favoured-Nation Clauses by Investor-State Arbitral Tribunals: Implications for the Developing Countries* (Springer 2020).
Silverman MM and PR Lee, *Pills, Profits, and Politics* (University of California Press 1974).
Stewart TP, *The GATT Uruguay Round: A Negotiating History 1986-1992: A Commentary* (Kluwer 1993).
Stoll PT and F Schorkopf, *WTO: World Economic Order: World Trade Law* (Martinus Nijhoff 2006).
Taylor MD, *International Competition Law: A New Dimension for the WTO?* (CUP 2006).
Whish R and D Bailey, *Competition Law* (OUP 2015).

Chapters

Adeola R, AO Jegede, and A Karibi-Whyte, 'Restructuring Nigeria's Federalism Post-1999: How Should Nigeria Federate and Share Resources?' in Romola Adeola and Ademola Oluborode Jegede (eds), *Governance in Nigeria Post-1999: Revisiting the Democratic 'New Dawn' of the Fourth Republic* (Pretoria University Law Press 2019) 145.
Blakeney M, 'DNA Patenting' in Harikesh B. Singh, Alok Jha, and Chetan Keswani (eds), *Intellectual Property Issues in Biotechnology* (CABI 2016) 128.
Chidyausiku BG, 'Plant Variety Protection and Patents on Life Forms' in Christophe Bellmann, Graham Dutfield, and Ricardo Meléndez-Ortiz (eds), *Trading in Knowledge: Development Perspectives on TRIPS, Trade and Sustainability* (Earthscan 2003) 101.
Cimoli M, G Dosi, R Mazzoleni, and BN Sampat, 'Innovation, Technical Change. And Patents in the Development Process: A Long-Term View' in Mario Cimoli, Giovanni Dosi, Keith E Maskus, Ruth L Okediji, Jerome H Reichman, and Joseph E Stiglitz (eds), *Intellectual Property Rights: Legal and Economic Challenges for Development* (OUP 2014) 57.

Drahos P, 'Making and Keeping Negotiating Gains: Lessons for the Weak From the Negotiations Over Intellectual Property Rights and Access to Medicines' in Larry Crump and S Javed Maswood (eds), *Developing Countries and Global Trade Negotiations* (Routledge 2007) 97.

Kampf R, 'Does Intellectual Property Belong to the Trade Family?' in Christoph Herrmann, Bruno Simma, and Rudolph Streinz (eds), *Trade Policy Between Law, Diplomacy and Scholarship* (Springer 2015) 87.

Kariyawasam K and M Tsai, 'Intellectual Property, Climate Change and Technology Transfer in South Asia' in Matthew Rimmer (ed), *Intellectual Property and Clean Energy: The Paris Agreement and Climate Justice* (Springer 2018) 207.

La Croix S and M Liu, 'Patents and Access to Essential Medicines' in Keith E Maskus (ed), *Intellectual Property, Growth and Trade* (Emerald Group 2007) 423.

Lo CF, 'A Proper Balance Between WTO's Members-Driven Nature and the Appellate Body's Role as an Adjudicator–Careful Exercise of Judicial Activism' in Chang-fa Lo, Junji Nakagawa, and Tsai-fang Chen (eds), *The Appellate Body of the WTO and Its Reform* (Springer 2020) 125.

Loizides F, B Diallo, A Pollard and A Mavri, 'Increasing the Discovery and Use of Non-Patent Literature (NPL): Scientific Publications in Patent Examination' in Leslie Chan and Fernando Loizides (eds), *Expanding Perspectives on Open Science: Communities, Cultures and Diversity in Concepts and Practices: Proceedings of the 21st International Conference on Electronic Publishing* (IOS 2017) 211.

Marsoof A, 'Local Working of Patents: The Perspective of Developing Countries' in Ashish Bharadwaj, Vishwas H Devaiah, and Indranath Gupta (eds), *Multi-Dimensional Approaches Towards New Technology: Insights on Innovation, Patents, and Competition* (Springer 2018) 315.

Mercurio B, 'TRIPS-Plus Provisions in FTAs: Recent Trends' in Lorand Bartels and Federico Ortino (eds), *Regional Trade Agreements and the WTO Legal System* (OUP 2006) 215.

Miyamoto T, 'International Treaties and Patent Law Harmonization: Today and Beyond' in Toshiko Takenaka (ed), *Patent Law and Theory: A Handbook of Contemporary Research* (Edward Elgar 2008) 154.

Mutasa C, 'Inspirations and Hesitations in Africa's Relations with External Actors' in Dawn Nagar and Charles Mutasa (eds), *Africa and the World: Bilateral and Multilateral International Diplomacy* (Palgrave 2018) 1.

Napollitano S, 'From TRIPS to Access to Medicines: What's There in Between?' in Srividhya Ragavan and Amaka Vanni (eds), *Intellectual Property Law and Access to Medicines: TRIPS Agreement, Health, and Pharmaceuticals* (Routledge 2021) 66.

Ncube CB, 'Three Centuries and Counting: The Emergence and Development of Intellectual Property Law in Africa' in Rochelle Dreyfuss and Justine Pila (eds), *The Oxford Handbook of Intellectual Property Law* (OUP 2018) 409.

Ng ESK, 'Global Health and Development: Patents and Public Interest' in Thomas Pogge, Matthew Rimmer, and Kim Rubenstein (eds), *Incentives for Global Public Health: Patent Law and Access to Essential Medicines* (CUP 2010) 101.

Ruse-Khan HG, 'IP and Trade in a Post-TRIPS Environment' in Hanns Ullrich, Reto M Hilty, Matthias Lamping, and Josef Drexl (eds), *TRIPS Plus 20: From Trade Rules to Market Principles* (Springer 2016) 163.

Taubman A, 'Genetic Resources' in Silke von Lewinski (ed), *Indigenous Heritage and Intellectual Property: Genetic Resources, Traditional Knowledge and Folklore* (Kluwer 2008) 181.

Watal J, 'Is TRIPS a Balanced Agreement from the Perspective of Recent Free Trade Agreements?' in Josef Drexl, Henning Grosse Ruse-Khan, and Souheir Nadde-Phlix (eds), *EU Bilateral Trade Agreements and Intellectual Property: For Better or Worse?* (Springer 2014) 41.

YU PK, 'The Non-Multilateral Approach to International Intellectual Property Normsetting' in Daniel J Gervais (ed), *International Intellectual Property: A Handbook of Contemporary Research* (Edward Elgar 2015) 83.

Legislation

Article 27, TRIPS Agreement
Article 31, TRIPS Agreement

Cases

ICSID, *Eli Lilly and Company v The Government of Canada*, UNCITRAL Case No. UNCT/14/2.

WTO *Canada - Continued Suspension of Obligations in the EC - Hormones Dispute* (16 October 2008) DS321.

Other

AfrIPI, 'AfrIPI Endorses Intellectual Property Cooperation Plan in Africa' (*AfrIPI*, 7 September 2020) <https://internationalipcooperation.eu/en/afripi/news/afripi-endorses-intellectual-property-cooperation-plan-africa>.

ARIPO, 'OAPI and ARIPO Sign New Cooperation Agreement' (*ARIPO*, 9 February 2017) <https://www.aripo.org/oapi-and-aripo-sign-new-cooperation-agreement>.

Bourla A, 'An Open Letter from Pfizer Chairman and CEO to Colleagues' (*Pfizer*, 2021) <https://www.pfizer.com/news/hot-topics/why_pfizer_opposes_the_trips_intellectual_property_waiver_for_covid_19_vaccines>.

David D, 'Covid: Germany Rejects US-Backed Proposal to Waive Vaccine Patents' (*BBC News*, 6 May 2021) <https://www.bbc.co.uk/news/world-europe-57013096>.

Elgot J, 'UK's Covid Vaccine Donations Alongside Move to Block Waiver "Shameful"' (*The Guardian*, 28 July 2021) <https://www.theguardian.com/politics/2021/jul/28/uks-covid-vaccine-donations-alongside-move-to-block-waiver-shameful>.

EU, 'Communication from the European Union to the Council for TRIPS: Urgent Trade Policy Responses to the COVID-19 Crisis: Intellectual Property' (4 June 2021) <https://trade.ec.europa.eu/doclib/docs/2021/june/tradoc_159606.pdf>.

EU Council, 'Infographic – COVID-19: the EU's Contribution to Global Vaccine Solidarity' (*EU Council*, 18 June 2021) <https://www.consilium.europa.eu/en/infographics/covid-covax-global-vaccine-solidarity/>.

European Parliament, 'Parliament Calls for Temporary COVID-19 Vaccine Patent Waiver' (*EU Parliament*, 10 June 2021) <https://www.europarl.europa.eu/news/en/press-room/20210604IPR05514/parliament-calls-for-temporary-covid-19-vaccine-patent-waiver>.

Gallagher J, 'Covid: Is There a Limit to How Much Worse Variants Can Get?' (*BBC News*, 12 June 2021) <https://www.bbc.co.uk/news/health-57431420>.

Gurry F, 'Intellectual Property for an Emerging Africa' (*WIPO Magazine*, October 2015) <https://www.wipo.int/wipo_magazine/en/2015/si/article_0001.html>.

Hughes L, H Kuchler, DP Mancini, and O Barnes, 'UK Purchases Additional 11m Coronavirus Vaccine Doses' (*FT*, 1 December 2021) <https://www.ft.com/content/b809c6e5-baa5-43d2-b666-6067d90ad3ed>.

Jack S, 'AstraZeneca Vaccine – Was it Really Worth It?' (*BBC News*, 30 March 2021) <https://www.bbc.com/news/business-56570364>.

Kibasi T, 'The Global Scale of the Coronavirus Disaster Demands a Global Response' (*The Guardian*, 22 September 2020) <https://www.theguardian.com/commentisfree/2020/sep/22/coronavirus-global-novel-virus-world-health>.

Kituyi M, 'The $2.5 Trillion African Economy: Why a Borderless Africa Offers Best Hope for Unleashing the Continent's Potential' (UNCTAD, December 2019) <https://unctad.org/news/25-trillion-african-economy-why-borderless-africa-offers-best-hope-unleashing-continents>.

Kuenssberg L, '"Greed" and "Capitalism" Helped UK's Vaccines Success, Says PM' (*BBC News*, 24 March 2021) <https://www.bbc.co.uk/news/uk-politics-56504546>; Elizabeth Cohen and Wesley Bruer, 'US Stockpile Stuck with 63 Million Doses of Hydroxychloroquine' (*CNN Health*, 18 June 2020) <https://edition.cnn.com/2020/06/17/health/hydroxychloroquine-national-stockpile/index.html>.

Mancini DP, 'AstraZeneca Vaccine Document Shows Limit of No-Profit Pledge' (*Financial Times*, 7 October 2020) <https://www.ft.com/content/c474f9e1-8807-4e57-9c79-6f4af145b686>.

Mayta R, KK Shailaja, and A Nyong'o, 'Vaccine Nationalism is Killing Us. We Need an Internationalist Approach' (*The Guardian*, 17 June 2021) <https://www.theguardian.com/commentisfree/2021/jun/17/covid-vaccine-nationalism-internationalist-approach>.

Moderna, 'Statement by Moderna on Intellectual Property Matters during the COVID-19 Pandemic' (*Moderna*, 8 October 2020) <https://investors.modernatx.com/news-releases/news-release-details/statement-moderna-intellectual-property-matters-during-covid-19>.

Moderna, 'United States Patent No. 10,703,789 B2' (7 July 2020) 2–5 <https://www.modernatx.com/sites/default/files/US10703789.pdf>.

Naidu S and B Vickers, *South Africa, Africa, and International Investment Agreements* (Centre for Conflict Resolution: Policy Advisory Group Seminar Report, 1 July 2014).

Newey S, '"Trojan Horse": Bulk of UK Vaccine Donations to Poor Countries Set to Expire in September" (*The Telegraph*, 28 July 2021) <https://www.telegraph.co.uk/global-health/science-and-disease/trojan-horse-bulk-uk-vaccine-donations-poor-countries-set-expire/>.

Nyaiage J, 'Could Quality Problems Unravel China's Coronavirus Mask Diplomacy in Africa?' (*South China Morning Post*, 11 August 2020) <https://www.scmp.com/news/china/diplomacy/article/3096908/africa-chinas-mask-diplomacy-will-rise-or-fall-quality-those>.

Olla A, 'Welcome to the New Colonialism: Rich Countries Sitting on Surplus Vaccines' (*The Guardian*, 14 April 2021) <https://www.theguardian.com/commentisfree/2021/apr/14/rich-countries-surplus-covid-vaccines>.

Oxfam, 'Small Group of Rich Nations Have Bought up More than Half the Future Supply of Leading COVID-19 Vaccine Contenders' (*Oxfam*, 17 September 2020) <https://www.oxfam.org/en/press-releases/small-group-rich-nations-have-bought-more-half-future-supply-leading-covid-19>.

Pfizer, 'Pfizer and Biontech to Provide 500 Million Doses of COVID-19 Vaccine to U.S. Government for Donation to Poorest Nations' (*Pfizer*, 10 June 2021) <https://www.pfizer.com/news/press-release/press-release-detail/pfizer-and-biontech-provide-500-million-doses-covid-19>.

Safi M, 'AstraZeneca Vaccine Price Pledge Omits Some Poor Countries, Contract Shows' (*The Guardian*, 17 June 2021) <https://www.theguardian.com/world/2021/jun/17/astrazeneca-vaccine-price-pledge-omits-some-poor-countries-contract-shows>.

Shah H, 'The Vaccine Most Widely Used in Africa and India isn't Part of Europe's Vaccine Passport' (*Quartz*, 29 June 2021) <https://qz.com/2026656/the-eu-digital-covid-certificate-excludes-the-covishield-vaccine/>.

Sullivan H, 'South Africa Paying More than Double EU Price for Oxford Vaccine' (*The Guardian*, 22 January 2021) <https://www.theguardian.com/world/2021/jan/22/south-africa-paying-more-than-double-eu-price-for-oxford-astrazeneca-vaccine>.

Tai K, 'Statement from Ambassador Katherine Tai on the Covid-19 TRIPS Waiver' (5 May 2021) <https://ustr.gov/about-us/policy-offices/press-office/press-releases/2021/may/statement-ambassador-katherine-tai-covid-19-trips-waiver>.

Thambisetty S, A McMahon, L McDonagh, HY Kang, and G Dutfield, 'The TRIPS Intellectual Property Waiver Proposal: Creating the Right Incentives in Patent Law and Politics to End the COVID-19 Pandemic' (LSE Legal Studies Working Paper, 2021) 21 <https://papers.ssrn.com/sol3/papers.cfm?abstract_id=3851737>.

Wingate S, 'Politicians Scuffle at African Union Parliament in Row over How to Elect New President' (*The Independent*, 1 June 2021) <https://www.independent.co.uk/tv/news/politicians-scuffle-at-african-union-parliament-in-row-over-how-to-elect-new-president-va25a294d>.

WHO, 'COVAX Joint Statement: Call to Action to Equip COVAX to Deliver 2 Billion Doses in 2021' (*WHO*, 27 May 2021) <https://www.who.int/news/item/27-05-2021-covax-joint-statement-call-to-action-to-equip-covax-to-deliver-2-billion-doses-in-2021>.

WTO, 'TRIPS Council to Continue to Discuss Temporary IP Waiver, Revised Proposal Expected in May' (*WTO*, 30 April 2021) <https://www.wto.org/english/news_e/news21_e/trip_30apr21_e.htm>.

5 Conclusion

5.1 Introduction

Patent law, in many ways, reflects the complex state of law and legal research in 2025. While from a narrow perspective it simply provides legal protection for technical innovations, its impact is at once political, societal, and legal in a way that undermines strict divisions in the way we talk about and analyse patent law. Patent law has been understood from a variety of different viewpoints – emphasising its property characteristics,[1] presenting it as a form of international regulation,[2] and this book that has centred the complex interactive dynamics that produce international patent law. Nevertheless, the challenge in each of these approaches is recognising the complexity and overlapping quality of law in a distinctly global setting. Understanding legal systems and their interactions as interfaces in which different values, objectives, and laws come into contact helps to produce a more contextual and nuanced analysis that centres the participants and their autonomy. The borders of a legal system are not found in the sharp lines produced by legislation or legal order, but instead are produced through the interactions of different bodies in a dynamic process. Crucial to this process, then, is the ability to meaningfully participate in the design and values of the binding obligations of a legal framework. Patent law in the contexts investigated in this book essentially focus on three different types of boundaries between legal systems: the EU and its Member States, bilateral or plurilateral trade partners, and state members of the multilateral trading system. In each of these, patent law becomes entangled with other forms of intellectual property and broader geopolitical forces that extend beyond a narrow technical patent analysis. Interpreting these developments and configurations through the lens of participation, accountability, and transparency reveals a more nuanced understanding of how patent law actually develops. The international, and perhaps even the national, setting prevents patent law from ever being truly

1 Though Travis argues that the US has actually departed from the private property model: Hannibal Travis, 'Patents, the Private Property Ideal, and the Public Interest in a Seamless Global Public Health System' (2022) 31(1) Federal Circuit Bar Journal 24, 25.

2 Henning Grosse Ruse-Khan, 'Intellectual Property and International Law: A Research Framework' in Irene Calboli and Maria Lillà Montagnani (eds), *Handbook of Intellectual Property Research: Lenses, Methods, and Perspectives* (OUP 2021) 15, 16.

DOI: 10.4324/9781003616856-6

isolated. Agreements and dispute resolution bodies do not simply affect patent law when they negotiate or modulate the functioning of patent provisions, but they also shape the broader relationship between these legal systems and the autonomy of participants within them. Patent law is then at once political, social, and cultural in a way that actively challenges domestic or technocratic isolation.

The book has focused on exploring how new patent frameworks are created, the distinct sense of global space in international patent law, and the processes through which different systems of patent law interact. In each of these, the role of dispute settlement bodies in enabling these systemic interactions reflects specific values drawn from work on global administration. Throughout, the book has used the global administration perspective to centre concerns of accountability, transparency, and participation to break from more conventional ways of understanding patent law. In this sense, the values of global and domestic administration provide a lens through which patent law can be freed from its technical vocabulary. A fundamental aspect of presenting patent law in this way is that, in the deeply contextual spaces produced in dispute resolution proceedings, the development of patent policy is impacted not only by other forms of intellectual property but by more social forces that shape, restrict, or influence the autonomy of its participants. Approaching international law in a way that emphasises the economic qualities of the patent may work for designing national growth plans; but in doing so, this approach minimises the dynamic qualities of patent law and fundamentally provides an incomplete understanding of how patent law develops.

The language of accountability, transparency, and participation enables a broader discussion as to the role and functioning of patent law. In some ways, the book has been about patent law for non-patent scholars. It has been an attempt at presenting international patent law in a way that opens it up to engagement to those outside of academic patent law scholarship. Continuing to speak about patent law in a way that predominantly emphasises its technical characteristics contributes to its isolation not only within a legal context but also in broader society.

The conclusion is split into five parts, with the first four reflecting on the material covered in each chapter of the book. The second part of each section is a more critical revisiting of the limitations and strengths of the chapter, particularly in terms of how the work could be improved and discussions on future work that would be beyond the current scope of the book. The chapter ends with a brief summation.

5.2 Revisiting the objectives and purpose of the book

In reflecting on the process of writing this book, three general objectives and contributions were central in guiding the text. The first of these is that it positions international patent law alongside the emerging system of global administration. As patent law has already been discussed extensively as a form of global regulation and an element of global trade regulation, the book instead focuses on using values from the administrative foundation of patent law and the emphasis in global administration on the creative potential of dispute resolution bodies. International patent law is indeed regulatory, but the administrative foundation of patent law means that legislation that modifies the ability of a state to freely grant patents can instead be considered in a similar way to more conventional administrative law scholarship. It has become almost cliché at this point to discuss the emergence of global patent law with the TRIPS Agreement without recognising that the negotiating dynamic between the developing and developed countries was unequal. More critical work takes a more overt stance in that the developing countries were misled, coerced, or otherwise taken advantage of.[3] Of course, the TRIPS Agreement was formally and procedurally consented to, but this does not provide a convincing case that the TRIPS Agreement did not (and does not) practically restrain state power. The book then provides a more nuanced understanding of international patent law as a part of global regulation and frames it through the vocabulary that has emerged prominently in global administration. In doing so, it provides a novel way of approaching international patent law that recasts tensions in patent law in a way that explicitly reaches out to other disciplines – it invites a reader from any background to have an opinion on patent law and recognise that it has never simply been an area of trade regulation. The book has taken complex legal problems in the development of international patent law and approaches them in a way that uses accessible concepts, a starting point for a dialogue between patent law and other fields. This approach, specifically in its deployment of participation, also helps to position international patent law alongside other initiatives in international regulation and law more generally. Issues of meaningful participation are not unique problems of patent law and are instead inherent tensions of legal development (whether national, international, or global).

The second objective in mind while writing the book is perhaps more abstract and connects several contemporary issues in international patent law. By constructing patent law as fundamentally related to administrative power and control, the book deconstructs it from the perspective of accountability, participation, and transparency in a way that can then be considered an *internal* critique of patent law. These concepts are fundamental to the study of administrative law, yet in patent law, the theoretical consequences of its administrative foundation are rarely considered outside of the bifurcation of validity and infringement. This approach also speaks to a more fundamental debate in administrative law, articulating precisely why administrative law is an essential feature of any legal system. The core of patent law is the exercise of state power in a way that cannot be replicated through private law means. Critical approaches, specifically on issues of access to medicine,[4] have analysed patent law from perspectives that

3 Though it is not frequent, there is writing that specifically uses the language of coercion when discussing the implementation of the TRIPS Agreement and developing countries: Ezinne Mirian Igbokwe and Andrea Tosato, 'Access to Medicines and Pharmaceutical Patents: Fulfilling the Promise of TRIPS Article 31bis' (2023) 91(5) Fordham Law Review 1795, 1796.

4 Anjali Vats and Deidré A Keller, 'Critical Race Theory as Intellectual Property Methodology' in Irene Calboli and Maria Lillà Montagnani (eds), *Handbook of Intellectual Property Research: Lenses, Methods, and Perspectives* (OUP 2021) 789, 790.

emphasise human rights or specific values but have done so in a way that puts them in contrast to the economic (orthodox) understanding of patent law and its role. Instead, the book attempts to position the patent's economic qualities alongside the values common to administrative law discussion. From this perspective, the economic dimension of patent law represents only a single aspect of a more complex whole. The book's approach has then not been the application of a non-patent framework of values to the development of international patent law, but rather a way of recognising the administrative foundation of patent law and suggesting that concerns around participation, accountability, and transparency are legitimate things to critique. The vocabulary of global administration was used to try and minimise the theoretical dissonance (in terms of legitimacy) that appears to be so fundamental to work analysing contemporary issues of international patent law. Why should patent law not be subject to the same value standards as other areas of administrative law? Why is the exercise of delegated state power overlooked so frequently when discussing patent law and evaluating its function in society?

The third contribution of the book is that it has, hopefully, provided a more nuanced and complete understanding of how dispute resolution bodies function in international patent law beyond their narrow and immediate role as a venue for legal disputes. Framing dispute settlement bodies using global administration concepts also helped highlight how these institutions are central in promoting (or undermining) the values of accountability, transparency, and participation. In doing so, the book also necessarily explored what exactly these values can mean – their normative content – in both a more general sense and in the context of international patent law. Throughout, though specifically in the Introduction and Chapter 1, the objective was to recognise that these three values are fundamentally joined and cannot easily be separated in practice. Yet in choosing to interpret dispute settlement bodies and their broader legal space through the artificial separation of these values, the analysis was trying to explore the specific function of each dimension in the development of patent law. This type of separation also reflects the broader objective of promoting communication beyond patent law because it helps to communicate different facets of the subject under consideration rather than presenting an amorphous whole. Even in the choice of language, of administrative values, a persistent objective in writing the book was to enable audiences, who typically perceive patent law as technocratic and complex, to actually engage with patent issues. There was certainly a difficulty in balancing between appropriately deconstructing issues of complex legal analysis and ensuring that the work went beyond the conventional way we discuss patent law. Though it was mentioned in the Introduction, this sense of accessibility framed much of the analysis and returned periodically in the process of writing. Readers from all backgrounds can relate to and interpret a subject through the values of accountability or transparency, and patent law should not be somehow immune to generalist intervention. Has a lack of extensive technical knowledge ever prevented someone from engaging in earnest discussion about human rights or politics?

5.3 Chapter 1: On Global Administrative Law and its themes, values, and objectives

5.3.1 Exploring the background of Global Administrative Law

Chapter 1 explored the development of global administration as an academic subject, contextualising its major features and discussions with the fundamentals of international patent law, which was the focus of the remainder of the book. An important aspect of this chapter is understanding the relationship between patent law, global administration, and administrative power more generally. This was important for framing the book since, conventionally, patent law has never been linked with global administration. As such, there was a discussion not only of how patent law connects with global administration concepts but also of defining to some extent how these concepts have been adapted within the book. Within intellectual property, patent law stands out as an area where the push towards increased international harmonisation has not yet resulted in a singular, global patent system.[5] Enforcement, in particular, has retained a distinctly national characteristic and provides a forum in which national, international, and global forces come into contact on issues of patent law.[6] In this, the book focused more on systemic interactions and the process of development in international patent law rather than substantive characteristics of law. Applying an administrative law lens to these patent law interactions also provides a way of highlighting how specific values can be used to deconstruct how the relevant actors are engaged in the process of developing patent law. Primarily, the administrative values were brought from their original administrative context and applied as a lens through which patent law can be viewed. What does patent law look like when we frame it in terms of meaningful participation? Does it emphasise dynamics or issues typically overlooked when using a more conventional approach to patent law?

The administrative perspective is applied to patent law, though the book in some way centres the role of Europe as a particularly influential actor in the development of international initiatives (in patent law and beyond). The European focus also provides a way of deploying the administrative lens to a series of specific contexts in a more graduated fashion. The book starts with the relatively narrow (though still international) interactions of the EU and the Member States before moving to environments which are more thoroughly global in character. Fundamentally, though, Europe also provides one of the few global examples of sustained close integration between states. It is an example of how tensions emerge (and are managed) when

5 Randy Campbell, 'Global Patent Law Harmonization: Benefits and Implementation' (2003) 13(2) Indiana International & Comparative Law Review 605. And while Rajec remains unconvinced by the explanatory value of harmonisation within international intellectual property (preferring maximalism instead), it remains that there is no global system that deals with the grant and enforcement of patent rights: Sarah R Wasserman Rajec, 'The Harmonization Myth in International Intellectual Property Law' (2020) 60 Arizona Law Review 735, 740.

6 Randy Campbell, 'Global Patent Law Harmonization: Benefits and Implementation' (2003) 13(2) Indiana International & Comparative Law Review 614.

legal systems interact at that particularly systemic level.[7] Europe has many non-intellectual property examples of mechanisms used to modulate or otherwise adjust how legal systems interact that specifically incorporate the language of administrative law concepts.[8] Intellectual property, and specifically patent law, has not typically been discussed as a form of administrative law despite the fundamental role of administrative power in granting the patent. Patents (and the process of granting a patent) are the result of an exercise of delegated state power – though, perhaps more fundamentally, it is the state power that is essential to the very existence of patent law. Patent systems and the retained national scope of patent law mean that international agreements, like the TRIPS Agreement, practically restrict a state's autonomy to freely grant patents. This can be constructed as simply the regulation of international patent law or technical standards of the patent grant process,[9] but these agreements should be recognised as having a fundamentally administrative dimension precisely because they produce a modification as to how delegated state power may be exercised. The rules and systems that affect national patent law are both regulatory *and* administrative.

Patent law presents a interesting opportunity for applying an administrative lens to the process of policy development in patent law since international patent law (and also national patent law) has often been framed in terms of its economic potential.[10] Even at this abstract level, the use of administrative vocabulary immediately shifts how we construct patent law and its development. This reframing and re-description of patent law provides a break with conventional work and creates a more open space that is open to other, potentially disruptive, perspectives from other disciplines. This economic framing in patent law has been used to drive discussions on the harmonisation of patent law,[11] of the role of efficiency,[12] and the stability of property rights.[13] Yet the reality of patent law is much more complex and should be open to engagement from diverse and varied audiences. Though

7 Günter Burghardt, 'The EU/US Transatlantic Relationship: The Indispensable Partnership' in Christoph Hermann, Bruno Simma, and Rudolf Streinz (eds), *Trade Policy between Law, Diplomacy and Scholarship* (Springer 2015) 197; Victor Rodriguez, 'Constructing a Unitary Title for the European Patent System' (2011) 6(8) JIPLP 576.

8 Giacinto Della Cananea, 'Administrative Law Beyond the State: The Influence of International and Supranational Organizations' in Peter Cane, Herwig CH Hofmann, Eric C Ip, and Peter L Lindseth (eds), *Oxford Handbook of Comparative Administrative Law* (OUP 2021) 359, 373.

9 P Sean Morris, 'Private Intellectual Property Regulation in Public International Law' (2020) 26(1) UC Davis Journal of International Law and Policy 148, 149.

10 Albert GZ Hu and IPL Png, 'Patent Rights and Economic Growth: Evidence from Cross-Country Panels of Manufacturing Industries' (2013) 65(3) Oxford Economic Papers 675, 676.

11 Jerome H Reichman and Rochelle C Dreyfuss, 'Harmonization Without Consensus: Critical Reflections on Drafting a Substantive Patent Law Treaty' (2007) 57(1) Duke Law Journal 87.

12 Vincent Chiappetta, 'Working Toward International Harmony on Intellectual Property Exhaustion (and Substantive Law)' in Irene Calboli and Edward Lee (eds), *Research Handbook on Intellectual Property Exhaustion and Parallel Imports* (Edward Elgar 2016) 139.

13 Amina Ahmed Lahsen and Alan T Piper, 'Property Rights and Intellectual Property Protection, GDP Growth and Individual Well-Being in Latin America' (2019) 28 Latin American Economic Review 2, 5.

the system does produce a legal right that necessarily has an economic impact,[14] the process of developing patent law and its binding obligations incorporates a much more contextual series of considerations. Patent law, within a legal single framework, brings together a rich and provocative set of normative perspectives that distinguish what is and what is not inventive,[15] how relevant constructions of public morality adjust its functioning,[16] and the appropriate role of the patent system in driving economic growth.[17] From this perspective, it seems clear that a technical or regulatory approach to patent law misses so much of what it *is* and how it comes to be.

5.3.2 Critically reflecting on the mapping of Global Administrative Law concepts and values

One of the major aspects of Chapter 1 was an attempt to contextualise the development of global administration, patent law, and the broader emergence of global systems of regulation. An essential part of this was highlighting that patent law, specifically through the grant of a patent, was fundamentally built on an exercise of delegated state power and can, therefore, be analysed from an administrative law perspective. Even within national administrative law, there are a number of discussions about the exact legal mechanisms and tools that control the exercise of state power as delegated to administrative agencies.[18] Yet one of the limitations of the chapter, and perhaps of the book more generally, is that properly exploring the administrative foundations of patent law would be beyond the book's scope. The book does not explore the precise administrative quality of the patent grant in a series of jurisdictions. It is not a survey or broad comparative study on the administrative processes involved in patent grant and review. Instead, it takes the values fundamental to administrative law and uses them to deconstruct international patent law. It is precisely this international setting that the book draws so heavily from global administration, where there are unique characteristics of

14 Discussing the utilitarian perception of patents as 'economic instruments' that should protect only the minimum term required to incentivise innovation: Federica Baldan, *Judicial Coherence in the European Patent System: Lessons from the US and Japan* (Edward Elgar 2022) 91.

15 Such as excluding mathematics from patentability: Hazel VJ Moir, *Patent Policy and Innovation: Do Legal Rules Deliver Effective Economic Outcomes?* (Edward Elgar 2013) 64.

16 The changing approach to 'products manufactured by an atomic transformation' in Japan is one example: Nobuhiro Nakayama, 'The Enforcement of the TRIPS Agreement in Japan' (1995) 38 Japanese Annual of International Law 58.

17 Like the reforms around universities and patent commercialisation that appeared around the world: Hiroyuki Odagiri, Akira Goto, and Atsushi Sunami, 'IPR and the Catch-Up Process in Japan' in Hiroyuki Odagiri, Akira Goto, Atsushi Sunami, Richard R Nelson (eds), *Intellectual Property Rights, Development, and Catch-up: An International Comparative Study* (OUP 2010) 120.

18 Where even edited volumes highlight, beyond the 'necessary control function and the significant role played by courts' in administrative law, the importance of interpreting 'the concept of control more inclusively': Carol Harlow, Päivi Leino, and Giacinto Della Cananea, 'Introduction: European Administrative Law – A Thematic Approach' in Carol Harlow, Päivi Leino, and Giacinto Della Cananea (eds), *Research Handbook on EU Administrative Law* (Edward Elgar 2017) 7.

administrative subjects that play out in an environment with no single legislator, executive, or judiciary. This intensive focus on the international aspects of patent law also reflects perhaps a broader limitation in the book, which is that the emphasis of patent law's administrative foundation and using that as an analytical lens is not a conventional approach. Other authors have produced excellent scholarship on how patent law develops from perspectives that focus on economics,[19] human rights,[20] and property law.[21] I believe that the administrative law perspective here helps to deconstruct patent law in a way that not only sheds light on the dynamic interactions which produce international patent law but in a more expansive or encompassing way.

The administrative perspective also provides an importantly *internal* critique of patent law that is aimed at challenging or destabilising the dominant economic narrative of patent law. As discussed in the Introduction and Chapter 1, a major theme within the literature – specifically work that critiques the distributive impact of patent law[22] – is the use of a non-patent perspective to analyse an issue of patent law. In this, there is a significant level of dialogue that appears to be aimed at legitimising this approach, of reconciling two different disciplines. Patent law, as fundamentally realised through the exercise of administrative power, dissolves this issue by producing a critique that is internal to patent law and draws on conventional administrative law values as tools of analysis. Despite this, it is clear that this tension in the legitimacy of applying different perspectives to issues of patent law is not necessarily a pressing issue in the literature. The administrative perspective that enables an internal critique of patent law is a novel approach, though the practical value of it for scholars engaged in specific issues (like access to medicine, the right to health) may be limited. If the book were to be focused entirely on the legal theory of administrative power in patent law, there is a risk that it becomes so detached from real-world issues of the international patent system. The book attempts to reconcile the theoretical administrative values with the specific interactions between actors in very grounded and embedded contexts. From this perspective, a discussion on the delegated state power of a patent grant is of very limited use for someone advocating for vaccine accessibility in specific marginalised communities.

Patent law as a form of administrative law can be seen in two specific elements, the first of which comes from the scope and means of execution in patent law. Yet there is also an important recognition that the discussion of how patent law is uniquely administrative runs in parallel to a similar conversation in administrative law – that administrative law is unique and cannot be replicated by other tools

19 Duncan Matthews, 'Patents in the Global Economy' (UKIPO Report 2010) 1.

20 Hans Morten Haugen, 'Patent Rights and Human Rights: Exploring their Relationships' (2007) 10(2) WIPOJ 97, 98.

21 Adam Mossoff, 'Patents as Constitutional Private Property: The Historical Protection of Patents under the Takings Clause' (2007) 87 Boston University Law Review 689.

22 Philippe Cullet, 'Patents and Medicines: The Relationship between TRIPS and the Human Right to Health' (2003) 79(1) International Affairs 139, 140.

of law. Patent law, and the enforcement of a patent, relies on state power for its authority and explains why it has retained such an emphasis on national borders for patent validity. A key part of a patent is that it is a negative right – a right to exclude all others[23] – and this effect cannot be replicated through ordinary contract law or commercial law tools precisely because it affects all actors in that legal system with no prior arrangement. Provisions in international trade law that control how this delegated power may be exercised (the type of patent that can be issued, the length of a patent) then have a functionally similar role to tools of administrative law. The issue of consent is crucial here. Discussions throughout Chapters 3 and 4 examined how formal consent, or more generally the 'thin' procedural understandings of administrative values, work to mask inequalities between trade partners. In a very real sense, does the formal consent of a developing country somehow make up for the negotiating imbalance and significant concessions made during the Uruguay Round? It also returns us to the sense of entanglement because patent law was not negotiated in isolation during this period (nor is it ever in international law). The issue is not whether the coercion reached the formal definition of an intervention (whichever construction one chooses to take),[24] but whether functionally these states adopted constraints to their ability to grant a patent that they would otherwise not have accepted. Though this is by no means an objective test, and surely remains unconvincing to some readers, any sense that the negotiations were produced in an environment in which there was a fundamental imbalance at least raises the question about the extent to which the resulting legislation can be seen to restrict the exercise of state power.

5.4 Chapter 2: On the development of European patent law

5.4.1 A new patent interface in Europe: The potential of 'participation' to interpret tensions in international initiatives

Chapter 2 explored the development and implementation of the European Patent with Unitary Effect (EPUE). Though it is specifically explored through the lens of administrative values, the EPUE is a fundamental evolution of patent law in Europe intended to significantly address the ongoing fragmentation of European patent law.[25] The fragmentation of patent law in this context has been discussed extensively elsewhere,[26] though it is important to recognise that the lack of harmonisation

23 Adam Mossoff, 'Exclusion and Exclusive Use in Patent Law' (2009) 22(2) Harvard Journal of Law & Technology 322.

24 On an in-depth exploration of the genealogy of 'intervention' and its range beyond armed conflict: Patrick Quinton-Brown, *Intervention Before Interventionism: A Global Genealogy* (OUP 2024).

25 With the objective of creating a specialised patent jurisdiction and promoting research, development and investment in innovation: EU Commission, 'Internal Market, Industry, Entrepreneurship, and SMEs: Unitary Patent' (EU Commission) <https://ec.europa.eu/growth/industry/strategy/intellectual-property/patent-protection-eu/unitary-patent_en>.

26 Specifically in terms of patent validation but also more generally: Amanda Odell-West, 'Exclusions in Patent Law as an Indirect Form of Regulation for New Health Technologies in Europe' in Mark

has typically resulted from a mix of substantive and procedural issues. Significant progress was made with the EPC and other specific Directives that helped promote a more unified European approach to patents (though specifically in applying for a patent).[27] Particularly for users, a European patent system that presents a single enforceable right effective throughout the EU would be a positive simplification over the multiple national approaches to application and enforcement generally required in Europe. However, despite this significant potential, the EPUE as currently constructed falls short of producing an effective and harmonised system for patent protection in Europe – specifically in the way that it constructs a new and concerning dynamic between the interests of different EU Member States and how they are represented in patent law. The EPUE is also a unique opportunity within patent law to observe the creation of a new interface and, from an administrative perspective, to explore how specific values can be used in an interpretative way to understand how that legal framework is developing and the interests it centres. The chapter specifically emphasised the role of transparency and participation in the development of the EPUE as fundamental concerns. The challenges of promoting participation were especially visible in the EPUE context because it was the result of enhanced cooperation rather than the ordinary legislative process of the EU.

Chapter 2 focused on how participation not only influenced the creation of a new legal framework in patent law but also how it can be used to look at the future development of European patent law. The EPUE is, of course, only one element of European patent law and the latter half of the chapter was devoted to exploring the UPC and its relationship to participation. The UPC, as the court structure that deals with both the administration and enforcement of EPUEs, is central to understanding how administrative values function within this system and the future trajectory of patent practice in Europe. The UPC also represents an important development for specialisation in European patent law, in line with a more general trend towards the specialisation of intellectual property courts globally.[28] Administrative values enable an understanding of the dynamic character of legal development that cannot be captured by simply looking at the legislative provisions. It is the interpretation, adaptation, and enforcement of these provisions through the creative process of dispute resolution that reveals a much more contextual experience of patent law.

L Flear, Anne-Maree Farrell, Tamara K Hervey, and Thérèse Murphy (eds), *European Law and New Health Technologies* (OUP 2013) 152.

27 On the complex role of the EPC in bringing together standards in patent law: Alexander Stack, *International Patent Law: Cooperation, Harmonization and an Institutional Analysis of WIPO and the WTO* (Edward Elgar 2011) 94.

28 On the increasing global attention that specialised intellectual property courts have attracted: Olga Gurgula, Maciej Padamczyk, and Noam Shemtov, 'Specialised IP Judiciary: What Are the Key Elements to Consider When Establishing or Reforming an Effective IP Court?' (2022) 71(3) GRUR International 206, 207.

5.4.2 Balancing the chapter: Between speculation and analysis

A strength of Chapter 2 is that it investigates an emerging legal development in patent law from a perspective that stresses the interconnected nature of law. As a new legal instrument and court, the chapter provides valuable analysis of the EPUE and UPC, even from a narrow patent law perspective. Yet it is in reframing the functioning of the EPUE and the UPC through the vocabulary of participation that provides an analysis which centres unconventional aspects of patent law. The very design of the EPUE is a direct response to established EU doctrine concerning the improper delegation of regulatory power to administrative agencies.[29] From this perspective, reflecting many discussions on the role of international patent law as an element of global trade regulation,[30] patent law clearly has a regulatory character in that it provides for specific boundaries of the patent and yet it is fundamentally reliant on an exercise of delegated state power. This chapter is important as it not only explores the EPUE from the perspective of administrative values, but also supports a broader argument on the abstract nature of patent law as deeply connected to administration even in an international setting. Participation was the central value in this chapter and unifies many different themes that appear in more implicit or isolated ways in other work on European patent law. This is particularly the case for the EPUE and enhanced cooperation since the focus on participation draws attention to the systemic dimensions of international cooperation rather than suggesting there is a unique quality to the EPUE development. The contextual analysis of other uses of enhanced cooperation in the chapter also supports this and works to distinguish the EPUE in a way that has generally not been explored in the literature so far.

Using the administrative values to guide the analysis throughout the book was useful in Chapter 2 because the emerging literature on the EPUE has generally focused on the technical character of patent law exceptions. There is some excellent work that does incorporate a broader perspective, particularly with the work of Lamping on the undermining of enhanced cooperation requirements and McMahon on the difficult process of balancing in the context of *l'ordre public* exceptions.[31] But by using participation as a lens through which to view patent law, the chapter effectively explores not only the EPUE as a legal development but also what it means for the process of legal development more generally. A core element that helped drive the analysis of the chapter was a questioning of *who* was important in this process. The global administration framing helps the chapter bring together the patent-specific disputes in the EPUE (in particular, the language challenges) with a

29 To avoid the *Meroni* doctrine from C-9/56, C-10/56 *Meroni v High Authority* [1957/1957].

30 Frederick M Abbott, 'Intellectual Property Rights in World Trade' in A Guzman and A Sykes (eds), *Research Handbook in International Economic Law* (Edward Elgar 2007) 444, 445.

31 Matthias Lamping, 'Enhanced Cooperation: A Proper Approach to Market Reintegration in the Field of Unitary Patent Protection?' (2011) 42(8) IIC 25, 26; Aisling McMahon, 'An Institutional Examination of the Implications of the Unitary Patent Package for the Morality Provisions: A Fragmented Future Too Far?' (2017) 48(1) IIC 42, 46.

broader critique of how EU Member States interact with each other in law-making. As developed in the chapter, the precise contours of the EPUE system were essentially beyond any serious threat of redesign since it was only the major patent jurisdictions that were necessary for the project to succeed. As long as the major patent jurisdictions were participating, there was very little room for smaller Member States to modify the EPUE framework, and even non-participation would not have shielded their national innovation contexts from the impact of the EPUE system.

One of the fundamental limitations of the chapter is that the analysis, of both the EPUE and the UPC, is necessarily quite speculative. Many variables could affect the eventual usage of the EPUE by industry and how the UPC approaches difficult questions of patent law. The speculative quality of the analysis is quite pronounced as the focus was on the *values* of an international patent system that has seen just under two years of functioning. In fairness, this applies to all work on the EPUE and UPC rather than something unique to the approach developed through the book. Yet this emphasis on participation and administrative values in the EPUE is important because it invites those who are typically not involved in patent law discussions to have a response. Patent law and the harmonisation of European patent law are undoubtedly technical – but so are many other areas of law that people feel comfortable with having a perspective on. Framing it in terms of participation asks an open question to the reader, using a more accessible vocabulary to not only connect with other scholarly backgrounds but to draw attention to issues that have been overlooked in conventional patent work. Patent law is an area of law like any other and should be subject to high standards of accountability and participation. This is specifically the case in Europe due to the frequency with which these values specifically appear in official EU materials,[32] and patent law should be no exception.

5.5 Chapter 3: Understanding the bilateral space and the entanglement of patent law

5.5.1 Exploring the values of EU bilateral trade agreements: The interconnected nature of transparency, accountability, and participation

Particularly in recent years, bilateral and regional trade agreements have become an increasingly prominent part of the global trade system.[33] These agreements contribute significantly to the trade relationship between global trading partners and represent, particularly in contrast to the perceived (lack of) speed of multilateralism, a

32 EU Parliament, 'Transparency and Ethics' (*Europarl*) <https://www.europarl.europa.eu/at-your-service/en/transparency>; though perhaps more explicitly declared through Article 15 TFEU, where the EU bodies and institutions 'conduct their work as openly as possible in order to ensure the participation of civil society and thus promote good governance'.

33 On the sharp growth of trade agreements since the 1990s: Silvia Sopranzetti, 'Overlapping Free Trade Agreements and International Trade: A Network Approach' (2018) 41(6) The World Economy 1549.

more efficient alternative.[34] The increased attention to the impact of bilateral trade agreements, within trade specifically and beyond, is a more recent trend (though their use has a much longer history).[35] The contentious events of the Cancún Ministerial Meeting and the conclusion of the Uruguay Round have emerged as significant drivers of this more central role that bilateral agreements have taken on in recent years.[36] As such, the chapter examines both how participation and transparency have been impaired in the context of bilateral trade agreements and explores more fully the distinct qualities of the bilateral space (in contrast to the national and global environments highlighted in global administration).[37]

Bilateral trade agreements, as individualised agreements between trading partners, produce a legal space in which disputes and negotiations take on a specific, bilaterally-inflected character. Disputes between trade partners are necessarily diffuse and reflect the more localised elements of their trade relationship, the agreement concerned, and how dispute resolution bodies are constructed within that agreement. Because of this, bilateral trade agreements and their relationship to localised dispute resolution and settlement provide an interesting context for exploring how participation and other administrative values function in those highly inflected spaces. Analysing bilateral trade agreements from this global administration perspective highlights the different ways that this process affects the specific characteristics of values, the first of which is their interconnected nature. This builds on some of the more conventional work in global administration that works to illustrate the mutually reinforcing effect of transparency, accountability, and participation.[38] Yet despite this interconnected quality, the bilateral trade environment space demonstrates that these localised values remain somewhat isolated

34 'The institutional machinery of the GATT/WTO system is cumbersome and slow. Multilateral rounds take many years to negotiate, and tend to address issues agreed upon by the parties at the inception of each round.': Thomas R Howell, 'The Multilateral Trading System and Transnational Competition in Advanced Technologies: The Limits of Existing Disciplines' in Göran Marklund, Nicholas S Vonortas, and Charles W Wessner (eds), *The Innovation Imperative: National Innovation Strategies in the Global Economy* (Edward Elgar 2009) 52.

35 On the long history of bilateral agreements (as well as the more general trends of liberalism and protectionism over time): Olivier Cattaneo, 'The Political Economy of PTAs' in Simon Lester, Bryan Mercurio, and Lorand Bartels (eds), *Bilateral and Regional Trade Agreements: Commentary and Analysis* (CUP 2015) 31.

36 On the subversive impact of preferential trade agreements on the GATT obligations before Uruguay: Marcelo de Paiva Abreu, 'Developing Countries and the Uruguay Round of Trade Negotiations' in Proceedings of the World Bank Annual Conference on Development Economics, April 1989 (1990) 28.

37 Drawing on perspectives and themes that were prominent in the early development of GAL, where much of the work deals with establishing that there is a 'global space' at all: Elisa D'Alterio, 'Judicial Regulation in the Global Space' in Sabino Cassese (ed), *Research Handbook on Global Administrative Law* (Edward Elgar 2016) 321.

38 Indeed, in the introduction to a symposium issue, Krisch and Kingsbury discuss administrative values and often group together accountability, participation, and transparency: Nico Krisch and Benedict Kingsbury, 'Introduction: Global Governance and Global Administrative Law in the International Legal Order' (2006) 17(1) EJIL 4, 5.

from their multilateral counterparts. This type of breakdown between each distinct value considered throughout the chapter reinforces the artificial character of any separation between transparency, accountability, and participation. Bilateral trade agreements highlight how, in practice, challenges to these values take on a distinctly overlapping and interconnected quality. This presents a dissonance between the very contextually sensitive bilateral environment and how values are supported or undermined in the multilateral context. As such, the themes of systemic isolation and insulation, of internal and external, throughout the chapter reflect many of the same tensions described in work on the increasing atomisation of international trade law.[39]

Turning to the treatment of intellectual property within bilateral trade agreements, the traditional approach has been to reference standards of intellectual property protection in major multilateral agreements rather than requiring the adoption of specific legal standards.[40] One of the breakdowns that occur when trying to explore patent provisions in bilateral agreements is that they are embedded in broader intellectual property agreements. From a practical perspective, this means that patent law – in its negotiation, its enforcement, and its development – is enmeshed and entangled with the way in which that agreement deals with other forms of intellectual property or trade disciplines. More recent years have seen major trade actors such as the EU and the US depart from the earlier and more general approach to bilateral intellectual property agreements.[41] Instead of references to the broad intellectual property standards in multilateral agreements, intellectual property is increasingly subject to elaborate chapters that establish much more specific obligations.[42] Reframing these agreements through the lens of administrative values reveals the complex dynamic between patent law and other subjects of the agreement. There is something almost deceptive about the increasingly specific patent provisions in that they draw attention, narrow the reader's focus, and create an almost self-contained space within the agreement. This masks the fact that

39 Though in reference to international investment law, Hamdani specifically discusses the negative impact of a patchwork of individual treaties between trade partners: Khalil Hamdani, 'Panel: Process and Value of Uniform Commercial Law: Proceedings of the Congress of the United Nations Commission on International Trade Law Held on the Occasion of the Fortieth Session of the Commission' (2007) 25.

40 One more recent example would be the agreement between the Central American Association Agreement where Article 78(g) refers simply to a commitment to 'the adequate and effective protection of intellectual property rights, in accordance with international obligations in force between the parties': Article 78(g) Agreement Establishing an Association between the European Union and its Member States, On the One Hand, and Central America on the Other; while Title VI of the same agreement (that deals with intellectual property) simply reaffirms the binding nature of the TRIPS Agreement in Article 229.

41 Chenguo Zhang, *Balance and Limitation of Intellectual Property Protection in China: The Latest Law Amendments and Judicial Developments Under Micro-Comparative Perspectives* (Springer 2022) 129.

42 Chenguo Zhang, *Balance and Limitation of Intellectual Property Protection in China: The Latest Law Amendments and Judicial Developments Under Micro-Comparative Perspectives* (Springer 2022) 129.

these patent-specific provisions were developed alongside, and therefore part of a broader political negotiation between these countries, every other provision of that agreement. There is something counterintuitive in that, to understand more fully how patent law is developing in the bilateral space, one must also look at how the provisions relate, contrast, and mirror those in the rest of the agreement. The bilateral space demonstrates the entanglement of patent law most clearly as it takes the social, cultural, and political aspects of the patent and contextualises them alongside all other forms of intellectual property and trade priorities in a given state relationship.

The interplay of disciplines, regulation, and trade provisions means that each individual trade agreement has a specific type of relationship with the grounding multilateral instrument (TRIPS). This localisation of the scope of international trade law (and intellectual property more specifically) presents a more abstract challenge to transparency. Transparency in this context is threatened not by the failings of formalist provisions that undermine legal predictability, but rather by an obscuring of the trajectory of international intellectual property law. The bilateral space(s) raise a simple question with no simple answer: How were these provisions in patent law arrived at? With successfully concluded bilateral trade agreements, it is not clear to observers or society more generally which provisions were the result of strategic trading.[43] As such, the values and principles that propel the development of international intellectual property through bilateral trade agreements are fundamentally obscured. This also reveals one of the weaknesses of a more traditional analysis of bilateral trade agreements and their provisions because it explicitly recognises (and denies in the same moment) the multifaceted nature of patent law. The negotiation and conclusion of patent law provisions are the product of a complex social process that is invisible to all but the participants. The inclusion of patent law provisions is not simply the result of a deliberation as to their efficiency or effectiveness, but instead effected by a complete range of non-economic factors that shape the future of international patent law and are masked by both the process and the output.

Here, the lack of transparency also undermines a more practical sense of participation in two specific ways. The first impairment to participation is reflected in the more conventional explorations of democratic accountability that appear in many elements of global administration.[44] Yet there is a second perhaps narrower way in which participation is minimised and centres on the role of state actors in the development of bilateral trade agreements. Even within the specific context of bilateral trade, state participation (and the bodies that would usually provide at least some

43 One multilateral example of this type of strategic trading of standards can be found in the Uruguay Round, with the dynamic between increased intellectual property standards and the possibility of greater market access in textiles and agriculture for developing countries: JH Reichman, 'The TRIPS Component of the GATT's Uruguay Round: Competitive Prospects for Intellectual Property Owners in an Integrated World Market' (1993) 4 Fordham Intellectual Property, Media & Entertainment Law Journal 178.

44 Martin Shapiro, '"Deliberative," "Independent" Technocracy v. Democratic Politics: Will the Globe Echo the E.U.?' (2005) 68(3/4) Law and Contemporary Problems 343.

administrative counterbalance) is restricted to a number of specialised national actors that together result in a system that fundamentally minimises accountability, transparency, and participation.

5.5.2 Reconciling state autonomy with a critique of meaningful participation in bilateralism

Perhaps one of the fundamental limitations of Chapter 3 relates to both global administration as a lens for patent law and the legal arrangement of bilateral trade agreements. Turning first to global administration as an area, Chapter 3 reflects some of the tensions identified in Chapter 1 around the precise scope of 'global' administration. International regulation is so complex that global administration work necessarily incorporates elements that are not just administrative, not just law, and not just global.[45] Bilateral trade agreements push this hazy construction of both 'global' and 'administration' the furthest of any chapter of the book because while it produces agreements with legal effect, it has a more contextual and nuanced relationship to conventional actors in global administration. The book has focused on patent law in a range of international contexts, though future work could instead centre fully the bilateral space and analyse how administrative values operate in this atomised space more generally.

In a related sense, one of the fundamental critiques of the chapter would be that bilateral trade agreements necessarily involve an exercise of autonomy. This is particularly relevant when discussing the negative dimensions of these trade agreements because developing countries often seek to actively engage in trade relationships with larger economies.[46] From this perspective, of economic potential, bilateral trade agreements reflect empowered national governments and a success of trade liberalisation. Yet this is perhaps tempered in the context of the book for two specific reasons. The book has focused on how accountability, participation, and transparency are present in a patent context and at least in these bilateral trade agreements, the chapter deconstructed several examples where the ability to grant a patent or exercise flexibilities was significantly impacted. Accountability for the binding obligations of the Paragraph 6 system and the TRIPS Agreement more generally are, in practice, being modulated by provisions in bilateral trade agreements that minimise their use. Looking at debates in access to medicine, GIs, and test data exclusivity, it would not be controversial to suggest that these agreements not only affect one partner more than the other, but that they function more generally to undermine the binding commitments in the TRIPS Agreement. It is, again, a more functional approach to understanding these trade relationships and the way in

45 Sabino Cassese, 'Global Administrative Law: The State of the Art' (2015) 13(2) ICON 465.

46 And not always for the economic gains – Gallagher discusses how Latin America's engagement with the US in trade agreements actually produces fewer economic gains than under global trade liberalisation efforts, instead emphasising the economic diplomacy dimension of these engagements: Kevin P Gallagher, 'Trading Away the Ladder? Trade Politics and Economic Development in the Americas' (2008) 13(1) New Political Economy 37.

which patent law becomes entangled. If the ability to freely make use of exceptions or flexibilities is being impaired in practice, clearly something is being negotiated for. We return to a discussion raised earlier about autonomy and the conclusion of the Uruguay Round – the consent of developing countries, whether partners in bilateral or multilateral trade, is valid. However, the entangled quality of patent law in these environments means that patent law is never negotiated alone. Participation and accountability provide a way of interpreting these arrangements by considering whether, if negotiating patent law alone, would the trade partners have accepted the limitations to their autonomy?

The second aspect that complicates whether the autonomy of trading partners can be used to critique the book more generally comes from the scholarship around the political economy of trade agreements. This manifests in trade agreements that work to facilitate some broader geopolitical objective (the US–Oman trade agreement is one example),[47] and also in more conventional contexts in intellectual property where higher standards are traded for market access in another area.[48] This trading of standards has been discussed extensively in the context of multilateral trade rounds and can also be seen in the bilateral context as well.[49] From this perspective, the autonomy of the parties involved – though particularly developing countries – could then be contextually understood as fundamentally tied to the economic potential of the agreement. The smallest of developing countries, in reality, have little capacity to negotiate the terms of an agreement with the EU and may indeed not want to challenge specific provisions (like patents) because the economic value of the agreement in terms of market access outweighs all other concerns. Trade partners, specifically in agreements with the EU, are then clearly exercising their autonomy in entering these agreements, but it reflects a qualified autonomy that is subject to a variety of external (to the trade agreement) pressures.

This also links with a further limitation of the chapter connected to how the issues within bilateral agreements are constructed. The book attempts to use the concepts of participation and accountability in an expansive way for patent law to integrate, rather than isolate, issues in patent law. Yet especially with problems emerging from bilateral agreements, a great deal of literature already focuses more on the discrete issues themselves from a rights perspective. Access to medicine and limitations on the exercise of flexibilities is one example,[50] though GIs and

47 Lucia M Rafanelli, *Promoting Justice Across Borders: The Ethics of Reform Intervention* (OUP 2021) 34.

48 Where the bilateral trade negotiation context itself 'easily enables trade deals that trade IP standards against concessions in other areas of trade that are perceived to be more important': Anke Moerland, 'Do Developing Countries Have a Say? Bilateral and Regional Intellectual Property Negotiations with the EU' (2017) 48 IIC 781.

49 JH Reichman, 'The TRIPS Component of the GATT's Uruguay Round: Competitive Prospects for Intellectual Property Owners in an Integrated World Market' (1993) 4 Fordham Intellectual Property, Media & Entertainment Law Journal 178.

50 Emmanuel Kolawole Oke, *Patents, Human Rights, and Access to Medicine* (CUP 2022) 93, 94.

the claw-back provisions are another reflection of a more contextualised discussion.[51] The administrative perspective in Chapter 3 is only one way of approaching these issues and is not intended as a definitive understanding. The chapter does, however, present the interconnected nature of these issues by emphasising the relationship between the bilateral and multilateral spaces and the way deficiencies in administrative values necessarily enable these more specific legal problems. By focusing on discrete issues, conventional patent work isolates those provisions to a degree because they are contextualised so specifically by the trade relationship of the individual trade partners. These issues and practice-focused approaches to patent law work are effective for articulating specific tensions and outcomes, but fail to identify and communicate the common foundation of these problems to patent and non-patent audiences.

This also links more generally with the way the book attempts to connect the values of global administration with the legal frameworks of international patent law. Chapter 3 questions both the accountability of bilateral trade agreements and the transparency of how international patent law is developing through this diffuse (and relatively opaque) system of trade agreements. The chapter concludes that there has been a significant impairment of transparency in how provisions of patent law are being developed that will have a long-term impact – and yet a difficult question emerges: Who can solve this transparency issue? The reality is that patent law is one small area of these large trade agreements and effective oversight, or the effective empowerment of accountability and transparency, would require a significant degree of consistent political will. Addressing the issue of opaque development in this area will not come from a simple or linear system of oversight. Instead, academic commentary that critically highlights the dysfunctional elements of bilateral trade agreements *in combination with* the work that focuses on discrete issues will at least provide a different, non-economic perspective on these agreements that prioritise broad communication and engagement with issues of patent law. Again, there is an almost counterintuitive conclusion that to address the concerning trajectory of international patent law, patent scholars must seek to actively engage non-patent audiences and get them to be interested, worried, or even enthusiastic about questions of how patent law is developing.

51 Anselm Kamperman Sanders, 'Geographical Indications as Property: European Union Association Agreements and Investor-State Provisions' in Irene Calboli and Ng-Loy Wee Loon (eds), *Geographical Indications at the Crossroads of Trade, Development, and Culture: Focus on Asia–Pacific* (CUP 2017) 179.

5.6 Chapter 4: The global space in patent law: Pre-Doha, post-Doha, post-COVID-19

5.6.1 Multilateral development in review: Recasting the structure of global patent law

Chapter 4 deals with the multilateral dimension of patent law and focuses on the WTO, TRIPS Agreement, and the broader trade environment. The TRIPS Agreement was an important context in which patent tensions can be reconstructed through the lens of participation because it essentially forms the basis of global patent law. Flexibilities such as compulsory licensing and *l'ordre public* exceptions enable the TRIPS Agreement to function effectively as an interface, wherein multiple competing tensions and forces can be negotiated without removing the actors from the multilateral system. Autonomy in the use of these flexibilities is a reflection of the broader concern of participation, where even more conventional work in patent law has explored the disconnect between the existence of patent flexibilities and the lack of use of them in practice.[52] Understanding these interactions through the lens of administrative values further contextualises the dynamic quality of the space produced through multilateral agreements, more concretely incorporating political and social dimensions to the development of patent law.

Participation is particularly complex in the multilateral environment because it relies on, at a fundamental level, an assumption that all parties have legally consented to the binding obligations of the WTO Agreements. And yet despite this, it is clear in practice that specific states have very little opportunity to meaningfully shape the development of international patent law. This essentially represents a global reflection of the dynamic discussed in Chapter 2 in which patent law, through the lens of participation, is understood as a configuration of power between the states, legislative power, and the dispute resolution bodies. The emphasis on participation problematises both contemporary and historical configurations and developments in multilateral patent law by framing them in a way that centres the practical outcome. Instead of asking how the subject matter eligibility provisions function, participation asks a more grounded question: Which actors have the power to meaningfully shape the binding obligations that make up patent law? Which actors are driving the values, priorities, and objectives of international patent law? This also raises questions that were explored in part through Chapter 3 regarding dispute resolution and *which* bodies are shaping the understanding of these provisions in practice. Dispute resolution in the multilateral setting is perhaps more concerning for participation issues because the dispute resolution, though falling short of official precedent,[53] operates in a much closer way to a court than

52 Particularly in the context of the Doha Health Declaration amendments to the TRIPS Agreement for countries without manufacturing capacity: Eric M Solovy, 'The Doha Declaration at Twenty: Interpretation, Implementation, and Lessons Learned on the Relationship between the TRIPS Agreement and Global Health' (2022) 42(2) Northwestern Journal of International Law & Business 256, 257.

53 Yet still retaining, in practice, an important role in future decisions: James Bacchus and Simon Lester, 'The Rule of Precedent and the Role of the Appellate Body' (2020) 54(2) JWT 185, 186.

the arbitral tribunals established through bilateral trade agreements. This means that the interpretation of binding obligations in patent law has a much greater potential in the multilateral setting to significantly alter the character or content of binding obligations.

Balance in the WTO and the potential of strategic coalitions in Chapter 4 also raises profound questions about the future of multilateral patent law when approached from the perspective of participation. These discussions often respond to specific issues such as biopiracy or access to medicine and appear throughout conventional patent law work. The chapter considers the role of the AU as a way of balancing not only these specific and potentially isolated issues of patent law, but how it can enable a genuine level of participation that allows states to more fully articulate their perspective or priorities. Patent law seen from this perspective is especially entangled with political and geographic considerations. The further development of the AU represents a future global trade space in which all members, whatever their economic size, have the ability to meaningfully participate in the development of trade obligations. Participation runs throughout these considerations since it integrates perspectives from within patent law and political science generally, emphasising the autonomy of WTO members and the important task of remedying the political legitimacy of the WTO.[54] Addressing the ability for all members to meaningfully participate is essential in not only addressing the discrete patent issues, but also in the fundamental sense of imposed trade obligations that was masked (and not resolved) by the successful conclusion of the Uruguay Round.

COVID-19 was also an important consideration in looking at international patent law and the future of the multilateral trading system. COVID-19, just as with HIV/AIDS, represents a complex set of tensions, which are at once legal, political, and social. The chapter explores the legal provisions of the TRIPS Agreement and how they relate to the COVID-19 pandemic, though the analysis moves to centre participation and autonomy in a way that shifts towards a more entangled understanding of the issues and away from technical patent discussions. One of the central issues explored in the chapter is vaccine donations and the problematic way it configures power relationships between states. By rejecting a more fundamental or radical review of how international patent law can exacerbate patent issues and instead relying on the language of donations and sharing, the COVID-19 pandemic demonstrated the limited success of the Doha Health Declaration. The formal language of the WTO and its members may suggest the importance of addressing vaccine inequality, but action remains limited. The WTO struggles, fundamentally, with its trade mandate and the degree to which issues external to trade can be incorporated – and so too with patent law. The fundamental tension in COVID-19 from a patent perspective was that the functioning of patent law was being interpreted through the lens of an external value framework and that this was somehow not legitimate. Understanding these tensions through participation instead draws on

54 Daniel C Esty, 'The World Trade Organization's Legitimacy Crisis' (2002) 1(1) World Trade Review 7, 8.

patent law's administrative foundation and presents the contemporary dynamic in a way that invites the reader, the public, and the politician to engage with patent law. It encourages these audiences to look at global patent law and focus on the *output* of these frameworks. Rules specifically exist in patent law for facilitating access to medicine or other patented information, and yet they have not be used to address the impact of COVID-19. Who exactly has the power to meaningfully shape the content of these patent flexibilities and the rules for their use?

5.6.2 *Critical reflections on further naturalising existing imbalances in global patent law and the risk of an isolated patent discourse*

Perhaps the most significant issue with focusing on the potential for the AU to (re) balance multilateral trade and patent law to respect participation is that it represents precisely that – a rebalancing. The lens of participation makes it clear that the contemporary issues in patent law are fundamentally linked and, though in practice they have distinct dynamics, the common tension is that certain participants lack the ability to meaningfully shape the content of binding obligations. While a more developed AU and greater strategic coalition building may achieve this type of participatory empowerment, it essentially legitimises the current structure of international trade. There is certainly a difficulty in striking an appropriate balance here, however. Just as with discussions in patent law that range from minor tweaks to a more radical amendment of its fundamentals,[55] the multilateral trade system has similar voices that propose large-scale and far-reaching reform.[56] International trade and the WTO are profoundly connected to colonial dynamics between countries,[57] the continued exploitation of low-wage workers,[58] and the tension between environmental initiatives and trade.[59] Enabling the meaningful participation of members through coalitions and AU-like structures does little to adjust the fundamental characteristics of the WTO, though it does raise the potential of these issues being at least identified in the global space. Instead, it simply reconfigures the relationship between members. A more long-term and perhaps optimistic view is that it is precisely through these rebalancing efforts and empowerment of

55 Such as a proposal for a startup immunity: Amy L Landers, 'The Antipatent: A Proposal for Startup Immunity' (2015) 93(4) Nebraska Law Review 951.

56 See for broader discussion on the future of the WTO: Robert Howse and Joanna Langille, 'Continuity and Change in the World Trade Organization: Pluralism Past, Present, and Future' (2023) 117(1) American Journal of International Law 2.

57 Danielle Robertson, 'EU–ACP Economic Partnership Agreements: Modern Colonialism Disguised in Violation of the WTO' (2017) 50(2) Vanderbilt Journal of Transnational Law 464.

58 With the continued rejection of labour standards by members of the WTO: Friederike Römer, Jakob Henninger, and Thuy Dung Le, 'International Organizations and Global Labor Standards' in Kerstin Martins, Dennis Niemann, and Alexandra Kaasch (eds), *International Organizations in Global Social Governance* (Springer 2021) 67, 68.

59 Harro van Asselt, 'Trade and Climate Disputes before the WTO: Blocking or Driving Climate Action?' in Ivano Alogna, Christine Bakker, and Jean-Pierre Gauci (eds), *Climate Change Litigation: Global* Perspectives (Brill 2021) 433.

overlooked members that over time international trade will develop in a way that is more responsive and more representative of the global diversity of conditions. There is certainly a legitimate concern that Chapter 4 either does not go far enough in restructuring the WTO or goes too far in distorting a sense of 'pure' trade autonomy between member countries.

The second area of critical reflection is the complex impact of COVID-19 and COVID-19 vaccines, which produced an effect that appears at once to be completely disruptive and almost entirely limited in scope. COVID-19 brought the world to a standstill and the health dimension brought patent law to public consciousness, at least temporarily. The academic response, and eventual WTO discussions, essentially focused on a waiver of the intellectual property rights related to COVID-19 vaccines to improve production and distribution.[60] This was met with a variety of claims as to the negative impact on business,[61] the importance of innovation and economic growth even in times of crisis,[62] and distribution concerns in developing countries.[63] The issue with the waiver approach, again, is that it represents a narrow modification of patent law. It does little to meaningfully resolve either the pressing health needs of vulnerable populations or the more fundamental issues in patent law structure that led to this situation. The Doha Health Declaration has undoubtedly positively impacted vulnerable communities, yet COVID-19 demonstrated the sense of compartmentalisation that occurs in these international spaces. The entanglement of patent law here extends beyond ordinary political tensions and economic objectives and instead becomes linked with national science policy. The continued lack of investment in science in countries around the world has created a space in which essential medicine – including vaccines – are sources of profit for private companies.[64] A temporary waiving of the intellectual property rights associated with a vaccine can only ever represent an imperfect and temporary response to a much more fundamental lack of funding and public role in science development. In terms of future pandemic preparedness, the proposed waiver should be a chilling sign of the unwillingness to fundamentally alter principles of patent law even in times of crisis. Addressing a future pandemic through a waiver of intellectual property rights would indicate that there has been a global failure to prepare, as patent law has remained essentially unaltered since the HIV/AIDS epidemic. The emphasis on greater public science and protection of

60 WTO, 'TRIPS Council Welcomes MC12 TRIPS Waiver Decision, Discusses Possible Extension' (*WTO*, 6 July 2022) <https://www.wto.org/english/news_e/news22_e/trip_08jul22_e.htm>.

61 Bryan Mercurio, 'The IP Waiver for COVID-19: Bad Policy, Bad Precedent' (2021) 52(8) IIC 983.

62 European Council, 'Council Conclusions on Intellectual Property Policy' (*European Council,* 18 June 2021) <https://www.consilium.europa.eu/media/50529/st-9932-2021-init.pdf> 4.

63 Victory O Olutuase, Chinwe J Iwu-Jaja, Cynthia P Akuoko, Emmanuel O Adequyi, and Vishnu Khanal, 'Medicines and Vaccines Supply Chains Challenges in Nigeria: A Scoping Review' (2022) 22 BMC Public Health 1.

64 Which, at this point, is a consistent element in the relationship between universities, industry, and medicine: Risa L Lieberwitz, 'Confronting the Privatization and Commercialization of Academic Research: An Analysis of Social Implications at the Local, National, and Global Levels' (2005) 12(1) Indiana Journal of Global Legal Studies 134.

existing publicly funded projects would also address the criticisms that the waiver would disincentivise private companies from engaging in vaccine development. Though it appears insignificant or somehow trivial in the face of global disease and death, a demonstrated willingness to undermine property rights *does* contribute to a negative business environment and would impact companies beyond the pandemic and outside of intellectual property. There is also something interesting about the way in which, during the pandemic, intellectual property (as a form of property) becomes somehow malleable (at least conceptually) in a way that would never be applied to real property.

5.7 Conclusion

This book attempts to do two things: to demonstrate that patent law can never truly be isolated from its broader political, cultural, and social context; and to further destabilise the tendency towards technocratic isolation by framing problems in international patent law through the language of accountability, transparency, and participation. It is important to recognise that the book, in supporting expansive understandings of patent law, is not aimed at exposing or stating an authoritative vision. Instead, it is a creative work that necessarily reflects my own approach to scholarship and the complexity of patent law. Even the values chosen from administrative law represent a specific positionality. A book could have just as easily been written in a way that centres legitimacy or authority. The book is, fundamentally, an offering to the reader of a different way of looking at international patent law. It is intended to actively reach out to non-patent audiences and stress the importance of broader engagement with patent law. As such, the perspective in this book represents only a single (and necessarily limited) interpretation of how patent law looks in 2025.

The entanglement of patent law is fundamental to this project because it pushes at the boundaries of patent scholarship. This is particularly apparent in Chapter 4 on the multilateral environment as it is clear that an understanding of patent law cannot be achieved through studying patent-specific provisions in isolation. It is profoundly connected to how other forms of intellectual property are treated, the political dynamic between parties involved, and the broader social context in which we experience patent law. Yet, it is in the context of dispute resolution that this entanglement becomes especially prominent. This is because in the dispute space – a creative environment that has the potential to reshape and rebalance law in an almost improvisational way – patent provisions are interpreted not only in terms of their legal content but with an implicit recognition of its context and the practical scope of its binding decisions.

The approach throughout the book has been to explore how patent law takes on different political or social characteristics alongside the legal content of patent provisions. This is, fundamentally, a challenge to the technocratic isolation of patent law and the idea that patent law can ever represent 'neutral' trade or regulatory policy. Approaching patent law from this apparently neutral perspective not only legitimises the value judgments it makes – specific interpretations of 'invention' and capitalist growth – but renders them invisible as it naturalises these perspectives. In doing so, the nuance and complex nature of patent law is overlooked. A focus solely on the economic dimensions of patent law or patent law as a trade tool misses how it has developed, how it functions, and how it can be reimagined to meet the evolving needs of global society.

This is fundamentally linked to the second intention of writing the book, which is to encourage and provoke a reader or audience outside the typical patent scholar profile. The language of administrative values is both a reminder of patent law's administrative foundation and a way of challenging how problems in patent law are typically framed. Framing patent law in terms of accountability, participation, and transparency invites the reader – no matter their background – to interact with substantive issues across a variety of different patent spaces. This is an approach that is rarely found in patent scholarship or patent practice. Though it was mentioned in the introduction, there is a persistent sense in both professional and academic circles that patent law is perceived as too specialist and complex for general audiences. This technocratic tendency of patent law is something that does not, in admittedly anecdotal experience, affect areas like human rights or constitutional law. A lack of technical expertise on the specifics of human rights law is no barrier to an ordinary reader meaningfully considering a specific issue, exploring their own response to it, and contextualising its relationship to law and society. Yet the issues that have emerged in patent law considered in the book, such as medicine and genetic resources, are fundamental concerns for society as a whole. The types of decisions being made in these contexts, and in international patent law more generally, reach far beyond the patent world and affect society itself. Incorporating the language of administrative values so prominently in an analysis of patent law has an integrating effect and provides a more accessible vocabulary that reaches out to those outside patent law. It is integrative in that rather than contributing to the existing approach of problematising issues in individual and discrete ways, it brings together these tensions in patent law. Access to medicine, use of genetic resources, and the substantive content of patent provisions are not actually separate concerns. They all result from a fundamental impairment of meaningful participation in patent law, demonstrating the importance of expansive and contextual approaches to critical patent scholarship. The vocabulary of administrative law is one way of encouraging communication between these different bodies of scholarship and advocacy, actively creating a space in which links between different perspectives, disciplines, and approaches can be facilitated.

Bibliography

Articles

Bacchus J and S Lester, 'The Rule of Precedent and the Role of the Appellate Body' (2020) 54(2) *Journal of World Trade* 184.

Campbell R, 'Global Patent Law Harmonization: Benefits and Implementation' (2003) 13(2) *Indiana International & Comparative Law Review* 605.

Cassese S, 'Global Administrative Law: The State of the Art' (2015) 13(2) *International Journal of Constitutional Law* 465.

Cullet P, 'Patents and Medicines: The Relationship Between TRIPS and the Human Right to Health' (2003) 79(1) *International Affairs* 139.

Esty DC, 'The World Trade Organization's Legitimacy Crisis' (2002) 1(1) *World Trade Review* 7.

Gallagher KP, 'Trading Away the Ladder? Trade Politics and Economic Development in the Americas' (2008) 13(1) *New Political Economy* 37.

Gurgula O, M Padamczyk, and N Shemtov, 'Specialised IP Judiciary: What are the Key Elements to Consider when Establishing or Reforming an Effective IP Court?' (2022) 71(3) *GRUR International* 206.

Haugen HM, 'Patent Rights and Human Rights: Exploring their Relationships' (2007) 10(2) *The Journal of World Intellectual Property* 97.

Howse R and J Langille, 'Continuity and Change in the World Trade Organization: Pluralism Past, Present, and Future' (2023) 117(1) *American Journal of International Law* 1.

Igbokwe EM and A Tosato, 'Access to Medicines and Pharmaceutical Patents: Fulfilling the Promise of TRIPS Article 31bis' (2023) 91(5) *Fordham Law Review* 1791.

Krisch N and B Kingsbury, 'Introduction: Global Governance and Global Administrative Law in the International Legal Order' (2006) 17(1) *European Journal of International Law* 1.

Lahsen AA and AT Piper, 'Property Rights and Intellectual Property Protection, GDP Growth and Individual Well-Being in Latin America' (2019) 28 *Latin American Economic Review* 1.

Lamping M, 'Enhanced Cooperation: A Proper Approach to Market Reintegration in the Field of Unitary Patent Protection?' (2011) 42(8) *International Review of Intellectual Property and Competition Law* 879.

Landers AL, 'The Antipatent: A Proposal for Startup Immunity' (2015) 93(4) *Nebraska Law Review* 950.

Lieberwitz RL, 'Confronting the Privatization and Commercialization of Academic Research: An Analysis of Social Implications at the Local, National, and Global Levels' (2005) 12(1) *Indiana Journal of Global Legal Studies* 109.

McMahon A, 'An Institutional Examination of the Implications of the Unitary Patent Package for the Morality Provisions: A Fragmented Future Too Far?' (2017) 48(1) *International Review of Intellectual Property and Competition Law* 42.

Mercurio B, 'The IP Waiver for COVID-19: Bad Policy, Bad Precedent' (2021) 52(8) *International Review of Intellectual Property and Competition Law* 983.

Moerland A, 'Do Developing Countries Have a Say? Bilateral and Regional Intellectual Property Negotiations with the EU' (2017) 48 *International Review of Intellectual Property and Competition Law* 760.

Morris PS, 'Private Intellectual Property Regulation in Public International Law' (2020) 26(1) *UC Davis Journal of International Law and Policy* 147.

Mossoff A, 'Exclusion and Exclusive Use in Patent Law' (2009) 22(2) *Harvard Journal of Law & Technology* 321.

Mossoff A, 'Patents as Constitutional Private Property: The Historical Protection of Patents under the Takings Clause' (2007) 87 *Boston University Law Review* 689.

Nakayama N, 'The Enforcement of the TRIPS Agreement in Japan' (1995) 38 *Japanese Annual of International Law* 1.

Olutase VO, CJ Iwu-Jaja, CP Akuoko, EO Adequyi, and V Khanal, 'Medicines and Vaccines Supply Chains Challenges in Nigeria: A Scoping Review' (2022) 22 *BMC Public Health* 1.

de Paiva Abreu M, 'Developing Countries and the Uruguay Round of Trade Negotiations' in Proceedings of the World Bank Annual Conference on Development Economics, April 1989 (1990) 21.

Rajec SRW, 'The Harmonization Myth in International Intellectual Property Law' (2020) 60 *Arizona Law Review* 735.

Reichman JH, 'The TRIPS Component of the GATT's Uruguay Round: Competitive Prospects for Intellectual Property Owners in an Integrated World Market' (1993) 4 *Fordham Intellectual Property, Media & Entertainment Law Journal* 171.

Reichman JH and RC Dreyfuss, 'Harmonization without Consensus: Critical Reflections on Drafting a Substantive Patent Law Treaty' (2007) 57(1) *Duke Law Journal* 85.

Robertson D, 'EU-ACP Economic Partnership Agreements: Modern Colonialism Disguised in Violation of the WTO' (2017) 50(2) *Vanderbilt Journal of Transnational Law* 463.

Rodriguez V, 'Constructing a Unitary Title for the European Patent System' (2011) 6(8) *Journal of Intellectual Property Law & Practice* 574.

Shapiro M, '"Deliberative," "Independent" Technocracy v. Democratic Politics: Will the Globe Echo the E.U.?' (2005) 68(3/4) *Law and Contemporary Problems* 341.

Solovy EM, 'The Doha Declaration at Twenty: Interpretation, Implementation, and Lessons Learned on the Relationship Between the TRIPS Agreement and Global Health' (2022) 42(2) *Northwestern Journal of International Law & Business* 253.

Sopranzetti S, 'Overlapping Free Trade Agreements and International Trade: A Network Approach' (2018) 41(6) *The World Economy* 1549.

Travis H, 'Patents, the Private Property Ideal, and the Public Interest in a Seamless Global Public Health System' (2022) 31(1) *Federal Circuit Bar Journal* 1.

Books

Baldan F, *Judicial Coherence in the European Patent System: Lessons from the US and Japan* (Edward Elgar 2022).

Moir HVJ, *Patent Policy and Innovation: Do Legal Rules Deliver Effective Economic Outcomes?* (Edward Elgar 2013).

Oke EK, *Patents, Human Rights, and Access to Medicine* (CUP 2022).

Quinton-Brown P, *Intervention Before Interventionism: A Global Genealogy* (OUP 2024).

Rafanelli LM, *Promoting Justice Across Borders: The Ethics of Reform Intervention* (OUP 2021).

Stack A, *International Patent Law: Cooperation, Harmonization and an Institutional Analysis of WIPO and the WTO* (Edward Elgar 2011) 94.

Zhang C, *Balance and Limitation of Intellectual Property Protection in China: The Latest Law Amendments and Judicial Developments Under Micro-Comparative Perspectives* (Springer 2022).

Chapters

Abbott FM, 'Intellectual Property Rights in World Trade' in A Guzman and A Sykes (eds), *Research Handbook in International Economic Law* (Edward Elgar 2007) 444.

von Asselt H, 'Trade and Climate Disputes before the WTO: Blocking or Driving Climate Action?' in Ivano Alogna, Christine Bakker, and Jean-Pierre Gauci (eds), *Climate Change Litigation: Global* Perspectives (Brill 2021) 433.

Burghardt G, 'The EU/US Transatlantic Relationship: The Indispensable Partnership' in Christoph Hermann, Bruno Simma, and Rudolf Streinz (eds), *Trade Policy Between Law, Diplomacy and Scholarship* (Springer 2015) 193.

Cananea GD, 'Administrative Law Beyond the State: The Influence of International and Supranational Organizations' in Peter Cane, Herwig Ch Hofmann, Eric C IP, and Peter L Lindseth (eds), *Oxford Handbook of Comparative Administrative Law* (OUP 2021) 357.

Cattaneo O, 'The Political Economy of PTAs' in Simon Lester, Bryan Mercurio, and Lorand Bartels (eds), *Bilateral and Regional Trade Agreements: Commentary and Analysis* (CUP 2015) 28.

Chiappetta V, 'Working Toward International Harmony on Intellectual Property Exhaustion (And Substantive Law)' in Irene Calboli and Edward Lee (eds), *Research Handbook on Intellectual Property Exhaustion and Parallel Imports* (Edward Elgar 2016) 125.

D'Alterio E, 'Judicial Regulation in the Global Space' in Sabino Cassese (ed), *Research Handbook on Global Administrative Law* (Edward Elgar 2016) 303.

Harlow C, P Leino, and GD Cananea, 'Introduction: European Administrative Law – A Thematic Approach' in Carol Harlow, Päivi Leino, and Giacinto Della Cananea (eds), *Research Handbook on EU Administrative Law* (Edward Elgar 2017) 1.

Howell TR, 'The Multilateral Trading System and Transnational Competition in Advanced Technologies: The Limits of Existing Disciplines' in Göran Marklund, Nicholas S Vonortas, and Charles W Wessner (eds), *The Innovation Imperative: National Innovation Strategies in the Global Economy* (Edward Elgar 2009) 50.

Odagiri H, A Goto, and A Sunami, 'IPR and the Catch-Up Process in Japan' in Hiroyuki Odagiri, Akira Goto, Atsushi Sunami, Richard R Nelson (eds), *Intellectual Property Rights, Development, and Catch-up: An International Comparative Study* (OUP 2010) 95.

Odell-West A, 'Exclusions in Patent Law as an Indirect Form of Regulation for New Health Technologies in Europe' in Mark L Flear, Anne-Maree Farrell, Tamara K Hervey, and Thérèse Murphy (eds), *European Law and New Health* Technologies (OUP 2013) 148.

Römer F, J Henninger, and TD Le, 'International Organizations and Global Labor Standards' in Kerstin Martins, Dennis Niemann, and Alexandra Kaasch (eds), *International Organizations in Global Social Governance* (Springer 2021) 57.

Ruse-Khan HG, 'Intellectual Property and International Law: A Research Framework' in Irene Calboli and Maria Lillà Montagnani (eds), *Handbook of Intellectual Property Research: Lenses, Methods, and Perspectives* (OUP 2021) 15.

Sanders AK, 'Geographical Indications as Property: European Union Association Agreements and Investor-State Provisions' in Irene Calboli and Ng-Loy Wee Loon (eds), *Geographical Indications at the Crossroads of Trade, Development, and Culture: Focus on Asia–Pacific* (CUP 2017) 168.

Vats A and DA Keller, 'Critical Race Theory as Intellectual Property Methodology' in Irene Calboli and Maria Lillà Montagnani (eds), *Handbook of Intellectual Property Research: Lenses, Methods, and Perspectives* (OUP 2021) 777.

Legislation

Article 15, TEU.

Article 78(g) Agreement Establishing an Association between the European Union and its Member States, On the One Hand, and Central America on the Other.

Article XXIV GATT.

Article V GATS.

Cases

C-9/56, C-10/56 *Meroni v High Authority* [1957/1957].

Other

EU Commission, 'Internal Market, Industry, Entrepreneurship, and SMEs: Unitary Patent' (*EU Commission*) <https://ec.europa.eu/growth/industry/strategy/intellectual-property/patent-protection-eu/unitary-patent_en>.

EU Parliament, 'Transparency and Ethics' (*Europarl*) <https://www.europarl.europa.eu/at-your-service/en/transparency>.

European Council, 'Council Conclusions on Intellectual Property Policy' (*European Council,* 18 June 2021) <https://www.consilium.europa.eu/media/50529/st-9932-2021-init.pdf> 4.

Hamdani K, 'Panel: Process and Value of Uniform Commercial Law: Proceedings of the Congress of the United Nations Commission on International Trade Law Held on the Occasion of the Fortieth Session of the Commission' (2007) 25.

Hu AGZ and IPL Png, 'Patent Rights and Economic Growth: Evidence from Cross-Country Panels of Manufacturing Industries' (2013) 65(3) *Oxford Economic Papers* 675.

Matthews D, 'Patents in the Global Economy' (UKIPO Report 2010) 1.

WTO, 'TRIPS Council Welcomes MC12 TRIPS Waiver Decision, Discusses Possible Extension' (*WTO*, 6 July 2022) <https://www.wto.org/english/news_e/news22_e/trip_08jul22_e.htm>.

Index

FSC
www.fsc.org
MIX
Papier | Fördert gute Waldnutzung
FSC® C083411

Kolibri 360 GmbH
Ferdinand-Jühlke-Straße 7
99095 Erfurt, Deutschland
produktsicherheit@kolibri360.de